JUST WAR

JUST WAR

Authority, Tradition, and Practice

Anthony F. Lang Jr., Cian O'Driscoll,
and John Williams

Editors

GEORGETOWN UNIVERSITY PRESS
Washington, DC

Library of Congress Cataloging-in-Publication Data

Just war : authority, tradition, and practice / Anthony F. Lang, Jr., Cian O'Driscoll, and John Williams, editors.
     pages cm
  Proceedings of a workshop held in the summer of 2010 in Washington, D.C.
  Includes bibliographical references and index.
  ISBN 978-1-58901-996-6 (pbk. : alk. paper)
  1. Just war doctrine—Congresses.   I. Lang, Anthony F., 1968–   II. O'Driscoll, Cian. III. Williams, John, 1969–
U21.2.J849   2013
172'.42—dc23

2012042486

♾ This book is printed on acid-free paper meeting the requirements of the American National Standard for Permanence in Paper for Printed Library Materials.

15 14 13   9 8 7 6 5 4 3 2   First printing

Printed in the United States of America

Contents

Preface

This book, the yield of an interdisciplinary workshop held in Washington in the summer of 2010, is an attempt to shine new light on an old topic: the just war tradition. This tradition has long served as a framework within which to explore matters of war and communal violence. It not only structures moral reflection on these matters but also informs the political and legal institutions that govern and constitute them. Our efforts, first during the Washington workshop and later through the production of this volume, have been directed principally toward re-orienting scholarly attention to a central but recently neglected element of the tradition: the question or problem of authority. As conveners of the workshop, we sought to drive this agenda by elucidating the key questions it raises and by responding to them with suggestions for how we think authority should be under-stood in the context of the tradition. We continued to play this role in our work as editors in writing the introductory and concluding chapters of this volume. Rising to this provocation, the volume's contributors have produced a very rich set of chapters, each of which represents a different perspective on, and raises distinct questions and concerns about, the practice of political authority as it speaks to the just war tradition. We hope and believe that it provides a unique and insightful contribution to the scholarly discussion of both the just war tradition and the ques-tion of authority in contemporary international politics.

The Washington workshop was both funded and hosted by the US Institute of Peace in August 2010. As editors we express our keen gratitude to that institution for its hospitality and financial support. Steve Riskin at the institute deserves special mention for his help in facilitating the use of the grant and the workshop itself. The grant for the workshop was obtained by Durham University, and its management by Lorraine Holmes is greatly appreciated. We would also like to thank Albert Pierce, who presented at the workshop but, due to his obligations at the National Defense University, was unable to contribute to this volume and Henry Shue, who for similar reasons presented at the workshop but was unable to contribute to the final volume.

Don Jacobs at Georgetown University Press carefully guided us through the process of turning the workshop papers into a publishable volume. We appreciate his patience and care in dealing not only with us as editors but also with our contributors. The comments of two peer reviewers are also greatly appreciated, as they helped us to better integrate the volume as a whole.

Tony Lang would like to thank his fellow editors for making this a truly enjoyable experience. Meetings in Glasgow, Durham, and St. Andrews were not so onerous when dealing with such easygoing colleagues. He would also like to thank his family for their patience while he worked on this volume. The smile and laugh of the newest addition to that family, Vivienne Luna, makes it somewhat easier to write about matters of war.

Cian O'Driscoll is also keen to thank his fellow editors for the efficiency, generosity, and intelligence with which they guided this project. Working with John and Tony was a pleasure and a privilege. Cian also greatly appreciated the cordiality of all the contributors to this volume, and the esprit de corps that they cultivated in Washington and nourished during the subsequent years. Cian would like to express his gratitude to Toni Erskine for supporting the project when it was still in its infancy, and to his family for their care, attention, and love. A special word of appreciation is offered here for Eamon, who generously devoted his time and talent to designing the posters and programs for the Washington workshop. Finally, he would like to dedicate his efforts on this volume to Jenny, with whom it is so much fun tripping through the four seasons of autumn that Glasgow has to offer.

John Williams echoes the appreciation for his fellow editors' work, dedication, and commitment to ensuring that this collection is successful. Although this volume might exist without his contribution, it would not exist without theirs.

Introduction

The Just War Tradition and the Practice of Political Authority

Anthony F. Lang Jr. and Cian O'Driscoll

THE JUST WAR TRADITION is the predominant moral language through which we address questions pertaining to the rights and wrongs of the use of force in international society. Boasting a lineage that is typically traced to the sunset of the Roman Empire, it furnishes us with a set of concepts, principles, and analytical devices for making sense of the moral-legal questions that war raises. Contemporary accounts of the tradition organize it around two independent but related poles of inquiry: the *jus ad bellum*, which speaks to the conditions under which the recourse to war might be justified; and the *jus in bello*, which treats the issue of how war might be conducted in a just manner once commenced.[1] Although scholars disagree over which principles should take priority within these poles of inquiry, and how they relate to one another, a certain amount of consensus endures regarding the principles themselves. Few scholars challenge the view that the *jus ad bellum* requires us to think in terms of "just cause," "proper authority," "right intent," and "last resort," whereas most agree that the *jus in bello* directs us to questions relating to "discrimination," "proportionality," and "double-effect." These categories have been covered extensively in the literature, so there is, we hope, no need to elaborate further on them here. Instead, we wish to draw attention to the fact that, when set out in these terms, the just war tradition may appear abstract and bloodless, removed from the rough and tumble of real-world international politics. This is both regrettable and misleading.

In actuality, the just war tradition is central to the practice of international relations. Its influence is evident in the legal codes that govern how modern militaries perform their duties, and it has featured prominently in the rhetoric surrounding the "War on Terror" and the recent military actions in Iraq, Afghanistan, and Libya. Most recently, President Barack Obama reaffirmed its significance in his December 2009 Nobel Peace Prize address, when he stated the centrality of just war precepts

1

to US foreign policy, and called on the international community to "think in new ways about the notion of just war and the imperatives of a just peace." He enjoined his audience to face "the hard truth that we will not eradicate violent conflict in our lifetimes. There will be times when nations—acting individually or in concert—will find the use of force not only necessary but morally justified."[2] However, as we shall see, the tradition is not uncontroversial, and its central role in contemporary international relations raises a series of searching questions.

The sense of tempered idealism and the reluctant acceptance of the element of force in human political life articulated by President Obama express the central concerns and continuing fascination of the just war tradition. From Augustine's mordant observations regarding humanity's incapacity to wield power justly to the celebrated *Rights of War and Peace* of Hugo Grotius, the just war tradition manifests, on the one hand, a tragic resignation to the necessity of war in this fallen world, and, on the other hand, a determination to restrict its destructiveness. It reflects an enduring effort to sustain the idea that, even when fighting in the trenches, humanity lives in a moral world. As such, the tradition should not be misconstrued as a simple *techne* or set of guidelines stipulating what is permissible in war. Rather, it comprises a tradition of political theory that invites us to think about war on a philosophical register. It challenges us to peer beyond the possibility of a narrowly defined "ethics of war," toward a broader engagement with the nature of rules and responsibilities, and rights and duties, as they relate to the violent edge of world politics. Underpinning this is a sustained inquiry into the relation between the use of force in international life and political authority, understood as a practice. With this in mind, this introductory chapter elaborates the dimensions of this relationship and, in so doing, provides a broad overview of the structure of this volume.

POLITICAL AUTHORITY IN FOCUS

Although most contemporary literature on the just war tradition focuses on questions of "just cause" (e.g., relating to humanitarian intervention or anticipatory defense) or considerations of "noncombatant immunity," the principle of "proper authority" has, with a few honorable exceptions, been largely overlooked.[3] This is a startling omission, not least for the reason that, as James Turner Johnson points out in chapter 1 of this volume, the requirement of proper authority must logically be the point of departure for any serious analysis of the ethics of war. Before one can evaluate the merits of a particular claim to just cause, or ascertain what order of military response it licenses, one must first determine whether the agent bringing the charge is entitled to do so, and if so, on what grounds. These are obviously very important but difficult questions, which only renders it all the more lamentable that they have received such scant attention in recent years.

It is not, however, difficult to work out why this has been the case. Since the early modern period, the principle of proper authority has been obscured, or even obviated, by the emergence of the sovereign state as the locus of Western political thought. Over time, the question of what constitutes proper authority to levy war—the subject of so much spilled ink in the period from Gratian to Grotius—came to be construed almost exclusively in terms of Max Weber's famous definition of the state as the agency that exercises the monopoly of legitimate violence within a given territory.[4] In lieu of this, the requirement of proper authority was rendered coterminous with the idea that only sovereign states were permitted to wage war. Translated into international law, the requirement of proper authority now came to mean that it was the state's prerogative to use force to advance its aims if it so pleased.

There are good reasons to be suspicious of the idea that the principle of proper authority is reducible to the concept of state sovereignty. Three reasons in particular stand out. A brief review of them will lay the foundations for the account of authority that is developed in the following sectors, and indeed chapters.

The first reason why we should regard the equivalence drawn between proper authority and sovereignty with a healthy dose of circumspection is that the just war tradition is, plainly speaking, more pluralistic than this. It incorporates a range of different approaches to what constitutes authority, not all of them consistent with the idea of the state, as we understand it today. For example, those who trumpet the natural law heritage of the tradition would remind us that the sovereign state is not the only, or even the primary, source of authority in international political life. We could cite other examples, but suffice it to say that authority can be, and indeed has been, understood apart from state sovereignty. The second reason is the pragmatic one that framing the principle of proper authority entirely in terms of sovereignty blunts its critical edge by subordinating it to the state system. On this account, the principle of proper authority reinforces the rights of states to deploy force while denying other forms of community the same license. If not quite amounting to a "might is right" formula, it renders the good a function of sovereignty. This is clearly problematic. The third reason is that the concept of state sovereignty has decreasing relevance to the realities of modern armed conflict, much of which takes the form of what Mary Kaldor has termed "new wars." This, incidentally, is the point of departure for chapter 12 of this volume, Michael Gross's "Just War and Guerrilla War."

Mindful of the three concerns we have just elucidated, this volume pursues a broader conception of authority. In particular, it seeks to develop a conception of authority that, rather than being rooted in a simplistic appeal to state sovereignty, emphasizes its institutional, discursive, and performative elements. Where to begin with such a task? We commence our inquiry by acknowledging the heart of the matter: Submitting to authority requires an individual not to make choices for himself or herself but to submit to the will of another. As Joseph Raz notes: "To be subjected to authority, it is argued, is incompatible with reason, for reason requires that one should always act on the balance of reasons of which one is aware. It is of the nature of authority that it requires submission even when one thinks that what is required is against reason."[5] On this account, it seems that respect for authority entails a suspension of judgment, something that is surely inimical to the character of the just war tradition. What are we to make of this tension? Perhaps it points to the fact that we need a more refined account of authority.

Recent debates in philosophy and political theory may help us in this regard. Some philosophers, such as Richard Friedman and Richard Flathman, identify two types of authority, practical and theoretical. Practical authority, or being "in authority," is a form of authority that arises from the execution of agreed-upon conventions or procedures. Theoretical authority is what some might call being "an authority," and it derives from the expertise or knowledge of the authority figure.[6] Plato's philosopher king is arguably the most celebrated example of theoretical authority. Conversely, most democratic theory, which stipulates that it is the procedure whereby an individual comes to office that matters, assumes practical authority. This typology, though analytically intriguing, is not of interest to us in its own right. Instead it is in relation to the debate it provoked between Friedman and Flathman—a debate that reveals some of the principal contours of political authority, understood both as a concept and as a practice—that it is useful for our purposes.

Let us start with Friedman. He expands upon Raz's concern that conforming to authority necessarily entails the suspension of private judgment, while at the same time claiming that authority does not mean the imposition of brute coercion to force compliance.[7] Following Hannah Arendt, he supposes that authority is located somewhere between brute force and persuasion through reason; though it has elements of both, it cannot be reduced to either.[8] As he develops this view, Friedman expresses a certain degree of disquiet about the utility of theoretical authority. Living as we do in a world fraught by stark moral disagreement, he writes, how can we agree upon, or even identify, what counts as the form of knowledge from which authority may be derived? Without access to some prior conventions regarding how to determine what counts as right knowledge, it seems, he cautions, that we are stuck. This leads Friedman to assert both the futility of theoretical authority in the modern, pluralized world and the primacy of practical authority. It is, he argues, the strength of practical authority that it is not reliant upon any common background, shared beliefs, or privileged access to right knowledge but is instead capable of overlaying them. It is, he writes, "in those circumstances in which a society has lost the sense of a common framework of substantive moral beliefs and has grown skeptical of the idea of a homogenous moral community, that the notion of being 'in authority' may present itself as the appropriate form of authority for defining the general rules all men must conform to."[9]

Friedman's observations resonate in the current international order, riven as it is, if not by putative clashes of civilizations, then at least by antithetical value systems and ideologies. For instance, when it comes to the use of military force, ongoing squabbles about the definition of terrorism, torture, and aggression suggest that there remains strong moral, legal, and political disagreement about these key elements of international affairs. If we cede that there is a lack of consensus even on these basic ideas, could it be that Friedman is correct? Should we defer to a conception of political authority that surrenders the ideal of theoretical authority as a lost cause and construes authority as a political concept and practice exclusively in terms of conventional arrangements?[10]

Richard Flathman refutes this. He contends that there must be some background of shared beliefs for those in authority to function effectively. In other words, there needs to be a level of theoretical authority in political matters for practical authority to make any sense. This is on account of Flathman's refusal to countenance the idea that conformity to authority demands a complete suspension of reason; rather, one chooses to acknowledge the character of the procedures that are constitutive of authority as fair and just. This formula is crucial for Flathman's argument. It ensures that individuals subject to authority are posited as retaining some level of agency and the capacity to determine their own actions.[11] Yet this reveals a further tension, this time in respect of the claim that individuals enjoy agency and are, simultaneously, subject to authority.

How does Flathman resolve this tension? He suggests that there is a need for some agreement among those who subscribe to authority, an agreement not just that this individual or institution should govern but also that this individual or institution must somehow reflect their constituents' shared beliefs and values about the political realm—beliefs and values that he calls "authoritative." These beliefs and values do not go as far as the modern communitarian might want them to; that is, they are not the teleological kinds of values that would direct a community toward a specific goal. Instead, they comprise a set of background conditions that make authority possible. These conditions will likely include certain broadly defined procedural elements, but they may also include values that reflect principles that define certain realms of life, certain distinctions between people and the rest of the world, or certain kinds of distinctions concerning social practices. In other words, authoritative values are partly procedural, but not entirely so. In effect, then, rather than abandoning theoretical authority, Flathman suggests that it can furnish a set of background conditions whereby practical authority can effectively function, and in which individuals can place their trust to be sure that they do not have to simply follow authority without any reasons for so doing. These background conditions include both the procedural ones by which an authority is chosen, and, more importantly for our purposes, norms that in part constitute what a community values.

Stepping back from the particulars of this debate and summing up, our point here is not to resolve the disputes about authority that Raz, Friedman, and Flathman have pursued. Rather, it is to introduce a set of approaches for how we might understand the contours of political authority, as both a concept and a practice. These approaches draw our attention to the conventional, procedural, and substantive aspects of authority, and how they may be viewed as mutually dependent, or at least interconnected in a host of subtle but significant ways. But perhaps more important, they alert us to the close connection between the production of knowledge and the practices whereby political authority is constituted. This is the *bene esse* of political life.

THE PRACTICE OF AUTHORITY

It is, as noted above, both surprising and disappointing that the issue of authority has received scant attention in contemporary just war studies. Few scholars, for instance, have taken the time to examine the authority of the just war tradition as a source of moral guidance for modern statecraft. Rather, the authority of the tradition is taken as a given. It is simply assumed that the various categories of the *jus ad bellum* and *jus in bello* constitute the appropriate frame for ethical deliberation about the use of force in international society.[12] And it is often further assumed that any verdict on a particular war reached by judicious engagement with these categories must, courtesy of its provenance, have a claim to authoritative status. If pushed, many of today's just war theorists would justify these assumptions on the grounds that the authority of the tradition is self-evidently derived from "right reason," "Christian love," or some other foundational value. Others appear to have hardly considered the matter at all.

Yet it is also the case that the just war tradition's putative authority, however it is justified, raises searching questions. Namely, how far does this authority range, and from whence is it ostensibly derived? These two questions require elucidation before we carry on. The first question, which focuses on the scope of the tradition's jurisdiction, is particularly complex. It invites us to reflect upon the limits of the tradition's applicability. Widely regarded as an artifact of Christian political theology, can the tradition have any salience beyond the boundaries of what was once known as Christendom? Can it provide a universal language in which a wider audience, of all creeds, can freely participate? Or, as the alleged property of Christians, is the tradition merely one more wedge in the so-called clash of civilizations, such that as the "West" is to "Islam," so "just war" is to "jihad"?[13] Put differently, is the just war tradition merely another particularist discourse in a world of rival value systems? One could put the issue even more sharply by jettisoning the reference to the clash of civilizations and instead inquiring what purchase can the just war tradition—a product of medieval Christian reflection on war—have in the contemporary secularized world. How can a tradition so deeply rooted in Christian tenets continue to dispense meaningful guidance to a flock that, in large part, has long ago strayed from the church?[14] These challenges are explicitly addressed by Nigel Biggar in chapter 3 of this volume, and resonate with many of the other essays gathered here.

The consensus—such as there is one—in the wider literature indicates that these challenges are not crippling.[15] David Fisher and Brian Wicker put it best when they write that though the just war principles were undoubtedly developed within a Christian framework, they were never intended to apply exclusively to that particular community of faith. Instead, they were intended to appeal to a universal audience of all "men and women of reason."[16] And with the institutionalization of just war precepts in the strictures of international law and the Law of Armed Conflict, this intention has apparently been realized, at least partially. The chapters that form part I of this volume do not tackle this orthodoxy in a direct fashion, but instead they offer a series of thoughtful (and often critical) reflections upon both its conditions of possibility and its implications.

In chapter 1 James Turner Johnson, as has already been noted, offers a rich and wide-ranging treatment of the principle of proper authority and its significance within the broader framework of the just war tradition. Johnson's core concern is to elucidate the nature of the relation between (in his words) "the classic just war conception of sovereign authority" and "the just use of armed force," understood in terms of its reasons, ends, and methods. In chapter 2, "Just War and Political Judgment," Chris Brown endorses and builds upon Johnson's argument. In particular, he is keen to assert that proper authority, and indeed the just war tradition more generally, should be approached not as a "rote algorithm" to be satisfied but as an "invitation to exercise judgment." This would involve the elevation of phronetic modes of reasoning at the expense of the modern desire for formal, abstract, logical rules. Taking on board Brown's call for a kind of just war thinking that rests upon "practical, care-based, experience-based reasoning," John Williams asks in chapter 4 what proper authority can and should mean in the context of contemporary liberal democratic societies. Adopting as his starting point the 2003 antiwar protests that formed the backdrop to Ian McEwan's novel *Saturday*, Williams examines the tensions between liberal just war theory and conventional accounts of sovereign authority and raises interesting questions related to the value of political community—issues taken up by Nicholas Rengger in chapter 16. Following Williams, Nahed Zehr also tackles the liberal conception of proper authority in chapter 6, particularly as articulated by Cecile Fabre. However, rather than relate Fabre's position to competing conceptions of sovereignty, as per Williams's approach, Zehr sets it in dialogue with variants of Islamic thinking on war and peace.

The second question inquires into the source of the just war tradition's authority. What arguments may be posited in support of the assertion that the just war tradition is the appropriate idiom through which we should think about the challenges posed by the use of force in the twenty-first century? From whence, in other words, does the tradition derive the force that Obama and so many others appear ready to grant it? As noted above, some theorists appear to assume that the authority of the just war tradition is predicated upon aspects of faith or abstract claims to access "right reason" or some other such anchorage. Others have, however, contested this view, and instead proposed the Burkean view that the authority of the just war tradition is derived from its rich historical lineage. According to this view, the status of the tradition is born of its role as a store of communal learning with respect to the rights and wrongs of war. It embodies and conveys, from one generation to the next, the wisdom of the ages, the sum of experiential knowledge as it bears on the use of military force. Putting it in a nutshell, then, the just war tradition carries the clout it does because it partakes in a "fund of practical moral wisdom" that has withstood the test of time.[17] This volume does not seek to resolve this debate. But what it does do is present a series of chapters in part I that profess that the authority of the tradition is predicated on social practice.

Although these chapters disagree on the particular framework of political authority—sovereignty, democracy, religion, or gender, to name a few proposals—to which it is indexed, they all share the view that the tradition's authority is constituted through usage, and more specifically, how it is invoked and deployed. This point is made powerfully by Tarik Kochi in chapter 7, "Problems of Legitimacy within the Just War Tradition and International Law," when he writes that "the violence of the so-called just war plays a productive role in creating and sustaining new historical forms of 'legitimate' governance while destroying others."[18] Viewed together, then, all these chapters challenge the reader to think about the just war tradition as a practice of political authority. In some cases—as with chapter 5, by Laura Sjoberg, "The Inseparability of Gender Hierarchy, the Just War Tradition, and Authorizing War"—they go even further, provoking the reader to consider whether the tradition is a beneficial or pernicious practice of political authority.

The chapters that make up part I of this volume reflect a healthy diversity of approach and opinion. But they all subscribe to the view that if the just war tradition is framed as a practice of political authority, it cannot be understood as a purely intellectual conceit that exists in isolation from the practical and material world. Rather, it must be understood as a body of thought that is informed by, and reflective of, a heterogeneous array of practices and actors—political, military, legal, and scholarly. For some of the contributors, most notably Anthony F. Lang Jr., it also involves a religious component. He argues in chapter 8 that scholars should pay more attention to the locales and settings in which just war ideas are discussed and circulated, suggesting that the pulpit and the pew are an underused resource in this regard. Returning to our main point, we might note that, when it is set out in these broad terms, it is apparent that the just war tradition does not denote a single, monolithic theory. Instead, it resembles a multiplicity of closely related but competing voices that, when combined, constitute a unified tradition of inquiry and practical judgment. It is, to borrow Terry Nardin's felicitous phrase, a "tradition of argument"—that is, a site of inquiry whose form and substance reflect the sum of its own contestation.[19] So it should not surprise us that very different and even antagonistic accounts of what we might call the "just war idea" occasionally emerge. How can we adjudicate between these different articulations of the just war idea?

AUTHORITY IN PRACTICE

The problem shifts, then, from identifying the source of the authority of the just war tradition to determining what qualifies as an authoritative account of this tradition. The chapters that make up part II of this volume speak to this particular difficulty. They draw attention to the way in which the authority of the just war tradition—and the various accounts of political authority it in turn invokes—is reflected in practices of various sorts, from military ethics education to counterterrorism. In doing so, they emphasize the dynamic and contested way in which authority is constituted both in and by the just war tradition, understood as a practice. This agenda provokes two related questions. First, can recognize one account of the tradition as more authoritative than another? And second, on what grounds might such a judgment be made?

Treating these questions as flip sides of the same coin, the moral philosopher Alasdair MacIntyre furnishes us with a way of discerning what counts as an authoritative account of a tradition.[20] He argues that all traditions contain within them a standard of some sort that enables us to determine what counts as a persuasive interpretation or extension of that tradition. Where an interpretation or extension contributes to the *telos*, or end point, toward which the tradition is oriented, it should be viewed as participating in the authority of the tradition. Conversely, where an interpretation fails this test, it should be regarded as lacking authority. Interestingly, MacIntyre believes that interpretation need not be a purely reflective endeavor. Interpretation may also take a practical form. That is, it may be carried out, not just by those engaged in scholarly reflection on a tradition but also by concrete social and political agents who, whether knowingly or unknowingly, act in that tradition's name. This aspect of MacIntyre's argument reveals a fundamental point underlying it: The locus of authority within any tradition relates to the interplay between its received understandings and what we might call its interpretative community.

Applying MacIntyre's ideas to the just war tradition, we open up an interesting issue pertaining to who exactly is in a position to act as an authoritative interpreter of the just war tradition. As its principal interpreters, should we privilege practical actors who engage the tradition in the course of their everyday practice (e.g., the military and political leadership) or academic actors who reflect upon it in a scientific or philosophical way (e.g., ethicists, theologians, political theorists)? Whose voice should carry more weight when we are engaged in the practice of just war argumentation? Do we have some way of making this determination? A useful way to think about these problems would be to return to MacIntyre's teleological conception of tradition and to think about the source of a tradition's authority in relation to the particular *telos* or purpose that the tradition in question is understood to serve. Adapting this idea to the just war tradition, one can explicitly identify four potential purposes to which the tradition might be oriented: political, prophetic, pastoral, and philosophical. Each of these purposes anchors the tradition in different conceptions of authority.[21]

The political purpose of the just war tradition denotes its utility as a guide to policymakers. This is particularly so with relation to the *ad bellum* side of the tradition, where questions of the rightness of particular wars are subject to critical inquiry. This purpose means admitting that the tradition must accept a more limited role for moral judgment, for the complexity of modern politics and warfare means that political leaders have difficult choices to make. James Turner Johnson articulates this position well in the following: "I hold that there is a fundamental difference between the roles and competencies of moralists and those in political responsibility. We moralists do not bear political responsibility, and in our reflection and in our advice, whether solicited or unsolicited, we need to take care that we do not act as if we do."[22] This conception, as captured in this passage and some other writings of Johnson, depicts the just war tradition as a source of guidance to policymakers that helps them frame their choices through an ethical prism, while recognizing that this is not the only prism they will employ.

A second way to understand the just war tradition is as a form of prophecy. For some, the tradition supplies a position or platform from which to critically challenge those in power. This does not mean necessarily being a pacifist or accepting a presumption against war; rather, it means that one might approach the just war tradition as a tool for compelling policymakers to confront their understandings of justice and violence—confrontations not designed to advocate particular policies but oriented toward an ongoing critical stance. In MacIntyre's approach to traditions, this would mean that the *telos* of just war thinking is not relative judgment but absolute judgment. This supposes that those who engage in just war debate might see their role as not giving solace to the prince but standing before him and demanding that he adhere to the laws of the land—something akin to the role played by the Old Testament prophet. Of particular importance, the prophetic voice is directed toward those with power, for it is they who need to be reminded of their responsibilities to a higher order. Neta Crawford undertakes a related task in chapter 13 of this volume, asking whether the just war framework, as institutionalized in international law and reified in US war-making practices, is an effective instrument in this regard.

A third way to approach the tradition can be called the pastoral. Those drawing on the just war tradition also answer specific moral dilemmas facing individuals who have to use force. Here attention would be more specifically focused on the *in bello* side of the tradition and would be oriented toward individual combatants. This might manifest itself as education for military officers, which would focus more on developing their ability to make judgments in cases where the law or military manuals do not provide clear guidance. Indeed, as Martin Cook explains in chapter 14, just war has long played an important role in the education of the officer corps in the US military establishment. This approach eschews larger questions about the justice of wars and instead helps those who must follow orders from policymakers develop their ability to confront difficult moral dilemmas.

A final purpose for the tradition is the philosophical. This approach is oriented toward asking questions about the internal coherence of the tradition and some larger questions about what should be the relationship between violence, justice, and politics. These kinds of questions are most often found in scholarly debate, academic journals, and conferences. Such debates do not presume to give guidance to policymakers at the first level, although they might eventually do so. Rather, they allow for thinking within the broad categories of the tradition about what does it mean to use violence and how does violence relate to political leadership in an age of the sovereign state system. In chapter 9 Gregory Reichberg offers an excellent example of this kind of engagement on the relation between proper authority and the right to punitive war in the writings of Thomas Aquinas, whereas in chapter 11 Brent Steele treats the proximate, not to say intriguing, matter of revenge as it pertains to (and indeed reinscribes) the requirements of both the *jus ad bellum* and *jus in bello*. Revenge, according to Steele, should be understood as an affective practice, one that speaks to the *intentionality* of actors, a concept that is then taken up and reconsidered by Joseph Boyle in chapter 10.

When considering from whence the authority of the just war tradition derives, then, and who should be regarded as an authoritative interpreter of it, we need to think carefully about the purpose for which the tradition is invoked and deployed in differentiated contexts. This way of thinking about authority in practice raises a series of interesting questions for each of us as individuals with an interest in the tradition. For example, it provokes us to ask whether or not the four purposes can coexist; that is, can one be both a prophetic critic of the tradition and yet also use it to influence political decision making? Or, if the tradition is subject to critical philosophical analysis, does this undermine of teachers of military officers to use the tradition in a pastoral way? This volume does not furnish any final answers to these questions. This lies beyond its scope. The essays gathered in part II, however, elucidate the scope of these questions, and examine their application across a range of military and political practices and contexts. This modest, but we hope significant, pursuit should hopefully lead us toward some new insights regarding how we think about how authority functions in relation to the just war tradition.

THE TRIUMPH OF JUST WAR

Part III of this volume comprises a pair of chapters, 15 and 16, by, respectively, John Kelsay and Nicholas Rengger, that address from different directions the so-called triumph of just war theory. More specifically, it debates whether this purported triumph—if that is what it in fact is—would be a good thing, that is, something to be celebrated. It asks whether the ascendancy of the just war idiom in the official rhetoric of political and military leaders, as well as in the public sphere more generally, is likely to serve a progressive end by restraining the more barbaric aspects of modern war. Or is it more likely to verge toward the opposite extreme and facilitate barbarism by providing it with a gloss of moral respectability? Has it become, in other words, a means for the Gullivers of this world to circumvent international law (where it is perceived to be too constraining) while still providing their otherwise illicit acts with a thin but effective veneer of legitimacy?

The idea that the just war tradition may serve as a political discourse that enables and constrains the actions of our leaders is probably best illustrated by recourse to an apocryphal tale.[23] It involves President George H. W. Bush and his decision to launch the United Nations–authorized military mission against Saddam Hussein's Iraq in January 1991. Before the declaration of war, Bush was apprehensive that he could not reconcile his role in declaring war on Iraq with his Christian faith. Seeking reassurance, he contacted a minister known to his family and asked the minister to summarize the basic points of the Christian just war tradition on an index card, so that Bush might reflect upon them at his convenience. As the story goes, the minister obliged and Bush kept the index card in his shirt pocket for the duration of the war. Although some scholars might be swayed to argue that this story illustrates the easy residence the just war tradition has taken up in the corridors and chambers of power—the "triumph of just war theory" as Michael Walzer would have it—a more cynical reading is also possible.[24] According to this perspective, this story cautions that the just war tradition must always be in danger of residing in the politician's pocket, to be drawn upon and exploited at his or her expedience. It is worth expanding these rival views in more detail.

Walzer's argument is attractively simple. Just one year after the September 11, 2001, terrorist attacks, and one year into the so-called "War on Terror," Walzer published an essay that celebrated what he termed the "triumph of just war theory." This referred to the trend by which the conceptual framework of just war has been adopted by soldiers and political leaders alike, and has been "incorporated into war-making as a real constraint on when and how wars are fought."[25] Evidence for this trend is readily available in the communications of military advisers and leaders, such as Rupert Smith and Michael Quinlan, as well as in the speeches of both President Bush and President Obama. A few reservations aside, Walzer's view would seem to be that the triumph of just war is, in general terms, a good thing. He contends that it heralds a long-term process whereby the norms of restraint governing war are further buttressed and consolidated, with the result that their constraining effect on military action is increased. Oliver O'Donovan has put forward similar sentiments in his monograph *The Just War Revisited*, where he argues that the prevalence of just war norms has contributed to rendering war a more civilized endeavor over the course of the past fifty years.[26]

Contra Walzer and O'Donovan, skeptics have frequently claimed that the prevalence of just war discourse does not indicate a civilizing process or constraining factor at work. Instead, they argue, just war is a language that invites abuse by providing unscrupulous politicians with a vocabulary of justice with which to mask their realpolitik. What this story calls our attention to is the potential for the transformation of just war theory into a strategic discourse, which serves rather than challenges realpolitik.[27] As the vocabulary of just war theory is internalized by military and political leaders, the possibility that this theory may be deployed as a strategic partner in battle is increased. Military lawyers have undoubtedly become adept at manipulating the language made available to them by just war theory, frequently using it to extend the range of action available to their commanders. By way of example, we might think of the manner by which the catchall term "collateral damage" was invoked by NATO lawyers as legal cover for the targeting of dual-use installations—power plants, radio stations, oil refineries, water treatment plants, and so on—in Kosovo in 1999. In such cases, the language of just war theory appears to be mobilized by the military as a strategic asset, serving to enable rather than constrain the violence of war.

There should be no surprise, then, these critics write, that those eras in which notions of just war enjoy currency also happen to have been among the bloodiest periods of human history. Subsequently, we are led to wonder whether the aphorism that the road to hell is paved with good intentions pertains acutely to the just war tradition? As Chris Brown wonders in chapter 2, are the critics (from Carl Schmitt to Ken Booth to Andrew Fiala) correct to decry the just war tradition as the handmaiden to imperialism?[28] By allying itself to power in order to restrain the "monstrous barbarity" that war sometimes unleashes, does it compromise too much and risk its own integrity? Or, to paraphrase Nicholas Rengger's riff on *The Lord of the Rings*, is the very project of just war theory in danger of falling prey to, and being consumed by, Sauron's ring of power?[29] These charges have haunted contemporary just war theorists, who have found themselves consistently decried as apologists of power. Are they fair?

If one wished to defend Walzer's position, one could argue that these charges overlook the deeper level at which his argument works. Walzer claims that the adoption of just war as the lingua franca of state leaders and generals is a good thing, not because it indicates that we are governed by righteous people but because it means that we, as critics and engaged citizens, have enhanced critical leverage on those in power. This is because we now possess a language of immanent critique that enables us to hold our military and political leaders to account; that is, to call them to task on the moral promises and pronouncements they make in the course of military struggles. The point here is that, even if military and political leaders invoke just war terminology in an insincere and/or opportunistic way, commentators and critics may turn these very claims against them. As Walzer writes, we can ascertain the legitimacy of the judgments and justifications people commonly make by seeking out their coherence and laying bare the principles they exemplify. We can "expose the hypocrisy of soldiers and statesmen who publicly acknowledge these commitments while seeking in fact only to their own advantage; . . . we hold such people to their own principles, though we may draw these out and arrange them in ways that they had not thought of before."[30] In this respect, the just war tradition provides us with a medium through which to challenge the actions of the powerful as they relate to the use of military force. Put in more grandiose terms, it offers us an avenue for speaking truth to power.

Is Walzer too sanguine in this assessment? Might it be the case that, far from vindicating the just war tradition as a critical tool, the adoption of just war vocabulary by those commanding the "War on Terror" instead contributes to its corrosion? These are clearly important questions that call upon us to think about the continuing capacity of the just war tradition to supply us with a moral vocabulary through which to evaluate the rights and wrongs of the use of force in international society and, beyond this, to speak truth to power.

CONCLUSION

Taken as a whole then, the chapters of this volume are intended to provoke readers to reconsider what it means to characterize the just war tradition as a practice of political authority. As such, they challenge scholars of the just war tradition to turn their minds, if not for the first time, then once again, to the twin categories that we have called the "practice of authority" and the "authority of practice." These, in turn, provide what we hope is a penetrating angle or perspective on the three key facets of political authority as it pertains to the just war tradition. First, it provides a platform from which to examine the authority *of* the tradition, where it derives from, and where it rests today. This line of inquiry invites scholars to treat the tradition in relation to its role and position in the wider political, military, and even academic world. Second, it exposes a series of thorny issues regarding the constitution of authority *in* the tradition. Teasing this out, it calls to our attention a set of questions about the proper interpretation of the tradition. Who, for instance, should be regarded as an authoritative interpreter of the tradition, and on what grounds? Third, and perhaps most obviously, it speaks to the relation between authority *and* the tradition. This is to say that it treats issues arising in connection with the tradition's understanding of the use of force in the context of the diverse battlefields of the contemporary security environment. Bringing all this together, the ambition behind this volume is to suggest a new research agenda that responds in a meaningful way to Obama's exhortation that, confronted by the challenges of the twenty-first century, we must learn to think in new ways about the notion of just war.

NOTES

1. Recent scholarship suggests that a third category, the *jus post bellum*, should be attached to the tradition. However, this is not universally accepted. For a recent treatment of this topic, though, see Eric Patterson, ed., *Ethics beyond War's End* (Washington, DC: Georgetown University Press, 2012).

2. President Barack Obama, "Remarks by the President at the Acceptance of the Nobel Peace Prize," December 10, 2009, Oslo City Hall, www.whitehouse.gov/the-press-office/remarks-president-acceptance-nobel-peace-prize.

3. Honorable exceptions include James Pattison, *Humanitarian Intervention and the Responsibility to Protect: Who Should Intervene?* (Oxford: Oxford University Press, 2010); and Eric A. Heinze and Brent J. Steele, eds., *Ethics, Authority, and War: Non-State Actors and the Just War Tradition* (Basingstoke, UK: Palgrave, 2009).

4. Max Weber, "The Profession and Vocation of Politics," reprinted in *Political Writings*, ed. Peter Lawson and Ronald Speirs (Cambridge: Cambridge University Press, 1994; orig. pub. 1919), 310.

5. Joseph Raz, *The Authority of Law: Essays on Law and Morality* (Oxford: Clarendon Press, 1979), 3.

6. Thomas Christiano, "Authority," *Stanford Encyclopaedia of Philosophy*, July 2004, http://plato.stanford.edu/entries/authority.

7. R. B. Friedman, "On the Concept of Authority in Political Philosophy," in *Authority*, ed. Joseph Raz (London: Basil Blackwell, 1990; orig. pub. 1973), 56–91.

8. Hannah Arendt, "What Is Authority?" in *Between Past and Future: Eight Exercises in Political Thought*, by Hannah Arendt (New York: Penguin Books, 1968), 91–142.

9. Friedman, "On the Concept of Authority," 84.

10. David Lake has recently argued that the United States does indeed provide such authority through its practical control of the international order. See David A. Lake, *Hierarchy in International Relations* (Ithaca, NY: Cornell University Press, 2009).

11. Richard Flathman, *The Practice of Political Authority* (Chicago: University of Chicago Press), 175–91.

12. This is the critique leveled at Michael Walzer by Hedley Bull, "Recapturing the Just War for Political Theory," *World Politics* 31 (1979): 588–99.

13. On the "clash of civilizations," see Samuel Huntington, *The Clash of Civilizations and the Remaking of World Order* (New York: Simon & Schuster, 1996). James Turner Johnson addresses it in relation to the just war tradition; see James Turner Johnson, *The War to Oust*

Saddam Hussein: Just War and the New Face of Conflict (Lanham, MD: Rowman & Littlefield, 2005).

14. For more on this, see Cian O'Driscoll, "Under an Empty Sky? Bruce Springsteen, Just War, and the War on Terror," *Critical Studies on Terrorism* 4, no. 2 (2011): 283–92.

15. David Fisher and Brian Wicker, "Editors Introduction," in *Just War on Terror: A Christian and Muslim Response* (Farnham, UK: Ashgate, 2010), 5.

16. Ibid.

17. James Turner Johnson, *Can Modern War Be Just?* (New Haven. CT: Yale University Press, 1984), 15.

18. See chapter 7 in this volume by Tarik Kochi, "Problems of Legitimacy within the Just War Tradition and International Law."

19. Terry Nardin, "Ethical Traditions in International Affairs," in *Traditions of International Ethics*, ed. by Terry Nardin and David R. Mapel (Cambridge: Cambridge University Press, 1992), 18–19. In a similar light, Michael Walzer contends that the just war tradition is the product of "many centuries of arguing about war." Michael Walzer, "The Triumph of Just War Theory," in *Arguing about War*, ed. by Michael Walzer (New Haven, CT: Yale University Press, 2004), 7–8.

20. MacIntyre deals with these issues in a number of works, but they are perhaps most clearly articulated in his *Three Rival Versions of Moral Inquiry* (London: Duckworth, 1990).

21. This four-part framing is drawn from Anthony F. Lang Jr., "The Just War Tradition and the Question of Authority," *Journal of Military Ethics* 8, no. 3 (2009): 202–16.

22. Johnson, *War to Oust Saddam Hussein*, 67.

23. Peter Temes, *The Just War: An American Reflection on the Morality of War in Our Time* (Chicago: Ivan R. Dee, 2003), 91.

24. Walzer, "Triumph."

25. Ibid., 12.

26. Oliver O'Donovan, *The Just War Revisited* (Cambridge: Cambridge University Press, 2003), 126.

27. See David Kennedy's recent analysis of the relationship between the practice of war and the discourse of international law. David Kennedy, *Of War and Law* (Princeton, NJ: Princeton University Press, 2006). Also see Tarik Kochi, *The Other's War: Recognition and the Violence of Ethics* (New York: Birkbeck Law Press, 2009), 1–23.

28. Carl Schmitt, *The* Nomos *of the Earth* (New York: Telos Press, 2003); Gabriella Slomp, "Carl Schmitt's Five Arguments against the Idea of Just War," *Cambridge Review of International Affairs* 19 (2006): 435–47; Ken Booth, "Ten Flaws of Just Wars," in *The Kosovo Tragedy*, ed. Ken Booth (London: Frank Cass, 2001); and Andrew Fiala, *The Just War Myth: The Moral Illusions of War* (Lanham, MD: Rowman & Littlefield, 2008).

29. Nicholas J. Rengger, "Just a War against Terror? Jean Bethke Elshtain's Burden and American Power," *International Affairs* 80 (2004): 107–16.

30. Michael Walzer, *Just and Unjust Wars: A Moral Argument with Historical Illustrations* (New York: Basic Books, 1992), xxix. Also see Michael Walzer, *Interpretation and Social Criticism* (London: Harvard University Press, 1987), 39.

PART I

~

The Practice of Authority

CHAPTER 1

The Right to Use Armed Force

Sovereignty, Responsibility, and the Common Good

James Turner Johnson

TWO CONCEPTIONS: CLASSIC AND CONTEMPORARY

THROUGH MOST OF THE HISTORY of the just war tradition, writers on just war, when listing the requirements for just resort to armed force, followed the example of the summary provided by Thomas Aquinas: first the authority of a sovereign ruler; then just cause, defined as retaking that which has been wrongly taken and punishing evildoing; and then right intention, defined negatively as avoiding intentions grounded in personal vice and positively in terms of aiming to secure peace.[1] Here the primary necessity for a just war is sovereign authority; the other necessities named not only follow in precedence but also depend importantly on that authority, for among the responsibilities included in those of sovereignty are determining when there is just cause for resort to armed force on behalf of the political community and maintaining right intention in the use of such force.

This is a conception placed squarely within the frame of an understanding of the ends of good politics. For the medieval writers, these were defined in the terms of the three interrelated "goods" of politics—order, justice, and peace—as taken over from earlier Classical thought by Augustine. The just war conception of sovereign authority reflected the good of political order; the conception of just cause reflected the good of justice within the political community; and the conception of right intention corresponded to the good of peace within that community. More broadly, this understanding also extended to relations between and among political communities, as disorder, injustice, and conflict in one community inevitably affected the well-being of neighboring communities.

There is a marked contrast between this conception and the majority of present-day just war thought. Present-day discussions of the idea of just war commonly give priority to the question of just cause in listings of the requirements for justified resort to force, while at the same time giving less weight to the matter of the authority required for resort to the use of armed force. A well-known and influential example of this is provided by the US Catholic bishops in their 1983 pastoral letter, *The Challenge of Peace*, and again in their 1993 statement marking the tenth anniversary of this pastoral, *The Harvest of Justice Is Sown in Peace*.[2] In both these statements, the listing of the just war criteria begins with "just cause," followed (in order) in the case of *The Challenge of Peace* by "competent authority," "comparative justice," "right intention," and three prudential criteria, "last resort," "probability of success," and "proportionality." The listing in *The Harvest of Justice* also begins with the category "just cause," but the next two requirements have swapped places, so "comparative justice" comes second; "legitimate authority" is demoted to third, followed by "right intention" and the three prudential criteria, whose order is also shuffled here: "probability of success," "proportionality," and "last resort."

Further stress on the importance of the just cause criterion in both the 1983 and 1993 listings is provided by the definition of "right intention," not as a distinct moral reference point but simply as having an intention in line with the just cause. No mention is made of avoiding evil intentions or aiming at peace, as in the classic definition of right intention.

In the context of all this emphasis on the importance of just cause, defined and drawn attention to in various ways, the question of the authority needed for just resort to armed force is presented with diminished strength. As noted above, the bishops' listings demote it to second place in 1983 and to third place in 1993, sandwiching it between the two criteria having to do with justice in 1983 and placing it after both these criteria in 1993. In both cases, moreover, the description of the authority required is formalistic: In 1983, the term used is "competent authority," defined as follows: "War must be declared by those with responsibility for public order"; in 1993, the term used is "legitimate authority," defined this way: "Only duly constituted public authorities may use deadly force or wage war." The issue in both statements is the formal role of the authority as legally defined for the political community in question. It is not clear what either of these formulations means when the referent is the US constitutional system, whereby the authority to declare war lies with the Senate, while responsibility for "public order" arguably lies with the president and the executive branch. The more general language used in 1993, "duly constituted public authorities," leaves room for the varieties of governmental systems across the world, but it also leaves open the question whether such authorities are national or must be international (e.g., the United Nations Security Council). But in both cases the ambiguity is trumped by the prioritization; what is of first importance is the question of justice, and then it is the role of those holding the appropriate legally defined roles to act accordingly. Their role is reactive. Who makes the decision regarding justice? That is left unclear; but perhaps it is the moralists, or perhaps it is public opinion, or perhaps it is the law itself and the lawyers who interpret it. In any case, the role of the political authority is secondary, reacting to whatever has been determined by the appropriate experts with regard to justice.

The case of the US Catholic bishops is typical rather than exceptional in regard to how justice and authority are treated across a broad spectrum of recent thinking on the justification of the use of armed force. Another prominent example, from a very different source, is provided by the "Six Conditions for Committing United States Military Forces," the so-called Weinberger Doctrine of 1984, where the first condition is a statement of just cause: "When [use of armed force] is vital to the defense of national or international interests."[3] Other examples abound.

My point in noting the difference in how the role of the requirement of authority is treated in classic and contemporary thinking about justified use of armed force is to suggest that something has been lost in the shift I have described and to argue for the importance of recovering it. The first step in this direction is to trace how the shift took place, the reasons for it, and the implications that followed.

THE HISTORICAL BACKGROUND OF THE CONTEMPORARY CONCEPTION OF THE JUST USE OF ARMED FORCE

The contemporary way of thinking about the justified use of armed force is not simply a recent phenomenon; it has its own deep history, made up of several interlinked elements. First came a shift in the conception of sovereignty, together with an emphasis on the defense of national territory as the primary justifying cause for the use of armed force. A bit later came the rise of internationalism, the idea that disputes between and among states could be ended by the creation of a new international legal and political structure taking precedence over states and their governments. And still later came a conception of modern war as inherently grossly indiscriminate and destructive, leading to the effort to abolish war altogether in relations among states.

The first of these, a shift in the conception of sovereignty, appears fully in the thought of Grotius; here, sovereignty, instead of being understood as associated with the person of the ruler of a political community, was redefined as a characteristic of the community itself, in terms of its geographic borders, its inhabitants, and their "ancient laws and privileges." Developed as part of Grotius's intellectual effort to justify Dutch independence from the rule of the king of Spain, this conception became the backbone of the system of international order associated with the Peace of Westphalia, a system based on a state system defined by specific national borders. In the Westphalian system, as in Grotius's thought, the defense of those borders against intrusion by others becomes the most important justification for resort to armed force, with other reasons (retained by Grotius from earlier just war tradition) reduced to derivative, supporting roles.[4] Positive international law took shape around this conception, and it is central to the system of international order defined by the United Nations Charter, in which Article 2 prohibits member states from "the threat or use of force against the territorial integrity or political independence of any state" and Article 51 clarifies that nothing in the charter impairs "the inherent right of individual or collective self-defense" against armed attack.[5] In this context what matters in defining whether a use of armed force is justified or not is whether it defends against armed attack; political authority's role here is effectively limited to coordinating the defense.

The second development, the push to create a new international structure of government above that of states so as to abolish war, first took shape in the form of the idea of "perpetual peace" developed in the thought of various writers from the early seventeenth to the late eighteenth centuries.[6] In the nineteenth century the resulting internationalist ideal contributed to the early development of positive international law; and in the twentieth century it took structural form, first in the League of Nations and then in the United Nations. On the internationalist conception the problem of war is understood as arising from the existence of states and competition creating friction among them; the new international system is posited as a form of world order that rises above the selfish interests of states and thus eliminates conflict among them.

The third development, the idea that war in the modern world has become inherently indiscriminate and destructive beyond all possibility of restraint, arose in the nineteenth century in response to two main influences: the growth of large national armies fed by conscription, first in France as a result of the Revolution, and then in other European societies as a result of the Napoleonic wars; and, by the 1860s and 1870s, the appearance of weapons in greater numbers and of more destructive capability than had earlier been the case. These influences came together in the two world wars, and the debates over nuclear weapons from the 1950s to the 1980s (including the contribution of the US Catholic bishops to this debate in *The Challenge of Peace*) were fed importantly by the assumption that subsequent wars would be fought on the model of these two conflicts.

The effects of all these developments are still very much in evidence in both thought and institutional form. At the same time, both the systems of moral thought and the international institutional system built on them have introduced problems of their own. The international system in both its institutional incarnations, the League of Nations and the United Nations, has proven unable to play the superstate role envisioned by the most ardent internationalists, and the importance of well-governed and robust states has reasserted itself since the end of the Cold War and in the face of international terrorism. The aggressor-defender model for the only proper use of force by states has turned out to be problematic in the face of conflicts involving nonstate actors, forms of aggression that are not military in nature, and new awareness of the importance of a role for armed force in reacting to heinous violations (often by ruling authorities within a society) of basic human rights. These problems suggest the importance of again looking closely at the conceptions of sovereignty, just cause for resort to force, their interrelation, and their bearing on the possibilities for peace in traditional just war thinking.

THE IMPORTANCE OF SOVEREIGN AUTHORITY UNDERSTOOD AS RESPONSIBILITY FOR THE COMMON GOOD

By contrast to the sort of recent just war thinking described above, in the idea of just war as it originally came together in the Middle Ages and continued into the early modern period the requirement of sovereign authority held first place. The difference between these two ways of thinking about justified resort to armed force is more than accidental or random; which of these two moral requirements has first priority is an essential part of the associated conception of just war, including what that conception intends to say about the role of the use of armed force in relation to political order and the practice of government and who are understood as the proper interpreters of the just war requirements. The nature and importance of this difference has drawn no particular attention among present-day just war thinkers, possibly because the current way of listing the defining requirements of just war fits well within the modern international system, but also perhaps because this way of thinking allows the moralists to take the role of judging when force is justified, with those in charge of governing given the secondary, pro forma role of acting on whatever has been determined to be just according to the judgments of the moral experts. The traditional or classic understanding of just war, by contrast, puts the focus on the sovereign ruler of each political community as the final repository of responsibility for the good of that community and for the nexus of relations among communities that serves to protect and reinforce the good of all. Here the responsibility to govern is understood as *moral* in character; it is to serve the good of the community for which the sovereign, and only the sovereign, has overall responsibility. Hence, on this conception, the idea of just war is not merely procedural or formal but also serves to establish that only the sovereign has the right to resort to armed force and thus has a monopoly on the use of such force within the political community or on behalf of that community in relations with others. Putting the requirement of sovereign authority first means both that the sovereign is the one who must judge whether a use of armed force in a given case would be just or unjust and whether it would serve peace, and that the sovereign is the one charged with using such force only with a right intention, and thus in the right way. Within this frame specialists in moral thinking, along with specialists working from other perspectives, may (and should) offer advice, but final judgment rests with the sovereign, because the responsibility for the good of the community rests on him (or her or, in rare cases, them). The conception of just war here, in a term used by Chris Brown in chapter 2 of the present volume, is that of a "praxis of judgment," not a list of criteria to be employed as a kind of checklist, whether by those with the responsibility of government or by others who may wish to advise or criticize them. Although this conception of politics is premodern, it also turns out to fit well the needs encountered in present-day circumstances (of the sort previewed above), in which the possibility of the use of armed force by individual states is placed on the table for decision and action. The deficiency of the inherited model of international order in the face of such challenges similarly argues for the need to recover what was lost when the premodern moral conception of sovereign authority was superseded by the modern, territorially defined conception of sovereignty.

As acknowledged earlier in the chapter, the historical or traditional understanding of the requirements for just war was given classic statement by Thomas Aquinas in *Summa Theologiae* II/II, Q. 40. His summary there of what is required for a justified resort to force, however, points both backward and forward. Looking backward, it reflects a long century of debate that began with Gratian's *Decretum* in the 1140s, continued in the two generations of canonical commentators known as the Decretists and the Decretalists, and reached a settled position not long before Aquinas wrote on the thinking of Pope Innocent IV and the canonist Hostiensis. Looking forward in time, the summary statement on just war provided by Aquinas remained a stable point of reference right up into the era of the Reformation, when it was employed by Protestant as well as Catholic thinkers writing about war. With Grotius, as noted above, this way of thinking was revised in important respects; our purpose now, however, is to examine in closer detail the classic idea of just war, its antecedents, and the benefits manifest in its long-term stability.[7]

THE CLASSIC CONCEPTION OF JUST WAR AND POLITICAL AUTHORITY: A CLOSER LOOK

In his classic statement, Aquinas summarized the three requirements of a just war (*bellum iustum*): the authority of a prince or sovereign ruler; a just cause, defined as to retake that which has been wrongly taken and to punish evildoing; and a right intent, defined negatively in terms of the avoiding of wrong intentions such as exemplified by Augustine in *Contra Faustum* (xxii.74) and defined positively as the obligation to aim at peace.[8] The canonical debate that had preceded Aquinas provided the meat for all three just war requirements, as well as for how they were conceived and how they were ordered.

The priority of sovereign authority came from two directions. First, the Decretists had concluded that only temporal rulers in positions of sovereignty could justifiably resort to armed force. Negatively, this required denying the right of the sword to two other varieties of possible claimants, the spiritual or ecclesiastical authorities and private individuals, especially those of the knightly class, who were not in positions of sovereign authority. Positively, the canonists' decision required explaining why sovereign rulers should have this right. In denying the right of resort to the sword to spiritual authorities, the canonists relied on the Gelasian distinction between the spiritual and temporal powers, with the right of the sword belonging to the temporal sphere. In denying this right to persons with temporal superiors, the Decretists concluded that such persons could appeal disputes to those superiors, all the way up to the sovereign, who had no superior and thus must possess the right to defend claims he judged justified by resort to arms. This was one direction of thinking behind Aquinas's formulation.

The second direction from which came the priority given sovereign authority in the requirements for a just resort to force was the development of thinking about the moral responsibilities and personal characteristics of the ideal or "good" ruler, which were already reflected in the canonists' thinking and developed in some detail in Aquinas's own thought by his brief work *On Princely Rule*.[9] On this account the prince or sovereign ruler was defined in moral terms as having ultimate responsibility for the overall good of the political community governed, and this responsibility requires the right of recourse to the sword to deal with both internal and external threats to this good. The meaning of sovereignty, on these terms, was fundamentally moral in nature and was located in the person of the sovereign ruler, being exercised through that sovereign's rule over the community for which he (or she, or occasionally they) bore responsibility. Aquinas's account summarizes this reasoning as follows:

> It is not the business of a private individual to declare war, because he can pursue his right before the judgment of his superior. Moreover it is not the business of a private person to summon together the people, which has to be done in wartime. And as the care of the common weal is committed to those who are in authority, . . . it is licit for them to have recourse to the material sword in defending the common weal against internal disturbances, as when they punish malefactors [according to the provisions of Rom 13:4], so too, it is their business to have recourse to the sword in protecting the common weal against external enemies.[10]

This is medieval language, but the issues addressed are still very much in evidence as problems needing to be dealt with in the practice of politics in the contemporary world: the existence of private armies or militias that exist to advance the personal interests of their leaders, as in insurgencies, or to serve claims of transcendent right, as in religiously justified terrorism, and the need for an orderly, secure life in community. I will return to this point below.

Part of what the sovereign must do to discharge his responsibility for the common good is to judge which issues justify resort to armed force. This is why, in classic just war reasoning, just cause comes after the requirement of sovereign authority. The canonists' language signals this explicitly in linking the discernment of just cause and the authorization of force to the act of a judge and, as is clear in Gratian, to the importance of personal rectitude on the judge's (or sovereign's) part: "For he is no judge who has not justice within himself."[11]

But what constitutes a just cause for resort to armed force on behalf of the good of the community? Aquinas's summary statement, drawn from Augustine, identifies two such causes: "A just war is wont to be described as one that avenges wrongs, when a nation or state has to be punished, for refusing to make amends for the wrongs inflicted by its subjects, or to restore what it has seized unjustly."[12] This echoes the language of Romans 13:4, a text widely cited in reference to the just war idea: The sovereign ruler "beareth not the sword in vain: for he is God's minister, an avenger to execute wrath upon him that doth evil." Thus a just cause for use of armed force exists when there is an unanswered need for punishment and/or restitution.

What about self-defense? That purpose is acknowledged as part of Aquinas's summary statement defining the sovereign's right to the sword, and it had been part of the definition of just cause in the *Decretum*, but it is not part of Aquinas's specific definition of just cause.[13] The reason for this is, again, the conclusion that had been reached in the debate among the canonists, and specifically in a judgment offered by Innocent IV around 1245 distinguishing between war and self-defense: "It is permissible for anyone to wage war in self-defense or to protect property. Nor is this properly called 'war' (*bellum*) but rather 'defense' (*defensio*). [One] may lawfully fight back on the spot (*incontinenti*) . . . before he has tuned his attention to other matters."[14] Everyone, including both private individuals and princes, has the right to use armed force in self-defense "on the spot"—that is, at the time the harm is being offered or done—but doing justice after such harm has been accomplished is another matter, which belongs to the judgment of sovereign authority. Just war, described in these terms, has to do precisely with the execution of justice in response to injustice. This is the function of just war, *bellum iustum*.

Consider, by contrast, how this matter is handled by Grotius. First, he explicitly distinguishes war from "judicial processes": "For where judicial processes fail, there war begins." Second, rather than finding the justification of resort to armed force in the need to establish or maintain justice, Grotius reasons upward from the individual's right of self-defense to that of the state. After some discussion, he reaches his definition of just cause: "Three justifiable causes for war are generally cited: defense, recovery of property, and punishment. . . . The first just cause of war, then, is an injury, which, even though not actually committed, threatens our persons or our property."[15]

These are two quite different forms of reasoning. Classic just war thought finds the justification for resort to force in the need to establish justice after a wrong has been done and reasons downward from the responsibility of the sovereign authority to protect justice; no special justification is thought to be needed for a response in force to a serious threat "on the spot," while the threat is being offered. Grotius, conversely, separates war from judicial process and reasons upward from the individual's right of self-defense against attack or the immediate threat of attack to the right of the political community to resort to armed force in the same circumstances. The right to continue to use force after this, to punish the aggressor and seek restitution for harm done, depends here on the first justifying cause, the right of self-defense. It is a small step, taken by others after Grotius, to argue that once the immediate danger is ended, then "war" gives way again to "judicial processes," so that justice after a clash of arms should be a matter for the courts, not a continuing justification for use of armed force. But such reasoning raises a problem: What if the original aggressor refuses to comply with the judgment? May arms then be used to enforce compliance? And if so, is this a new case of aggression, justifying resort to arms in self-defense? And so on.

A quick word should be added about the conception of right intention and its function. As noted earlier in the chapter, in the US Catholic bishops' reasoning, the category of "right intention" serves to reinforce their giving highest priority to just cause while reducing the authority requirement both by demoting its place in the listing and by describing it formalistically. By contrast, in classic just war thought it reinforces the conception of sovereignty in moral terms, requiring the sovereign who authorizes the resort to armed force to avoid evil intentions and to orient the use of force toward the service of peace. Once again, the proper exercise of sovereignty, understood as responsibility for the common good, is the key concept for classic just war thinking and the tradition it defines, whereas for recent just war thinking just cause, understood in terms oriented to restricting the right to war, is the key concept.

THE CLASSIC IDEA OF SOVEREIGN AUTHORITY AND TWO CONTEMPORARY ISSUES

In classic just war thought the requirement of sovereign authority for any just use of armed force holds first priority among the requisites for moral use of such force. This is so for two reasons: first, because of how such authority is understood—as the final seat of responsibility for the common good of the political community in question and of the relations among political communities; and second, because logically, the person or persons with such responsibility must determine whether the cause is just, ensure that any use of armed force does not proceed from wrongful intentions, and ensure that the use of such force is directed toward protecting or reestablishing a just, peaceful order. Much recent just war thinking, working from the very different conception of sovereignty and the right to use armed force established in the Westphalian system of world order, prioritizes the requirement of just cause and defines this narrowly in terms of the self-defense of one's own national territory against armed aggression from outside. In this thinking the role of political authority becomes secondary and largely formalistic; the authority needed is whatever is "competent" or "legitimate" in the case in question, and its function is effectively only to respond to acts needing to be defended against. Such a conception of just war closely follows the shape of international law, but it also reflects a judgment that the use of armed force is itself bad and is to be avoided except perhaps in extreme situations. Just as the origin of the Westphalian system was an effort to prevent another Thirty Years' War, and its adaptation into the present system of world order was an effort to prevent another world war, so the shape of such present-day just war thinking reflects the desire to avoid nuclear war and a desire to limit the options available to political leaders so that they may not resort to armed force except in extreme situations. But this way of seeking to restrain resort to use of armed force limits the options of statecraft in dealing with the actual kinds of injustice manifest in the world today—including some that are arguably the result of the territorial protections given to tyrants under the Westphalian–United Nations system. The need to deal with such injustice calls for new attention to the classic just war conception of sovereign authority, the responsibility it entails, and the possibility of the use of armed force in carrying out the implications of this responsibility.

In the following pages I discuss the classical conception of sovereign authority as applying to two pressing contemporary issues: egregious violations of basic human rights, and the breakdown in protection of noncombatants during asymmetric warfare.

THE RIGHT OF STATES TO EMPLOY ARMED FORCE IN RESPONSE TO EGREGIOUS VIOLATIONS OF BASIC HUMAN RIGHTS

Beginning in the 1990s a serious moral and legal debate developed over the question of the use of armed force to respond to cases of egregious violations of basic human rights. This debate reached a kind of climax with the report of the International Commission on Intervention and State Sovereignty, *The Responsibility to Protect*.[16] Since then, however, the moral and legal debates have shifted to other issues, and the tension in the positive international legal structure remains unresolved. This tension is between the idea of sovereign inviolability on the one hand and the rise of human rights law on the other. The first is rooted in the conception of sovereignty coming out of the thought of Grotius and established in the Westphalian and United Nations systems: that the borders of sovereign states are sacrosanct, and what goes on inside those borders is a matter for the government of that state to deal with. In general terms, so long as there is reasonably good government in all states, this rule serves well as a barrier to cross-border interference for other reasons as well. But where there is not reasonably good government—when the rulers seek to enrich themselves or a particular class at the expense of the society as a whole, when the government of a state oppresses or persecutes the people over whom it has power, or when there is internal strife leading to significant oppression or worse and the government will not take steps to remedy this or is unable to do so—then the rule of sovereign inviolability turns out to protect evildoing. Not without irony, the restraints on the use of force by states defined in the UN Charter reinforce this protection. But the rise of human rights law after the Universal Declaration of Human Rights and the Genocide Convention (both adopted in 1948) has increasingly established a challenge to this, defining positive obligations and the idea of responsibilities for states and the community of nations to oppose systematic violations of basic human rights. Exactly how far these responsibilities extend and how they apply were the central questions in the debates over humanitarian intervention occasioned by the conflicts of the 1990s, particularly the wars of the breakup of Yugoslavia and the Rwandan genocide of 1994. The indictment of high government officials by the International Criminal Tribunal for Rwanda and the International Criminal Tribunal for the Former Yugoslavia (particularly the indictment of former Yugoslav leader Slobodan Milošević), together with the position taken in *The Responsibility to Protect* has, at least so far, tilted resolution of this tension in the positive law in favor of the right of intervention and against the rule of sovereign inviolability in the case of gross and systematic abuses of basic human rights. There is also now a history of states acting to deal with major human rights abuses (not usually called that) in neighboring states, including the examples of Vietnam in Cambodia, Tanzania in Uganda, Nigeria in Sierra Leone, and NATO in Kosovo. But it is far from clear that, in practice, there is now agreement that armed force can be used in response to such abuses, or what the aims of intervention involving the use of force should be: to stop the abuses (a short-term matter), to provide protection to the endangered population (a matter for longer-term military and/or police presence in the affected state), or to reshape the government of the society to avoid such abuses in the future (a very long-term affair involving many other kinds of interventionary involvement than simply the military). The United Nations is ill equipped on its own to perform any of these tasks; it lacks the necessary resources in itself, has insufficient command and control capabilities to deal effectively with military forces, and has achieved only a middling record of success, at best, in past efforts of this kind. Functionally, the UN Security Council is in a position similar to that of medieval popes: It can authorize the use of armed force in the name of the UN itself, by ad hoc or treaty-based groups of states, or by individual states, but in any of these cases it is dependent on the agreement of states and the use of the resources of states. This fact argues that a new ingredient is needed for a functional resolution of the tension described above, one that returns to consideration of the pre-Grotian conception of sovereignty understood as responsibility for the common good, both of the sovereign's own political community and of the community of such communities, that is, the regional and/or international pattern of order among individual political communities. In any case, consideration of such moral responsibility as a necessary ingredient of good statecraft is necessary wherever any political community confronts such manifestations of injustice as the egregious violation of human rights.

Precedent for this, historically, is found in the treatment of tyranny as not simply an internal matter for the political community afflicted but also for its neighbors, and thus for their sovereign rulers. But while dealing with a tyrant—or, in present-day terms, a government that fails its people in one or more of the sorts of ways described above—is a matter that affects the interests of neighboring states and the international system as a whole, it is easy for states to accept the status quo (especially when an offending government is "on one's own side") or for opponents of involvement to ignore the negative effects, arguing that involvement would serve no pressing national interest. The state of international law on sovereignty provides cover for inaction and downplaying responsibilities to protect human rights, as when members of the US Clinton administration assiduously avoided use of "the G-word" (genocide) when speaking of the 1994 Rwandan massacre, lest using that term be understood as obligating the United States to intervene militarily to stop the slaughter. Similarly, we may consider the reticence of European states and also the United States to become involved in dealing with the human rights abuses accompanying the wars of the breakup of Yugoslavia. And further, there is the fate of US president George W. Bush's citing the egregious humanitarian abuses of the Saddam Hussein regime as one of his three reasons for use of military force to remove Saddam and his regime:[17] This argument discomfited military leaders, who did not regard action for such reason as an appropriate mission for US military forces, and it was simply ignored by moralists, pundits, and others who wanted to oppose the use of armed force in this case by focusing on the deficits in the argument from preemption. Today Bush's argument for protection of human rights has entirely been forgotten as a justification offered for that use of armed force, as attention has shifted to criticism and rejection of the preemption argument.

So state behavior is far from catching up with the aggressive attitude toward punishing human rights violations found in the international criminal tribunals for

Rwanda and the former Yugoslavia and toward protecting human rights found in *The Responsibility to Protect*. But serious just war thinkers also have a role to play in seeking to educate state behavior, reflecting on the responsibilities of sovereignty as traditionally conceived and their implications for dealing with tyrants, who in present form are political leaders who engage in human rights abuses or facilitate such abuses by favored portions of their populations.

THE BREAKDOWN OF NONCOMBATANT PROTECTION IN ASYMMETRIC WAR

The major form taken by warfare since 1945 has not been that of "World War III," major international conflicts between alliances of states carried out by massive armies using heavily destructive means including weapons of mass destruction, but local conflicts and spot uses of terrorist strikes involving nonstate actors on one or both sides. Such warfare, called by various names—"low-level" conflicts, "small wars," insurgencies, irregular warfare, guerilla warfare, asymmetrical warfare, and of course terrorism itself taken as a general phenomenon—has typically involved relatively small groups of fighters, arms ranging from knives and machetes through the ubiquitous Kalashnikov-type automatic rifles and mortars to the explosive vests of suicide bombers, car and truck bombs, and different types of mines and improvised explosive devices. Sometimes the fighting groups live apart under their leaders and operate as coherent units, but in other cases they live among the civilian population and try to blend in with it. Often women and even children are recruited to join the fighters; at other times they may be effectively enslaved, coerced into joining the fighters or serving them in other ways. The groups involved in such warfare fight in ways that disregard the laws of armed conflict, and indeed a hallmark of such warfare is the direct, intended targeting of noncombatants as a means of war combined with efforts to create collateral harm to noncombatants by their opponents, who are often regular armed forces or police and paramilitary forces. This style of fighting is, of course, in direct contradiction to the idea central to both just war thinking and international law on armed conflicts that noncombatants should, so far as possible, be spared harm in armed conflicts and in any case ought not to be the object of direct, intended harm or efforts to draw collateral harm. This is one reason why just war thinkers need to give more sustained attention to this kind of war.

In fact, it is arguable that both international law and just war thinking have helped to encourage the growth of such warfare, or at least have done little to restrict it. In trying to "level the playing field" between irregular fighters and the organized armed forces of states, international law has been reshaped in a way that allows the irregulars more latitude in their means of fighting than was the case in the earlier law, focused on state armed forces.[18] The results, however, tend to make the noncombatant population more vulnerable. Some just war thinkers, aiming at restricting the use of armed forces by states (and particularly the United States) and severely criticizing instances of harm to members of the civilian population, apply moral and legal restraints unevenly, not holding the irregulars to the same high standards laid on the states. This tendency is reinforced by the nature of such conflict: The irregulars are hard to get at (by intention); they do not wear uniforms, so that there is easy deniability if desired, and if they are closely allied with elements of the civilian population in the area, they can easily deflect blame to the organized armed forces that they are fighting against. Their records of actions may be only oral, if they exist at all, and oral records can easily be forgotten or reshaped for a particular purpose. By contrast, organized armed forces wear uniforms, use weapons of distinctive types, and may not be able, in practice, to distinguish irregular fighters from nonfighters. Moreover, such forces keep careful records, and these records may be mined for evidence against them. These factors tend not to level the playing field between the irregulars and regular armed forces but rather tilt it against the latter while leaving the former undeterred in the endangerment of the civilian population or direct, intended attacks against its members.

Another issue raised by the endangerment of noncombatants—whether by direct, intended action or by efforts to draw collateral harm against them—is tied closely to the classic just war idea of sovereignty and its definition in terms of responsibility for the common good of the society. The leaders of irregular fighting groups, by their characteristic mode of fighting, show utter disregard for such responsibility. The only noncombatants whose good interests them are those they identify as on their side; everyone else is regarded as part of the enemy, and no responsibility at all is taken for their lives, health, or property. This, too, needs to be explored from within the frame of just war thinking; yet of course to do so it would first be necessary for contemporary just war thinkers to adopt the classic understanding of sovereignty and its role in determining the just use of armed force. The sort of present-day just war thinking discussed above simply misses the point of the evil of the actual nature of such irregular warfare.

For centuries, the just war tradition maintained a strong bias against the kinds of irregular, nonstate fighting groups found in contemporary asymmetric warfare. Their leaders were, in the first place, understood as not having the right to authorize the use of armed force: They were not persons with responsibility for the common good of their communities and others affected by the conflict in which they were involved. Accordingly, their taking arms meant that there was no distinction between them and criminal bands, for both operated outside the law. Second, their means of fighting, even in the premodern era, tended to increase the amount of death in war; this was because of the kind of weapons they used, the fact that they gave no quarter (and took no prisoners, except as hostages), and the larger numbers of people that might take arms in popular uprisings. Opposing them, moreover, could lead to the use of no-holds-barred means against persons and groups involved in such armed conflict, as in Luther's message to the German nobility on how to deal with the German peasants' rebellion: "Smite, stab, kill."[19] In the present day a similar attitude has fed numerous efforts to deal with insurgencies, including the use of intensive interrogation techniques in the fight against radical Islamist terrorism.

But the central point remains: Classic just war thinking was right to hold that the use of arms is just only when authorized by a ruler responsible for the common good, employed for the purposes of protecting the common good and punishing threats to it, and intended to produce or restore peace, so that the use of such justified force therefore must not aim at directly, intentionally harming noncombatants and must not cause harm out of proportion to the good achieved. The classic just war conception of sovereign authority thus is central to understanding what constitutes the just use of armed force: its reasons, its ends, and its methods.

NOTES

1. Thomas Aquinas, *Summa Theologiae*, II/II, Q. 40, A. 1, in *The Ethics of War*, ed. Gregory Reichberg, Henrik Syse, and Endre Begby (Oxford: Basil Blackwell, 2006): 177–78. To anticipate further discussion below, what Aquinas says here directly reflected the outcome of the canonical debates before him reaching back to Gratian's *Decretum*. On this conception, the authority necessary was that of a temporal ruler with no temporal superior. Aquinas's word for a ruler of this sort was *princeps* (prince), but in contemporaneous English and French the word "sovereign"/*souverain* was already being used for such a ruler. The sovereign, on this conception, was the person who had final responsibility for the common good of the political community governed; this is why sovereign authority had priority among the requirements for a just use of armed force. This conception differs in fundamental ways from the conception of sovereignty in the modern state system, which is defined in terms of the territorial integrity of a political community and the ascription of self-determination to that community. The requirement of just cause as listed by Aquinas was reparative and punitive; there was no mention of self-defense as a category of just cause. This was because, in the outcome of the canonical debate, defense was understood as being a natural right of every person and community. The right of immediate defense against an attack, though, did not extend to repairing and punishing injustices already accomplished; this right (and responsibility) belonged to the ruling authority. Finally, the end of peace here is not the *pax* of the heavenly City of God but the peace of the political community (and among such communities) in this world, defined by Augustine as "well-ordered concord' and "the tranquility of order": It was the peace that resulted from maintaining a just order. On this conception of just war, *bellum iustum*, force is not understood as inherently morally tainted, but rather the use of force is morally good or bad depending on whether it satisfies the listed requirements, and thus the overall goods of politics.

2. National Conference of Catholic Bishops, *The Challenge of Peace* (Washington, DC: US Catholic Conference, 1983), 72f; National Conference of Catholic Bishops, *The Harvest of Justice Is Sown in Peace* (Washington, DC: US Catholic Conference, 1993), 5.

3. The Weinberger Doctrine, defined by Caspar Weinberger, secretary of defense under President Ronald Reagan, laid out six conditions for commitment of US military forces: that

the commitment be vital to US national interests, that force should not be committed without a clear intention of winning, that the commitment of force should be done only with
clearly defined military and political objectives, that force must be adjusted continually to
serve the objectives of the action, that force should not be committed without the support of
the American people and their representatives in Congress, and that the commitment of
force should be a last resort. These conditions were first presented by Weinberger in a speech
given in November 1984, and he laid them out in their final form in his "Annual Report to
the Congress for Fiscal Year 1987." The doctrine was much discussed at the time—for a
sampling, see the essays in *Small Wars and Insurgencies* 1, no. 2 (August 1990): 95–201—and
it formed the basis for the later Powell Doctrine, named after General Colin Powell at the
time of the Gulf War of 1990–91.

4. Hugo Grotius, *The Law of War and Peace* Book II, 2 (Roslyn, NY: Walter J. Black,
1949), 72.

5. United Nations Charter, www.un.org/en/documents/charter/index/shtml.

6. James Turner Johnson, *The Quest for Peace* (Princeton, NJ: Princeton University Press,
1987), 176–98.

7. For more on this history of the development of the tradition of just war, see James
Turner Johnson, *Ideology, Reason, and the Limitation of War* (Princeton, NJ: Princeton Uni-
versity Press, 1975); and *Just War Tradition and the Restraint of War* (Princeton, NJ:
Princeton University Press, 1981).

8. Reichberg, Syse, and Begby, *Ethics of War*, 177.

9. Thomas Aquinas, *Selected Political Writings* (Oxford: Basil Blackwell, 1959).

10. Reichberg, Syse, and Begby, *Ethics of War*, 177.

11. Gratian, *Decretum* in *Ethics of War*, ed. Reichberg, Syse, and Begby, 113.

12. Reichberg, Syse, and Begby, *Ethics of War*, 177.

13. Ibid.

14. Ibid., 150.

15. Grotius, *The Law of War and Peace*, book II, 72.

16. International Commission on Intervention and State Sovereignty, *The Responsibility
to Protect* (Ottawa: International Development Research Centre, 2001).

17. In his speech to the United Nations General Assembly on September 12, 2002, President Bush laid out three reasons for using force to remove Saddam Hussein: the need to
preempt the possible use of weapons of mass destruction, which the Bush administration at
that time was convinced Iraq possessed; the need to stop, alleviate, and punish the Saddam
Hussein regime's repeated and severe violations of basic human rights of portions of its own
population and others; and the need to enforce and punish Iraq's systematic and repeated
violations of Security Council resolutions including the cease-fire that ended the fighting in
the 1990–91 Gulf War responding to Saddam's aggression against Kuwait. This speech was
published in full in the *New York Times* on September 13, 2002. On two later occasions—his
State of the Union Address and his brief speech at the beginning of the invasion of Iraq—he
restated these same three reasons more briefly. Also see my discussion in James Turner
Johnson, *The War to Oust Saddam Hussein* (Lanham, MD: Roman & Littlefield, 2005),
chap. 3.

18. This was explicitly the aim of the 1977 Protocols to the 1949 Geneva Conventions; see
particularly the changes in the rules regarding irregular fighters: 1949 Geneva Convention
III, Article 4, and 1977 Protocol I, Article 43, all reprinted by Adam Roberts and Richard
Guelff, *The Laws of War*, 3rd ed. (Oxford: Oxford University Press, 2000), 246, 444–45.

19. See Clyde L. Manschrek, *A History of Christianity* (Englewood Cliffs, NJ: Prentice Hall,
1964).

CHAPTER 2

Just War and Political Judgment

Chris Brown

T HE AIM OF THIS CHAPTER is to defend the position that while the categories associated with just war *thinking* may help us to exercise judgment in particular cases,
we should avoid just war *theorizing* altogether. The intended distinction here is best,
if somewhat crudely, summarized by saying that whereas those who look to just
war theory expect to be given *answers*, those who prefer to talk of just war thinking
hope to discover good *questions*. In the first case, the expectation is that just war
theory properly applied will tell us whether a particular war, or a particular action
in a war, is just; in the second case, the hope is that just war thinking, and the
canonical categories of the just war, will help us to make the wider judgment as to
whether, in the particular circumstances of the case, a resort to force, or a particular
forceful action, would be the right thing to do, all things considered. In the first
section of the chapter, this latter conception of the just war will be employed to
defend the notion from its enemies, but also from some of its friends. The second
section examines the conventional categories used in just war thinking, with a view
to showing that they are best understood as the basis for some good questions
rather than as providing good answers. Finally, some wider conclusions about the
nature of ethical thinking and social science theory are drawn.

FRIENDS AND ENEMIES OF THE JUST WAR

The position defended here is, I believe, consistent with the just war tradition as
articulated by St. Augustine and St. Thomas Aquinas, for example, although I argue
that it does not need this support. However, it runs counter to modern expectations,

at least as those expectations are expressed in popular discourse. To illustrate the point, consider the debate on the justice of the Gulf War 1990–91 in the United Kingdom—interesting because this was the first time in recent British history when classical just war thinking/theorizing was deployed in a quite heated political debate, to the extent that the religious correspondent of the London *Times*, Clifford Longley, felt it necessary to enlighten the public by publishing a center-page op-ed piece titled "Going by the Aquinas Book"![1] In the war of the Oxford Anglican theologians, Richard Harries, then bishop of Oxford, opined that the coming war to evict Saddam Hussein from Kuwait met the standard criteria for a just war; the then professor of divinity at Oxford University, Rowan Williams, later to become archbishop of Canterbury from 2002 until 2013, argued that it did not.[2] The two learned doctors expressed opinions on whether the "last resort" had actually been reached, on the proportionality of the coalition war effort in response to the Iraqi offense, on the level of civilian casualties to be expected, and so on—all subjects upon which there was no reason to believe they possessed the expertise or knowledge to make informed judgments. The point is that both controversialists seemed to assume that just war theory would tell them whether or not the war was just. My argument is, first, that just war thinking cannot provide unambiguous answers of this sort, and should not be expected to; and second, that the judgments called for by just war thinking are varied in nature, and require expertise and experience that is not confined to, or often possessed by, theologians and moral theorists.

In the case described above, just war thinking needed to be protected from its putative friends, but understanding just war thinking as an aid to judgment allays some (but only some) of the concerns of enemies of the notion of a just war. The most serious of such enemies is, I judge, Carl Schmitt, who, unlike modern critics from the left, is clear about the implications of rejecting just war thinking, yet still wishes to do so. Schmitt's position—expressed most clearly in *The* Nomos *of the Earth*—is that to describe a war as "just" encourages a self-righteous fury that will demonize the enemy and stand in the way of establishing limits in warfare.[3] Every war becomes a total war, because every war is a war between good and evil, and with evil there can be no compromise. This is strikingly similar to the argument put forward, in different terms, by some modern students of "critical security studies," who write of just war theory as delegitimizing "the Other," encouraging a Manichaean worldview, and so on.[4]

The difference between these superficially similar critiques is that Schmitt is hostile to the notion of a just war because of his nostalgia for an era when (allegedly) interstate war was regarded as a kind of duel between legitimate enemies, whereas modern critics are unclear on what alternative to the just war they propose. Schmitt wants to clear the space for war as an act of state within a European states system, the Jus Publicum Europaeum, and he understands, correctly, that just war thinking is incompatible with the idea that war is *simply* a political act of this kind (even though, I would argue, state interest is a legitimate component of the wider judgment that war is the appropriate response to a particular state of affairs). Schmitt clearly cannot accept the notion that war can only be waged for a just cause, and for that reason he is right to see his approach as incompatible with the tradition; but he is wrong to think that just war thinking automatically leads to the demonizing of enemies and the end of restraint. He may be right that it sometimes has this effect on people who think of themselves as just warriors—not difficult to find contemporary examples from all points on the political compass—but this self-satisfied approach is, or ought to be, contrary to a good understanding of what using just war criteria as a basis for political judgment ought to involve.

Modern critics of just war thinking from a left perspective, such as Ken Booth, are rather less clear-sighted than Schmitt. They make the same misjudged critique of just war thinking as Schmitt, but crucially without the endorsement of war as an act of policy. The result is either a pacifist stance or an attempt to distinguish between "progressive" and "reactionary" uses of violence. Pacifism is, of course, a very well established position with a long and distinguished pedigree, from Jesus to Tolstoy and Gandhi, but it is open to the obvious objection that an absolute rejection of violence, whatever the circumstances, puts power in the hands of those who are not similarly disposed and can lead to the perpetuation of injustice. Belief in a God who will provide an ultimate guarantee that justice will prevail may make this position tenable for some, but this is an argument that cuts no ice with nonbelievers, or, for that matter, with a majority of believers.[5] In practice most "pacifist" thinkers are, actually, "pacifistic," to adopt a term of Martin Ceadel; that is, they are predisposed against violence but prepared to countenance it in some circumstances, which of course opens the door to just war thinking, properly understood.[6]

The alternative position on the left is to distinguish between the progressive and the reactionary use of violence, supporting the former and opposing the latter. At one level, this is simply an instrumental, Clausewitzian approach to violence in which matters of justice are irrelevant or, perhaps, predetermined—one side in a conflict is, by definition, just and therefore no further questions need to be asked about its conduct. This is also an argument that works in reverse; figures such as Noam Chomsky and John Pilger regard the United States (US) as axiomatically unjust and therefore any state or group is justified in opposing US policy by violence (and justified also in using whatever tactics they think likely to be effective).[7] This position, of course, is vulnerable to exactly the charge of promoting a Manichaean view of the world, and legitimating the crusading spirit. Perhaps rather more interesting, and certainly more Clausewitzian, is the position exemplified by Karl Marx and Friedrich Engels in their writings on the Crimean War in the 1850s.[8] Rather than attributing justice to any particular country, their judgments were entirely based on a utilitarian calculation as to the implications of the war for the Revolution; on this basis they opposed the nascent peace movement of the day and broadly supported the Anglo-French position, Czarist Russia being the great opponent of the Revolution. Marx and Engels read and admired Clausewitz, as did Mao Zedong, whose *On Protracted War* quotes Clausewitz liberally, albeit without citing him.[9] These writers, along with other figures in their tradition such as Lenin and Trotsky, regard violence in purely instrumental terms, as a means to an end, neither morally superior nor morally inferior to other means. This being so, their opposition to just war thinking is as understandable as the opposition of Schmitt, and as unacceptable as is his position to anyone who is not prepared to see violence in this light.

Although the remedies they offer are, I think, unacceptable for one reason or another, it would be wrong to dismiss out of hand all the criticisms of just war *theory* offered by Schmitt, Booth, and other figures on both the right and left. As noted above, it would be right to be skeptical of a just war theory that purported to tell us whether a particular war was just and therefore to be supported, or unjust and therefore to be opposed. This sort of certainty is rarely provided by even the best-developed ethical theory and, as the critics allege, constitutes a standing invitation to engage in the demonization of one's enemies. Conversely, if we understand just war thinking as providing a set of questions that act as an aid to the exercise of political judgment, these dangers are much less apparent. If we reject the pacifist position that violence is never justifiable (which we should, because we have no reason to believe that violence is always and necessarily the greatest evil), and if we reject the Clausewitzian view that violence is simply one tool to be used whenever it might be effective (which we should because although violence may not be the greatest evil, it is an evil nonetheless), then we will need to exercise judgment as to when violence is indeed the appropriate response to a situation, and the classic just war questions will help us to perform this task.

THE CANONICAL CATEGORIES OF THE JUST WAR

The canonical questions ask of any particular action whether the force employed, or to be employed, is intended to right a wrong, is the last resort, is proportional to the offense, has reasonable prospects of producing a successful outcome, is undertaken with proper authority, and with care being taken, as far as possible, to protect the innocent. We should ask these questions not because that is what just war theory or the just war tradition requires us to do, but because they are the appropriate questions to ask. There is every reason to be interested in what, say, Thomas Aquinas had to say about these questions, because of the undoubted power of his intellect—but the questions are not important because he, or anyone else, asked or answered them. As will be apparent in the following discussion, they are not necessarily the only questions that need to be asked, and perhaps some of them are not as important as they once were, but, taken together, they constitute a good starting point.[10]

An important point to understand, and again a source of confusion to both friends and enemies, is that the questions posed above require not just the exercise of "judgment" per se but also the exercise of different kinds of judgment. Thus, what constitutes a "wrong" that should be righted involves legal and political as well as moral considerations. The "Legalist Paradigm" set out in part I of Michael Walzer's very influential, and generally excellent, book *Just and Unjust Wars* defines the wrong to be righted in legal terms—that is, as an act of interstate aggression—but this is too restrictive.[11] Both the tradition, as James Turner Johnson has argued, and common sense dictate that a wider judgment needs to be made here.[12] It may well be the case that, contra David Rodin, as a general rule national sovereignty and territorial integrity should be protected, but the exercise of judgment involves precisely deciding when such general rules should be broken in response to other, more compelling, considerations.[13] Walzer acknowledges this by instancing genocide and mass enslavement as examples of state behavior that would justify violating sovereignty, and this opens up the possibility that there are other just causes of this kind. As always, judgments must be made.

Judgments concerning "right intention" will (or should) involve a distinction between motives and intentions; thus, in the context of the Iraq War of 2003, Fernando Tesón supports what he takes to be the laudable *intention* of removing Saddam, a dictator who had murdered his own people and invaded his neighbors, and he argues that this would not necessarily have been vitiated had the *motive* for the intervention been, say, to gain control of Iraq's oil.[14] It is not necessary to follow him all the way with this argument to see the distinction he is drawing. From another angle, "right intention" is, perhaps, one area where one might well argue that a judgment is not actually required; the stress the just war tradition lays on intentions could be seen as generated by theological concerns, as expressed, for example, by the Catholic philosopher Joseph Boyle in chapter 10 of this volume. Clearly, intentions are important if the fate of one's immortal soul is at stake, but if this consideration is no longer salient, then intentions are only really significant in consequential terms. Thus, to return to Iraq in 2003, the alleged desire for oil would be relevant if and only if it led the Coalition to do things that were otherwise undesirable, or to undermine the intention to remove a tyrant (e.g., by striking a deal with Saddam or his sons to allow him to stay in power in exchange for oil concessions).

Whether action is a "last resort" relies on a judgment as to the diplomatic-strategic realities of a given situation, which only those with relevant knowledge or expertise may be in a position to make. The notion of last resort very clearly does not require all other options to be tried before force is employed—what it requires is a judgment about the plausibility of nonviolent measures in achieving the desired goal. Last resort could in fact be the first resort, if only one course of action is viable. A "reasonable prospect of success" is, again, a matter for the exercise of diplomatic-strategic expertise. Both these notions are widely misused, as the afore-mentioned debates between Richard Harries and Rowan Williams illustrated. Neither of these clerical gentlemen was actually in a position to be able to make the kind of judgment required—although it would have been perfectly proper for them to have demanded that those who were in this position should take these factors into account.

"Proportionality" is another difficult notion; once again, the root idea is simple—folk wisdom is full of warnings against taking sledgehammers to crack nuts, and modern game theory finds "tit for tat" the best strategy for playing iterated Prisoner's Dilemma—but putting it into effect is not so easy. It requires a judgment about outcomes that may be difficult to make; we never know what the consequences of our actions will be, or, equally important after the event, what the consequences of our inaction might have been. And our actions are rarely a response to a discrete act in the way that the principle of proportionality seems to suggest they are, or should be. Thus, for example, setting into motion a European-wide war might be thought a disproportionate response to the German invasion of Poland in 1939, but the latter took place in the context of a series of German aggressions and the judgment that this could not go on seems reasonable, in spite of the misery that followed. Again, perhaps more controversially, it might be argued that the dispatch of an expeditionary force to retake the Falkland Islands in 1982, with the consequent loss of more than a thousand lives, was a disproportionate response to the bloodless occupation of a sparsely inhabited territory, but it could equally be said that there was an important principle at stake that should be weighed in the balance along with other costs. Similar points could be made, on a larger scale, about the response to Saddam's invasion of Kuwait in 1990.

The wider point here is that a judgment as to the effects of forceful action needs to be made. A calculation must be made, and into the balance are thrown both the direct and indirect consequences of action, as well as those of inaction. One of the standard critiques of humanitarian interventions is that appropriate cases are selected not in accordance with the seriousness of, say, the human rights violation involved but in response to essentially political criteria; powerful states get away with things that the weak would not, friends and allies are treated differently from those with whom the interveners have no such connections. This is certainly the case; but there is no reason to be surprised that this should be so, nor to regard this as delegitimizing particular actions. Calculations of political interest always feed into judgments as to whether there is "a reasonable prospect of success"; "success" has to be understood in the context of the maintenance of medium- or long-term political relations as well as that of solving particular problems.[15] Even the most vigorous critics of selectivity usually acknowledge that starting World War III in response to China's behavior in Tibet, or Russia's in Chechnya, would not be a good idea; and it should be equally obvious that the fact that one cannot act in these cases does not constitute a reason for not acting in other circumstances where such dire results would not be forthcoming.

"Proper authority" is a difficult notion and, as the introduction to this volume suggests, one that is often neglected in otherwise comprehensive accounts of the just war. The root idea, that force should not be used when an appeal to a superior authority is available as an alternative, is quite simple—domestically, this is what distinguishes the rule of law from a system built on blood-guilt and vendetta. In the medieval context of St. Thomas Aquinas and the Schoolmen, the private use of force was a constant possibility—indeed reality—given the decentralized nature of political power, and the requirement of proper authority constituted a real limitation on the legitimate use of force (or would have, had it been widely obeyed). Nowadays, the term reeks of ambiguity. Are sovereign states the proper authority for the use of force? The positivist account of international law that dominated in the century before 1919 certainly took that view, albeit with the occasional nod in the direction of the importance of arbitration. Or has the United Nations—or perhaps the Security Council thereof—taken over this role? The UN Charter can certainly be read to this effect, but the record of the United Nations Security Council (UNSC) over sixty-five years is not encouraging in this respect—those who have looked to this body to right an injustice have almost always been disappointed. Michael Glennon argues cogently that the attempt to impose international law on the use of force via the UN has failed, and failed repeatedly.[16] Even if such a blanket judgment seems a step too far, it is generally the case that in the democracies an appeal to the UN is usually made as an expression of opposition to action, in the realistic expectation that the UN will never legitimize the resort to war. It is interesting that on the one occasion in recent history where the UN did support military action by the US and its allies—over Saddam's aggression in Kuwait in 1990—it was denounced by opponents of the action as having been manipulated by the Americans.[17] The Security Council's decision to authorize NATO to protect Libyan civilians in March 2011 (UNSC Resolution 1973) produced similar denunciations.

Perhaps "proper authority" resides neither in the sovereign state (because this would make the state a judge in its own cause) or the UN (because this would imply that the UN had a capacity to right wrongs that, in fact, it lacks) but in some notion of international public opinion, amorphous though this notion may be. Consider, for example, NATO's Kosovo intervention in 1999; *pace* some forced legal interpretations by the British Foreign and Commonwealth Office, this was not authorized explicitly by the UN. Conversely, it was supported by all of NATO's members and the members of the European Union (with varying degrees of enthusiasm, admittedly), and a resolution to condemn the action was defeated in the UN Security Council by twelve votes to three—all of which suggests that this was not simply an example of states inventing their own justifications for action.[18] It was such facts that led the Independent International Commission on Kosovo to describe the intervention as "illegal but legitimate."[19] This rather fuzzy approach to proper authority also gives due recognition to the fact that international law usually provides no arbiter when it comes to matters of interpretation of UNSC resolutions and the like. Thus, for example, the British government's position that previous UNSC resolutions covered the use of force in Iraq in 2003 without the need for further specific authorization was certainly a minority view among international lawyers, but, *pace* rhetoric about an "illegal" war, there is no definitive way of determining whether the argument was valid.

The final traditional question concerns the protection of the innocent, which once again requires quite complex moral reasoning and the exercise of different kinds of political judgment. Conventionally international humanitarian law understood innocence in terms of the combatant/noncombatant distinction, and this is broadly reflected in Walzer's notion of the "War Convention."[20] The idea that wearing a uniform makes one a legitimate target has an appealing simplicity; but, predictably, things are not actually that clear-cut.[21] Not all people who wear uniforms can be considered legitimate targets all the time, and, conversely, there may be some people who do not wear uniforms but who are not in any moral sense innocent. Compare, for example, the position in 1942 of a conscripted, socialist-leaning, pay clerk in the German Army in an office hundreds of miles behind the lines with that of a Nazi party member and munitions worker—the fact that the former wears a uniform while the latter does not hardly seems the most relevant difference between them. Again, there may be innocent civilians who are protecting combatants, deliberately or against their will. The situation is greatly complicated in guerrilla wars and putative wars of national liberation, which are much more characteristic of contemporary armed conflict than conventional interstate wars.[22] The notion of "double effect" comes into play here—in some circumstances it may be legitimate to use force, even though one knows that the result will be unintended harm to the innocent.[23] This is a disturbing idea, but one that is difficult to avoid without adopting policies that reward the unscrupulous; the alternative—an absolute prohibition on harm to the innocent—could easily result in, for example, weapons facilities being situated in school playgrounds or hospitals by those who are prepared to be less absolutist in their approach (or who regard the notion of "innocence" with suspicion or disfavor).

These are the conventional questions that just war thinking suggests we should ask of any potential use of force. There is no reason to think that these questions are the only ones that we should ask, or that all of them remain relevant. As to the latter, as noted above, one might, for example, take the view that questions of "right intention" are of little value in the absence of an explicitly theological context. Similarly, there may be pertinent questions that arise today that did not loom as large in the past. One such might concern the role of domestic public opinion in circumstances where violence is deployed; it is clear that in the Western democracies any act of state violence needs to be justified to the people, and the terms of such justification are not necessarily aligned with the kind of questions asked by the tradition. Thus, for example, military operations that are perfectly legitimate within the terms of the traditional questions posed by just war thinking may be unacceptable to Western public opinion because of the casualties involved—and such opinion nowadays is not simply oriented toward "friendly" casualties but is often also concerned with "enemy" casualties. This, I suspect, is one reason why some Catholic theologians whose tradition originated just war thinking as a moral praxis have now adopted a more legalistic conception of the notion.[24]

Finally, before moving on, it should be noted that although the term just *war* nowadays points us toward interstate violence on a largish scale, the questions that just war thinking suggests we should ask are relevant in any situation where violence or coercion is under consideration. At the interstate level, such coercion includes economic sanctions, which are often put forward as a morally acceptable alternative to violence but which frequently harm the innocent—but the just war questions are equally salient in the case of domestic and intersocietal conflicts. This position is actually true to the tradition, which was developed at a time when the current distinction between "international" and "domestic" could not be drawn. There is an analogy here between just war thinking and the Clausewitzian account of the dynamics of conflict. As noted above, revolutionaries from Marx and Engels to Lenin and Mao have explicitly employed Clausewitz's ideas to advance their cause, and students of industrial relations have been similarly impressed by his understanding of the relationship between politics and conflict and limited and absolute war. Clausewitzian understandings of conflict, of course, concentrate on cause and effect, whereas just war thinking focuses on the moral dimension of action; but both modes of thought are relevant outside the areas where they were first developed.

JUDGMENT AND PRACTICE: AGAINST THEORY

The discussion offered above of notions such as "just cause" and "right intention" could have been extended at much greater length, and, of course, has been in the standard texts on the subject, and elsewhere in this volume. But it is not my intention to add anything more on these matters. Instead, in the last section of this chapter, I wish to focus on *the way* in which we think about these matters rather than *what* we think about them. My core argument is that just war thinking should not be approached as though it could provide us with an algorithm to determine what course of action to follow. An algorithm is a method of solving a problem by following a series of well-defined steps. An algorithmic approach to just war theory would approach a particular situation where violence was contemplated with a checklist of questions rather similar to those that used to be found on the back of a US visa waiver form—in that case, half a dozen questions where the answer to each must be an unambiguous "no" (as in "no, I am not a convicted war criminal"). In the case of an algorithmic approach to just war theory, the answer always has to be "yes"—Is there a just cause? Yes. Right intention? Yes. Proper authority? Yes. And so on—and if every box can be ticked, we have a just war and can get on with it. Conversely, one "no" causes the algorithm to produce a negative verdict.[25] This is the wrong approach at a fundamental level; none of the questions that just war thinking invites us to ask can be answered in this way, and the attempt to do so impoverishes the notion.

There is a still wider point here about the nature of the social sciences and of ethical thinking on social problems. Bent Flyvbjerg has much of interest to say on this subject in an important but somewhat neglected text (neglected at least by scholars of international relations), *Making Social Science Matter*.[26] Drawing heavily on Aristotle, Flyvbjerg contrasts general, theoretical, context-independent knowledge with concrete, practical, context-dependent knowledge; his thesis is that the modern social sciences wrongly privilege the former over the latter. Aristotle, in the *Nicomachean Ethics*, distinguishes three "virtues of thought": *episteme* (scientific knowledge), *techne* (craft knowledge), and *phronesis* (prudence, or practical wisdom).[27] The desire to produce general, context-independent theory corresponds to Aristotle's account of science, but is generally inappropriate in the social sciences, and wholly inappropriate when it comes to action-guiding knowledge of the sort that just war theory purports to provide. This is, or should be, the province of *phronesis*, of deliberation not about "things that cannot be otherwise or about things that cannot be achieved" but about "the truth, involving reason, concerned with action about things that are good or bad for a human being" (Book VI, 5, § 3, 1140). Prudence (*phronesis*) is not just about universals but also about "knowledge of particulars, since it is concerned with action and action is about particulars" (Book VI, 7, §7, 1141b). It is also about experience; Aristotle has interesting things to say here, reassuring to the graying part of the population:[28] "[Prudent] young people do not seem to be found. The reason is that prudence is concerned with particulars as well as universals, and particulars become known from experience, but a young person lacks experience, since some length of time is needed to produce it" (Book VI, 8, §5. 1142a).

In our world, we are not altogether comfortable with this way of proceeding. It is interesting that whereas there are terms in English to describe those who follow the virtues of *episteme* and *techne*—"scientist" and, in different contexts, "technician" or "artisan"—there is no obvious word for those who exercise the virtue of *phronesis*. In some ways this is not surprising; in terms of the history of thought, Stephen Toulmin has given a compelling account of how, in the seventeenth century, the moral insights of renaissance humanism and the classical world were put aside.[29] Under the influence of Descartes and Hobbes, along with many lesser talents, formal logic came to displace rhetoric, general principles and abstract axioms

were privileged over particular cases and concrete diversity, and the establishment
of rules (or "laws") that were deemed of permanent as opposed to transitory applicability came to be seen as the task of the theorist—in other words, although Toulmin does not put it this way, matters properly within the purview of *phronesis* came
to be seen, wrongly, as matters of *episteme*. Toulmin suggests that at this time moral
reasoning became "theory-centered" rather than "practically minded"—that is, a
matter of following a theoretically validated rule, rather than of making a practical
judgment—and was thereby impoverished.

The shift to which Toulmin refers is of considerable significance for the argument of this chapter. The seventeenth-century writers who effected this reorienta-
tion were not simply rejecting the generous, open-minded thinking of humanists
such as Montaigne but also, and very explicitly, they were rejecting Aristotle and
also Aquinas and the Schoolmen—in the latter case, that is, the very scholars who
took a few thoughts of Augustine on war and society and applied Aristotelian
methods to create the basis for just war thinking. Hobbes—a consistent anti-
Aristotelian—has nothing directly to say about just war, but his near contemporary
Grotius, from a standpoint similar to Hobbes, had a lot to say on the subject and
can, I think, be seen as the author who does most to turn the medieval notion of
just war thinking into just war theory, impoverishing it thereby.[30]

A further victim of the seventeenth century shift away from context-dependent
knowledge—in this case suffering "collateral damage" as it were—was the Augustinian tradition of realism, as exemplified in our age by writers such as Hans J.
Morgenthau. By reifying the complex thought of Augustine and Aquinas into a set
of rules, the producers of just war theory have lost contact with the observations
on political life and political psychology that make Augustine in particular such a
fascinating writer, even for those, such as the present author, who find it impossible
to accept his concepts of original sin, atonement, and predestination.[31] In what was
perhaps his best book, *Scientific Man vs. Power Politics*, Morgenthau castigated the
desire to find abstract, logical moral rules that would somehow enable the process
of judgment to be circumvented; this was very much part of the mindset of "scientific man," and fundamentally untrue to the texture of the moral life that Morgenthau always tried to illuminate.[32] Although certainly not a just war theorist, there is
much in Morgenthau's work that contributes to just war thinking, in ways that are
clearly not true of, say, modern structural realism.

Still, the move toward a *phronetic* social science does not simply rely on Aristotelian formulations or nostalgia for classical as opposed to structural realism. Flyvbjerg draws quite substantially on Pierre Bourdieu's understanding of the "theory of
action," and Bourdieu is a major influence on the "practice turn" in contemporary
international studies—see, for example, the work of Vincent Pouliot.[33] Pouliot
stresses the inarticulate, tacit nature of the "logic of practicality," which is certainly
not Aristotelian; but his emphasis on experience and learning how to proceed by

doing is consistent with the approach advocated in this chapter, and in general the practice turn has very positive implications for just war thinking.[34] Of course, those committed to the generation of a context-independent theoretical account of human behavior will always be dissatisfied with the kind of practical, case-based, experience-based reasoning that underlies just war thinking—they will look to developing a just war theory that provides answers rather than an invitation to exercise judgment. And many of the critics of the just war theory assume that this is indeed the purpose of just war thinking and criticize it accordingly.[35] But if we can wean ourselves away from this mode of thought, and accept that the just war thinking is an aid to judgment—nothing more; but also, and very importantly, nothing less—we will find much within the tradition that is valuable, and we will find the questions it has generated indispensable.

NOTES

Thanks for comments to Stephanie Carvin, Toni Erskine, Andrew Jillions, and Pietro Maffettone, and to the participants in the colloquium "The Just War: The State of the Art," US Institute of Peace, Washington, August, 2010; any errors that remain are, of course, my responsibility.

1. *The Times*, November 3, 1990. In World War II there was an understandably somewhat muted debate about area bombing that used just war terminology.

2. Richard Harries, "The Path to a Just War," *The Independent*, October 31, 1990; and Richard Harries, "A Just War Not a Crusade," *The Observer*, January 20, 1991; Rowan Williams, "Onward Christian Soldiers?" *The Guardian*, November 1, 1990.

3. Carl Schmitt, *The Nomos of the Earth in the International Law of the Jus Publicum Europaeum*, trans. G. L. Ulmen (New York: Telos Press, 2003; orig. pub. 1950). I have written at greater length on Schmitt and just war theory; see Chris Brown, "From Humanised War to Humanitarian Intervention: Carl Schmitt's Critique of the Just War Tradition," in *The International Political Thought of Carl Schmitt: Terror, Liberal War, and the Crisis of Global Order*, ed. Louiza Odysseos and Fabio Petito (London: Routledge, 2007).

4. A classic statement of this position is given by Ken Booth, "Ten Flaws of Just Wars," *International Journal of Human Rights* 4 (2000): 314–24; see also, partly in response, Chris Brown, "A Qualified Defence of the Use of Force for Humanitarian Reasons," *International Journal of Human Rights* 4 (2000): 282–88.

5. A good account of Christian pacifism is offered by Theodore J. Koontz, "Christian Nonviolence: An Interpretation," in *The Ethics of War and Peace*, ed. Terry Nardin (Princeton, NJ: Princeton University Press, 1996); in the same collection Michael G. Cartwright offers an alternative reading, "Conflicting Interpretations of Christian Pacifism."

6. Martin Ceadel, "Pacifism and Pacificism," in *The Cambridge History of Twentieth-Century Political Thought*, ed. Terence Ball and Richard Bellamy (Cambridge: Cambridge University Press, 2003): 473–92. A similar position is defended by Richard Norman, *Ethics, Killing, and War* (Cambridge: Cambridge University Press, 1995). It is fair to say that for both Ceadel and Norman the circumstances in which the use of force could be considered justified are so circumscribed as to be virtually impossible of achievement; but, still, the door to just war thinking has been opened.

7. See, e.g., Noam Chomsky, *Failed States: The Abuse of Power and the Assault on Democracy* (Harmondsworth, UK: Penguin, 2007); and John Pilger, *Hidden Agendas* (New York: Vintage, 1998).

8. Karl Marx and Friedrich Engels, *The Eastern Question* (London: Cass Reprints, 1994); see also "Articles by Marx in the *New-York Daily Tribune*," www.marxists.org/archive/marx/works/subject/newspapers/new-york-tribune.htm.

9. "Selected Works of Mao Tse-tung: On Protracted War, *May 1938*," www.marxists.org/reference/archive/mao/selected-works/volume-2/mswv2_09.htm.

10. The approach to these canonical questions adopted here differs somewhat from that of James Turner Johnson in chapter 1 of this volume, but we are in broad agreement that they must be approached as matters of practical judgment rather than in any mechanical manner—on which see the next section of this chapter. More fundamental differences are to be found when my position is contrasted with that of Joseph Boyle, as expressed in chapter 10, especially with respect to "right intent" on which, again, see below.

11. Michael Walzer, *Just and Unjust Wars*, 3rd ed. (New York: Basic Books, 2006). Walzer does acknowledge that there are some limited additional circumstances where force might be justified.

12. See chapter 1 of this volume and James Turner Johnson, *The War to Oust Saddam Hussein: Just War and the New Face of Conflict* (Lanham, MD: Rowman & Littlefield, 2005). One does not have to accept Johnson's argument in this particular case to agree that in some circumstances the use of force might be an appropriate response to human rights violations.

13. David Rodin, *War and Self-Defence* (Oxford: Clarendon Press, 2004), argues against the conventional view that states are entitled to defend themselves.

14. Fernando Tesón, "Ending Tyranny in Iraq," *Ethics & International Affairs* 19, no. 2 (2005).

15. I have discussed this issue at length; see Chris Brown, "Selective Humanitarianism: In Defence of Inconsistency," in *Ethics and Foreign Intervention*, ed. Deen Chatterjee and Don Scheid (Cambridge: Cambridge University Press, 2003), 31–50.

16. Michael Glennon, "Why the Security Council Failed," *Foreign Affairs*, May–June 2003. Edward C. Luck, Anne-Marie Slaughter, and Ian Hurd, "Stayin' Alive: The Rumours of the UN's Death Have Been Exaggerated," *Foreign Affairs*, July–August 2003, put forth the opposing point of view.

17. See, e.g., Noam Chomsky, *World Orders, Old and New* (London: Pluto Press, 1997). Not everyone on the left went down this route; see Fred Halliday, "The Gulf War and Its Aftermath: First Reflections," *International Affairs* 67, no. 2 (1991).

18. The contrast with Iraq 2003 is striking; then the Coalition gave up the attempt to gain a positive resolution from the UNSC not because of the certainty of several vetoes but because, unlike in 1999, there was no majority in their favor.

19. Independent International Commission on Kosovo, *The Kosovo Report: Conflict, International Response, Lessons Learned* (Oxford: Oxford University Press, 2000).

20. Walzer, *Just and Unjust Wars*. Modern IHL defines a legitimate target as someone "directly participating in hostilities"; but this, of course, requires interpretation (are soldiers held in reserve "directly participating"?)

21. See the essays collected by David Rodin and Henry Shue, eds., *Just and Unjust Warriors: The Moral and Legal Status of Soldiers* (Oxford: Oxford University Press, 2008).

22. On this, see Michael Gross, *Moral Dilemmas of Modern War* (Cambridge: Cambridge University Press, 2009); and chapter 12 in the present volume.

23. See P. A. Woodward, ed., *The Doctrine of Double Effect: Philosophers Debate a Controversial Moral Principle* (Notre Dame, IN: University of Notre Dame Press, 2001); and T. A.

Cavanaugh, ed., *Double Effect Reasoning: Doing Good and Avoiding Evil* (Oxford: Oxford University Press, 2006).

24. See, e.g., Joseph Boyle, "Traditional Just War Theory and Humanitarian Intervention," in *Humanitarian Intervention: Nomos XLVII*, ed. Melissa Williams and Terry Nardin (New York: New York University Press, 2006), 31–57.

25. Actually, nowadays there are usually two algorithms in play, one for whether to go to war (*ad bellum*), the other for the conduct of a war (*in bello*). This distinction is unknown to Aquinas, and an unhelpful product of theoretical thinking about just war theory. For an example of this kind of reasoning, see Craig White, *Iraq: The Moral Reckoning* (Lanham, MD: Lexington Books, 2010); I am grateful to James Turner Johnson for this reference.

26. Bent Flyvbjerg, *Making Social Science Matter: Why Social Inquiry Fails and How It Can Succeed Again* (Cambridge: Cambridge University Press, 2001).

27. Aristotle, *Nicomachean Ethics*, trans. Terence Irwin (Indianapolis: Hackett, 1999), book VI, 1138b ff. References in the main body of the text are to this edition/translation.

28. Perhaps it should not be reassuring because in war young people (e.g., junior officers and noncommissioned officers) will often have to make important decisions about, e.g., specific targets and tactics; here there is perhaps a limited role for checklists and box-ticking. Thanks to Andrew Jillions for this point.

29. Stephen Toulmin, *Cosmopolis: The Hidden Agenda of Modernity* (Chicago: University of Chicago Press, 1990).

30. Richard Tuck, *The Rights of War and Peace: Political Thought and International Order from Grotius to Kant* (Oxford: Oxford University Press, 1981), sets out the similarities between Hobbes and Grotius, but without endorsing the position argued for here. James Turner Johnson, whose position on just war thinking as a moral praxis is, in most respects, similar to mine, presents a more favorable account of Grotius in chapter 1 of the present volume.

31. A prominent modern Augustinian who has contributed much to just war thinking is Jean Bethke Elshtain. See Jean Bethke Elshtain, *Augustine and the Limits of Politics* (Notre Dame, IN: University of Notre Dame Press, 1997); and Jean Bethke Elshtain, *Just War against Terror: Ethics and the Burden of American Power in a Violent World* (New York: Basic Books, 2003).

32. Hans J. Morgenthau, *Scientific Man vs. Power Politics* (Chicago: University of Chicago Press, 1947). Morgenthau's interest in Aristotle is evident in the lectures he gave on the Aristotle's *Politics*; see Anthony F. Lang Jr., ed., *Political Theory and International Affairs: Hans J. Morgenthau on Aristotle's The Politics* (Westport, CT: Greenwood Press, 2004).

33. Pierre Bourdieu, *Practical Reason: On the Theory of Action* (Cambridge: Polity Press, 1998); Vincent Pouliot, *International Security in Practice* (Cambridge: Cambridge University Press, 2010).

34. I have written elsewhere on these matters; see Chris Brown, "The 'Practice Turn': *Phronesis* and Classical Realism—Towards a *Phronetic* International Political Theory," *Millennium: Journal of International Studies* 40, no. 3 (2012): 439–56.

35. However, this does not apply to Schmitt, who had a very clear understanding of just war thinking, and who rejected it for reasons that have nothing to do with the distinction between theoretical and practical reasoning.

CHAPTER 3

Natural Flourishing as the Normative Ground of Just War

A Christian View

Nigel Biggar

THE IRREDUCIBLE PLURALITY OF SECULAR
DISCUSSION ABOUT JUST WAR

WE MIGHT ACHIEVE a universal language about the ethics of war. It might be that warrior cultures will vanish from the world, and that no one will ever again suppose that the ecstasy of violence is its own justification, or that domination is war's obvious and intrinsic end. It might be that the terms in which the just war tradition speaks will become the global lingua franca. I doubt it, but it might be. If it were so, we would have achieved a measure of consensus about how to view war morally—but still only a measure. Common terms are susceptible of diverse information. Different people can use the same language and still mean significantly different things by it. Controversy is here to stay; and salvation lies, not in aspiring to transcend it, but in growing the virtues to handle it well.

Some might think that in this supposedly secular world, the moral essence of just war thinking needs to be liberated from its premodern, theological husk and translated into universally accessible philosophical language. Well, when I last looked, there was no such language—not even among philosophers. There is no language that is beyond provoking moments of bafflement. And besides, surely bafflement is a normal feature of human conversation, around which we have learned to maneuver in a familiar variety of ways. No doubt ethical discourse about war that is silent about God, the afterlife, and eschatological justice, and which

49

makes no reference to holy scriptures, will seem neutral to atheists and agnostics. But it will not seem so to religious believers, whose rising number worldwide discomfits the secularization thesis, and not all of whom belong to the Great Unwashed—or at least to the Great Uneducated. So with due respect to just war Habermasians, the search for a universally acceptable "secular" language is a narcissistic illusion. The same applies, *pace* just war Rawlsians, to the search for an overlapping consensus that transcends controversy. Even the very late Rawls admitted that consensus contains such dissensus as to require, sometimes, crude resolution by majority vote.[1]

THE *RELATIVE* DISTINCTIVENESS OF CHRISTIAN JUST WAR THEORY

I take it that, like any other, the tradition of just war discourse contains a diversity of construals, which are nevertheless sufficiently similar to be considered members of a single family. Quite where lies the bottom line will, of course, be controversial. One man's heretic is another man's Protestant. Nevertheless, heresy there must be; otherwise definition is lacking, and if definition, then identity. There can be no doubt, however, that orthodox construals of the just war tradition include Christian ones. And in what now follows, I offer a Christian, theological account of the grounds of the authority of just war discourse, and of their moral implications.

A Christian account will have its proper characteristics. What is characteristic, however, need not be absolutely distinctive. Not everything that a Christian affirms will every non-Christian feel the need to deny. This is so for one of several reasons: Either the non-Christian depends on a Christian intellectual heritage, or she shares with Christians the same moral conviction but for different reasons, or the Christian view incorporates an empirical element that commands broad assent. The fact that an account of just war is Christian, therefore, is no good reason for non-Christians to shut their ears and turn away, as if it had nothing to do with them. Some characteristic features of a Christian account of just war will elicit their agreement, whether qualified or wholehearted; other features will baffle them. It was ever thus in human conversation. What reaction something provokes depends upon who is listening and where they are listening from. Accessibility is unpredictable. The only thing to do is to speak one's mind, and then negotiate.

FROM THE COMMAND OF NEIGHBOR-LOVE TO THE GOOD OF HUMAN LIFE

The practical norm that immediately generates Christian just war thinking is Jesus's command that we should love our neighbors, whom he then specifies as including our enemies.[2] No command, however, is ever its own justification; every duty serves a good. We should love our neighbors because it is good for us to do so—because it profits us.[3] The relevant profit, however, is not extrinsic but intrinsic, and its currency is not money but virtue. It is good that we should grow in the virtues of benevolence and justice; it belongs to our own good or flourishing that we should become benevolent and just. And that will remain true, even if it should cost us our very lives; for God—judging by his resurrection of Jesus—will recover the righteous (or, better, the faithful) from death.

As I see it, then, a Christian ethic should be basically eudaemonist.[4] Therefore, the rationale of the normative authority of Jesus's love command needs to refer to the flourishing of the one who is commanded. Nevertheless, it also needs to refer to the good or value or flourishing of the one who is to be loved. For we should only love what, being valuable, deserves to be loved. The command to love presupposes that the human neighbor is valuable—and given Jesus's own information of the concept of love by his practice of self-giving unto death—the neighbor is very valuable indeed. The love command, then, presupposes the biblical view of the human individual as made in God's image to respond to a unique calling to play an inimitable part in the history of the salvation of the world. In this respect all human beings possess—despite their manifest inequalities of physical power and beauty, of intellect and virtue—an equal dignity. Jeremy Waldron observes that John Locke's classic expression of this counterempirical form of basic human equality is irreducibly theological.[5] He also doubts that a plausible nontheological account is possible.[6] A number of other contemporary atheist philosophers tend to agree with him: Jeffrie Murphy, Raymond Gaita, and Jürgen Habermas.[7]

So the human neighbor is valuable and deserves love. But in order to know how to love him, we need some idea of what is valuable about him. One basic feature that is valuable is his life, for without that no response to God's call is possible. Almost as basic is his health, for ill health impedes responsiveness. Love of neighbor, therefore, requires that we protect his life against evils, including those evils meted out by other humans, especially those that are unjust. Evils are bad, but unjust evils are worse.

CHRISTIAN JUST WAR AS BASICALLY PUNITIVE

From a Christian point of view, then, the use of coercion, though sometimes lethal, is justified if it is necessary to protect neighbors from unjust evils. Note the reactive, defensive posture. It might be that the natives of the sixteenth-century Caribbean would have been better off with the Christian religion, and that the inhabitants of nineteenth-century China would have benefited from the free trade of opium. The conferring of such benefits, however, cannot amount to a just cause for waging war on them. Why not? One reason is that some benefits can only be enjoyed when held sincerely, and sincerity cannot be coerced. Another is that no people is likely to appreciate a benefit that has been forced on them at gunpoint and over the corpses of their kith and kin.

Christian just war is reactive against injustice and defensive of justice. It is there-fore—as Gregory Reichberg further discusses in chapter 9 of this volume—also punitive. One cannot rectify injustice without punishing its perpetrator—by forcing him to stop, by deterring him from resuming, and ideally by provoking him to think again and change his aggressive ways forever. By this definition punishment is retaliatory, but it is not vengeful or vindictive; for it has no interest in the suffer-ing of the enemy—far less his annihilation—*as such.*

While this punitive conception of just war is thoroughly embedded in Christian tradition, it is now very controversial.[8] Contemporary critics accuse it of fostering moral self-righteousness, loosening the reins of war, and flouting proper authority. I find none of these criticisms ultimately cogent. Holding fire on the last charge until the fifth section, I fend off the first two here.

The basic point of thinking of war in terms of punishment is to say that it is about justice and that therefore it is a *moral* enterprise. It is not just about defending whatever borders history or positive law happens to have posited, nor about main-taining a stable regional status quo, regardless of the evils being perpetrated behind those borders or the justice that could be done in transgressing them.

Yes, this moralized conception of war does encourage intervention, and therefore conflict, where those engaged in postmoral realpolitik decry the naïve, messianic moralism that would disturb the peace. But naïveté attends their own distinction between war and peace. The fact that the West turned its back on Rwanda in 1994 meant that it spared itself war and left the Hutus in peace—to slaughter the Tutsis. And the fact that Europe spared itself war in Bosnia until August 1995 left Ratko Mladić at peace to supervise the July massacre at Srebrenica. Less conflict was good for the West, of course, but not so good for those whom it declined to defend. If peace were always simple, then war could never be preferable. But peace is seldom simple.

It is true that those who make moral judgments against others risk becoming "judgmental."[9] They risk buying into a Manichaean vision of things where the basi-cally good (the judges) battle against the basically bad (the judged), and where the bad, being basically so, deserve to be fought without restraint. Just wars do stand in danger of becoming crusades. Nevertheless, just wars need not become crusades; and if they remain faithful to the logic of Christian just war thinking, then they will not. As a Christian the just warrior cannot stand to the unjust perpetrator as clean to unclean, righteous to unrighteous, good to evil. He can only stand as one sinful creature to another. Even the enemy partakes of an equal dignity that deserves respect. According to the Christian view, therefore, cleansing the world of wicked-ness cannot be an aim of just war, because wickedness lies within as well as without, *here* as well as *there.* Just war is only ever a police action, never a crusade—always proximate, never ultimate.

HUMANITARIAN INTERVENTION AS PARADIGMATIC

This Christian, punitive conception of just war does tend to favor "humanitarian intervention" over mere self-defense, and thus it diverges from those conceptions that take their cue from post-Westphalian international law. Although Augustine was prepared to justify the use of force out of love for the neighbor, he was disinclined to sanction it in self-defense. So in his letter, *Ad Publicolam* (47), he writes that killing in self-defense is permissible only to a soldier or public official, who does it "not . . . for his own sake, but for others or for the state to which he belongs."[10] Similarly, in *De libero arbitrio* (I.5) he tells us that self-defense is morally permissible to a soldier or public servant acting for "the protection of the people," but not to someone acting out of a passionate (and so excessive) attachment to his own life.[11] This discovers the reason for Augustine's suspicion of self-defense: its propensity to become a vehicle for sinful self-love or selfishness.

Aquinas both agrees and disagrees with Augustine. He disagrees in holding that "it is natural for anything to want to preserve itself in being as far as it can," that "a man is under a greater obligation to care for his own life than for another's," and therefore that a private person may kill another, if in so doing he intends to save his own life rather than to kill his assailant.[12] Nevertheless, he agrees with Augustine that killing by public authorities "charged with the care of the whole community" is straightforwardly legitimate.[13]

When Augustine and Aquinas discuss self-defense, they do so in terms of a national society, contrasting the public servant's concern for the common good with the private person's concern for his own life. They agree that the latter can be excessive and therefore vitiated; but whereas Augustine thinks that that is always so, Aquinas thinks that it need not be (if the intention is right). We need to be careful in transposing these views directly onto discussion about relations *between* national societies. This is because the *self* that a national government seeks to defend is not simply a private individual, but a body of people for whose common good the government has public responsibility. In this sense, then, national self-defense is always a public act. However, that does not make it right; for, as history tells us, there is such a thing as corporate selfishness. Indeed, if Reinhold Niebuhr is correct, selfishness is even more likely at the corporate level than at the interpersonal one.[14] Going to war in national self-defense, therefore, may well be selfish. In contrast, going to war to prevent or to stop the gross oppression of another people is not obviously selfish. Accordingly, Christian just war thinking smiles upon the latter more readily than upon the former.

But surely no nation will go to war, and bear its costs, *simply* to liberate a foreign people? Surely Niebuhr was right in observing that the light of human sympathy flickers and fades the further removed it becomes from kith and kin? Surely belligerency out of love for distant neighbors is a phenomenon that occurs somewhere between rarity and impossibility? The more anthropologically pessimistic reaches of Protestant theology, together with Hobbesian "realism," would tell us so. There are, however, less dismal views—for example, that of the Anglican bishop and moralist Joseph Butler, who insisted that human beings have a natural propensity toward benevolence (as well as to self-love).[15] Experience suggests that he is correct. In the nineteenth century many British people were deeply moved by the distant plight of slaves in the West Indies and of Christians in the Turkish Balkans; and in the twenty-first century their counterparts have supported military interventions to rescue faraway peoples in Sierra Leone and Libya.

It remains true, however, that one national people is unlikely to bear very heavy costs *simply* to save another. If military intervention for humanitarian purposes is to have their support, then the expenditure of blood and treasure will have to find adequate justification in terms of national interest. But does this not compromise— indeed corrupt—the altruistic, humanitarian motive and intention? That would appear so, if we assume a popular Kantian view of morality, which, applied to international affairs, deems national interest as such to be immoral.[16] Accordingly, the fact that such interest motivated Britain's interventions in Kosovo and Iraq counts against their moral justification. I myself reckon this view of morality mistaken, and I prefer the alternative provided by the ethical tradition stemming from Aquinas. Combining the Book of Genesis's affirmation of the goodness of creation with Aristotle, Thomist thought does not view all self-interest as selfish and immoral. Indeed, as I have shown above, it holds that there is such a thing as morally obligatory self-love. The human individual has a duty to care for himself properly, to seek what is genuinely his own good. As with an individual, so with a national community and the organ of its cohesion and decision, namely, its government: A national government has a moral duty to look after the well-being of its own people—and in that sense to advance its genuine interests. Such a duty is not unlimited, of course. There cannot be a moral duty to pursue the interests of one's own nation by riding roughshod over the rights of others. Still, not every pursuit of national interest does perpetrate injustice. Therefore, the fact that national interests are among the motives for military intervention does not by itself vitiate the latter's moral justification.

Christian just war doctrine prefers military intervention for humanitarian purposes to self-defense—prima facie. This is not to say, however, that it lacks appreciation for the prudence embodied in post-1945 international law, which reserves to collective authority the right to sanction war for purposes other than self-defense. The intention here is laudable: namely, to get beyond the situation where every nation is judge in its own case and so free to fabricate humanitarian pretexts for acts of selfish aggression. Moreover, disposed by their monotheism to believe in the moral coherence of the world of God's creating, Christians will support the development of international law that reflects the universal moral order.

Nevertheless, Christians also appreciate the creaturely fallibility of human institutions and the sinful propensities of those who operate them. Accordingly, more than the starry-eyed children of the Enlightenment, they will be inclined to acknowledge the structural problems that afflict current international law and its operating institutions. What I have in mind here, in particular, is the fact that the ability of the Security Council of the United Nations to authorize the enforcement of international law against a transgressing state lies at the mercy of a single veto, which may be cast in the service of vicious national interests. The result is that the current international order often ends up protecting atrocious tyrants from interference. To illustrate this problem, let me deploy an analogy that I have used elsewhere.[17] A neighbor a few houses away is beating his own children to death. It is against the law for us to intervene directly, so we call the police and ask them to intervene instead. Before they can intervene, however, the police have to get authorization from a committee, any member of which can veto it. In this case a member of the committee is allied with the neighbor in some way. He therefore casts his veto and prevents the police from intervening. What are we to do? Shall we break the law and intervene unilaterally? Or shall we abide by the law and watch the children being done to death? This is the predicament into which current international law can deliver us.

Because Christian proponents of just war recognize a moral order that transcends international law (and is therefore "natural"), they find it conceivable that the moral obligation to rescue grossly oppressed neighbors may sometimes warrant military intervention without the UN Security Council's authorization, and so the breaking of the law. In other words, they find it conceivable that morality may warrant illegality. Nevertheless, if Christian just warriors do countenance moral illegality, they do not countenance wanton illegality. The authority of law is important and is sustained by the respect that is paid it. Accordingly, transgression can only be moral where it has first done its utmost to remain within the letter of the law, and where its reasons for violating it are proportionately strong.[18]

Further, in the absence of an impartial global court to decide cases, what *is* the law is somewhat determined by international opinion. So even though NATO's 1999 intervention in Kosovo was conducted without UN Security Council authorization and was therefore literally illegal, the fact that the council subsequently refused to pass a condemnatory resolution backed by Russia gave the intervention something approaching retrospective legality. Accordingly, the more widespread and diverse the international support for a transgression of the letter of international law, the more legal authority it accrues. Thus it was morally significant that the Kosovo intervention was backed by France as well as the United States, and by Turkey as well as Greece.

THE RESTRAINTS OF INTENTION, RESPECT, AND PRUDENCE

It belongs to the tragic nature of secular things that defending innocent neighbors against unjust evils sometimes cannot be done without inflicting further evils on unjust neighbors. What makes this infliction just is that its primary intention is to protect the innocent, not to hurt the harming. Although the just warrior must and should behave toward unjust aggressors in a hostile manner—because not to resent harm to valuable things is not to care for them as they deserve—his hostility is governed and restrained by this basic intention. It is also restrained by respect for the enemy as equal before God in creaturely calling and as subject to a measure of sinful fate, which is humanly inscrutable—"There, but for the grace of God and an accident of history, went we all."

The hostile behavior of the Christian just warrior is also reined in by a certain prudential concern for moral and spiritual self-preservation. To some extent this prudence is this-worldly. Aware that hostility can become disproportionate—indeed, can become a passionate hatred to which the agent is helplessly subject—and aware also of how unruly passion generates its own injustices, which are sometimes atrocious, the just warrior will take care to monitor and discipline his motives. And this secular prudence will be intensified by the agent's religious concern to form his character to make himself fit for life beyond the grave.

The justified use of violent force, then, is motivated first and last by a care for human dignity and a concomitant desire to fend off injustice. From this virtuous motive follows right intention, namely, the achievement of just peace. If there is hostility—as there must and should be—then it will be subordinate to this species of benevolence and its ends. Christian just war thinking, therefore, is not simply consequentialist; it does not operate only in terms of consequences. Whether or not going to war or waging war is just depends on motive and intention, as well as on the supposed balance of costs and benefits.

JUST WAR ANALYSIS AS ALTERNATIVE TO RIGHTS DISCOURSE

Nor, I think, does Christian just war doctrine operate basically in terms of human rights. My impression—as yet not fully tested—is that human rights discourse is strongly inclined to preempt the kind of moral reasoning in which just war thinking wants to engage. The rights advocate wants to secure for the individual certain immunities—say, from torture or attack or a failure of the duty of care—that are *ab initio* absolute, noncontingent, and nonnegotiable. Rights talk forecloses the very questions that just war thinking has been developed to answer. What is right, according to just war doctrine, depends on motive, intention, and circumstance—and can only be determined at the end of a laborious process of moral reasoning that considers all the various factors. Amateur, journalistic rights talk asserts baldly that Afghan civilians have a right not to be injured by NATO bombing; but just war analysis only says that they have a right not to be injured maliciously or wantonly. More professional rights talk asserts a universal right against torture. However, the just warrior (if he were prepared to lose all his right-thinking friends) would reply that, if terrorists' use of a weapon of mass destruction were correctly known to be imminent, if there was very good reason indeed to suppose that this captured enemy did in fact know its whereabouts, if the desire to save innocents from mass destruction were one's governing motive, if sadistic hatred of the enemy were entirely lacking, if the coercive methods applied were known to be effective in eliciting the truth, and if only such coercion as was necessary were applied, then proportionate "torture" would be just. Those are a lot of "ifs," of course; and the just warrior might conclude that meeting them would be practically impossible or improbable, or that to permit the practice of torture at all would tend to invite the proliferation of abuse. Nevertheless, this would be the conclusion of a set of empirical and prudential judgments, and it would always be vulnerable to the emergence of fresh contingencies, which rights talk abhors.

Thus, Christian just war thinking is realistic. It requires the prudential consideration of circumstances, even the "weighing up" of goods and evils, albeit within the terms set by moral norms of conduct. When it is (as it should be) more Aristotelian than conventional-Kantian—and when it is more Thomistic than Augustinian—it recognizes that the prudent pursuit of genuine self-interest is, within the bounds of justice, not only permissible but also obligatory. It is therefore disinclined to assume that what passes for realpolitik is ipso facto immoral. It does not consider "the ethical prism" as something separate from the pursuit of policy goals or the management of differential power relations.

CONCLUSION: THE SOURCES
OF NORMATIVE AUTHORITY

In conclusion, let me return to some of the questions posed in the introduction to this volume and state straightforwardly the Christian answers I would give to them. What is the source of the just war's normative force? My construal of Christian just war thinking reaches back through and behind the biblical, dominical command of neighbor love to a "natural law" account of the human good or flourishing. It then combines this with a theological account of high equal human dignity, which explains why human flourishing deserves especially careful treatment, and why even enemies deserve a certain respect.

Who may be regarded as an authoritative interpreter of the just war tradition? If by "authoritative interpreter" is meant "genuine member," then surely anyone belongs who thinks that war should be governed by considerations of *justice*, and that it is not justified merely by its intrinsic ecstasy or by the aim of glorious domination—or simply by *positive law*. Having said that, the differences between versions that operate in terms of the complex moral reasoning exemplified by double-effect analysis and those that take a more Kantian or rights line might be very great; and advocates of one might harbor very serious reservations about the other. Still, a tradition ought not to be identified with its earliest expression, and families have been known to contain even violent disagreements. Conversely, later developments do need to show considerable continuity with earlier expressions, if their claim to belong to a tradition is to stand. Where a tradition lacks definition, it lacks identity. But if it has definition, then heresy must be possible. Not any claim to belong can stand. It is unlikely, however, that we will agree about where to draw the line. Some Christians, for example, think that a Christian atheist is possible; I do not.

Given rivals that are indeed members of the just war tradition, how should we adjudicate between them? Certainly not, I submit, on the ground that religious versions are "inaccessible" and secular ones are "neutral." That is neither true nor genuinely liberal. Presumably we should judge in terms of correspondence to basic intuitions (critically sifted), internal coherence, and empirical grip—and perhaps also in terms of moral beauty.

NOTES

1. I allude here to the claim of Jürgen Habermas that public deliberation in an ideologically plural society should operate in nonreligious, "secular" language; and to the claim of John Rawls that it should operate in terms of a liberal consensus about justice, which overlaps multiple "comprehensive doctrines." For a fuller, critical account of the debate about the propriety of religious references in the public discourse of plural societies, see Nigel Biggar, "Not Translation, but Conversation," in *Religious Voices in Public Places*, ed. Nigel Biggar and Linda Hogan (Oxford: Oxford University Press, 2009), 162–84, 191–93.

2. See, e.g., Matt 5:43–44, 19.19b; Mk 12:31a; Lk 6:27–28, 6:35, 10:27. It is true that those two towering patriarchs of the Christian tradition of just war thinking, Augustine and Aquinas, do not always open their justification of war by citing Jesus's love command. Sometimes they do; but even when they do not, they affirm it implicitly by consistently describing just war as a benevolent response to injustice, which intends just peace. In his letter *Ad Marcellinum* (138), Augustine initially argues that Christians should eschew the passion for revenge; Augustine, *Political Writings*, ed. E. M. Atkins and R. J. Dodaro (Cambridge: Cambridge University Press, 2001), 35 (s.9). Augustine also argues that Christians should intend to persuade the wrongdoer to repent and embrace peace; ibid., 36 (s.11). Further on, Augustine articulates what lies implicit here—namely, that just war is waged out of a benevolent concern for the interests of the unjust enemy; ibid., 38 (s.14). In his letter *Ad Bonifacem* (189),

he does quote Jesus's love command; ibid., 215 (s.2). He then proceeds shortly afterward to discuss the propriety of a Christian serving as a soldier; ibid., 216 (s.4). And he prescribes peace as the proper end of a just war; ibid., 217 (s.6). In *Ad Bonifacem* (220), he refers to the dominical command that one should love one's enemies, when enjoining "single-minded love," even while treating them with "an unpleasant severity"; ibid., 222 (s.8). And in the *City of God*, he defines just war as a necessary response to injustice (XIX.7), which intends just peace (XIX.12). Likewise, Aquinas defines just war as that which responds to an injustice and intends the good of peace; *Summa Theologiae*, 2a2ae, q. 40, art. 1.

3. Matt 16:24–26.

4. Following Aristotle, eudaimonism understands the fundamental rationale of morality to be that of promoting human *eudaimonia*, which is variously translated as "happiness," "well-being," or "flourishing." The ethics of Augustine and Aquinas—and so the ethical hinterland of the tradition of just war thinking that they developed—are eudaemonist.

5. Jeremy Waldron, *God, Locke, and Equality: Christian Foundations in Locke's Political Thought* (Cambridge: Cambridge University Press, 2002), 80–81.

6. Waldron comments: Lockean equality "is a conception . . . that makes no sense except in the light of a particular account of the relation between man and God"; Waldron, *God, Locke, and Equality*, 82. Further: "I believe that Locke's mature corpus . . . is as well-worked-out a theory of basic equality as we have in the canon of political philosophy" (p. 1). Further still: "Locke's religious premises help to make sense of or give shape to a certain cluster of human characteristics that might seem arbitrary, shapeless, even insignificant apart from the religious context" (p. 48). Even further: "I am inclined to believe . . . that a commitment to human equality is most coherent and attractive when it is grounded in theological truth, truths associated particularly with the Christian heritage" (p. 236). Furthest: "I actually don't think that we—now—*can* shape and defend an adequate conception of basic human equality apart from some religious foundation" (p. 13).

7. When he was an atheist, Jeffrie Murphy wrote: "[For me it is] very difficult—perhaps impossible—to embrace religious convictions," and yet "the liberal theory of rights requires a doctrine of human dignity, preciousness and sacredness that cannot be utterly detached from a belief in God or at least from a world view that would be properly called religious in some metaphysically profound sense"; Jeffrie Murphy, "Afterword: Constitutionalism, Moral Skepticism, and Religious Belief," in *Constitutionalism: The Philosophical Dimension*, ed. Alan S. Rosenbaum (New York: Greenwood Press, 1988), 239. Raimond Gaita has written along similar lines: "The secular philosophical tradition speaks of inalienable rights, inalienable dignity and of persons as ends in themselves. These are, I believe, ways of whistling in the dark, ways of trying to make secure to reason what reason cannot finally underwrite. Religious traditions speak of the sacredness of each human being, but I doubt that sanctity is a concept that has a secure home outside those traditions"; Raimond Gaita, *A Common Humanity: Thinking about Love and Truth and Justice* (London: Routledge, 2000), 5. Though more cautious in his concessions, Habermas has nevertheless admitted recently that religious traditions "have the distinction of a superior capacity for articulating our [liberal, humanist] moral sensibility" ("Habermas entre démocratie et génétique," *Le Monde*, December 20, 2002), and that when the notion of the value of the individual's authenticity—which is a form of equal human dignity—is translated out of theological terms and into "secular" ones, an important dimension is lost. Jürgen Habermas, "Are There Postmetaphysical Answers to the Question: What Is the Good Life?" in *The Future of Human Nature* (Cambridge: Polity, 2003), 5–11, esp. 10, 11; see also Biggar, "Not Translation, but Conversation," 163–66.

8. I owe my understanding of the controversy very largely to Anthony Lang, "Punitive Intervention: Enforcing Justice or Generating Conflict?" in *Just War Theory: A Reappraisal*,

ed. Mark Evans (Edinburgh: University of Edinburgh Press, 2005); and Cian O'Driscoll, *The Renegotiation of the Just War Tradition and the Right to War in the Twenty-First Century* (New York: Palgrave MacMillan, 2008), esp. chap. 3 and 134–38. O'Driscoll traces the punitive conception of just war from St. Paul, through Augustine, Aquinas, Vitoria, and Suárez, to Grotius; and he lists as its contemporary champions only the moral theologians Oliver O'Donovan and Jean Bethke Elshtain; O'Driscoll, *Renegotiation*, 52–54, 60–65.

9. For more on the idea of judgment, as approached from a practice-based perspective, see chapter 2 in this volume by Chris Brown.

10. Augustine, *Letters, Volume I (1–82)*, in *The Fathers of the Church*, vol. 12, ed. Wilfrid Parsons (Washington, DC: Catholic University of America Press, 1951), 230.

11. Augustine, *The Teacher; The Free Choice of the Will; Grace and Free Will*, trans. Robert P. Russell, in *The Fathers of the Church*, vol. 59 (Washington, DC: Catholic University of America Press, 1968), 81–83.

12. Thomas Aquinas, *Summa Theologiae*, 2a2ae, q. 64, a.7, Responsio. Because our bodily nature is created by God, it deserves our love; *Summa Theologiae*, 2a2ae, q.25, a. 5, Responsio.

13. Ibid., a.3, Responsio.

14. See, e.g., Reinhold Niebuhr, *Moral Man and Immoral Society* (New York: Scribner, 1932).

15. Joseph Butler, "Sermon 1: Upon Human Nature," in *Fifteen Sermons*, intro. W. R. Matthews (London: G. Bell & Sons, 1953), 29–45.

16. The ethics of Immanuel Kant are usually held to be simply "deontological," viewing the only truly moral act as one that is done out of a pure sense of duty or reverence for the moral law. So conceived, the truly moral act stands in stark contrast to a merely prudential one, which seeks to promote the agent's interests. Whether this common, deontological view of Kant fully captures his thought I doubt. I think that a better reading has him argue that truly moral acts are those where the duty of justice as fairness disciplines—rather than excludes—the pursuit of interest.

17. E.g., see Nigel Biggar, "Iraq: What Are the Morals of the Story?" *International Affairs*, January 2011; and Nigel Biggar, "Was Iraq an Unjust War? A Debate on the Iraq War and Reflections on Libya," *International Affairs*, May 2011.

18. Christian just war thought in the sixteenth and seventeenth centuries did consider the issue of proper jurisdiction as it bears on military intervention on behalf of third parties. Francisco Suárez opined that "the assertion made by some writers, that sovereign kings have the power of avenging injuries done in any part of the world, is entirely false, and throws into confusion all the orderly distinctions of jurisdiction"; Francisco Suárez, "A Work on the Three Theological Virtues of Faith, Hope, and Charity," "On Charity, Disputation XIII: On War," Section IV.3, in *Selections from Three Works of Francisco Suárez, SJ*, vol. II, trans. Gwladys L. Williams et al. (Oxford: Clarendon Press, 1944), 817. Nevertheless, he judged intervention on behalf of "allies or friends" to be just, provided that the victim of wrongdoing is morally justified in avenging himself and that he consents to being helped; ibid.

Next, Francisco de Vitoria held that Christian princes may not wage war against other princes, Christian or otherwise, to stop their subjects committing "sins against nature" (e.g., pederasty or buggery) or, more broadly, offences against natural law (e.g., adultery, fornication, perjury, or theft); Francisco de Vitoria, "On Dietary Laws, or Self-Restraint," in *Political Writings*, ed. Anthony Pagden and Jeremy Lawrance (Cambridge: Cambridge University Press, 1991), Q.1, Art. 5, 218–19, 224. Nevertheless, he wrote, such princes may wage war against the barbarians in order to defend the innocent against the *injustice* of being made to suffer cannibalism or human sacrifice—even if (pace Suárez) the victims do not ask for help (ibid., 225).

Then Hugo Grotius argued "that Kings, and those who are invested with a Power equal to that of Kings, have a Right to exact Punishments, not only for Injuries committed against themselves, or their Subjects, but likewise, for those which do not peculiarly concern them, but which are, in any Persons whatsoever, grievous Violations of the Law of Nature or Nations"; Hugo Grotius, *The Rights of War and Peace*, book II, ed. and intro. Richard Tuck (Indianapolis: Liberty Fund, 2005), chap. XX, "Of Punishments," s.XL.1, p. 1021; that (echoing Augustine) "it is so much more honourable, to revenge other Peoples [*sic*] Injuries rather than their own" (ibid.); and that "I may make War upon a Man, tho' he and I are of different Nations, if he disturbs and molests his own Country, as we told you in our Discourse about Punishments, which is an Affair often attended with the Defence of innocent Subjects" (ibid., chap. XXV, "Of the Causes for which War is to be undertaken on the Account of others," s.VIII.4, 1162).

It seems to me that all three of these Christian just war theorists argue that military intervention in the affairs of a foreign state can be justified on the ground of a natural justice or law that transcends positive civil jurisdiction. Therefore, I do not see the tension between Grotius on the one hand, and Suárez and Vitoria on the other, of which Cian O'Driscoll writes. I do not think that "both Vitoria and Suarez are keen to attach the caveat that this right to [punitive] war as a form of judgment is only operative in those instances where the prince's own commonwealth is the injured party on whose behalf justice is sought"— O'Driscoll, *Renegotiation*, 64—or that "Vitoria and his scholastic brethren claimed that license to punish is conditional upon proper civil jurisdiction, while Grotius countered that it may be understood as derived from the law of nature"; ibid., 62. O'Driscoll later qualifies his view in a footnote, where he writes that "Vitoria . . . did actually allow for intervention on behalf of third parties, but only to protect the innocent rather than to uphold natural law"; ibid., 182n65. The problem lies in Vitoria's confusing view of "natural law" here. On the one hand, he tells us that the reason that cannibalism and human sacrifice provide grounds for intervention is not that they are "against natural law," but rather that they "involve injustice to other men"; Q.1, Art. 5, 225. This distinction is odd, however, because the kinds of wrongdoing that he earlier describes as offences against natural law—adultery, fornication, perjury or theft; ibid., 218—also involve injustice to other people. On the other hand, by sanctioning intervention to stop cannibalism and human sacrifice, he implies that the obligations of justice transcend the borders of civil jurisdictions—and are, in that sense "natural" rather than positive. One way to resolve this tension is to read Vitoria as saying that only *grave forms* of injurious offence against natural law warrant military intervention.

CHAPTER 4

"Not in My Name"?

Legitimate Authority and Liberal Just War theory

John Williams

THIS CHAPTER AIMS TO EXPLORE one aspect of the massive controversy generated by the 2003 invasion of Iraq. The war, occupation, and postwar political fate of Iraq and Iraqis have occasioned enormous debate on a whole range of important political questions and still cast a lengthy shadow over the political reputation of the two leaders most closely associated with the invasion, George W. Bush and Tony Blair, and their administrations. The failure of the war to achieve its stated goals, the inaccuracy of the intelligence on which the case for war rested, the incompetence of postwar reconstruction efforts, the deaths of tens or possibly hundreds of thousands of Iraqis, and the uncertainty over the future of Iraq as a state and the quality of its citizens' lives are all topics worthy of detailed consideration—but are all ignored by this chapter.

Instead, the focus here is on what, on the face of it, may appear to be a minor and esoteric concern—a slogan carried on thousands of banners in February 2003 during the largest demonstration in London's history, when upward of 1 million people expressed their opposition to the impending invasion. Opinion polls in the period preceding the war were contradictory, often because of the variety of conditions under which war might have begun, which were reflected in the framing of the questions, and thus the opinion polling evidence was debated.[1] However, support for the war in the United Kingdom rose to more than 60 percent of the population as the initial military campaign made rapid progress. Nevertheless, it was the antiwar marchers who captured the iconic image of British public opinion on the war. And it was one slogan that has stuck in the political consciousness—"Not in my name."

As with any such mass demonstration, there was doubtless a great mixture of reasons explaining why people had chosen to join the protests. Some may have wanted to express their opposition to the government and its policies in toto; others their personal dislike for the prime minister; some a notion of religious solidarity with fellow Muslims who were to be on the receiving end of Western military "shock and awe"; and some their rejection of war in all circumstances. However, this is not a chapter on the sociology of public demonstration. Nor is it an assessment of the political significance of this particular march, or of political demonstrations in general. Instead, I look at what lies behind the slogan "Not in my name": what is claimed by the withdrawal of consent by an individual to the actions of a government. In particular, the chapter poses the question of how the authority to take a state to war, often seen as a classic example of a sovereign prerogative, should be understood in a democratic context. It uses the idea of "Not in my name" as an explicit challenge to this prerogative, exploring that claim as a way into debates within contemporary just war theory, which has taken an increasingly liberal turn in recent years.

There is more to this slogan, I shall argue, than Ian McEwan allows in his novel *Saturday*: "Its cloying self-regard suggests a bright new world of protest, with the fussy consumers of shampoos and soft drinks demanding to feel good or nice."[2] This implies, at least to my eye, that McEwan sees a political naïveté on the part of such protesters, a desire to wash their hands of difficult or dangerous decisions, and to insulate themselves from the hard world of politics and of war. This chapter argues that in fact the slogan should be seen as a profoundly and importantly political claim. The desire to dissociate oneself from a war through the slogan "Not in my name" takes a form that is different from a traditional pacifist rejection of the possibility of a just war. Brandishers of such placards need not be pacifists; nor are they necessarily mounting a critique on the basis of what, in the eyes of some contemporary just war theorists, is the key principle of just cause.[3] Instead, the question of the authority of the government to pursue such a war is what is called into doubt. The authority claim of the government to speak in the name of its citizens is what is being disputed.

At one level, that dispute raises questions about the mechanisms through which citizens participate in the political process. The institutional and constitutional settings vary, of course, from state to state, and the UK government took unprecedented steps, including the first ever parliamentary vote on military action, in relation to the decision to invade Iraq. This constitutional novelty looks likely to become permanently enshrined in the way that British governments go about the process of going to war, but the idea of "Not in my name" is about much more than an uneasiness over the constitutional arrangements for such decisions. Securing parliamentary majorities, whether in the face of the largest revolt by members of Parliament of the governing party since the repeal of the Corn Laws in 1846, or with almost universal acclamation, seems unlikely to ameliorate the claims that are made by the slogan "Not in my name." Again, these are issues that this chapter notes but now sets to one side. Instead, it is the claims that ring out well beyond the British context that are important, as they address some fundamental questions with serious implications for sovereignty.

Political authority is, of course, a huge subject, and any sort of comprehensive survey, let alone inquiry, lies beyond the scope of this chapter. Even within the just war tradition a thorough account of legitimate authority would be impossible in a single chapter.[4] Thus the focus here is on recent accounts of and debates within the just war tradition, where legitimate authority provides one of the classic tenets of the *jus ad bellum*. "Not in my name" challenges established notions of legitimate authority in just war thinking—that this is the authority of the sovereign. The slogan is striking because it reflects the common idea in liberal accounts of sovereignty that the authority of the state is derived from its citizens, typically via some sort of notion of consent, tacit or otherwise, rooted in contract. "Not in my name" marks a clear desire to withdraw that consent in relation to war, arguably the most fundamental arena of policy for the idea of sovereignty. Can this be done, and what are the implications of such an attempt to do so, for how we should conceive of legitimate political authority in just war theory? Should we, as Cecile Fabre argues, suggest that the concept is no longer relevant in an era of cosmopolitan ethics?[5]

The chapter ultimately rejects Fabre's position, and it does so by proceeding in three principal sections and approaches the question from what at first sight is an unusual angle. The first section looks at a distinctive critique of the idea of legitimate authority as being sovereign authority within contemporary just war theory's discussion of the ethical challenges of terrorism and counterterrorism via C. A. J. Coady's analysis of Michael Walzer's idea of a "supreme emergency."[6] Coady develops part of the argument that I want to explore, which is the privileging of the state's claims to legitimate authority. Coady's argument for the intellectual incoherence of limiting the supreme emergency claim to states alone causes him to argue for its complete rejection. However, the argument here is that the "Not in my name" claim gives us a different way of thinking about claims to exceptions from powerful moral prohibitions, such as those made by the "supreme emergency" idea, in a way that is more attuned to the politics of such issues.

The second section examines what is labeled a "liberal" just war approach that ought, in principle, to be better able to respond to the challenge of "Not in my name" because it makes the individual the centerpiece of political and ethical theory. However, despite this, such theory deploys a generally conventional account of sovereign authority, indebted to a stereotypical Westphalian position. This misses the full critical potential of the "Not in my name" claim, but it also points to the way that the dispute here is political rather than philosophical. Therefore, the chapter concludes with a discussion of the political significance of challenging a standard idea of legitimate authority as sovereign authority.

LEGITIMATE AUTHORITY, THE STATE, AND SOVEREIGNTY

C. A. J. Coady offers a relatively rare analysis of the way that a privileging of the state as legitimate authority can and should be challenged within an otherwise conventional account of just war theory. His defense of the admissibility of appeals by nonstate actors to the idea of "supreme emergency" as a basis for derogation from the rules of *jus in bello* is significant for the argument that this chapter advances. However, it is noteworthy that Coady sees the admissibility of such claims as a reason to reject the "supreme emergency" exception for all political actors, including states.[7] This is in order to rule out of court indiscriminate targeting strategies, which he sees as an essential element of the terrorism that is the focus of his analysis.[8]

Walzer's well-known argument for a supreme emergency exemption to the *jus in bello* rules of discrimination and proportionality appeals, argues Coady, to the "dirty hands" approach to the facing of grave ethical dilemmas in political life. Essentially, for Coady, dirty hands argues that political leaders sometimes have to make decisions that fly in the face of ethical prohibitions, either because of the serious consequences that would flow from upholding the prohibition or because they are faced with a similarly serious ethical obligation that can only be met through such violation. The role of political leader may often demand hard choices are made in circumstances where there are no realistic options available that do not produce ethical dilemmas.[9] Coady notes three distinctive elements of the "dirty hands" idea and the way that it addresses such dilemmas:

> The first is its emphasis on the political realm as the principal focus for the making of exceptions to . . . powerful moral prohibitions; the second is its common emphasis upon the extreme nature of the situations in which the powerful moral rule must be disregarded; and the third . . . is its stress upon the abiding wrongness that is done by the necessary violation of the moral prohibition. . . . Dirty hands theorists . . . treat such moral prohibitions as . . . far more than prima facie or presumptive. They think them profound. . . . Nonetheless, . . . there comes a point at which the gravity of the consequences or the gravity of the conflicting duty can demand the regrettable but morally painful choice to violate such deep norms.

Unlike Coady, who sees the third of these features—the gravity of conflicting duties—as the most important characteristic of the dirty hands approach, I want to highlight the first of these—the political realm where such decisions must be made. In this I follow Alex Bellamy's account of the dirty hands approach in which he argues that a defense of the breaching of powerful moral prohibitions on these grounds rests upon a separation between public and private morality—that the hands of political leaders are dirtied by the necessity of the choices that they must make in the name of the public good and, in particular, in response to the necessity that they face of privileging those whom they are charged with representing.[10] "Not in my name" can be read, as I think McEwan does, to be a rejection of that kind of logic—political leaders do not (or at least did not in the case of the invasion of Iraq) have to dirty their hands in such a way and that public dissociation from such a move can demonstrate the unacceptability of those claims.

Coady and Bellamy, however, part company on whether the "supreme emergency" argument presented by Walzer is indeed an instance of dirty hands.[11] Bellamy places it within a second category, that of "lesser evil."[12] This chimes closely with the third of Coady's characteristics of dirty hands arguments: "the abiding wrongness that is done by the necessary violation of the moral prohibition." The finer-grained approach to categorizing these kinds of arguments that Bellamy develops appears, on the face of it at least, to be preferable. However, it is also the subject of a critique by Bellamy because of the way that the two strategies for justifying actions that offend against powerful moral prohibitions neglect the politics of such decisions and their debate and presentation.[13] This is an issue to which we shall return as it is an important part of the case made against a certain sort of authority claim by the slogan "Not in my name" and is at the heart of the problem it presents for liberal just war theory. This helps us to understand why the reading suggested by McEwan is limited in its insight.[14]

Both Coady's and Bellamy's analyses identify the survival of the state as the issue most closely and clearly associated with the overriding of moral prohibitions on political action.[15] It is also Walzer's key example of "supreme emergency."[16] The idea of a profound and serious threat to the survival of the way of life that is made possible by the existence of a certain sort of state has been at the heart of justifications of the war on terrorism," and has been used to defend the necessity of actions such as preventive war and torture that raise the gravest moral questions.[17] The argument of "Not in my name" may be read as a defense of moral prohibitions against these kinds of actions, a stand against the appeal to political necessity—dirty hands—that characterizes such arguments and in defense of deontological moral precepts that stand above consequentialist reasoning, becoming peremptory norms that permit no derogation. That, however, is to fall into the trap of forgetting the politics of the issue, that it is in the political realm in which the resolution of such issues is sought.

An appeal to the politics of these questions appears to give an easy victory to the dirty hands position—that necessity characterizes public morality, especially in times of emergency or serious threat, and that responsible political leadership is about doing what is necessary, rather than what may be right by the standards of private moral principle. This is, however, as Bellamy shows, to grant carte blanche to political leaders to literally get away with murder (and torture, maiming, willful destruction, etc.).[18] The claim of "Not in my name" also possesses a different, more complex, and more powerful logic. It questions political leaders' claims to exercise authority and license in the name of the necessity of protecting the state and its citizens. As Coady argues, a dirty hands argument of this sort "dangerously opens the door to the identification of the state's survival with that of its political leadership."[19] "Not in my name" instead reminds the political leaders that they are beholden to a political process and that the authority that they claim derives from the people whom they ostensibly represent and to whom they should be accountable. The ethical foundations of this claim to representation in the idea of consent cannot be easily set aside, even in the name of national security or the emergency of transnational, fundamentalist mass-casualty terrorism. Or at least the case for such a setting aside must be carefully and convincingly made in order to fulfill the demand for accountability as the quid pro quo of consent.

Walzer limits the right to claim the supreme emergency to states or, more precisely, their leaders who have to make the decisions, on the basis that the state's claim to sovereignty grants it a privileged position.[20] The idea of legitimate authority as being sovereign authority is something of a commonplace in most accounts of just war theory.[21] The outcome of this, however, is a contemporary ethical privileging of the state as the only form of political community and authority that is entitled to level such arguments. Implicit in this is a moral privileging of sovereignty over other forms of political association.

This helps to highlight the political nature of the realm within which dirty hands claims are made and the tendency to frame the admissibility of such claims in statist terms. Fighting to protect a way of life from a murderous threat whose triumph would destroy Western civilization and threaten the security and value of peoples all over the world is how Walzer characterizes the position in which Britain found itself in the summer of 1940. This is also not too far from the position that the UK and US governments asked their citizenries to accept in relation to transnational terrorism in 2003. Again, both the US and UK governments have seen this as reason to argue for a very significant changing of the rules in response to claimed fundamental transformations of circumstances.[22]

The claim that the extent and character of the threat necessitates the overriding of the prohibition is, however, an empirical and a political argument rather than a straightforwardly moral or ethical one. There must be a degree of probability, although how great a degree is a matter of significant debate that we shall have to set aside, that the threat may come to pass and the feared consequences will emerge if it does.[23] As Elshtain argues, we should take the terrorists at their word when they tell us what they have in store for our societies.[24] But we must also assess the risk that they will be in a position to bring about such a society. The "supreme emergency," therefore, marks a turn toward a political claim about the supremacy of the authority of the sovereign to make the decision on when the rules can be set to one side and the necessity of action takes over. "Not in my name" denies the political permissibility of that move, at least in relation to the circumstances of February 2003, and insists on the need to remain within the established ethical realm for the resort to and conduct of warfare. However, it is also a political claim, because the struggle is over the political framing of the situation and the need to maintain a particular and established political narrative against efforts to set that aside in favor of a claim to exceptionality via emergency. It reasserts the "normality" of the politics of whether Iraq should have been subjected to military action. It may, for many individuals, have also expressed their moral distaste for the proposed invasion, but it carried en masse one message: that this was political business as normal, not a "supreme emergency" entitling state leaders to get off the hook of fulfilling established expectations.

Here I am in accord with Bellamy in his analysis of the limitations of the ethical arguments of dirty hands and lesser evil to fully capture what is most important in debates about military responses to terrorism.[25] Our ethical analysis of the claim to authority must go hand in hand with an assessment of the politics of the situation, asserting the mutually constitutive character of politics and ethics, as opposed to their separation. As Bellamy argues, "Necessity does not overcome 'right.' . . . When they [political leaders] ostensibly prioritise necessity over right, what they are in fact doing is weighing one set of values (say, national security) over another (for example, non-combatant immunity)."[26] The sovereign claim to authority over warmaking cannot, therefore, be above ethics; nor can it be outside political debate about which ethical frame to apply.

Privileging the state in analysis of supreme emergency needs to be more thoroughly explored if we are to get to the bottom of the importance of the "Not in my name" claim. We have seen so far how it is that this slogan contains a challenge to the authority claim of the state that is skeptical about a potential conflation of the survival of the sovereign state with the survival of its political leaders.

More than this, however, is skepticism about the distinctiveness of war as a political activity that is in some way outside of the processes of consent and accountability that govern "ordinary" politics. The idea of an overarching duty on the part of the state to protect its citizens from external attack as an essential element of its claim to sovereignty cannot straightforwardly justify exceptional actions that challenge deeply rooted moral prohibitions. These two things—the ideas of the right embedded in the prohibition, and the idea of the necessary that privileges security as the duty of the sovereign—are not separable and are not hierarchically arranged such that necessity acts as a trump card. For the state to go to war, it needs to do more than appeal to an idea of sovereignty that confers that authority upon its leaders as a matter of course. It needs to legitimize this claim through the retention of the consent of its citizens, and thus its leaders must remain accountable. The domestic aspect of sovereignty cannot be assumed to play second fiddle to the Westphalian notion whereby sovereignty is predicated upon simple claims of territorial control and international recognition. As Ian Clark argues, international legitimacy is a complex and multifaceted concept involving morality, legality, and what he calls "constitutionality"—the interplay of politics, power, and interests.[27] The balance between these factors, and their content, is historically dynamic and has been deeply affected by social and political trends that extend beyond the diplomatic and military interplay of sovereign states. "Not in my name" is a part of one of these trends—the growing emphasis on the consent of the governed as a basis for sovereignty seen in other areas, such as the responsibility to protect.[28]

These claims point in the direction of the significance of a liberal version of just war theory that has emerged in response to and been significantly shaped by the War on Terror. Such a theory aims to give much greater weight to individuals, to human rights, and to the classic liberal ideal of the state as servant rather than master of the people. Sovereignty is popular—rooted in the sovereignty of the individual as rights holder—and government claims to lead the people into war must therefore be accountable to the will of the people. As already argued, however, this does not mean that constitutional and procedural innovation can satisfy the claims of "Not in my name." There is a need for a deeper rethinking of the nature and scale of the authority claimed by sovereigns as they pursue the ultimate sovereign power—the right to make war. It is therefore to the idea of liberal just war theory that we now turn.

LIBERAL JUST WAR THEORY AND THE BORDERS OF LEGITIMATE AUTHORITY

Some of the strongest accounts of the centrality of liberal conceptions of individual rights in contemporary just war theory come from figures such as Fernando Tesón and Jeff McMahan.[29] They offer accounts of various *jus ad bellum* principles, including legitimate authority, that are fundamentally predicated on the idea of individual and universal human rights and how these are most effectively instantiated and institutionalized in international relations. This section looks at the relationship between legitimate authority and sovereignty to argue that despite the potential that such a rights-based approach offers to critique state-centric accounts of legitimate authority, the opportunity is not fully taken. The critique of the state as the sole claimant of legitimate authority through the possession of sovereignty endures and the critical potential of "Not in my name" goes unanswered. This, however, need not be the case, because the assertion of autonomy from the state made by the claim

"Not in my name" opens space between the claim of the liberal sovereignty of the individual and the sovereignty of the state and insists on a contingent rather than necessary link between the two.

A useful way into this space is through the idea of self-defense, which is central to contemporary just war thinking, to the international law that governs war, and to the idea of the sovereign individual.[30] The UN Charter (Article 51) identifies self-defense as an "inherent" right of states, and self-defense against actual armed attack is generally portrayed as the only unambiguously legal instance for war. Its definition is therefore crucial, and debates have raged over whether self-defense can be served by preemptive and—especially since the September 11, 2001, terrorist attacks on the United States (US)—preventive war.[31] The claims by the US government to preventive war in the 2002 and 2006 national security strategies demonstrate the policy significance of debates about when self-defense is permitted, but the issue of the self being defended has received less popular attention, although scholarly analysis is significant.[32] However, it is in itself a critical issue that relates closely to the argument here about the state as the insufficiently questioned centerpiece of legitimate authority and the depth of the challenge posed by the idea of individuals seeking to distance themselves from the state's authority.

Government assertions that "a government has no higher obligation than to protect the lives and livelihoods of its citizens," or that "providing security for the nation and its citizens remains the most important responsibility of government," hint at the problems that exist here. An obligation or a responsibility is not a right.[33] The obligation of the government stems from the need to respond to the rights-based claim to protection from the primary rights holders—citizens in this case. For the kind of liberal theorists discussed in this chapter, the state as the actor entitled to make the moral claim to the right of self-defense makes only a limited amount of sense. The ability of the state to be the possessor of moral agency in and of itself is fraught with intellectual difficulty,[34] despite the apparent simplicity of the legal claim evidenced in Article 51 and assumed in popular debates about sovereignty, and in some academic ones, too, through the claim that "states are people, too."[35] Instead, for liberal just war theorists, the state's right to self-defense derives from the right to self-defense possessed by individual citizens and how those citizens create, usually through some implicit notion of social contract, the state. Jeff McMahan stands as one of the most powerful advocates of the importance of individual self-defense as the basis of just cause in just war theory, using this claim to develop a powerful argument in favor of seeing just cause as the paramount principle of *jus ad bellum*.[36]

This chapter does not intend to dwell for long on the philosophical conception of the self that McMahan deploys in this analysis, or consider in detail whether there are good reasons for challenging his portrayal of self-defense as the only permissible form of just cause and the *grundnorm* of any just war analysis.[37] These are more properly the concern of philosophy, rather than an inquiry, such as this, into the political context within which claims to authority are made, recalling my focus on the first of Coady's three points about dirty hands. Nevertheless, McMahan's account, and others in the analysis of self-defense that address complex issues connected with it, are notable for the way in which the state is the institutional beneficiary of the ethical entitlement to wage war in the name of self-defense. The "self" that is being defended is not just a classic notion of the liberal sovereign self; it is also one that is located within a certain institutional context—that of the liberal state as the principal and premium location for the possibility of fulfillment for such selves.

However, what is important here is the sense that alternative institutional locations are not considered and dismissed. Instead, the primacy of the state is generally assumed. Here we can come back to McEwan's critique of "Not in my name"—the "cloying self-regard" of individuals seeking to duck the difficult decisions of politics in the name of their individuality denies a seemingly necessary embedding of the possibility of such individuality in a community manifested in and represented by the state. Where the possibility of nonstate institutional forms exists, then these are understood as what we might label "proto-states"—national self-determination movements, secessionist groups, or insurgents, perhaps, that aim at establishing a new state or seizing control of the power of an existing one. These, at least in the context of wars of national liberation from colonial oppression, can have the status of legitimate authorities entitled to wage war.[38] Nonstate-based political projects are excluded from the analysis of self-defense as just cause and as entitled to the claim of legitimate authority. This brings us back to Coady's argument against the "supreme emergency" exception: It grants too much to the state in terms of permitting the use of terrorist tactics on an inadequate basis for explaining the exceptional character of the state.

Walzer's political theory offers a richer account than liberal rights theorists like McMahan, Téson, and Rodin of the significance of political community to individuality and the ethical significance of the state as a result.[39] Yet it is a position such theorists wish to reject. Therefore, the defense of the state that these liberal just war theorists offer cannot be because of the "romance of the nation-state" and the admissibility of the transcendent importance of this particular form of political community.[40] Neither, given their commitment to rigorous philosophical logic, can it be because of pragmatic political considerations about the lack of credible alternative locations of political activity. Instead, it must be a principled commitment to this particular geographical framing of self-defense and the commensurate legitimate authority arguments. Yet we look in vain for a systematic account of these principles.

Cecile Fabre goes furthest in critiquing the connection between legitimate authority and sovereignty.[41] Her position, essentially, is that a cosmopolitan ethical position, of whatever stripe, ultimately places the ability of individual human beings to live meaningfully flourishing lives at the center of its conception of ethics. Any collective institution, like the state, has value only insofar as it furthers that potential; where it does not, the individual has the inherent right to take action, by violence if that is the only appropriate mechanism, to defend their right. That is, the individual retains a right to go to war against other individuals, collectives and institutions.[42] As a result, states cannot claim any kind of special entitlement over the recourse to war and the kind of constitutional wrangling that took place in the period preceding the invasion of Iraq in an effort to demonstrate consent was, in essence, a waste of time given that consent is not an effective measure of legitimacy.[43]

Thus, restricting the right to wage war to states is indefensible, at least on foundational ethical grounds, but it may be pragmatically desirable in the light of other considerations.[44] This effort to "dispense with the requirement of legitimate authority" certainly takes liberal cosmopolitan ethics very seriously.[45] However, Fabre's argument requires us to accept as war actions that intuitively many would see as something else. Her example is the use by an individual of a weapon of mass destruction on an underground rail system in the name of resisting and overthrowing a government that this individual believes to be persecuting a minority. Terrorism or mass murder may be the label many would attach. It would appear far from obvious, at least to my eye, to go along with Fabre's assertion that "it would seem odd to maintain that he [the train bomber] is *not* committing an act of war."[46]

The problem here, as with other accounts of liberal just war theory, is the search for a philosophical solution that may not be available. Fabre's argument ignores, and not just in this instance, the issue of the political context and framing of actions. Nahed Artoul Zehr takes this issue up at length in chapter 6 of this volume in relation to the "al-Qaeda model of war" and the efforts by al-Suri, al-Qaeda's principal strategic theorist, to develop an account of the legitimate authority of individual Muslims to wage war against the United States and others. This is based on a particular account of jihad that sees it as being a communal duty in which Muslims have a responsibility to defend the Muslim peoples and faith against Western aggression. Zehr highlights how such an account can, on the face of it, seem to fit with Fabre's rejection of the traditional conception of legitimate authority within the just war tradition because of the disconnect it establishes between an exclusive authority to go to war and the possession of political office. Yet the political ramifications of this surface similarity are radically different because of the context in which these accounts of the decentralization of authority are located.

As Zehr goes on to discuss, Fabre relies on a rather limited account of legitimate authority, neglecting the distinctive elements of authority that find their way into the just war tradition through Aquinas. This leads Zehr to stress the distinctive purview of holders of high political office and the associated responsibilities. This does not produce an account of the sovereign's legitimate authority that is unlimited, but it does highlight that Fabre's account of authority assumes a specific and narrow definition: "only an organization that has the authority to make and enforce laws over a given territory, and has a claim to be recognized as such by other comparable institutions holds the right to wage war."[47] This is restricted by the prior and necessary condition of the maintenance of the rights of the individuals who are the ultimate ethical units of any human society and grants these individuals an authority to resist through "war" if necessary. What ought, however, to point to the necessity of retaining an account of legitimate authority is the idea of the claim to recognition by others of a right to wage war. As Zehr concludes in chapter 6, the radical decentralization of legitimate authority to individuals brings with it grave dangers because it neglects the contextual account of recognition that is essential to the legitimate authority criterion in both asserting the retention of such authority by an established authority, like the state, and its loss.

Retaining a more contextual account of the just war and the necessity of a legitimate authority criterion as a means for identifying when such authority is decentralized also serves to remind us of a distinctive claim about just war: that it is an ethics of the abnormal, a way of maintaining an ethical perspective in the face of circumstances where the normal rules of ethics do not apply. This is, for example, an argument Walzer defends but that most liberal just war theory sets to one side.[48] The context in which we understand certain forms of political activity, like war, and how we intellectually, discursively, and politically frame these actions does make a difference to the ethical assessment that we deploy. Liberal, civic-republican, Marxist, and a host of other traditions of theorizing the relationship between the state and the individual have yet to deliver definitive answers to questions such as the nature of political obligation, even in specific contexts such as the obligation to fight for the state in time of war.[49] Therefore, we should not look to a philosophical reconciliation of these arguments but to a political one—or, more likely, instead of reconciliation, we should look for an appreciation of the different understandings of political context that inform the various positions. It is through politics that the challenge posed to the idea of Westphalian sovereignty by the slogan "Not in my name" will be accommodated.

THE POLITICS OF AUTHORITY AND THE AUTHORITY OF POLITICS

The deployment of just war theory by Tesón and other advocates of military action to prevent terrorist attacks, like Buchanan and Keohane, tends to reinforce support for states, or at least liberal democratic states, as the legitimate authorities of the international community.[50] The question of authority in these cases is primarily about the authority of certain sorts of states to make a case and to take action that ought to meet with the approval of the other states in the international community.

The appeal of "Not in my name" is to a far less statist form of liberalism (or other cosmopolitanisms) that typically emphasizes the most significant claim to authority is that which a particular government makes over its own citizens, emphasizing the complexity of the legitimate authority criteria in just war theory. It also points to the durability, at least in terms of political action, of the domestic/international divide. Sovereignty as domestic supremacy versus sovereignty as international autonomy, or an assumed easy coincidence of the two, is, of course, the classic Westphalian mix, and just war theory continues to struggle with its tensions, inconsistencies, and conservative tendencies at a time when the move within the theory seems to be toward a more explicitly cosmopolitan conception.[51]

The "Not in my name" claim is thus a valuable reminder of the importance of the legitimate authority criteria and the need to treat it as being more than the ability of state governments to establish their case in the court of the society of states. It is also about the ability of governments to carry their citizens with them. The philosophical questions surrounding the nature of self-defense start us along this path in useful ways and probably played an important part in the reluctance of many to support their governments in the absence of a compelling self-defense case. But "Not in my name" is also a powerful political rejection of the claim to legitimate authority by a government over its own people. Just war theory and the debates of just war theorists need to carefully balance the philosophical rigor and precision of their arguments against the political contexts of specific conflicts.

The desire of so many people to dissociate themselves from their government's actions was not, on the whole, a philosophical claim about the complex relationship between authority and obligation in a democratic state on the brink of war. It was a political protest about the proposed course of action, the way in which that course had been decided upon, and a perceived lack of accountability to those whose authority was being invoked. Withholding consent, even if only rhetorically, was a powerful statement because of the way it highlighted the tendency to take such consent for granted, to see the decision over war as being something that takes place at the level of national governments negotiating in what are now the smoke-free rooms and corridors of power. The democratic, individualist, rights-based form of just war promoted by the literature considered here generally fails to give us a good account of the legitimate authority principle from this perspective. A statist focus and an uncritical set of assumptions about the questions posed by the legitimate authority principle lead this literature down a path that is all about intergovernmentalism, with institutional questions focused on the international level.[52] The principal exception—Fabre—however, arguably goes too far the other way by neglecting any political issues other than those raised by cosmopolitan ethics.

National constitutional and institutional contexts vary too much to make explicit and universal prescriptions for what the process of establishing legitimate authority ought to be in this regard. However, just war theory needs to engage with the challenge posed by the claim that war is "Not in my name" and the alternative political scale to which it appeals. Liberal just war theory has to take the liberal part seriously, and that includes recognizing not just the philosophical importance of liberal notions of rights and individuality to its arguments about the justifiability of war against terrorism and the inadmissibility of terrorist forms of violence.[53] It also must deal seriously with the liberal politics of legitimacy if it is to find ways in which the political challenge of "Not in my name" can be met effectively and the philosophical potential of rooting just war theory in liberal philosophy is to be fulfilled. This effort demands maintenance of the political sphere and an appreciation for the power of political framing.

CONCLUSION

The marchers in February 2003 did not stop the invasion of Iraq. The power of the state prevailed. Why this was the case and the significance of the Iraq invasion for the conduct of politics in the United Kingdom are important questions, but they have not been the ones considered here. Equally, the context of protest in other states, both those participating in and opposed to the invasion of Iraq, has also, doubtless, been shaped to this day by those events. The concern here has been with the idea of legitimate authority in just war theory, which, I have argued, has been deeply affected by the controversy surrounding the war and its aftermath, at least in terms of highlighting the complexity of an issue that is often taken for granted, certainly in comparison with other just war issues such as self-defense and noncombatant immunity.

This chapter has tried to argue that the just war literature has missed the full significance of the challenge printed on thousands of placards that day in London in February 2003—"Not in my name." The location of political authority and the nature of the political process by which individuals are able to access decision making on key issues of war and peace were called into doubt. Instead, an increasingly liberal just war theory has focused on the authority claimed by liberal states vis-à-vis nonliberal states in the international system. The authority that was challenged that day—the authority over the citizenry—has generally been neglected.

The scale and scope of the debates about legitimate authority and its relationship to a generally assumed Westphalian notion of sovereignty is a pressing topic, however, adding to the wider challenges presented to just war theory by issues of space and scale.[54] Some, like Bellamy, see such protests as part of the wider notion of global civil society and its ability to provide an element of Clark's constitutionality element of legitimacy: Ideas of power, politics, and interest are being cut adrift from exclusively statist moorings.[55] However, the argument here is less empirical than that claim and more normative in its assessment of the politics of legitimate authority.

"Not in my name" is neither necessarily self-indulgent nor necessarily corrosive of sovereignty at a time when the sovereign state is portrayed by some as the principal bulwark against a threat that supposedly carries the potential to destroy a meaningful category of politics.[56] Instead, it is an invitation for just war theory to reengage with the idea of legitimate authority and its connection to one of the most fundamental of all political concepts—sovereignty—and to do so not only in a philosophical manner but also with an appreciation for political context and the possibilities of political action. Indeed, such an approach is exactly in tune with the strengths of the just war tradition, which repeatedly demonstrates an ability to frame critical political thinking in the face of technological, political, and social dynamics while retaining a common set of core questions of enduring importance.

It is also attuned to practice, appreciative of the fact that how wars are fought changes and the social and political role that war plays—its legitimacy, in Clark's terms—is embedded in wider questions of legality, morality, and constitutionality. These questions are only in part worked out in relation to the logical demands of the cosmopolitan ethical principle, the route that Fabre follows almost exclusively.[57] This certainly provides stimulating and provocative insights, but this chapter's defense of the politics of the issue of legitimate authority is skeptical of the ability of the force of the better philosophical argument to always carry the day in the political arena. A contextualized account that sees political protest, among other activities, as being in part about how we frame and locate the significance of issues like legitimate authority is preferred here. As in other analyses of high-profile and important political protests, there is an assertion here of the significance of political participation itself in the making and shaping of a community's self-understanding and how it frames its politics.[58] This is not necessarily tied to the state, as Lang's example of the Seattle antiglobalization protests shows, but it recognizes the significance and inertia of the state as a political institution that is impossible to ignore.

Therefore, "Not in my name," as a call to political practice and action, should be heard not just in the bald terms of individuals seeking to distance themselves from their government's policies. It is also an opening to thinking about the legitimacy of authority, and not only within the just war theory that has been the focus here, at a time when ideas about sovereignty as a paradigmatic instance of a claim to legitimate authority are in flux. This is not just through empirical changes in the structures and processes of politics, but also because of the normative desirability of engaged political action that sees the political resolution of questions such as legitimate authority as being an ongoing process and practice, rather than a somewhat sterile exercise in pure reason. The enormous wealth of intellectual resources on which the just war tradition can draw gives cause for optimism about its ability to continue to lead thinking about the response to the challenge of "Not in my name," even if this chapter has been skeptical about the way in which this has been done thus far.

NOTES

A very early version of this chapter was presented at the British International Studies Association conference in Cambridge in December 2007. I would like to thank the participants, particularly Chris Brown, for their encouragement in developing the idea. A second draft was presented at the International Boundaries Research Unit conference on "The State of Sovereignty" in Durham in April 2009. Thanks go to Tony Lang, Cian O'Driscoll, and Peter Stirk for reading that version and for their constructive suggestions on improvement. Responsibility for the chapter's persistent shortcomings remains, of course, my own.

1. E.g., Paul Baines and Robert M. Worcester, "When the British 'Tommy' Went to War, Public Opinion Followed," *Journal of Public Affairs* 5, no. 1 (2005): 9–14; Justin Lewis and Rod Brookes, "How British Television News Represented the Case for War in Iraq," in *Reporting War: Journalism in Wartime*, ed. Stuart Allen and Barbie Zellizer (Abingdon, UK: Routledge, 2004), 284.

2. Ian McEwan, *Saturday* (London: Jonathan Cape, 2005), 72.

3. E.g., Jeff McMahan, "The Ethics of Killing in War," *Ethics* 114, no. 4 (2004); Jeff McMahan, "Just Cause for War," *Ethics & International Affairs* 19, no. 3 (2005).

4. Ilan Baron, *Justifying the Obligation to Die* (Lanham, MD: Lexington Books, 2009); James Turner Johnson, "Aquinas and Luther on War and Peace: Sovereign Authority and the Use of Armed Force," *Journal of Religious Ethics* 31 (2003).

5. Cecile Fabre, "Cosmopolitanism, Just War Theory and Legitimate Authority," *International Affairs* 84 (2008). See also the discussion of Fabre's argument by Nahed Artoul Zehr in chapter 6 of this volume.

6. C. A. J. Coady, "Terrorism, Morality and Supreme Emergency," *Ethics* 114, no. 4 (2004).

7. Ibid., 788–89.

8. Ibid., 772–73.

9. Ibid., 779–80.

10. Alex J. Bellamy, "Dirty Hands and Lesser Evils in the War on Terror," *British Journal of Politics and International Relations* 9, no. 3 (2007): 512–13.

11. Michael Walzer, *Just and Unjust Wars: A Moral Argument with Historical Illustrations*, 3rd ed. (New York: Basic Books, 2000), 255–63.

12. Bellamy, "Dirty Hands," 514–15.

13. Ibid.

14. McEwan, *Saturday*, 72.

15. Coady, "Terrorism," 781; Bellamy, "Dirty Hands," 513.

16. Walzer, *Just and Unjust Wars*, 255–63.

17. On the war on terrorism, see, e.g., Jean Bethke Elshtain, *Just War against Terror: The Burden of American Power in a Violent World* (New York: Basic Books, 2004). On preventive war, see US National Security Council, *National Security Strategy of the United States of America 2002*, http://ics.leeds.ac.uk/papers/pmt/exhibits/378/NSS.pdf; and US National Security Council, *National Security Strategy of the United States of America 2006*, http://ics.leeds.ac.uk/papers/pmt/exhibits/2628/nss2006.pdf. For further discussion, see Whitley Kaufman, "What's Wrong with Preventive War? The Moral and Legal Basis for the Preventive Use of Force," *Ethics & International Affairs* 19, no. 3 (2005); and Nicholas J. Rengger,

"The Greatest Treason? On the Subtle Temptations of Preventive War," *International Affairs* 84, no. 5 (2008). On torture, see Alex Bellamy, "No Pain, No Gain? Torture and Ethics in the War on Terror," *International Affairs* 82, no. 1 (2006); Uwe Steinhoff, "Torture: The Case for Dirty Harry and against Alan Dershowitz" in *War, Torture and Terrorism: Ethics in the Twenty-First Century*, ed. David Rodin (Oxford: Wiley Blackwell, 2007); and D. Sussman, "What's Wrong with Torture?" *Philosophy and Public Affairs* 33, no. 1 (2005).

18. Bellamy, "Dirty Hands," 515.

19. Coady, "Terrorism," 781.

20. Walzer, *Just and Unjust Wars*, 251–68.

21. E.g., James Turner Johnson, *Morality and Contemporary Warfare* (New Haven, CT: Yale University Press, 1999), 52–57.

22. US National Security Council, *National Security Strategy of the United States of America 2002*; US National Security Council, *National Security Strategy of the United States of America 2006*; UK Cabinet Office, *National Security Strategy of the United Kingdom: Security in an Interdependent World*, http://interactive.cabinetoffice.gov.uk/documents/security/national_security_strategy.pdf.

23. Perhaps the best-known example of such reasoning in this context is the so-called 1 percent doctrine advocated by Vice President Dick Cheney: that if there was a 1 percent chance of Pakistani nuclear scientists helping al-Qaeda acquire a bomb, the US government should treat it as a certainty. See Ron Suskind, *The One Percent Doctrine: Deep Inside America's Pursuit of Its Enemies since 9/11* (London: Simon & Schuster, 2006), 62.

24. Elshtain, *Just War*, 85–98.

25. Bellamy, "Dirty Hands."

26. Ibid., 516.

27. Ian Clark, *Legitimacy in International Society* (Oxford: Oxford University Press, 2005).

28. International Commission on Intervention and State Sovereignty, *Responsibility to Protect* (Ottawa: International Development Research Centre, 2001); United Nations, *2005 World Summit Outcome* (New York: United Nations, 2005), www.responsibilitytoprotect.org/.

29. Fernando Téson, "Ending Tyranny in Iraq," *Ethics & International Affairs* 19, 2 (2005); McMahan, "Ethics of Killing."

30. David Rodin, *War and Self-Defense* (Oxford: Oxford University Press, 2002).

31. David Rodin and Henry Shue, eds., *Preemption: Military Action and Moral Justification* (Oxford: Oxford University Press, 2007).

32. E.g., Rodin, *War*.

33. The first quotation here is from US National Security Council, *National Security Strategy of the United States of America 2006*, 12; the second is from UK Cabinet Office, *National Security Strategy*, 3.

34. E.g., Toni Erskine, ed., *Can Institutions Have Responsibilities? Collective Moral Agency and International Relations* (Basingstoke, UK: Palgrave Macmillan, 2003).

35. Alexander Wendt, *Social Theory of International Politics* (Cambridge: Cambridge University Press, 1999), 215–24.

36. McMahan, "Ethics of Killing in War"; McMahan, "Just Cause."

37. E.g., Rodin, *Self-Defense*.

38. Fabre, "Cosmopolitanism," 964.

39. E.g., Michael Walzer, *Spheres of Justice: A Defense of Pluralism and Equality* (Oxford: Robertson, 1983); Michael Walzer, *Thick and Thin: Moral Argument at Home and Abroad* (Notre Dame, IN: Notre Dame University Press, 1994).

40. David Luban, "The Romance of the Nation State," in *International Ethics*, ed. Charles R. Beitz, Marshall Cohen, Thomas Scanlon, and A. John Simmons (Princeton, NJ: Princeton University Press, 1985). For a far more detailed discussion of understandings of the relationship between individual and state and the development of these in the context of just war, see chapter 16 in this volume by Nicholas Rengger.

41. Fabre, "Cosmopolitanism."

42. Ibid., 968–71.

43. Ibid., 973–74.

44. Ibid., 975–76.

45. Ibid., 975.

46. Ibid., 970.

47. Ibid., 967.

48. Walzer, *Just and Unjust Wars*.

49. Baron, *Justifying the Obligation*.

50. Allen Buchanan and Robert O. Keohane, "The Preventive Use of Force: A Cosmopolitan Institutional Perspective," *Ethics & International Affairs* 18, no. 1 (2004).

51. For a discussion of varieties of sovereignty, see Stephen D. Krasner, *Sovereignty: Organized Hypocrisy* (Princeton, NJ: Princeton University Press, 1999). On cosmopolitan conceptions, see, e.g., Fabre, "Cosmopolitanism," 964–66.

52. E.g., Buchanan and Keohane, "Preventive Use of Force"; Allen Buchanan and Robert O. Keohane, "The Legitimacy of Global Governance Institutions," *Ethics & International Affairs* 20, no. 4 (2006).

53. E.g., Noam J. Zohar, "Innocence and Complex Threats: Upholding the War Ethic and the Condemnation of Terrorism," *Ethics* 114, no. 4 (2004).

54. John Williams, "Space, Scale and Just War: Meeting the Challenge of Humanitarian Intervention and Trans-National Terrorism," *Review of International Studies* 34, no. 4 (2008).

55. Bellamy, "Dirty Hands," 519; Clark, *Legitimacy*; Ian Clark, *International Legitimacy and World Society* (Oxford: Oxford University Press, 2007).

56. Elshtain, *Just War*, 18–19, 152.

57. Fabre, "Cosmopolitanism."

58. E.g., Anthony F. Lang Jr., "Governance and Political Action: Hannah Arendt on Global Political Protest," in *Hannah Arendt and International Relations: Readings across the Lines*, ed. Anthony F. Lang Jr. and John Williams (New York: Palgrave Macmillan, 2005).

CHAPTER 5

The Inseparability of Gender Hierarchy, the Just War Tradition, and Authorizing War

Laura Sjoberg

WHEN US PRESIDENT GEORGE W. BUSH justified the US military invasions of Afghanistan and then Iraq in part by proclaiming that "brutality against women is always and everywhere wrong" and mixing that proclamation with the language of just cause in the just war tradition,[1] the gendered nature of his justifications was neither coincidental nor aberrant to the tradition itself.[2] Instead, the just war tradition has been built on, and I argue is inseparable from, a gendered idea of the dichotomy between civilians and combatants that stereotypes men as "just warriors" (righteous defenders of the innocent) and women as "beautiful souls" (innocent of wars but a justification for fighting them).[3] This gendered dichotomy, which I argue is the underlying logic of the noncombatant immunity principle, serves at once to justify war-making and motivate war-fighting, despite the deployment of discourses of civilian immunity in the just war tradition as an effort to moderate and humanize war(s). The *jus in bello* principle of civilian immunity, and particularly its reliance on "civilian" as a proxy for a gendered (feminine) notion of the protected, serves to authorize not only individual wars in political practice but also war conceptually.

The editors' introduction to this volume invites authors to consider the situation of, and questions of, authority relating to the just war tradition in the twenty-first century. Noting that "the just war tradition is the predominant moral language through which we address questions pertaining to the rights and wrongs of the use of force in international society," Cian O'Driscoll and Anthony Lang ask tough questions about the variegated practices of authority, ranging from the philosophical to the political. Though the editors note that it is "regrettable and misleading" that the just war tradition often looks "abstract and bloodless" in wars and conflicts when it is intimately bound up in (and often complicit in) violent political decision making, they are nonetheless interested in the value of the tradition, particularly as it allows "sustained inquiry into the relation between power and authority in international life."

In this chapter I am interested in the question of the *authority of* the just war tradition, particularly as it relates to a function of legitimating wars.[4] Particularly, I explore whether the authority of just war tradition is net positive or net negative for international society, normatively or practically. To do this, I look at the gendered narratives of the just war tradition generally and the civilian immunity principle specifically (which I argue are intrinsically interlinked).[5] This chapter, then, starts by identifying a fifth potential *telos* for just war theorizing in performativity. It then introduces a gender-based approach to understanding just war theorizing, leading into a feminist critique of the noncombatant immunity principle. The next section links a feminist reading of the noncombatant immunity principle to the *jus ad bellum* deployment of the just war tradition. The chapter then lays out a road map for how to evaluate whether these gendered problems with the just war tradition are cosmetic and mutable or fundamental and immutable. I make the case that the gendered pathologies of the noncombatant immunity principle specifically and just war theorizing generally are inseparable both from the tradition and from its role in authorizing or legitimating war(s). Having made the case that, through gendered lenses, the just war tradition is a net liability, the conclusion of this chapter briefly explores potential alternative directions.

PERFORMANCES OF JUST WAR

In the introduction to this volume, Cian O'Driscoll and Anthony Lang articulate and provide evidence for four potential purposes or *telos* for just war theorizing: political, prophetic, pastoral, and philosophical. I argue that, together, these ideas of *how just war theorizing works* are limited both by a unidirectional assumption of agency (that just war theorizing is deployed consciously and purposively) and a literalist notion of transmission (that our deployments of just war theorizing communicate clearly, consciously, and directly our intents). I suggest that there is at least a fifth *telos* for just war theorizing—and that it should be thought of as performative.[6] Seeing the just war tradition as performative suggests that it is not a pre-given subject or the product of a historical evolution of political, philosophical, pastoral, or prophetic traditions. Instead, the just war tradition is itself an ontological effect of processes that are performatively enacted.[7] In Judith Butler's words, there is a "reiterative and citational practice by which discourse produces the effect it names."[8] Just war theorizing, in this view, is not traceable to its provenance and available for evaluation on the basis of its written or spoken tenets. Instead, there is no just war theorizing beyond expressions of just war theorizing, and just war theorizing is performatively constituted by its employment, its deployment, and its manifestations in practice.[9]

Therefore, it is possible to see that war is as much a product of just war discourses as just war discourses are a product of grappling with and dealing with war(s). As much as it is anything else, just war theorizing is a set of "operative" abstractions that *operate as if they are reality*, particularly through discursive seduction, which "extracts meaning from discourse" in what Baudrillard calls discursive seductions, where a discourse "absorbs meaning and empties itself of meaning in order to better fascinate others."[10] In this interpretation, just war is not a (purely) agential discourse in the traditional sense, and we are not to assume that its signs and referents relate directly. As such, it is important to look for the meanings of the just war tradition not only in the straightforward account of its words and symbols but also in its narratives, logics, performances, emotional triggers, and manifestations.

GENDER ANALYSIS OF JUST WAR PERFORMANCES

It is these often-neglected elements that feminist analysis has often started with in order to make sense of just war theorizing through "gendered lenses."[11] Looking through "gendered lenses" is less an essentialist method of claiming that gender is all things to everything, and more a careful, examined, journeyed account of what looking for gender shows about our research subjects.[12] As Jill Steans has explained, "To look at the world through gendered lenses is to focus on gender as a particular kind of power relation, or to trace out the ways in which gender is central to understanding international processes."[13] Looking through gendered lenses encourages us to "ask what assumptions about gender (and race, class, nationality, and sexuality) are necessary to make particular statements, policies, and actions meaningful."[14] This chapter asks these questions with a performative notion of gender, where "gender is a system of symbolic meaning that creates social hierarchies based on perceived associations with masculine and feminine characteristics.[15] Therefore, in Marysia Zaleweski's words, "The driving force of feminism is attention to gender and not simply to women; . . . the concept, nature, and practice of gender are key."[16]

Feminist scholars, then, have looked at the question of the ways that the concept, nature, and practice of gender are key in just war theorizing.[17] They have identified masculinist practices of state violence,[18] the gendered nature of the noncombatant immunity principle and its resultant "protection racket,"[19] and rape as a weapon of war,[20] as relating to and with the just war tradition in gendered ways, finding traditional assumptions about gender roles to be necessary for just war theorizing to be formulated and to operate in the ways that it does. Starting from these critical observations, a number of feminist scholars have looked to rebuild just war theorizing with an eye toward degendering its concepts, nature, and practices, whereas others have looked outside the just war tradition for solutions to some of its gender biases.[21]

GENDER, JUST WAR, AND PERFORMANCES OF CIVILIAN IMMUNITY

This chapter looks to engage in a part of this debate about how to degender just war theorizing in more depth, looking at the noncombatant immunity principle through gender lenses as (at least in part) a performative structure of gender subordination. In so doing, it looks to contribute to answering the question of whether the authority of the just war tradition generally is a net negative or a net positive—a question that feminist work has not fully addressed so far, and a question regarding which just war theorists rarely consider feminist perspectives.[22]

Such an effort necessarily begins by engaging previous feminist work on the noncombatant immunity principle, which has engaged in critically interrogating what the combatant/civilian distinction really means, both in theory and in practice. Particularly, feminists asked who the ideal-typical "combatant" was as well as who the ideal-typical "civilian" was in just war narratives about combatants who fight to protect civilians. Research has found that the ideal-typical combatant was a masculine image of the "just citizen-warrior," a man who serves in militaries and fights wars, not because he would like to kill but because he is obligated to protect.[23] The just citizen-warrior's masculinity is tied to his ability to protect—some men actually protect; others are potential protectors should they be needed, but masculinity and service as a soldier are linked.[24] The just citizen-warrior's sacrifice does not go unrewarded, however—gratitude for his service is expressed with thanks, with honor, and with a link between military service and full citizenship in most societies. Still, inability or unwillingness to serve in a protective role is punished by emasculation and shame.[25]

The ideal-typical combatant, the just citizen-warrior, does not exist in a vacuum, however. The ideal-typical civilian is a necessary part of his story, because his honor comes from protection, not aggression.[26] So a key question is—who is he protecting? The ideal-typical civilian is a woman, who has been described in feminist terms as a "beautiful soul."[27] A beautiful soul is a woman who is innocent of whatever cause the threatening enemy might have for the war. She is apolitical, but the essence of what the state and/or nation needs to protect—families, ways of life, innocence, and purity. Though she does not fight in the war, she is crucial to the fighting of the war and to war-fighting narratives, because protecting her is not just part of the noncombatant immunity principle but an integral part of the state's self-image (and what Brent Steele would call ontological security).[28] So the beautiful soul—the woman, often with a baby, who could be threatened by war but must be (at least seen as) immune, is the "civilian" in civilian immunity.[29]

Feminists have argued that these dichotomized gender roles are necessary to making sense of the noncombatant immunity principle, which constitutes a gendered "protection racket."[30] This racket is that the signification of the gender roles in the immunity principle comes to trump the *actual provision of protection*, especially to women.[31] Because these gender roles at once fiat that protection is taking place and support the immunity principle, there is a significant risk that the performance of "protection" not only fails to provide it but comes at a hefty cost, in terms of both war security and gender subordination, to those who appear to be protected.[32]

JUS AD BELLUM AND THE
PERFORMANCE OF PROTECTION

Recent feminist work has argued that the "protection racket" does more than create a (possibly false) appearance of protection and perpetuate traditional, subordinating gender roles. Feminists have observed that the (gendered feminine) civilian in civilian immunity actually plays a double role in war-justificatory narratives.[33] She is the noncombatant who must be distinguished and made immune, but she is also the thing that must be protected at all costs. Protecting her, then, can serve as an essential *casus belli*. Much like the Trojan War was fought over and for Helen, modern wars are fought to protect "our" way of life, "life back home," "innocent women and children," and other proxies for the beautiful soul.[34]

The gendered image of the beautiful soul, then, serves as an authorizing force in the making and fighting of wars—a legitimation both contained in and absent without the just war tradition. This legitimating force reproduces (and is reproduced in) gendered conceptions of the state/nation and the gendered nationalisms these beget. Anne McClintock explains that "despite nationalisms' ideological investment in the ideal of popular *unity*, nations have historically amounted to the sanctioned institutionalization of gender *difference*."[35] This is because women, as beautiful souls in the story of the noncombatant immunity principle specifically and gendered nationalisms generally, play a reproductive role in nation/states, biologically, culturally, and symbolically.[36] Biologically, women reproduce national collectives; culturally, women reproduce the boundaries of national groups and transmit national cultures; symbolically, women (as beautiful souls) signify national self-identity and national differences.[37]

If wars are legitimated by protecting the (feminized other) beautiful soul, then "women's bodies, relations, and roles become the battleground for different idealized versions of the past and constructions of the nationalist project for the future."[38] There are, then, violences committed in the name of protecting, honoring, or building the nation/woman, particularly as they make women's violence vulnerable. Feminist scholars of the just war tradition and war more generally have expressed concern about these violences, because "nationalism is naturalized, and legitimated, through gender discourses that naturalized the domination of one group over another through the disparagement of the feminine."[39] As Mostov observes, "these ideas of women as potential repositories of future-soldier sons, symbols of the nation yet properties of the nation, mean women are vulnerable in conflict, particularly to sexual violence."[40] Recent feminist work has linked this vulnerability to intentional civilian victimization.

GENDER AND INTENTIONAL CIVILIAN VICTIMIZATION

If the "ideal-typical" civilian (as a performed proxy for "woman" or "beautiful soul") doubles as a motivator for the ideal-typical combatant or just citizen-warrior to fight, the "enemy" knows that. The enemy knowing the symbolic importance of women-as-beautiful souls matters not only in which wars are fought but in how they are fought. Strategists since Clausewitz have argued that belligerents looking to win wars should look for what their enemy is "fighting for," a center of gravity, and destroy that. Therefore, "it follows that a group's desire to 'protect' their women motivates them to attack the women seen as belonging to the "enemy.'""[41] The principle of civilian immunity, then, paradoxically but still really, carried to its logical end, makes it strategically beneficial to attack (enemy) civilians intentionally and in large numbers.

And belligerents do. States attack civilians in 35 percent of the wars in which they are militarily capable; the numbers are higher for interstate wars.[42] Recent research suggests that when belligerents attack "civilians," they are doing so as a proxy for women, not *as women* but as beautiful souls whose identification has its roots in the noncombatant immunity principle.[43] Feminists have long understood some violations of the noncombatant immunity principle (e.g., wartime rape) as gendered. For example, Jindy Pettman has noted that there is a "long history of associating actual women's rape with national, communal, and male dishonor."[44] This work has argued that raping women is attacking the nation in two key ways: It serves as an attack on men's virility/protective ability, and it is a material attack on women as symbolic centers of state and/or nation. Recently, feminists have argued that it is not just wartime rape that is aimed *at women* as symbolic centers of the state/nation. Instead, intentional civilian victimization is not only gendered—but the gendered result of the gendered noncombatant immunity principle.

THE GENDERED LOGIC OF THE IMMUNITY PRINCIPLE AS LEGITIMATING WAR *AD BELLUM*

This analysis suggests that war-fighting parties attack enemy "civilians" (as women) for the same reasons that they "protect" their own—because the protection racket *authorizes* war. It serves at once as states' license to make war(s) through the authority of the just war tradition, and as the logical path to winning an absolute victory by taking away the authorization to make war for the enemy. Whether or not the noncombatant immunity principle (and its related protection racket) is historically a structural or fundamental feature of just war theorizing, I argue that it has become inexorably linked, through gendered notions of nationalism and sovereignty in the Westphalian state system, to current manifestations and performances of just war(s), particularly just cause claims.

This chapter argues, then, that the noncombatant immunity principle serves three functions: first (and the one we think of most often) as an *in bello* limiting principle, but second (and as important) as an *ad bellum* permissive logic, and third (perhaps least considered so far) as a logic to motivate belligerents to violate it directly. In other words, I argue that the internal logic of the principle is fundamentally contradictory—key both to civilian protection and intentional civilian victimization. The argument that it is key to civilian protection is fairly straightforward—the "good guys" fight wars to protect the "beautiful souls" in their protection, and "beautiful soul" is a proxy for "civilian" in patriotic imaginaries.[45] The argument that it is key to civilian victimization is less easily accessible but as important, if not more so. If the raison d'être of the "good guys" is to provide beautiful souls with protection, then opponents looking to attack those good guys will look to interrupt, handicap, or demonstrate as false their protection narrative. Therefore, the "civilian" in intentional civilian victimization is inexorably linked to the "civilian" in civilian immunity—one man's beautiful soul is another man's target, and for the same fundamental reasons. Here, "civilian" is a proxy for "beautiful soul" in strategic accounting, and the noncombatant immunity principle's gendered logics justify attacking "civilians."[46]

If just war theorizing serves not only to legitimate war(s) but also to motivate intentional civilian victimization, then gendered performances of the noncombatant immunity principle tip the balance between just war theorizing as limiting and just war theorizing as permissive, encouraging, supportive, or complicit in war(s). This is because "implicit in the patriarchal metaphor is a tacit agreement that men who cannot defend their woman/nation have lost their "claim" to that body, to that land."[47] The protection racket within the immunity principle is bound up in ideas about the ownership of women (civilians) that legitimate attacking them in war(s), a permissive function. If just war theorizing functions as permissive, there is reason to be concerned that it may be counterproductive and backward, doing more harm than good, especially given the salience of just war theorizing in policy discourses and of just war tropes in popular cultures, especially in the states with the military power to cause the most damage to human life.

CAN JUST WAR BE SAVED?

To me, the question of whether just war theorizing is a net good or a net cause of harm turns on whether it is separable from the symbolic logic of the gender hierarchy it constitutes and is constituted by in the "just warrior/beautiful soul" dichotomy of the noncombatant immunity principle. In other words, if gendered understandings of women as in need of protection that at once serve as a *casus belli* and a fundamental part of just war theorizing *are mutable in or separable from just war theorizing*, then just war theorizing has potential as a critical tool. If not, then whatever is changed in, added to, or transformed within just war theorizing, it will remain potentially (and sometimes actually) counterproductive in both restricting wars and limiting civilian deaths.

Just war theorizing is a restrictive, limiting tradition *in bello* insomuch as it says that combatants and civilians can and should be distinguished and only combatants should be attacked. But exploring the beautiful soul trope more shows that it has an *ad bellum* impact, too, even though little work in just war theorizing really explicitly states or acknowledges it. Particularly, the elevated role that the innocent, feminine other has in the noncombatant immunity principle and the links between honor, masculinity, virility, citizenship, and her protection mean that protecting her can be articulated or felt as a "just cause" in belligerents' representations and performances of war if not in the explicit, textually articulated standards of just war theory.

This assertion is not without foundation in discussions of just cause, even when they do not explicitly mention gender. Many just war theorists have been curious about what it is that is worth "defending" when a just cause is defensive, or for whom punishment is to be exacted. In these musings, words associated with beautiful souldom—our women, our children, their innocence, our "future," our "way of life"—come up again and again. Seeing a performative *telos* for just war theorizing helps reveal these complexities and their related potential pathologies.

This means, in my understanding, that the civilian immunity principle is (at least formally) limiting *in bello* but is potentially permissive *ad bellum*, because the woman/civilian serves as a center of gravity that can (and does) serve to justify warmaking. The incentive that the gendered logics of immunity principle create to attack civilians (particularly, civilians as a proxy for women as a proxy for state and nation) leads one to be concerned that the civilian immunity principle is ultimately permissive not just *ad bellum* but also *in bello*.

Still, just war theory is only net harmful as an authority about war if, first, the noncombatant immunity principle cannot be delinked from just war performances; and second, the gendered logic of the noncombatant immunity principle is necessary to the existence and survival of the principle itself. The next section of this chapter argues that both conditions are met, and that, therefore, just war theorizing is a fundamentally conservative and net harmful influence on the making and fighting of wars.

THE INSEPARABILITY OF GENDER HIERARCHY AND THE JUST WAR TRADITION

This section argues that just war theorizing is a conservative tradition, the noncombatant immunity principle is on balance *not* a public good, and the gender hierarchy of/in just war theorizing is fundamentally linked to historical and contemporary justifications of not only war-fighting but also civilian victimization. The symbolic positioning of combatants and civilians where combatants protect civilians who are at once innocent and must be fought for is necessary for jus *in bello* rules about civilian immunity, which are crucial to the logic of just war performances.

I suggest that it is possible that the "problem" of the just warrior and beautiful soul tropes is not incidental to or layered on an existing, gender-neutral, fixable just war tradition. Instead, it is a "problem" that cannot be remedied within the logics and symbolisms of just war theorizing. Current deployments of just war theorizing are as much manifested in pictures, images, and signifying words and phrases in the claims and speeches of political and military leaders. In these deployments, themes of protecting homeland, "way of life," and innocent women and children are increasingly prevalent, as is the intentional victimization of civilian/women in the fighting of wars. This is because just war narratives rely on the existence of a feminized other, who plays the double role (and lives the double life) of "protected" and *casus belli*. It is possible that this paradox is inherent in the idea of discriminating between combatants and noncombatants.

Feminist work has tried to rescue and reformulate the just war tradition by seeing the "problem" of these gendered narratives in just war theory and by trying to deconstruct them. Feminists have worked to popularize the idea that women can be combatants and men can be civilians.[48] They have therefore contended that the images of masculinity and femininity in just warriors and beautiful souls are (and should be) understood as more complicated.[49] Feminist scholars have argued that no one should have to rely on masculinity for validation or on the ability or willingness to kill to validate masculinity.[50] That work is important, but it does not fully take account of that crucial second aspect of the double role played by the beautiful soul in just war narratives: as a motivation—or, more cynically, an excuse—for making war.

This work also neglects the possibility that gendered stereotypes constitute the immunity principle. Just war theorists have previously pointed out the practical difficulties distinguishing civilians and combatants, even if all belligerents agree that such a distinction is not only ethically appropriate but also ethically necessary. This is partly because, in order to know who to protect and who is a legitimate target, the noncombatant immunity principle needs to be able to distinguish between the innocent and the guilty. Making this distinction, and particularly identifying innocence, is controversial within the just war literature.[51] Some identify innocence as harmlessness (and guilt as dangerousness);[52] others define innocence as good behavior (and guilt as bad behavior);[53] and still others identify innocence and guilt by role (soldiers are guilty and nonsoldiers are innocent).[54] Michael Walzer focuses on consent to bad behavior as a key factor in guilt (and a lack of complicity signifying innocence).[55] Even if there were some clear way to identify a class of persons who merit "immunity," however, it is practically difficult to identify the people who ought to be immune during wars and separate them from the people who ought to be targeted.[56] Some theorists have also expressed a concern that the only effective mechanisms for discrimination, uniforms and battlefields, have become outdated in the practice of fighting wars.[57] There are those who believe that precision technology is the answer to effective civilian immunity; but others are skeptical about the practical possibilities of using technology to isolate civilians.[58]

In the midst of all these difficulties identifying civilians and combatants, practical and theoretical, war-fighting parties must resort to shortcuts, visual associations, metaphors, and other ways to make the distinction manageable and identifiable both generally and in the short-term decision-making frame necessary in the context of the fighting of wars.[59] These shortcuts and cues identify the innocent as feminine, as "womenandchildren" who are helpless at the hands of the (monstrous) guilty of the enemy.[60] They then place the burden of protection (and the honor received from protecting) on valorous, tough-but-tender just warriors, who fight the monstrous guilty of the enemy for the protection of their feminine/innocent/other. Research has shown that, even when belligerents do not explicitly identify men as guilty and women as innocent, they use (perceived) biological sex as a shortcut for identifying civilians and combatants.[61] Feminist work has argued that the intelligibility of the noncombatant immunity principle relies on its translation and simplification into images of just warriors protecting beautiful souls.[62]

This, of course, would not be dooming to the limiting and/or protective function of just war theorizing if we could picture just war without the current civilian immunity principle, and replace its intended (but, I have argued, impossible) function to make enforceable rules about who can be injured or killed *in bello* and who cannot. I have tried to accomplish that in earlier work, where I have suggested that this is instead more appropriately an *ad bellum* issue to supplement the *ad bellum* principle of proportionality. I have alternatively called it "empathetic war-fighting" and a "responsibility-for" approach.[63] These approaches ask belligerents to refrain from fighting wars that would not mainly or exclusively have an impact on the people who are directly responsible for the just cause, changing civilian immunity into an *ad bellum* priority. These approaches "fix" part of the problem—instead of saying "fight your wars, just do not hit civilians when you can help it," as a code for using civilians to justify war and attacking civilians seen as belonging to the "enemy," these approaches require belligerents to think seriously about the question of who will suffer from the war as a primary question in making decisions about whether to fight war as well. These approaches ask who it is acceptable to target a priori, rather than noting who should be protected if possible while going about the business of war.

But that corrective is not enough because, though it makes the combatant/civilian dichotomy more primary to war decision making, and presumes civilian-ness instead of presuming combatant-ness, it is still fundamentally homed in the untenable combatant/civilian dichotomy, despite moving away from its specific language.

Thinking about what just war would look like without the civilian immunity principle, then, is a difficult (if not impossible) prospect. This is because civilians *to protect from war* form part of the *authority of* just war discourses. The moral mandate of justice in war is reliant on the idea that there are levels of guilt in (and even complicity in) the just cause and later the war, which require treating potential participants and potential victims with different approaches based on their differential roles, positions, and moral culpabilities. Without the ability to distinguish between different people who should be treated differently in war(s) (which is made shorthand with the immunity principle, which is made accessible by the "just warrior"/"beautiful soul" dichotomy), just war theorizing loses not only its pretense to civilian immunity, but a fundamental source of its moral mandate in contemporary politics. For these reasons, the task of "saving" just war discourses from the gendered pathologies of the immunity principle seems difficult, both in theory and in practice.

CONCLUSION

If the gendered nature of the noncombatant immunity principle is a necessary feature of this principle, and the gendered noncombatant immunity principle is a necessary element of the just war tradition, then the just war tradition is internally contradictory, because it encourages its own violation and serves as a force not only to legitimate and authorize both war and the civilian victimization therein. If this is true (and not changeable within the current structure of just war narratives), then the just war tradition is itself a net cause of public harm that ought to be discarded and replaced not only in scholarly circles but also in policymaking circles.

The question of the alternative, however, is more difficult. If the purpose of just war theorizing is to serve as a moderating influence in war-making and war-fighting, and, despite that intent, it functions as a permissive force in war-making and war-fighting, then it needs to be supplanted to fulfill the intent of those who see the ethical importance of moderating the making and fighting of wars. Still, endorsing pacifism as an alternative does not moderate war but rejects it. Embracing pacifism as an alternative to just war theorizing would mean that there is no oppression less just than the most just war that could be imagined as necessary to defeat it, which is a position I could not imagine taking—logically, as a scholar; ethically, as a feminist; or practically, as an activist.

Yet the other extreme is equally problematic. It would make as little sense instead, with Clausewitz, to throw the ethics out of war in favor of a strategy uninhibited by morality.[64] This is precisely because an amoral position on the making and fighting of wars does not recognize the need for the authorization of war, whether it be by just war theorizing or some other moral framework. Yet for this very reason, it is important to find a moral framework for theorizing war ethics that does not appear to be restrictive without actually restricting, because that would create a moral hazard for war-making similar to the one that I argue current just war performances evoke.

So what is the alternative? To me, an ethics of war without civilians is one without us/them and public/private dichotomies, fundamentally altering the "us" that might decide, ontologically, to make wars, and act to fight them. It is an ethics of war that needs an alternative justification for war than those who it cannot and will not be able to protect. In other words, the gendered "protected" civilian other cannot serve as a cause to fight wars *ad bellum*, a motivation to fight *in bello*, a (symbolic or actual) target either *ad bellum* or *in bello*, or an authorizing narrative for violence more generally. A war ethics framework where the gendered, "protected" civilian plays any of those roles would find the deconstruction of the combatant/civilian dichotomy necessarily involves the deconstruction of the "us/them" dichotomy not only inherent in the immunity principle but also assumed in *jus ad bellum* rules about what motivates "us" to fight "them." This is because the separation between "us" and "them" both relies on and reifies the gendered dichotomies in the immunity principle. I argue that presuming such a separation between "us" and "them" is not only gendered but fundamentally unrepresentative. Instead, the "us" that fights wars can/should be seen as dependent on, and co-constituted with, the "other" that "we" have previously been understood as not only adversarial to but independent of. This realization, I contend, demands that war ethics be re-theorized from the ground up; taking into account this co-constitution and interdependence. In this view, decisions such as who is targeted in

war can be seen as complex and interrelated rather than unidimensional, dichoto-
mous, and ultimately reliant on gendered shorthand. War performances would need
to be understood as victimizing both the *self* and the *other*. Perhaps a starting point
of intersubjectivity, interdependence, and relationality for a communicative ethics
of war would avoid the net cause of public harm that the just war tradition is/has
become.[65] Such an approach would pay as much attention to war ethics' current
(gender) blind spots as to its well-rehearsed emphases, and as much attention to
the *international* implications of war decision making as to its *domestic* dilemmas,
in an attempt to deconstruct both dichotomies simultaneously as the basis for a
stronger overall ethical formulation.

NOTES

1. This is from George W. Bush's May 30, 2002, speech at the graduation at West Point;
the text was published in the *New York Times*, June 1, 2002. The relevant text is on page 3 of
the online publication: www.nytimes.com/2002/06/01/international/02PTEX-WEB.html?
pagewanted = 3. The surrounding text to the sentence cited above is worth quoting at some
length here to show the context of just war language (sentence cited above in italics; the
emphasis is added: "Moral truth is the same in every culture, in every time, and in every
place. Targeting innocent civilians for murder is always and everywhere wrong. *Brutality
against women is always and everywhere wrong.* There can be no neutrality between justice
and cruelty, between innocent and guilty. We are in a conflict between good and evil. And
America will call evil by its name."

2. See the discussions by Laura Sjoberg, "The Gendered Realities of the Immunity Principle: Why Gender Analysis Needs Feminism," *International Studies Quarterly* 50, no. 4 (2006):
889–910; Laura Sjoberg, *Gender, Justice, and the Wars in Iraq* (Lanham, MD: Lexington
Books, 2006); and recent discussion of the parallels to the Obama administration by Laura
Sjoberg, "'Manning Up' and Making (the Libyan) War," March 23, 2011, blog post at the
Duck of Minerva, http://duckofminerva.blogspot.com/2011/03/manning-up-and-making-
libyan-war.html.

3. The original articulation of this idea was by Jean Elshtain, "On Beautiful Souls, Just
Warriors, and Feminist Consciousness," *Women's Studies International Forum* 5, nos. 3–4
(1982): 341–48, which was expanded on by Jean Elshtain, *Women and Wars* (New York: Basic
Books, 1987), in dialogue with Judith Stiehm (and Nancy Huston), ed., *Women and Men's
Wars* (London: Pergamon, 1983), which serve as a foundation for contemporary feminist
thinking about this dichotomy.

4. See Sjoberg, *Gender, Justice, and the Wars in Iraq*, chap. 2.

5. See discussions in the contemporary literature on gender and the noncombatant
immunity principle, supra note 1, as well as Lucinda Peach, "An Alternative to Pacifism?
Feminism and Just-War Theory," *Hypatia* 9, no. 2 (1994): 152–72; Chris J. Cuomo, "War Is
Not Just an Event: Reflections on the Significance of Everyday Violence," *Hypatia* 11, no. 2
(1996): 30–45; J. Ann Tickner, *Gender in International Relations* (New York: Columbia University Press, 1992), chap. 2; and Laura Sjoberg, "Why Just War Needs Feminism Now More
Than Ever," *International Politics* 45, no. 1 (2008): 1–18.

6. See Judith Butler, *Excitable Speech: A Politics of the Performative* (New York: Psychology Press, 1997); as relates to international security law and ethics, see Laura J. Shepherd,
Gender, Violence, and Security: Discourse as Practice (London: Zed Books, 2008).

7. Cynthia Weber, "Performative States," *Millennium: Journal of International Studies* 27, no. 1 (1998): 77–95.

8. Judith Butler, "Contingent Foundations: Feminism and the Question of 'Postmodernism,'" in *Feminists Theorize the Political*, ed. Judith Butler and Joan W. Scott (London: Routledge, 1992).

9. For other discussions of performative constitution in international relations, see Roxanne Lynn Doty, *Imperial Encounters: The Politics of Representation in North–South Relations* (Minneapolis: University of Minnesota Press, 1998); Laura Shepherd, *Gender, Violence, and Security*; Laura Shepherd, ed., *Gender Matters in Global Politics* (London: Routledge, 2010); Cynthia Weber, *Simulating Sovereignty: Intervention, the State, and Symbolic Exchange* (Cambridge: Cambridge University Press, 1995); and Jean Baudrillard, *The Gulf War Did Not Take Place* (Bloomington: Indiana University Press, 1995).

10. Baudrillard, *Symbolic Exchange and Death* (London: Sage, 1979).

11. V. Spike Peterson and Anne Sisson Runyan, *Global Gender Issues* (Boulder, CO: Westview Press; 1st ed., 1992; 2nd ed., 1999). More recently, see Marysia Zalewski, "Feminist International Relations: Making Sense . . .," in *Gender Matters in Global Politics: A Feminist Introduction to International Relations*, ed. Laura J. Shepherd (London: Routledge, 2011), 28.

12. See, e.g., its use by Laura Sjoberg, "Introduction to *Security Studies*: Feminist Contributions," *Security Studies* 18, no. 2 (2009): 183–213.

13. Jill Steans, *Gender and International Relations: An Introduction* (New Brunswick, NJ: Rutgers University Press, 1998), 5.

14. Lauren Wilcox, "Gendering the Cult of the Offensive," *Security Studies* 18, no. 2 (2009): 214–40.

15. Sjoberg, "Introduction," 187.

16. Marysia Zalewski, "Well, What Is the Feminist Perspective on Bosnia?" *International Affairs* 7, no. 2 (1995): 339–56. See also Helen Kinsella, "For a Careful Reading: The Conservativism of Gender Constructivism," *International Studies Review* 5, no. 2 (2003): 287–302.

17. See Kimberly Hutchings, "Feminist Ethics and Political Violence," *International Politics* 44, no. 1 (2007): 90–106; Helen M. Kinsella, "Gendering Grotius: Sex and Sex Difference in the Laws of War," *Political Theory* 34, no. 2 (2006): 161–91; Judith Gardam, "Gender and Non-Combatant Immunity," *Transnational Law and Contemporary Problems* 345 (1993); Sjoberg, *Gender, Justice, and the Wars in Iraq*; Sjoberg, "Gendered Realities"; and Sjoberg, "The Paradox of Double Effect," *Women's Policy Journal* 6, no. 1 (2011).

18. E.g., V. Spike Peterson, ed., *Gendered States* (Boulder, CO: Westview Press, 1992).

19. See Sue Rae Peterson, "Coercion and Rape: The State as a Male Protection Racket," in *Feminism and Philosophy*, ed. M. Vetterling-Braggin, F. A. Ellston, and J. English (Totowa, NJ: Littlefield, Adams, 1977).

20. E.g., Hutchings, "Feminist Ethics."

21. On degendering its concepts, nature, and practices, see, e.g., Peach, "Alternative to Pacifism?"; J. Ann Tickner, *Gender*, chap. 2; and Sjoberg, "Why Just War Needs Feminism." On solutions to gender biases, see, e.g., Cuomo, "War Is Not Just an Event."

22. Dealing with the question of whether the just war tradition is a net negative or positive is inspired in part by one of the framing questions asked by the conference organizers at the conference that inspired this book: "Is just war a critical or conservative tradition?" It is also inspired by a conversation with R. Charli Carpenter at the 2006 Annual Meeting of the American Political Science Association, where, responding to my critiques of the immunity principle, Carpenter asked me whether I thought the noncombatant immunity principle is a public good or not—arguing herself that it is. I did not answer the question; here I attempt to.

23. Nancy Huston, "Tales of War and Tears of Women," *Women's Studies International Forum* 5, nos. 3–4 (1982): 271–82; Joshua Goldstein, *War and Gender* (Cambridge: Cambridge University Press, 2001).

24. Stiehm, *Women*.

25. R. W. Connell, *Masculinities* (London: Polity, 1995); Sjoberg, *Gender, Justice, and the Wars in Iraq*.

26. Peterson, "Coercion."

27. Elshtain, "Just Warriors, Beautiful Souls."

28. Brent Steele, *Ontological Security in International Relations: Self-Identity and the IR State* (London: Routledge, 2008). See also Jennifer Mitzen, "Ontological Security in World Politics: State Identity and the Security Dilemma," *European Journal of International Relations* 12, no. 3 (2006): 341–70.

29. See Sjoberg, "Gendered Realities."

30. Peterson, "Coercion."

31. See, e.g., Anne Sisson Runyan, "Gender Relations and the Politics of Protection," *Peace Review* 2, no. 4 (1999): 28–31.

32. See Iris Marion Young, "The Logic of Masculinist Protection: Reflections on the Current Security State," *Signs* 29, no. 1 (2003): 1–25.

33. See Laura Sjoberg and Jessica Peet, "A(nother) Dark Side of the Protection Racket," *International Feminist Journal of Politics* 13, no. 2 (2011): 162–81.

34. Ibid.

35. Anne McClintock, "Family Feuds, Gender, Nationalism, and the Family," *Feminist Review* 44 (Summer 1993): 62.

36. Nira Yuval-Davis, *Gender and Nation* (London: Sage, 1997), 2.

37. Nira Yuval-Daivs and Floya Anthias, *Woman-Nation-State* (London: Palgrave, 1989); Jan Jindy Pettman, *Worlding Women: A Feminist International Politics* (London: Routledge, 1996). McClintock argues that "all nationalisms are gendered, all are invented, and all are dangerous"; McClintock, "Family Feuds," 71.

38. Pettman, *Worlding Women*, 193. Ruth Seifert has described the effect as women's bodies becoming a "second front" for conflicts; see Ruth Seifert, "The Second Front: The Logic of Sexual Violence in Wars," *Women's Studies International Forum* 19, nos. 1–2 (1996): 35–43.

39. V. Spike Peterson, "Sexing Political Identity/Nationalism as Heterosexism," *International Feminist Journal of Politics* 1, no. 1 (1999): 34–65.

40. Cited by Cindy S. Snyder, Wesley J. Gabbarf, J. Dean May, and Nihada Zulcic, "On the Battleground of Women's Bodies: Mass Rape in Bosnia Herzgovina," *Affilia* 21, no. 2 (2006): 190.

41. Carl von Clausewitz, *On War*, 1832. The quotation is from Sjoberg and Peet, "A(nother) Dark Side," 169.

42. Alexander Downes, *Targeting Civilians in War* (Ithaca, NY: Cornell University Press, 2008); Alexander Downes, "Desperate Times, Desperate Measures: The Causes of Civilian Victimization in War," *International Security* 30, no. 4 (2006) 152–95.

43. See Sjoberg and Peet, "A(nother) Dark Side"; and Laura Sjoberg and Jessica Peet, "Targeting Women in Wars," in *Feminism and International Relations: Conversations about the Past, Present, and Future*, ed. J. Ann Tickner and Laura Sjoberg (London: Routledge, 2011).

44. Pettman, *Worlding Women*, 191.

45. Sjoberg, *Gender, Justice, and the Wars in Iraq*. The "good guy" and "bad guy" logics here are references to Huston, "Tales of War."

96   Laura Sjoberg

46. Sjoberg and Peet, "A(nother) Dark Side."

47. Peterson, "Sexing Political Identity," 48.

48. See, e.g., Laura Sjoberg and Caron Gentry, *Mothers, Monsters, Whores: Women's Violence in Global Politics* (London: Zed Books, 2007); and also see other work on women's participation in combat, terrorism, and other forms of political violence.

49. See, e.g., Annica Kronsell and Erika Svedberg, "The Duty to Protect: Gender in the Swedish Practice of Conscription," *Cooperation and Conflict* 36, no. 2 (2001): 153–76.

50. See, e.g., Joshua Goldstein, *War and Gender* (Cambridge: Cambridge University Press, 2001).

51. George R. Mavrodes, "Conventions and the Morality of War," *Philosophy and Public Affairs* 4, no. 2 (1975): 117–31, at 121.

52. Jenny Teichman, *Pacifism and the Just War: A Study in Applied Philosophy* (Oxford: Basil Blackwell, 1986), 66.

53. Richard Shelly Hartigan, *The Forgotten Victim: A History of the Civilian* (Chicago: Precedent Publishing, 1982).

54. Fritz Kalshoven, *The Law of Warfare: A Summary of Its Recent History and Trends in Development* (Leiden: A. W. Sijthoff, 1973), 35.

55. Michael Walzer, *Just and Unjust Wars: A Moral Argument with Historical Illustrations*, 2nd ed. (New York: Basic Books, 1977), 147.

56. Hartigan, *Forgotten Victim*, 7.

57. Donald A. Wells, "How Much Can 'the Just War' Justify?" *Journal of Philosophy* 66, no. 23 (1969): 819–29.

58. Walzer, *Just and Unjust* Wars, 156.

59. See, e.g., the arguments made by George Lakoff and Mark Johnson, *Metaphors We Live By* (Chicago: University of Chicago Press, 1980); and Yuen Foong Khong, *Analogies at War: Korea, Munich, Dien Bien Phu, and the Vietnam Decisions of 1965* (Princeton, NJ: Princeton University Press, 1992). These books share the argument that people use particular (metaphorical, visual, or analogic) shorthands to make accessible complicated concepts and situations.

60. Cynthia Enloe, "Womenandchildren: Making Feminist Sense of the Persian Gulf Crisis," *The Village Voice*, 1990; discussed in detail by Helen Kinsella, *The Image before the Weapon: A Critical History of the Combatant and Civilian* (Ithaca, NY: Cornell University Press, 2011).

61. R. Charli Carpenter, *Innocent Women and Children* (Aldershot, UK: Ashgate, 2007).

62. Kinsella, *Image before the Weapon*; Gardam, "Gender."

63. See Sjoberg, *Gender, Justice, and the Wars in Iraq*; and Sjoberg "Gendered Realities."

64. See Clausewitz, *On War*.

65. The use here is borrowed from Hayward Alker's discussion of conflict as communication, borrowing heavily from Jürgen Habermas. Hayward Alker, *Rediscoveries and Reformulations* (Cambridge: Cambridge University Press, 2001); Jürgen Habermas, *The Theory of Communicative Action* (Cambridge: Polity Press, 1981).

CHAPTER 6

Legitimate Authority and the War against Al-Qaeda

Nahed Artoul Zehr

SINCE THE EARLY TWENTIETH CENTURY, irregular and nonstate actors have demonstrated not only their political relevance but also increased levels of military capability and sophistication.[1] Such developments have spurred a reexamination of the legitimate authority criterion, leading certain theorists to argue that this criterion—as it serves to determine the justice of wars—ought to be reconsidered or dropped altogether.[2]

Cecile Fabre is especially helpful in understanding these arguments. Grounding herself in cosmopolitan theory, she claims that it is untenable to argue that individuals have rights that merit and require protection, while at the same time denying individuals the authority to use force in defense of those rights.[3] In particular, she is concerned about situations where a standing government is abusing the rights of its citizens while denying these citizens any legal channels for recourse. Under such circumstances, Fabre argues, it is clear that groups representing aggrieved political communities, along with individuals themselves, have the right to declare war or undertake the use of armed force in protection of their rights. Of particular importance, for Fabre, this demonstrates that judgments about the justice of war can be determined outside state-defined standards—leading her to conclude that the criterion of legitimate authority ought to be dropped.

In thinking about positions such as Fabre's, it seems necessary to discuss the most visible manifestation of both the capabilities and significance of irregular actors: the war against al-Qaeda. Now into its second decade, the "Long War" provides both a theoretical entry point as well an empirical context for examining the legitimate authority criterion. Although there are a variety of issues to discuss regarding legitimate authority and the Long War, I limit this piece to one issue: the justificatory claims to the use of force put forward by al-Qaeda's major ideologues.

According to al-Qaeda's most prolific theoretician and strategist, Abu Mas'ab al-Suri, Islam, its lands, and its people are under attack on every level from Western forces and influence.[4] Additionally, all standing governments in the Muslim world (with the exception of the Taliban) have acquiesced to the pernicious policies of the West, leaving Muslims without an appropriate figure to provide a formal declaration of war. The Muslim world, he argues, is under attack; and the war is a *defensive* one. Moreover, the lack of representative governments from which to seek redress leads him to argue that—in light of the current circumstances of the Muslim world—the authority to undertake the use of arms in redress is within the purview of every individual Muslim.[5] By *decentralizing* legitimate authority in this way, al-Suri's model effectively discards the notion of legitimate authority—culminating in a strategic framework that is diffuse, highly irregular in tactics, and only minimally interested in restrictions on the use of force.[6]

Al-Suri's thinking is cause for reflection regarding positions such as Fabre's—positions seeking to critique the saliency of the legitimate authority criterion *en masse*. Some may object that a group like al-Qaeda is outside the jurisdiction of her argument. However, though Fabre appears focused on what we might term "traditional" insurgencies, it remains the case that al-Qaeda's model illuminates a series of questions that ought to be seriously considered.[7] More specifically, al-Suri's thinking creates a space in which the just war theorist may reflect on the significance, importance, and utility of the legitimate authority criterion in both the Western and Islamic just war traditions.[8]

Now, Fabre's concern for appropriate recourse in the face of injustice is legitimate. Especially when accounting for the reluctance of states and large portions of the international community to grant authority (legitimacy) to nonstate actors. Fabre's concerns, then, speak clearly to the contestation of legitimate authority highlighted in Lang and O'Driscoll's introduction to this volume. As they note, the assumption that "the principle of proper authority is reducible to the concept of state sovereignty" denies the plurality of the tradition. This denial, they argue, appears to reject "a range of different approaches to what constitute authority, not all of them consistent with the idea of the state, as we understand it today." At a fundamental level, the argument put forward in this chapter is in agreement with both Fabre's and O'Driscoll and Lang's contestation of a *static* understanding of legitimate authority. However, it remains concerned with the ramifications of dismissing the category in its entirety—in the way that Fabre suggests. To this end, it seeks to demonstrate the importance of the legitimate authority criterion—whose intention is to place *limits* on warfare by demarcating a class of figures who may declare that the use of force is appropriate for the settlement of specific disputes.[9] Consequently, within the just war tradition there is both concern and recourse for the types of circumstances that Fabre worries about. As demonstrated through the work of its theorists, modern just war thinking grants authority to a class of irregular actors, particularly those who are rising up against a government that has lost its claim to use force through acts of tyranny and injustice toward its citizens. Its purpose is not to encumber the road to justice but to ensure that those taking up the sword have the proper authority and justification to do so—for the sake of justice.

Moreover, in an international arena in which irregular actors are more and more prominent, the criterion acquires increased importance. Therefore, this chapter argues that evaluating the moral standing of positions like those of al-Suri *requires* a moral category through which the grievances of irregular actors not only acquire meaning but might also be evaluated. This is primarily because the determination of when such circumstances exist—that is, circumstances in which irregulars are legitimately and appropriately granted the authority to use force—cannot be made meaningfully without the direction provided by the criterion.

In light of the above, I begin by sketching al-Qaeda's model of war as articulated by al-Suri, and focus specifically on how this model *departs* from historical Islamic thinking on the just use of force. Second, I discuss just war thinking on both the utility of the legitimate authority criterion as well as issues related to irregular actors. I conclude with a discussion of the relevance of the al-Qaeda model for current debates on the legitimate authority criterion.

CHANGING NOTIONS OF AUTHORITY:
THE AL-QAEDA MODEL OF WAR

Understanding al-Suri's position as a "departure" requires that we first explicate historical Muslim thinking on the proper use of force. Referencing the example of Muhammad and the earliest Muslims, medieval Islamic jurists developed a theory of statecraft that both directed and limited the use of force.[10] Within this historical tradition, war—or "jihad"—is a moral activity; one that is waged for certain ends and restricted by certain means.[11] As various tracts and treatises were written on the subject, directives were established for a range of activities and circumstances related to warfare: determining the status of noncombatants, the distribution of treasure, and appropriate behavior for Muslims in enemy lands.[12]

Of significant importance for our purposes is the discourse on legitimate authority as it relates to the justice of war. The jurists organized jihad under two classifications of God's commands: *fard 'ayn* and *fard kifaya*. *Fard 'ayn* designated duties that were incumbent on *every* individual (and physically able) Muslim.

These included obligations such as prayer, fasting, and charitable acts. In contrast, *fard kifaya* designated duties that were required of the community *as a whole.* If the community, as a whole, did not provide the necessary means for the *fard kifaya* duties, then the community—again, as a whole—was held responsible.[13] For example, the community was tasked with providing someone to recite the appropriate prayers at funerals, and for the raising of armies. However, these duties, as *fard kifaya*, were not necessarily incumbent on every individual Muslim. So long as the community provided the necessary means for the *fard kifaya* class of duties to be appropriately carried out by *some* members of the community, the obligation had been met.

Offensive jihad, within the classic juristic tradition, was a *fard kifaya*—a community obligation that was undertaken only under the authority of the political head of the community, and in light of his or her determinations that the use of force was necessary in pursuit of the community's welfare. Defensive jihad, in contrast, was a *fard 'ayn.* If a specific portion of Muslim land came under attack, then every capable Muslim—beginning with those closest, geographically, to the attack—was responsible for coming to its defense.[14] Although this second conception of jihad, as *fard 'ayn*, appears to open the way for the decentralization of authority, it is important to note that the juristic thinkers were concerned with a specific set of circumstances—an emergency situation when a specific Muslim community was attacked on its own soil. Therefore, the individual authority to take up arms was triggered only when there was an immediate attack on Muslim land.[15]

It is here—the notion of defensive war and legitimate authority—that al-Qaeda's model demonstrates a clear departure from the juristic understanding of the proper use of force.[16] Before moving to al-Suri's model, however, it is important to note that describing al-Suri's position as a "departure" from Islamic thinking is not to claim that the jihad tradition is a monolithic thing. Quite the contrary; Muslim thinking on war is varied and complex. Whether one reads a medieval text or the positions of contemporary thinkers, there tends to be more disagreement than agreement on the topic of war.[17] This is the clear mark of a discourse that has changed, adapted, developed, and responded to various historical events and circumstances. In other words, it is the mark of a religious *tradition.* As a *tradition*, however, Muslim discourse on war demonstrates common denominators that are called upon by various Muslim thinkers as they form their positions. This is not to make a case for a certain essence of the tradition. Rather, it is to argue that there is a loose yet discernible framework upon which we may hang the marker of jihad, and to further claim that this tradition is characterized by certain restrictions—one of which is the idea of legitimate authority, as described above.

AL-SURI'S MODEL

To demonstrate al-Suri's model, we turn to his 1,600-page treatise on jihad, *The Global Islamic Resistance Call* (hereafter, *The Call*) (دعوة المقاومة الاسلامية العالمية).[18] The text is widely understood as a tactical manual, though this is a relatively limited view of the nature and purpose of *The Call*. In this text al-Suri provides both a diagnosis of the major ills confronting the Muslim world and a comprehensive, militant solution to its set of problems.

For al-Suri contemporary Muslims are facing what he terms the "New World Order" (النظام العالمي الجديد).[19] Although he does not provide a precise definition of this term, an explanation of what he means by it may be surmised through his writing. According to al-Suri, the New World Order is rooted in three issues.

The first issue is the absence of proper religion among the majority of Muslims in both public and private life. Muslim nations, he argues, have failed to properly implement God's laws into public institutions, and have chosen to arrange their civic and social life through the guidelines of secular models. Furthermore, these secular institutions have transported what al-Suri argues is the moral depravation and decadence of Western society into the Muslim world.[20] As a consequence, Muslim societies are failing to abide by—and therefore living in contradiction to—the laws that God has decreed.

Second, the "abandonment" of religion is responsible for the weakness and decline of Muslim societies—demonstrated by their military deficiency and economic depravity. For al-Suri, the occupation of Islam's holy sites is the most visceral symbol of the shortcomings of the Muslim world—both the presence of foreign troops in Saudi Arabia and the continuing occupation of Jerusalem are testaments to its impotence. The lack of adherence to God's law, and the continuing loyalties to foreign systems of government and influence, have crippled the Muslim world's ability to resist foreign encroachment.

This leads to al-Suri's third issue. He claims that the New World Order is the result of a deliberate and concerted effort by the United States and Europe to dominate the region. Furthermore, these forces are in partnership with Arab governments and leaders who are more interested in maintaining their individual power then in promoting the liberation of Islam, its land, and its people. For example, al-Suri argues that Saudi Arabia has been a client government of the British and of the United States since its inception, leading Saudi Arabia to make foreign policy decisions that are contrary to the best interests of the Muslim people. It was under American influence and pressure, he argues, that Saudi Arabia allowed American presence on its soil during the First Gulf War. And this same influence and pressure lead Saudi Arabia to make continuing overtures toward the state of Israel.[21] Additionally, this program on the part of the West, and specifically the United States, has magnified in its intentions since 9/11—as the wars in Iraq and Afghanistan are the new entry points for a comprehensive occupation of the Muslim world. Under the guise of a "War on Terror," and with the military cooperation of the heads of Arab states, the United States has sought to eliminate any resistance to its program:[22]

> As we established in the first section below titled "The Situation of Muslims Today," it has become recognized among the Muslims today, as all those who are sane of mind have understood, that the entirety of our lands, from border to border is occupied by the enemies. And on behalf of their deputies, and the heavy military presence of the crusaders, they spread bases with complete economic occupation; [an occupation] that exceeds the economic power of monopolies. . . . And here is America today reoccupying the Muslim world from anew (من جديد) in the clear light of day (جهارا/ نهارا). It has occupied Afghanistan directly. It has spread its control to Pakistan and central Asia. And now it has occupied Iraq. It has placed hundreds of thousands of soldiers in the Arabian Peninsula and Turkey and the southern Levant as well as in Egypt and the Horn of Africa and North Africa. . . . And now Bush is announcing that he will direct onto Muslim lands a "crusade" (حملة صليبية) and he is supported by the European NATO allies and also through an alliance with the Israeli President whom occupies Palestine, and who is also preparing to demolish the sacred mosque and to expel the rest of the Muslims there (وتبقا فيها من المسلمين طرد).[23]

For al-Suri, the forces directing the New World Order must be resisted. Only in this way might the Muslim world regain its strength and execute God's decrees. Therefore, al-Suri calls for a "global confrontation"—a military response that can effectively combat the forces of the New World Order. This, according to al-Suri, is the purpose of *The Call:* To provide the means and instruction to construct and direct a large-scale resistance on the part of the Muslim world that will liberate Muslims and Muslim lands from the occupation of Western forces. The Muslim world, he insists, must in its entirety rise up and wage the jihad.[24]

Two points need to be noted here. First, according to al-Suri, the jihad against the forces of the New World Order is a *defensive* one, imposed upon the Muslim nation as a result of foreign occupation and influence. Construing the current jihad espoused by al-Suri (and al-Qaeda) as a *defensive* jihad allows him to claim that the authority to wage this war is transferred to the individual Muslim—effectively *decentralizing* the notion of legitimate authority from the head of a political community to the individual Muslim. The Muslim world—in its *entirety*—he argues, is under attack and subject to immediate danger. In this situation, where the life of the tradition is at stake, the duty to fight is mandated.[25] The jihad is imposed upon the Islamic nation—again, in its *entirety*—as a religious and individual duty. As this current jihad is a defensive one, he argues, permission from an emir or other such political authority is not necessary to determine the appropriate use of force. The individual Muslim—*every* Muslim who is able—he argues, is obligated to partici-pate in the jihad.[26] Therefore, the Muslim world is subsequently under an *immediate* obligation to resist. He writes: "And this is the truth: A national resistance to this foreign infidel occupation and the apostate forces collaborating with it, who are plying into the chests of Muslims is a required duty [فرض واجب] determined by the Islamic Sharia, and is a truth, furthermore, that is perceived by a sound mind."[27]

Although it may sound a bit fantastical to the current reader, al-Suri's sincerity is difficult to doubt. Although he does not characterize himself as a theologian, he goes to significant lengths—quoting (albeit selectively) from the Qur'an, the Hadith, and various juristic commentaries—in an attempt to establish a theological foundation for his claims. For example, referring to the Qur'an, he writes that,[28]

> as stated by God, Great and Almighty, "If two parties among the believers fall into a quarrel, make ye peace between them. But if one of them transgresses beyond bounds against the other then fight ye against the one that trans-gresses until it complies with the command of God; but if it complies then make peace between them with justice, and be fair: for God loves those who are fair (and just)." If God prescribed categories of combat against Muslims to preserve the unity of the Muslims and their religion and the protection of their land and their resources, then how must it be that the laws in regard to combat of the nation of the aggressive infidels? Is it not the first and more likely [obligation]?[29]

The second important point is al-Suri's understanding of individual authority as it is used to construct a tactical framework. Al-Suri sought to provide a *new* model of jihad for the global confrontation; one capable of responding to an environment characterized by a deep power asymmetry between the Muslim world and the West. In this end, he argued that in the post–September 11 environment, one character-ized by the New World Order, the "old ways" of secret, regional, and hierarchical jihadi organizations are no longer possible. Pointing to examples like Egypt, Syria, and Algeria, he argues that government intelligence and antiterror initiatives make such hierarchical models too easy to find, dismantle, and to destroy. In addition, the West's (specifically America's) military superiority has made the previous models ineffective and untenable: "The times have changed, and we must design a method of confrontation, which is in accordance with the standard of the present time. So I repeat again: . . . The main weakness is not in the structure of the secret organiza-tion or their internal weakness, although they were underlying reasons. The main weakness is caused by the fundamental revolutionary change of the times and the current premises, which has altered the course of history, the present, and conse-quently the future."[30]

In light of this, the military theory of al-Suri's global resistance calls for the application of what he terms "individual terrorism jihad." The individual jihad is both a key component of al-Suri's theory, and the most drastic departure from the juristic tradition on war. Here, al-Suri states that the jihad is to be conducted by highly decentralized cells, consisting of one to ten individuals. These cells participate in an exceedingly disconnected method of training and recruitment, such that most members are never aware of one another's existence. Their operations include "light guerrilla warfare, civilian terror, and secret methods."[31] Through this model, he argues, the resistance will not only be decentralized but will also expand significantly through its territorial reach: "It opens up the possibility to participate for thousands, say hundreds of thousands or millions, of Muslims sympathizing with jihad and with their Islamic Nation's causes. The constricted jihadi secret organizations did not have room for all of them. Moreover, most of them do not want to be linked to this commitment with all its security-related personal consequences. . . . Also they are not able to, or they do not want to get burned security-wise, by joining the Open Fronts which also have limited capacity to absorb them."[32]

This model, al-Suri argues, retains the ability to unite those with a common cause, and the desire to engage in the global resistance against the West.[33] Yet it significantly reduces the risks involved in the older methods of organization. For example, as al-Suri notes, the decentralized component of this method makes it extremely difficult to combat. Focusing on a theory of "system, not secret organization," al-Suri determined that minimizing the organizational bonds between members—to those of "beliefs, a system of action, a common name, and a common goal" would also minimize the security risks. Furthermore, the potential to destroy this model is significantly decreased, as destroying one cell does not eliminate the ability of other cells to undertake the jihad. Under this method of organization, "any Muslim, who wants to participate in jihad and the Resistance, can participate in this battle against America in his country, or anywhere, which is perhaps hundreds of times more effective that what he is able to do if he arrived at the open area of confrontation."[34]

As is now clear, al-Suri's decentralization of legitimate authority has constructed a model of jihad that allows any member of al-Qaeda or its affiliates to undertake armed resistance through terrorist means wherever they may be. While referencing the history, concepts, and terms of the juristic tradition, al-Suri's model does not require a declaration of war by a legitimate authority. Rather, *all* Muslims may— and are religiously required to—immediately take up arms against the West. Furthermore, the jihad is to be waged in any place possible—striking at Western interests in both the Muslim world and the United States and Europe, and with minimal restriction on noncombatants.

The ramifications of al-Suri's model—of his decentralization and effective dismissal of legitimate authority—are real and serious, and have significantly affected al-Qaeda and its affiliates. Reeling from the destruction of its training camps, al-Qaeda has found serious utility in al-Suri's organizational vision as it has allowed al-Qaeda to transform into a highly diffuse and decentralized network. The most observable effect has been a growing line of "lone wolf" jihadis, such as Richard Colvin Reid (the "shoe bomber"), Umar Farouq Abdulmtallab ("Christmas Day attacks"), Nidal Hasan ("Fort Hood shooting"), and Faisal Shahzad ("Times Square attack").

In particular, there is a remarkable affinity between Shahzad's story and al-Suri's recommendations. According to media reports, Shahzad asked his father's permission to fight in the jihad (his father refused). He consequently spent five months in Pakistan and claimed that it was during this period that he received the necessary training from the Pakistani Taliban for the Times Square attack. He then returned to the United States (leaving his wife and family in Pakistan), presumably with the express intent of coordinating and executing the attack.

This influence of al-Suri's model has also been noted by analysts and military figures. They argue that al-Qaeda's decentralization is leading to an organization with a wider breadth—an organization that is capable of reaching further into the Western world in both recruitment and operational capabilities. Additionally, such an organization will form links between movements affiliated with al-Qaeda, with an "invisible bridge" already established between al-Qaeda in Yemen and militant Islamists in Somalia.[35] Al-Qaeda has stated the same in its own outlets. In July 2010, al-Qaeda in the Arabian Peninsula (known as AQAP) released its first edition of *Inspire*—an English-language online magazine whose mandate revolves around recruiting English-speaking Muslims to the worldwide jihad. According to analysts, "*Inspire*'s primary message to its readers is that they too can be part of al-Qaeda and its mission, but from the comfort of their own home. Instead of traveling thousands of miles to join the jihad, the reader need only turn on their computer and visit websites to receive training—i.e., viewing videos and listening to sermons of their favorite leaders, and learning to handle weapons, explosives and even planning attacks."[36]

What, then, are the implications of al-Suri's model of war for the legitimate authority criterion?

CONTEMPORARY DEBATES ON
LEGITIMATE AUTHORITY

With this question in mind, let us turn to current debates within just war thinking on the legitimate authority criterion. Fabre, in particular, argues that the criterion is untenable in light of other assumptions and commitments made by the international community—specifically that "human beings are the fundamental units of moral concern and have equal moral worth, irrespective of group membership (cultural, ethnic, and national).[37] From this, it is clear that human beings not only have

a "right to the freedoms and resources they need in order to live a minimally flourishing life" but also that these rights are "held by all wherever they reside, and,
more controversially, are held *against* all, wherever they reside."[38] Just as important,
she argues, the state's authority is directly contingent upon its ability to serve and
protect the fundamental rights of its individual citizens.[39]

Fabre argues that the right to protect oneself against the violations of one's fundamental rights trumps the legitimate authority criterion's claim that only those in
positions of legal authority may undertake the use of force.[40] Of particular concern
are circumstances in which individual or communal rights are being threatened,
but individuals have no legal or political recourse against these forms of injustice.
Insofar as the fundamental rights of individuals are being violated, she argues, the
state has thereby renounced its political authority. Under such circumstances, she
argues that individuals have the authority to use force against the state and in protection of these rights.

In this way, the authority to wage war—assuming that the other requirements
of *jus ad bellum* are satisfied—is extended to a variety of classes: those who represent
a political community (e.g., national liberation movements); those who rise up
against a tyrannical state (but are not formally organized); to nonpolitical groups;
and to individuals who undertake the use of force in order to defend against violations of their human rights.[41] For Fabre, then, a war's moral standing may be determined by the circumstances at hand, and is not contingent upon a declaration by a
legitimate authority. As far as this is the case, she argues, the requirement has lost
its cogency and ought to be dispensed with.

A proper discussion of Fabre's position directs us to recount the reasoning
behind the requirement of legitimate authority.[42] For Fabre, individual authority is
understood as follows: "only an organization that has the authority to make and
enforce laws over a given territory, and has a claim to be recognized as such by
other comparable institutions holds the right to wage war."[43] It is certainly the case
that the classification of "individual authority" is often given to those who are
charged with enforcing the positive law of a political community. However, the just
war tradition interprets this requirement to go beyond this purview.

As understood by a number of its theorists, this criterion is a moral and ethical
category, serving to *place limits* on the use of force by *restricting* the pool of candi-
dates who may legitimately undertake the use of arms in the service of the political
community. To this end, the legitimate authority criterion plays the vital role of
delineating which members of a political community have the necessary authorization to utilize the military resources of the society in question, under the determination (and further limits imposed) by the criterion of just cause.

The process of determining who may undertake the use of force was premised
on a specific understanding of the role and responsibility of those in positions of
authority and, by extension, to those who are charged with the specific responsibilities of statecraft. The classic, and perhaps paradigmatic, statement on this issue is

from Thomas Aquinas, who noted: "For it is not the business of the private individual to declare war, because he can seek for redress of his rights from the tribunal of his superior. Moreover, it is not the business of a private individual to summon together the people, which has to be done in wartime. And as the care of the common weal is committed to those who are in authority, it is their business to watch over the common weal of the city, kingdom or province subject to them."[44]

As argued by James Turner Johnson, the sovereign's right to war flows directly from his "positive responsibilities as the one given charge for the common weal."[45] For the classic just war thinkers, the sovereign's responsibility for the general welfare of the political community was not only limited to its physical protection but also directed toward its welfare. In other words, the sovereign's responsibility was not limited to the enforcement of laws, as he or she was additionally—and just as importantly—tasked with the community's overall welfare. Regarding war specifically, the sovereign was to direct the use of force so that it both served the good and moved the political community toward the good.[46]

To put it plainly, the tradition's position is rooted in the notion that those in authority—who are responsible for the welfare of a political community—gain and hold a different vantage point from which to make decisions—a vantage point that is theirs *by way* of their position, and the responsibility and perspective that are acquired *through* it. Those in positions of responsibility have sight of the complex web of commitments that are involved in determining any proper course of action—including the determination of when it is appropriate to use force. Individual citizens are not typically afforded the same perspective.[47] The criterion, then, is *intentionally* restrictive, seeking to mitigate those whose motivations are individual and private, and not subject to the instructive capabilities that are the inheritance of those in positions of authority.

However, as Fabre is correct to argue, there are circumstances in which the state loses its legitimacy, and hence, its authority. Just war thinking is responsive to such conditions, and takes note of their significance to the maintenance of justice in war. To begin, this concern was embodied in the publication of two documents. The first was the US Army's *General Orders No. 100*, published in 1863. This document recognized confederate forces as legitimate belligerents (as opposed to rebels or criminals) and granted them the associated rights of soldiers. Second was the annex to "The Hague Convention IV, Laws and Customs of War on Land," which stipulated that the "laws, right, and duties of war" were not just the purview of armies but also extended to "militia, and volunteer corps" who demonstrated a set of provisions.[48] By recognizing the authority of irregulars, these documents were also recognizing that the state's sovereignty is not absolute.

Furthermore, these ideas are echoed in the work of contemporary just war theorists. For the sake of space, I limit this discussion to the work of Michael Walzer, whose ideas on this issue are exceptionally lucid. For him, the status of irregulars is directly contingent on whether the irregular forces represent the political community in question. In a frequently cited essay on counterinsurgency, Walzer argues that a soldier acquires war rights in light of his or her status as a "political instrument"—as a member of a community that exists in a reciprocal relationship with the citizenry. Therefore, the war rights of soldiers may be extended to the guerrilla fighter under the determination that specific conditions exist. Specifically, such rights might be extended under the determination that the guerrilla fighter also exists in a reciprocal relationship—living as a member of the citizenry and fighting as their military representative.

Therefore if, Walzer argues, the guerrilla fighters are not accorded support and recognition by the masses, they do not acquire the rights of war. However, under the determination that such support and recognition are apparent and are freely given by the citizens, the guerrillas ought to be guaranteed certain rights and treatment—like benevolent quarantine in the case of capture.

Importantly, Walzer argues that if political support for the irregulars is determined to be such that the "guerrillas cannot be isolated from the people," then a counterinsurgency war can no longer be fought on moral grounds. He writes that "it cannot be fought because it is no longer an anti-guerrilla but an anti-social war, a war against an entire people, in which no distinctions would be possible in the actual fighting."[49] It is critical to note here that the category of legitimate authority has not been removed. Rather, in the interest of justice, it has been *transferred* to an irregular force that is both representing a political community and contesting the legitimacy of a standing government in the interest of its welfare. The recognition of the "war rights" of irregulars is acknowledgment of their position as the proper and legitimate representatives of a political community. The rights afforded here, then, are symbolic of the fact that under certain circumstances, particularly those in which justice is threatened, irregulars may take on the rights and responsibilities typically afforded to heads of state—including the right to declare war.

Returning to Fabre's position, it is clear that the criterion of legitimate authority is not constructed as an obstruction to justice. Although it is certainly the case that one cannot speak on behalf of all perspectives and thinking that falls under the tradition's reach, Walzer's work on this issue gives clear indication that just war thinking is responsive to the circumstances that Fabre worries about.

Beyond this, however, is a second and critical point. Fabre argues that individuals may legitimately take up force only if all the other requirements of *jus ad bellum*— just cause, right intention, and so on—are satisfied. The notion that all individuals have the authority to determine a category like just cause is attractive, particularly to those of us who have been intellectually reared to value the principles of democracy. However, it also effectively eliminates the requirement—established by the legitimate authority criterion—that those undertaking the use of force must be able to demonstrate recognition on the part of those whose interests they claim to represent, advance, and protect. This claim is critical to the limits provided by the legitimate authority criterion.[50]

With this established, we can more appropriately evaluate al-Suri's claims to a defensive jihad—one that requires and legitimates the participation of every Muslims in individual terror operations against Western targets, wherever they may be. As we noted in the sections on historical Muslim thinking on war, and the Western just war tradition's understanding of legitimate authority, only certain individuals may undertake the use of force. The aim of this, in both traditions, is to restrict the pool of individuals—with such authority—to those who held the proper vantage point from which to more clearly understand the path to justice.

How, then, might we evaluate al-Suri's (and al-Qaeda's) claims for a pernicious New World Order that demands a defensive jihad? As noted above, in the Islamic tradition the authority to undertake the use of force in defense was granted to those Muslims who were closest, geographically, to the point of attack. This, however, was not meant to be a blank check for the use of force—such as that which would allow any individual Muslims to "to participate in jihad and the Resistance . . . in this battle against America, in his country, or anywhere."[51]

In addition to this, however, al-Suri's model demonstrates the importance of the legitimate authority criterion to the Western just war tradition. As noted, the legitimate authority criterion requires that those who undertake the use of force have the appropriate authority to do so. This authority can be transferred from standing governments (or political leaders) to a group of irregular actors once certain provisions have been met—specifically provisions demonstrating that the standing government has lost that authority (through acts of tyranny and injustice) and that the irregulars hold popular support. However, al-Suri specifically—and al-Qaeda more generally—do not represent any state, political space, or distinct community from which they might claim popular support or that could legitimate their grievances.[52] They cannot acquire legitimate authority because there is no authority for them to claim. In this way, the criterion categorically refutes the notion that al-Suri's arguments on the proper use of force are legitimate or justified. Even if we concede that al-Suri's accusations are verifiable, or even arguable, the legitimate authority criterion restricts his use of those arguments as basis for the legitimate use of force—as his argument sits outside the authority to use force on behalf of a discernible political community.

CONCLUSION

Fabre argues that citizens of a political community may acquire the right to rise up against tyranny and injustice. Insofar as this is the case, the justice of wars is not dependent on a declaration by those who fall under the traditional definition of legitimate authority. Consequently, for Fabre, the criterion loses its utility. As noted above, just war thinking shares this position. However, through the legitimate authority criterion, the tradition maintains the need to designate the authority to undertake war to a select group of people, and maintains that directing the use of force toward justice requires doing so.

Highlighting the criterion's ability to provide guidance is not to dismiss the fact, noted by Fabre and others, that states are extremely reluctant to grant authority to irregular actors. This is undoubtedly true. Yet it seems prudent to investigate the criterion's ability to deal with the tyranny and injustice of standing groups than to drop it altogether. As noted, if it becomes the case that those who are responsible for the welfare of the political community are no longer adhering to their responsibilities, particularly in the case where they are threatening the fundamental rights of their citizens, the authority to wage war is transferred to the citizens. However, for the historical tradition of just war thinking, determining *when* this is the case cannot be done without the criterion. As noted, there are certainly cases in which nonstate actors have both the legitimacy and cause to use force against a standing government. However, a judicious analysis of any use of force must begin from the assumption that war is not a weapon to be undertaken by every party who brings a grievance to the international arena. Al-Suri's model is evidence for the importance of this claim.

Furthermore, such an examination demonstrates that the just war criteria ought to be understood as interconnected. Although each requires separate consideration and analysis, the just war criteria work in concert to inform all interested parties about the overall character of a particular use of force. Anything short of this truncates the ability of the tradition to provide an ethical framework—one that maintains a clear purpose, as well as discernible limits, for the use of force.

NOTES

The positions expressed in this chapter are my personal views. I do not represent the Naval War College, the Department of Defense, or the US government, and my views are not necessarily shared by them.

1. Although recent events have once again brought the notion of guerilla warfare into prominent view, the notion of insurgency is traced to the ancient world, as specialists date guerilla tactics to as far back as 516 BCE. However, the understanding of insurgents as legitimate combatants is a concept dating back only a century or so. See Robert Aspery, *War in the Shadows: The Guerrilla in History Volume I and II* (Garden City, NY: Doubleday, 1975); and John Ellis, *A Short History of Guerilla Warfare* (New York: St. Martin's Press, 1976).

2. See Brent J. Steele and Eric A. Heinze, eds., *Ethics, Authority and War: Non-State Actors and the Just War Tradition* (New York: Palgrave Macmillan, 2009), esp. the chapters by Cian O'Driscoll, "From Versailles to 9/11: Non-State Actors and Just War in the Twentieth Century," and Anthony F. Lang, "Authority and the Problem of Non-State Actors."

3. Cecile Fabre, "Cosmopolitanism, Just War Theory, and Legitimate Authority," *International Affairs* 84, no. 5 (2008): 967.

4. He is also known as Mustafa bin Abd al Qadir Setmariam Nasar.

5. For al-Suri, the "Muslim World" refers to all lands that were under Muslim control at any point in Islamic history.

6. See Nahed Artoul Zehr, "Just War and Jihad in the War against Al-Qaeda" (PhD diss., Florida State University, 2011).

7. Irregular actors challenging the authority of *a particular* state in order to install a different governing order. The peculiar combination of al-Qaeda's military tactics renders it an organization that defies straightforward categorization. Though it displays certain elements typically attributed to insurgency groups, its global reach makes the insurgency category problematic. And though it privileges the use of terror as a tactic in its military arsenal, its penetration into Iraq, Afghanistan, and Pakistan (among others)—in other words, its global agenda—lends it qualities that make the terrorist label appear too restrictive. Michael L. Gross makes similar claims in chapter 12 of this volume, "Just War and Guerilla War."

8. This chapter understands the Western just war tradition as one that takes a multitude of voices, perspectives, and arguments into its fold. However, it also understands the tradition, as such, to be, in the words of James Turner Johnson, a "repository" of the various ways that the Western world has thought about issues of force, peace, statecraft, and justice. For a discussion of both points, see Cian O'Driscoll, *Renegotiation of the Just War Tradition and the Right to War in the Twenty-First Century* (New York: Palgrave Macmillan, 208), 91–116. The differences between the Islamic and the Western just war tradition's categories of legitimate authority are noted by this chapter. However, this chapter also notes that there is a significant overlap between them as categories denoting a just war, and therefore they may be juxtaposed for the purposes of this chapter. For a discussion of similarities and differences between Islamic and Western just war traditions, see John Kelsay, *Islam and Just War: A Study in Comparative Ethics* (Louisville: Westminster John Knox Press, 1993); John Kelsay, *Arguing the Just War in Islam* (Cambridge, MA: Harvard University Press, 2007); and James Turner Johnson, *The Holy War Idea in Western and Islamic Traditions* (University Park: Pennsylvania State University Press, 2005).

9. See also chapter 1 in this volume by James Turner Johnson, "The Right to Use Armed Force: Sovereignty, Responsibility, and the Common Good."

10. Note here that Fred McGraw Donner argues that the Islamic conception of war was influenced by pre-Islamic conceptions of warfare. See Fred McGraw Donner, "The Sources of Islamic Conceptions of War," in *Just War and Jihad: Historical and Theoretical Perspectives on War and Peace in Western and Islamic Traditions,* ed. John Kelsay and James Turner Johnson (New York: Greenwood Press, 1991), 31–69; and Fred McGraw Donner, *The Early Islamic Conquests* (Princeton, NJ: Princeton University Press, 1981), 11–49.

11. The word "jihad" has multiple meanings—all oriented around the struggle to fulfill God's will. This struggle is manifold and varied, and includes activities such as prayer, fasting, and the intentional attempt to purify one's mind and heart in a manner that is pleasing to God. In addition, however, it also has historically been used to designate a class of warfare that is waged in the path of God and religion and oriented toward the achievement of justice and peace as understood through the Islamic tradition. For a more detailed account, see Kelsay, *Islam and Just War.*

12. See Muhammad al-Shaybani, *The Islamic Law of Nations,* trans. Majid Khaduri (Baltimore: Johns Hopkins University Press, 1966).

13. Majid Khadduri, *War and Peace in the Law of Islam* (London: Oxford University Press, 1955).

14. The duty to defend was extended to Muslims who were outside the immediate area of attack only in the case where those closest to the attack were unable to repel the invading forces successfully.

15. Khadduri, *War and Peace*; Muhammad al-Shaybani, *The Islamic Law of Nations*, trans. Majid Khadduri (Baltimore: Johns Hopkins University Press, 1966); Donner, *Early Islamic Conquest.*

16. It is important to mention that the aims of this chapter are not to discuss al-Suri's theological credentials or merits. In other words, the purpose is not to answer whether or not his understanding is "real" Islam. Rather, the goal is to demonstrate the manner in which al-Suri draws upon the theological building blocks of a historical tradition in order to interpret international politics, and to determine a proper—and *novel*—course of action in light of the theological commitments of a religious subcommunity that he claims to represent.

17. See Ibn Jarir al-Tabari, *Al-Tabari's Book of Jihad*, trans. Yasir S. Ibrahim (Lewiston, ME: Edwin Mellen Press, 2007); and Abdulaziz A. Sachedina, "The Development of Jihad in Islamic Revelation and History," in *Cross, Crescent, and Sword* (New York: Greenwood Press, 1990), 35–50.

18. This treatise can be downloaded at www.archive.org/details/The-call-for-a-global-Islamic-resistance.

19. Al-Suri, *The Global Islamic Resistance Call* (Arabic), 52.

20. Although al-Suri is particularly focused on the contemporary issues, he mentions that this process of decline (due to foreign dominance) was initiated with the fall of the Abbasid caliphate, and has continued uninterrupted until the present, save for a reprieve during the Ottoman Caliphate, when the Muslim world once again experienced a period of strength and regeneration. See Jim Lacey, *A Terrorist's Call to Global Jihad: Deciphering Abu Musab al-Suri's Islamic Jihad Manifesto* (Annapolis, MD: Naval Institute Press, 2008), 30–47.

21. Ibid., 30–32.

22. Ibid., 39–47.

23. Al-Suri, *Global Islamic Resistance Call*, 138; author's translation.

24. Lacey, *Terrorist's Call*, 16.

25. Ibid., 175–76.

26. Ibid., 25–26; Brynjar Lia, *Architect of Global Jihad: The Life of al-Qaida Strategist Abu Mus'ab al-Suri* (New York: Columbia University Press, 2009), 428.

27. Al-Suri, *Global Islamic Resistance Call*, 137; author's translation.

28. English-language translations of quotations from the Quran are from the Abdullah Yusuf Ali translation.

29. Al-Suri, *Global Islamic Resistance Call*, 41; author's translation.

30. Lia, *Architect of Global Jihad*, 359.

31. Ibid., 373.

32. Ibid., 419.

33. Ibid., 422–23.

34. Ibid., 370.

35. E.g., Navy SEAL Admiral Eric T. Olson has talked of an "al-Qaeda 2.0," a derivative of Osama bin Laden's "al-Qaeda 1.0"; "Special Ops Chief Warns of Al Qaeda 2.0," *San Jose Mercury News*, July 28th, 2011.

36. Middle East Media Research Institute, Jihad and Terrorist Studies Project, Inquiry and Analysis 698, June 22, 2011.

37. Cecile Fabre, "Cosmopolitanism, Just War Theory, and Legitimate Authority," *International Affairs* 84, no. 5 (2008): 965.

38. Ibid.

39. Related to Fabre's point, here, John Williams notes that the authority of the state is not only contested by irregular actors, but—as demonstrated by the February 2003 protests in London against the impending invasion of Iraq—it is also contested by regular citizens. See chapter 4 in this volume by John Williams, " 'Not in My Name'? Legitimate Authority and Liberal Just War Theory."

40. Fabre, "Cosmopolitanism," 967.

41. Ibid., 967–71.

42. For a discussion of legitimate authority in the just war tradition, I am deeply indebted to James Turner Johnson. In particular, see James Turner Johnson, "Aquinas and Luther on War and Peace: Sovereign Authority and the Use of Armed Force," *Journal of Religious Ethics* 31, no. 3 (Spring 2003): 9; and chapter 1 in this volume by James Turner Johnson, "Right to Use Armed Force."

43. Fabre, "Cosmopolitanism," 967.

44. ST II/II, Q. 40, A. 1 See Johnson, "Aquinas and Luther," 9.

45. Johnson, "Aquinas and Luther," 9.

46. Ibid.; Johnson, chapter 1 in this volume, "Right to Use Armed Force."

47. This term was brought to my attention by Martin L. Cook.

48. This set of provisions is as follows: (1) to be commanded by a person responsible for his subordinates; (2) to have a fixed distinctive emblem recognizable at a distance; (3) to carry arms openly; (4) to conduct their operations in accordance with the laws and customs of war; and (5) in countries where militia or volunteer corps constitute the army, or form part of it, they are included under the denomination "army."

49. Michael Walzer, *Just and Unjust War: A Moral Argument with Historical Illustrations* (New York: Basic Books, 1977), 187.

50. Nicholas Rengger also notes the danger involved when the just war tradition's emphasis on the limits of war are eroded, and particularly through teleocratic inclinations that are present in popular public appeal to the just war tradition's moral concepts and language. See chapter 16 in this volume by Nicholas Rengger, "The Wager Lost by Winning: On the 'Triumph' of the Just War Tradition."

51. See note 31 above.

52. For a discussion on al-Qaeda's claims to authority in reference to the just war tradition, see O'Driscoll, "From Versailles to 9/11."

CHAPTER 7

Problems of Legitimacy within the Just War Tradition and International Law

Tarik Kochi

It's not a war. It's a naughty boy.

—graffito, Belfast

Justice removed, then, what are kingdoms but great bands of robbers? What are bands of robbers themselves but little kingdoms? The band itself is made up of men; it is governed by the authority of a ruler; it is bound together by a pact of association; and the loot is divided according to agreed law. If, by the constant addition of desperate men, this scourge grows to such a size that it acquires territory, establishes a seat of government, occupies cities and subjugates peoples, it assumes the name of kingdom more openly. For this name is now manifestly conferred upon it not by the removal of greed, but by the addition of impunity. It was a pertinent and true answer which was made to Alexander the Great by a pirate whom he had seized. When the king asked him what he meant by infesting the sea, the pirate defiantly replied: 'The same as you do when you infest the whole world; but because I do it with a little ship I am called a robber, and because you do it with a great fleet, you are an emperor'.

—Augustine, *City of God against the Pagans*

"JUSTICE REMOVED, THEN, what are kingdoms but great bands of robbers?"[1] Augustine's question does not go away. It calls forth the problem of the "just war"—when can a human kill without sin, what separates a legitimate act of killing from murder, what separates the violence of maintaining public "order" and "security" from mere banditry? The just war tradition, first as a theological tradition, and then in many secular variants, makes the distinction between "just" and "unjust" wars through the use of moral principles or criteria. In relation to the *jus ad bellum*, these criteria sometimes include the requirement that a war be waged by a "legitimate authority," for a "just cause," with "right intention," and carried out with "proportionality." Further, a war must be carried out only if there is a "reasonable chance of success," as a "last resort," and for the purpose of "securing peace."[2]

Through moral judgment guided by these criteria, the just war tradition attempts to introduce some concerns of justice into the haze of war, making the question of whether an act of war is legitimate or illegitimate a moral question and not abandoning such a decision solely to the status quo of legal positivism or to the so-called realism of power politics. Through these criteria just war scholars across the tradition have built a tower of arguments in which the moral theory of just war has historically been used to condemn acts of brutality and aggression, *and* used to justify uncountable acts of aggression, killing, and violence, especially within the colonial sphere. For some, the use of just war theory has "triumphed," though not unproblematically, on the international stage. Its language and criteria have been widely adopted by statesmen, generals, political theorists, and international lawyers.[3] For others, just war theory was and has become the language of "empire," a dominant moral rhetoric and charade that hides contemporary imperial and neo-colonial aggression.[4]

However, underneath each of these views resides the question raised by Augustine that does not go away. Justice removed, what separates the "morally legitimate" act of war from the violent tantrum of a naughty boy? The question troubles the traditional criteria set up by the just war tradition and does so by unsettling the concept of "right," "proper," or "legitimate" "authority." Within just war theory, and within aspects of contemporary international law, for a war to be considered "just" it must be waged by a legitimate authority. But who or what is a legitimate authority?

In this chapter I discuss three problems of legitimacy within the just war tradition. First, I argue that the question of legitimacy cannot easily be separated from a history of colonialism within which the just war tradition is heavily complicit. Second, I argue that the just war tradition needs to be understood not merely as a form of advice given to princes and sovereigns but also as forming part of a praxis of political theory drawn upon by international actors to attempt to trump the legitimacy claims of their rivals. Third, I argue that the violence of the so-called just war itself plays a productive role in creating and sustaining new historical forms of "legitimate" governance while destroying others. My general argument is that a contemporary tendency within just war theory and international law to use just war concepts either as a form of (quasi-Kantian) universal, abstract moral theory or as a form of (neo-Aristotelian) practical (prudential) wisdom to guide policymakers, often ignores these three problems of legitimacy that trouble the just war tradition.[5] When the tradition is approached uncritically—that is, when these and other similar questions are ignored, suppressed, or forgotten—then just war theory ceases to be a form of valid moral reasoning and drifts into the domain of dogma. As dogma, the tradition is easily mobilized by those in power as a tool to legitimate political ends.[6] If the tradition is to have any value, if it is worth thinking about the concept of the *jus ad bellum* at all, then the tradition cannot be approached uncritically; the tradition cannot be separated from, and thought in isolation of, the problem of legitimacy.

JUST WAR AS COLONIALISM

It was not for merely early-morning grumpiness that Immanuel Kant in his essay "Perpetual Peace" (1795) denounced the theories of just war and international law proposed by Grotius, Pufendorf, and Vattel as being those of "sorry comforters."[7] For Kant these thinkers produced a moral theory of war that abused the right of "hospitality" and mobilized moral philosophy to justify wars of colonial appropriation waged by European powers.[8] For Kant sorry comforters were those who used a moral theory to serve and promote the interests of the state and who attempted to render legitimate the theft, bloodshed, and occupation of the European practice of colonialism. Kant was not merely criticizing those "realist" statesmen who thought morality was absent in world affairs, but more so, his critique was directed against moral theorists—just war theorists and early-modern international law-yers—whose moral theory expressed a claim about the legitimacy of certain actions that either directly or indirectly supported the practice of European colonization in the non-European world.

However, Kant's remark does not condemn the whole of the just war tradition nor the role of moral theory in coming to terms with the problem of war. What it does is to draw into focus a historical link between the *use* of just war theory and the *practice* of colonialism. To draw attention to this link is not to condemn all theorists or political actors who draw upon the just war tradition as rabid, blood-thirsty (or gold-thirsty, or oil-thirsty) colonial adventurers. Rather, it is to think about how a particular tradition of moral theory has been used throughout history to justify various colonial projects and, then, to pause and consider whether particular instances of the use of such a moral theory today continue to justify forms of neocolonialism.

The ways in which the content of the concept of legitimate authority was pro-duced by just war theorists historically often drew heavily upon assertions about the nature of political authority in which non-Europeans were either excluded or trumped. Often, because the just war tradition drew heavily upon the universalist tradition of natural law, the possibility of groups holding legitimate political author-ity (and therefore viewed as immune from merely having their lives and possessions confiscated and able to wage a defensive just war) was open to non-Europeans. Yet for many just war theorists, the concept of legitimate authority still operated as a key tool for justifying colonialism. Two examples help to illustrate this point.

One example of a not-unproblematic link between the just war tradition and a history of colonialism is the work of the theologian and scholastic philosopher Francisco De Vitoria. In *On the American Indians* (1539) and *On the Law of War* (1539), Vitoria approaches a set of theological questions relating to what constitutes a "just war."[9] These respond critically to various arguments used to justify the Spanish conquest of much of the Western Hemisphere and also relate to concerns held by some Spaniards about the brutal treatment of the Amerindians. Vitoria considers the issue of whether the Amerindians lack political authority over themselves or ownership over their lands and possessions. In this respect he asks whether the Amerindians can be considered in an Aristotelian sense as either "true masters" or "natural slaves."[10] Vitoria's conclusion is that the Amerindians are rational, that they are true masters and cannot be disposed without just cause, and that they are deprived of their dominion neither by way of being sinners nor because of unbelief.[11] He insists that they exercise judgment in their affairs, such as through the organization of cities, laws, industry and commerce, and religion—all of which indicate the exercise of reason.[12] By establishing that the Amerindians are rational humans who are not to be considered natural slaves, Vitoria is able to extend his theory of natural law to govern the relations between Spanish and Amerindians and thus argue for a need to respect and recognize their property rights and political institutions.[13]

Vitoria's recognition of the political authority of the Amerindians has sometimes been held up as a model of a liberal, civilized moment in international law—that is, when a non-European people are recognized as holding independent and equal legal status with European peoples regardless of cultural differences.[14] Yet such a view is not entirely correct. Vitoria's account, though recognizing a general level of legitimate political authority held by different Amerindian peoples, still ends up justifying the Spanish colonial project through a formal legal strategy that elevates certain European values to a higher level of legitimacy, which then acts to trump particular non-European claims.

Vitoria keeps in reserve a number of higher rights that he recognizes the Spanish as holding but does not (or could not) recognize the Amerindians as holding in reciprocity. For example, he argues that on the authority of the law of nations, which is derived from natural law, the Spanish have a right to travel and dwell in America as long as they do not harm the local inhabitants.[15] That the Spanish have a right to lawfully trade (i.e., carry out commerce), and they possess forms of property that are held in common (i.e., digging for gold on common land or in rivers).[16] He argues that if the Amerindians deny the Spanish these rights and do not listen to the reasoning and persuasion of the Spanish and instead inflict violence (even if only out of fear), then the Spanish have a just cause to go to war in self-defense to redress or avenge the injury done to them.[17] Further, Vitoria grants the Spanish a right to preach the gospel and consequently a just cause to go to war if they are attacked or harmed when doing so.[18] In addition, he claims that if the political leaders of the Amerindians are tyrants or carry out oppressive laws such as human sacrifice, then the Spanish have a lawful right to intervene, and if necessary, to depose their political leaders and their laws and set up new ones.[19]

Under such an account the recognition of Amerindian political authority is limited by Vitoria's broader theory of legitimate authority grounded within natural law. His account of natural law does not simply privilege commerce and Christianity but also offers Europeans a right (and duty) of intervention when aspects of natural law are seemingly violated by non-Europeans (i.e., the duty to intervene to stop human sacrifice). The argument involves a sleight of hand privileging the colonial agency of Europeans via recourse to a theory of legitimacy grounded in a "universal" and "neutral" doctrine of international law as a component of natural law.[20]

A second example of the link between just war theory and colonialism can be found in the work of Hugo Grotius. In contrast to Vitoria, Grotius's theory of just war relied upon a "secular" account of political authority that could be proposed as acceptable to warring religious and civil factions in Europe in the seventeenth century.[21] For Grotius, natural law was secularized so as to delink it from religious institutions. He argued (in a terminology that echoes throughout the history of liberal political theory) that because natural law is based upon "human nature" and "human reason," it remained valid even if God did not exist.[22]

Grotius jettisoned much of the thick content of the Aristotelian "good" found in Aquinas and Vitoria in favor of a minimalist natural law. The legitimate authority of the sovereign was grounded upon its ability to secure and safeguard its subject's natural rights. This shift (later inherited and further developed by Hobbes and Locke) enunciated a modern form of liberal legal-political "legitimate" authority whereby the sovereign's right to rule was derived from its subject's "natural" or "human rights" and from the metaphorical "contract" in which some individual rights are given up so that the sovereign may ensure peace, security, good order, and safety from external threat.[23] By grounding legitimate authority upon natural rights, Grotius's conception developed a secular account of legal-political authority that, as described by Max Weber, the sovereign held a "monopoly upon the legitimacy of violence" within its territory.[24]

Such a conceptual innovation helped to articulate the "Westphalian" model of sovereignty upon which modern international law is built and developed an account of right or legitimate authority that could be adapted to fit a variety of peoples regardless of their religious beliefs and cultural differences. A political body could be recognized by others as a legitimate authority, as sovereign, as long as it could ensure a degree of peace within its territory and secure its subject's natural rights to life and property.[25]

However, again, the specter of colonialism hangs over Grotius's secular reformu-
lation of just war theory. The form of international law whereby sovereigns gain
their legitimacy through their ability to protect natural rights opens the door for
Grotius to argue for a host of European colonial interventions in the territory of
non-Europeans so as to "defend" natural rights. In this respect, the early-modern
Grotian account of natural rights presents a theory of political legitimacy that claims
to be "universal" and culturally "neutral" and yet is drawn upon in particular cases
to trump the claims of non-European peoples who are portrayed as abusing these
rights. Grotius develops a just war theory of "humanitarian intervention" of very
wide scope that is used to foster and offer legitimacy to a variety of European
colonial ends.

Grotius, in *The Rights of War and Peace* (1625), argues:[26]

> We must also know, that Kings, and those who are invested with a Power
> equal to that of Kings, have a Right to exact Punishments, not only for Injur-
> ies committed against themselves, or their Subjects, but likewise, for those
> which do not peculiarly concern them, but which are in any Persons whatso-
> ever, grievous Violations of the Law of Nature or Nations. For the Liberty of
> consulting the Benefit of human Society, by Punishments, which at first, as
> we have said, was in every particular Person, does now, since Civil Societies,
> and Courts of Justice, have been instituted, reside in those who are possessed
> of the supreme Power, and that properly, not as they have an Authority over
> others, but as they are Subject to none. For, as for others, their Subjection has
> taken from them this Right. Nay, it is so much more honourable, to revenge
> other Peoples Injuries rather than their own, by as much as it is more to be
> feared, lest out of a Sense of their own Sufferings, they either exceed the just
> Measure of Punishment, or, at least, prosecute their Revenge with Malice. . . .
> For the same Reason we make no Doubt, but War may be justly undertaken
> against those who are inhuman to their Parents, as were the *Sogdians*, before
> *Alexander* persuaded them to renounce their Brutality; and against those who
> eat human Flesh, from which Custom *Hercules* compelled the ancient *Gauls*
> to desist, as *Diodorus* relates and against those who practice Piracy.[27]

Following this:

> And so we follow the Opinion of *Innocentius*, and others, who hold that War
> is lawful against those who offend against Nature; which is contrary to the
> Opinion of *Victoria*, *Vasquez*, *Azorius*, *Molina* and others, who seem to
> require, towards making a War just, that he who undertakes it be injured
> himself, or in his State, or that he has some Jurisdiction over the Person
> against whom the War is made. For they assert, that the Power of Punishing
> is properly an Effect of Civil Jurisdiction; whereas our Opinion is, that it
> proceeds from the Law of Nature.[28]

Commenting on these passages, Richard Tuck argues:

> It is remarkable—and, I think, completely unrecognized by modern schol-
> ars—that Grotius specifically aligned himself with Innocent IV against Vitoria
> on this crucial issue. The idea that foreign rulers can punish tyrants, cannibals,
> pirates, those who killed settlers, and those who are inhuman to their parents
> neatly legitimated a great deal of European action against native peoples
> around the world, and was disconcertingly close to the extreme pre-Vitorian
> arguments used by the Spaniards in America. . . . The central reason why
> Grotius had developed his argument in this direction was, I think, that the
> Dutch had begun to change the character of their activity in the non-
> European world since his earlier works, and in particular had begun to annex
> territory.[29]

It does not take a great leap of one's imagination to substitute the formal legal
arguments about political and legal legitimacy given by Vitoria and Grotius to those
given by many international lawyers and just war scholars today arguing for acts of
war on the basis of "humanitarian intervention" and the "responsibility to protect."[30] Central components of the modern international order (state sovereignty,
human rights) are the descendents of the theories of natural law developed by figures like Vitoria and Grotius—indeed, the shadow of their theories of just war hang
heavily over our modern understanding of the laws of war and the principle of
humanitarian intervention. As such, just as it would be wrong to dismiss the links
between the theory of legitimate authority and practice of colonialism in the history
of the just war tradition, it would be naive to ignore the possible links between
contemporary uses of just war theory and neocolonial practices today. This colonial
history troubles the just war tradition, and to ignore it or wish it away would be to
accept too quickly the sometimes-convincing rhetoric of today's sorry comforters.

JUST WAR AS CONTESTING AUTHORITY

In one sense different instantiations of the just war tradition appear as efforts of
theologians, philosophers, and moral theorists to give advice to the prince or sovereign about what might be a just or unjust course of violent action. Understood in
this way, the conceptual apparatus of the tradition is used as a tool whereby moral
theory attempts to guide the art of political action and may even be used by sovereigns to reflect upon the moral justifications and limitations of war when faced with
difficult political decisions.[31]

However, another and not-unconnected sense of the tradition is its role as a
praxis of political theory whereby the theorist develops an account of legitimate
authority for a particular sovereign or legal order in the effort to trump the legitimacy claims of rival political communities. The just war tradition, when viewed as

a whole, constitutes a set of texts involving continual moments of challenge and contestation as each thinker attempts to rethink, shift, and reorder what counts as the ground or basis of legal and political authority. Just war theory can be viewed as a form of legal and political theory that seeks to establish what counts as "moral authority," and often this is what the category of "legitimate authority" is reflecting within the tradition.

Viewed in this way one can reread the canon of key texts within the tradition as diverse efforts of theologians, philosophers, and moral theorists attempting to reconceptualize the grounds for what counts as legal and political authority. Such a practice is more than merely giving advice to the prince; it involves determining who might rightfully claim to be a prince (or sovereign state) in the first place—that is, positing the criteria whereby a particular group might be recognized or acknowledged as holding the status of a "legitimate authority" and establishing the limits of any such authority in light of an existence (or absence in the case of a "state of nature") of some higher form of authority.

Thought of in this way, the writings of Augustine, Aquinas, Vitoria, Grotius, and so on all offer differing accounts of what constitutes legal and political authority in a broad sense and point to particular actors in concrete cases whose claims to holding "legitimate authority" (and hence the right to use violence) may or may not be recognized. Significantly, what counts as being recognized as a legitimate authority in the concrete case (the barbarian, the Protestant, the Amerindian, the pirate, or the rebellious peasant army) depends upon the broader, background theory of legitimacy that is assumed or articulated by each particular theorist. In turn, each theorist is writing against a host of other views of legitimacy, and these views may not merely be differing attempts to advise the prince but, rather, competing philosophical and moral visions asserting a sovereign claim of rival princes or rival legal orders.[32]

To ignore this function is to miss much of the core of the just war tradition and to misunderstand its practical function historically. The just war tradition is a history of contestation over the nature of legal and political authority, and the criteria of legitimate authority are the least stable aspect of the tradition. To think about how this occurs today, one merely needs to look briefly at how the category of legitimate authority is contested within contemporary international law.[33]

By 1945 Kant's cosmopolitan dream of an international federation of states bound by law and directed at the preservation of peace and human rights found itself pushed into some semblance of reality by the victorious powers through the Constitution of the United Nations.[34] In many ways the structure built upon Grotius's protoliberal conception of the founding of the secular state's authority upon the preservation of internal peace and protection of natural rights.[35] In the new international law's model, the authority of the federation was constituted through the metaphor of the "contract" between states that gave up particular rights (i.e., the absolute right to war) in favor of an executive body (the United Nations Security Council, UNSC) whose role was to protect the rights of states, act as judge between their disputes (in concert with the International Court of Justice), and decide when force should be used to "maintain or restore international peace and security."[36]

The UN Charter developed a dual system of international legitimate authority shared between individual states and the UNSC. The extent to which the authority to use violence is given up by states under the UN Charter is a matter of continued contention and disagreement for international lawyers. Those lawyers taking the "wider view" consider the language of the UN Charter in Article 51 to preserve and not erode a right to self-defense held by states under customary international law, which for some allows a concept of anticipatory self-defense. Others taking the "narrow view" consider the UN Charter to limit the state's right to self-defense to merely the conditions of an "armed attack,"[37] to generally prohibit the use of force by states, and limit their authority to use force to situations clearly mandated by the UNSC.[38] The level of fundamental disagreement between international lawyers over the scope and boundaries of these two forms of legitimate authority was seen most clearly in the endless debates about the invasion and occupation of Iraq by the United States and Britain (2003).[39] According to "positive" international law, there is no clear and agreed-on conception of what constitutes and delineates these spheres of legitimate authority; there is only legal argument, disagreement, rhetoric, and counterrhetoric. In this context, states and their international lawyers often switch their rhetorical positions over time, justifying their actions by differing sources of authority when it promotes their diverse set of interests.[40]

A similar position exists in relation to the emergence of a "higher" form of authority in the shape of human rights. First, there is no consensus within international law as to the exact content of "human rights," no agreement over whether "civil and political rights" have any priority over "economic and social rights," and no agreement over the nature of the "human" who is affirmed by such rights.[41] Second, international lawyers continue to be divided over the question of to what extent human rights constitute a form of "authority" that mandates the use of force. One position is that the collective security arrangements under UN Charter Article 1 (3) (the promotion of human rights) authorize the UNSC to use force to prevent grave human rights violations. This norm, sometimes labeled the "responsibility to protect," is linked to a developing, so-called "human security" turn within international law, the position well stated in the language of many international reports:[42] "We endorse the emerging norm that there is a responsibility to protect, exercisable by the Security Council authorizing military intervention as a last resort, in the event of genocide and other large scale killing, ethnic cleansing, or serious violations of humanitarian law which sovereign Governments have proved powerless or unwilling to prevent."[43]

Such a source of authority granting the UNSC the right to use violence to protect human rights is not expressly stated in the UN Charter, and it remains a matter of some contention within customary international law. Further, legal disagreement extends to the case in which individual states claim to act under the authority of human rights in the absence of express UNSC authorization, such as during NATO's bombing of Kosovo (1999).[44] The claim by states to act in accordance with the responsibility to protect contradicts the "narrow view" of the collective security arrangements of the UN Charter and radically expands the scope of authority under which states might legitimately use force, even aggressively, in the "defense" of human rights. Significantly, many international law arguments in favor of such a norm repeat an overtly moral language and set of justifications reminiscent of seventeenth-century natural law.[45]

What is contested within contemporary international law is not simply the scope of any particular "just cause" (i.e., arguments over the nature and limits of self-defense and intervention) but, more centrally, the issue of who has the *authority* to decide when violence should be used to maintain "peace and security" internationally or to protect against grave violations of "human rights." This issue is sometimes framed as a Hobbesian or Schmittian question, yet this question has a long history, and concerns and troubles the whole of the just war tradition.[46] Maintaining domestic and international order and protecting individuals who live both inside and outside a sovereign's territory are primarily questions of legitimate authority residing at the core of the just war tradition. As was seen with the examples of Vitoria and Grotius, each produced differing interpretations of international law (derived from natural law) that gave particular sovereigns the authority to intervene in matters beyond their territory. Each acted as an "adviser" to their respective governments, attempting to define the scope of legitimate authority against competing visions in the hope of limiting action in some cases and expanding it in others. Contemporary debates within international law (drawn upon by just war theorists) continue a tradition of political theory that attempts to articulate the scope and limits of such authority against rival accounts. The shift from natural rights to human rights still involves a praxis whereby the theorist or the lawyer as "adviser" proposes an argument for one normative, institutional, or metaphysical *form* of legitimacy in the effort to trump historical or rival contemporary accounts.[47]

Such advice giving is sometimes rendered further problematic when arguments about the defense of human rights are extended to include nonsovereign actors that use violence, such as rebels, revolutionary movements, self-determination movements, partisans, and terrorists.

Within twentieth-century international law and its contemporary form, states retain their role as agents recognized as holding the primary authority to use violence within their own territory. Although human rights norms imposed limits upon the extent to which a state could legitimately use violence against its citizens in the case of grave human rights abuses, the state's right to maintain peace and security within its territory is broadly affirmed.[48] The development of human rights norms during the twentieth century did not generally revive within international law a right to private violence or right to violent resistance by nonstate groups or individuals. Generally, the delegitimization and criminalization of nonstate violence by seventeenth-century natural law have carried through and up into contemporary international law. In this respect international law has privileged the authoritarian aspects of Grotius's (and later Hobbes's) theory of natural law and pushed to the side radical elements of the tradition, which, as in aspects of Locke's natural law theory, upholds a "right of resistance" and considers individuals (and groups of individuals) as possessing a "legitimate authority" to use violence against the monarch who violates their natural rights.[49] This is not to say that such a right to resistance is completely suppressed by international law; but its status remains controversial and contested, as with the example of the right to "self-determination."[50]

The extent to which violent resistance authorized by the right of self-determination forms part of customary international law is a matter of disagreement between international lawyers who take diverging views.[51] After the bombings in the United States in 2001, the rhetoric of many international lawyers has often moved quickly to conflate the right of resistance with the label of "terrorism."[52] However, the legitimate authority of nonstate groups to violently resist an oppressive state or occupying power in the name of a differing conception of "human rights," "freedom," or "justice" remains an open question for international law.[53] The issue of violent resistance in the name of human rights by nonstate actors will not go away, at least as long as international law and the UN Charter hold onto the claim that human rights and the right to self-determination form part of its "purposes and principles." Given that contemporary international law has been built upon natural law foundations, it will be continually troubled by the more radical aspects of the natural law/human rights tradition that does not accept that dignity or freedom or justice is something that descends from above but is something authorized, demanded, and realized from below. In the words of Ernst Bloch: "Genuine natural law, which posits the free will in accord with reason, was the first to reclaim the justice that can only be obtained through struggle; it did not understand justice as something that descends from above and prescribes to each his share, distributing or retaliating, but rather as an active justice of below, one that would make justice itself unnecessary."[54]

The flip side of the Kantian, natural law, cosmopolitan dream of an international law securing peace and human rights is an active "subaltern cosmopolitanism" constituted by the resistance and struggle of nonstate actors against hegemonic colonial and neocolonial forms of "legitimate authority."[55] It is a radical reworking of the cosmopolitan hope in which Kant's categorical imperative, the modern rational spirit of a denaturalized natural law, grounds its authority in the demand to realize human dignity. In the words of Karl Marx, also an inheritor of the natural law tradition, it is "the categorical imperative to overthrow all conditions in which man is a degraded, enslaved, neglected, contemptible being."[56] This line of thinking finds itself in the hands of nonstate groups—liberation movements, revolutionaries—that claim also the notion of the just war. This is a claim of a just war fought against the authority of God, against the state, against colonialism, and against capitalism. Such a theory of just war may also locate its source of legitimate authority in the idea of communism.[57] In the words of Bloch, this occurs as the "categorical imperative with revolver in hand."[58]

What this reading of the contemporary laws of war and the right to resistance suggests is that the concept of legitimate authority, today, remains contested. Contemporary international law inherits not simply the abstract rules and categories of natural law and the just war tradition but also a praxis of political theory that attempts to redefine the grounds of what constitutes legal and political authority and does so via the writing of charters, through legal advice to governments and through the calls of the dispossessed to higher forms of authority.

From this perspective the just war theorist who gives "advice" to the government of a sovereign state or to a revolutionary social movement can be situated within a broader historical tradition of natural law. At the core of the natural law tradition is an intellectual and social praxis of contesting one form of authority by positing a claim to a *higher* authority.[59] This may involve a critique of positive laws and customs via an appeal to a higher law, or it may involve the attempt to justify positive laws and existing institutions through their instantiation of a higher law. The history of natural law plays out continual appeals to forms of authority that may legitimate earthly action—nature, reason, divine law, natural rights, human rights. Each is taken on and used at differing times to challenge existing authorities and to propose an alternative future, *or* to justify the continued existence of particular institutions that safeguard peace and order in the present. Both the just war tradition and modern international law inherit this dual aspect of natural law; it is the "Janus face," as Bloch calls it, whereby appeals to the authority of a not-yet-realized liberty and social justice (i.e., the slogan "another world is possible") are pitched against a global legal order aimed at protecting "international peace and security."

JUST WAR AS CREATIVE-DESTRUCTIVE FORCE

One way of thinking about the role of violence in the just war tradition, perhaps one that is most common for moral theorists and international lawyers, is to think of violence as a tool, an instrument, something used to achieve certain legal or moral ends—violence as a sword, used (sometimes reluctantly, sometimes aggressively) by a legitimate authority. In this sense the notion of a legitimate authority and the act of violence are held apart, separate. One is viewed as a question of appropriate agency, the other as a question of the appropriate moral cause and ends (and means) of the violence used by the appropriate agent. The notions of authority and moral cause are held separate by Aquinas in his definition of the concept of legitimate authority within the just war. Aquinas in *Summa Theologiae* (1266–73) relates:[60]

> The ruler under whom the war is to be fought must have the authority to do so. A private person does not have the right to make war since he can pursue his rights by appealing to his superior. In addition a private person does not have the right to mobilize [*convocare*] the people as must be done in war. But since the responsibility for the commonwealth has been entrusted to rulers it is their responsibility to defend the city or kingdom or province subject to them. And just as it is legitimate for them to use the material sword to punish criminals in order to defend it against internal disturbances—as the Apostle [Paul] says in Romans 13, "He does not bear the sword without cause, for he is a minister of God, an avenger in wrath against the evildoer"—so they also have the right to use the sword of war to defend the commonwealth against external enemies.

However, the "*he*" (or *she*, or *it*, if we are talking about an institution) who does not bear the sword without cause is also a creator of worlds, a historical agent whose acts of violence may play a productive role in defending, sustaining, and realizing a particular concrete form of legal order and destroying or inhibiting another that opposes it. For example, the act of a "just war" carried out by a medieval Catholic monarch in punishing an internal rebellion of heretics or fighting a non-Christian "barbarian" also possessed a productive function, that is, the act of violence helped to sustain and further a specific form of legal order (privileging a set of values and suppressing others) over a particular territory over a period of time. In this sense the act of violence is not simply a tool used by a legitimate authority but also plays a constitutive role in creating and sustaining earthly forms of "legitimate authority." Another example is the colonial context of the Spanish conquest of America. In this case the just war subtly supported by Vitoria displaced indigenous forms of legal, political, and religious authority over American territory and extended Spanish, Catholic control and law over the region. It was not by moral argument that the old forms of institutional, legitimate authority were displaced but by the violence of those who were bearers of the sword, "ministers" of Spanish colonial authority.

Again, in the contemporary case of humanitarian intervention and "regime change," it is the act of violence that displaces one form of authority over territory and establishes a new form under the rule of (international) law and human rights. Or to think of an act of revolution, anticolonial national liberation, or self-determination, the act of violence that destroys the old tyrannical or colonial regime helps to create, found, establish, and realize a new one. In this context violence is as much productive as destructive; it is a creative force, not simply used like a tool by a "legitimate authority" but also complicit in the foundation and birth of new ones.

In part this is a sense of Goethe's words "In the beginning was the deed."[61] And this understanding of violence is sometimes ignored by moral theorists and international lawyers, although it is remembered by so-called realists.[62] The lesson would be to think of the "bearer of the sword" not merely as a potential moral actor but also as a destroyer and founder of worlds, a creator and sustainer of legal and political orders whose violence founds historical institutions, which after the foundational violence are then identified within legal and moral texts as a "legitimate authority."

Approaching the issue of violence in such a way can cause something of a problem for the category of legitimate authority within the just war tradition, at least in relation to institutions. The problem concerns the fact that the act of violence that destroys one "legitimate authority" and helps to create and support another is often itself *illegitimate* in some sense. An example would be the act of revolution, or act of aggressive war, that establishes a new government. The revolution would be illegitimate in the sense of breaching the previous government's Constitution, and the act of aggressive war would be illegitimate in the sense of breaching the laws of war. Of course, the legitimacy of the foundational act of violence of the revolutionary or the invading liberator/conqueror would be contestable and could involve a whole set of conflicting moral arguments drawn from a tradition of natural law to justify the act. Yet judged at least against a positive legal code of the relevant era, the act that founds what would later become a "legitimate authority" would take place initially as "illegitimate" (and illegal) violence.

Here resides something of a dilemma for the concept of legitimate authority within the just war tradition. Institutionally at least, the concept is troubled by a paradox—*The rightful bearer of the sword had (wrongly, illegally) stolen the sword from its rightful owner*. In other words, an institution that calls itself right, or legitimate, was founded on an illegitimate act, a wrong.[63] The existence of such a paradox pops up in cases of the right to resistance, self-determination, and terrorism. The common approach to dealing within this paradox by many moral theorists and international lawyers is, following Kant, to pretend it does not exist and to ignore or hide the illegitimacy of otherwise grand beginnings.[64] Jacques Derrida makes the point quite forcefully:

> *All* Nation-States are born and found themselves in violence. I believe that truth to be irrecusable. Without even exhibiting atrocious spectacles on this subject, it suffices to underline a law of structure: the moment of foundation, the instituting moment, is anterior to the law or legitimacy which it founds. It is thus *outside the law*, and violent by that very fact. But you know that this abstract truth could be illustrated (what a word, here!) by terrifying documents, and from the history of all states, the oldest and the youngest. . . . This

> foundational violence is not only forgotten. The foundation is made in *order* to hide it; by its essence it tends to organize amnesia, sometimes under the celebration and sublimation of the grand beginnings.[65]

Forms of moral reasoning that ignore or suppress this paradox often overlook more generally the productive (or creative, or constitutive) role of violence. One consequence of this is to arbitrarily cut off the process of moral reasoning from social and political action. When moral reasoning is abstracted from the historical and social context in which it takes place, then issues of power and violence are erroneously disconnected from moral arguments and moral claims to authority. Kantian moral reasoning and legal positivism are examples of forms of thinking that generally display such a disconnection, and many just war theorists often also follow this error in thought.[66]

One way out of this dilemma is by locating the formation of moral claims within a Hegelian theory of intersubjective and intercommunal recognition.[67] This involves understanding forms of moral reflection as a praxis of communicative action that takes place within the context of concrete, historical, cultural worldviews and involves the assertion of power, struggle, contestation, exclusion, and physical and symbolic violence. Legitimacy is an outcome of recognition, a shared normative standpoint that is produced between mutually affirming subjects, and between groups and institutions. It is a form of negotiated agreement—the construction of a shared norm or value jointly posited as having the status of *right*.

Legitimacy in this sense is arrived at via communicative and material action that is at all times speculative, reflective, and inclusive, and also limited, antagonistic, and exclusionary. Legitimacy is created and held in place both by consent and by strategies of exclusion and domination. Cultural and moral triumphalism—especially economic and religious fundamentalism (including liberal and secular versions of these)—plays a heavy role in excluding alternative claims of right; labeling them deviant, irrational, or wrong; and suppressing them through legal and political institutions that claim "legitimate authority."

Further, acts of personal and political violence play a central role as moral norms, criteria of legitimacy, and functioning institutions are produced as the outcomes of "struggles for recognition." In this manner both the broader concept of legitimacy and institutions that claim to be a "legitimate authority" are not disconnected from the acts of violence that helped to produce and sustain them in a violent world. Moments of contestation over the nature of authority and legitimacy within the various Janus faces of the natural law tradition are grounded in social struggles for recognition. The demand and struggle for human rights or social justice, just like the assertion of a state's authority over its territory, are moral claims not disconnected from the everyday workings of power and violence. Rather than suppressing a paradox of legitimacy, a form of moral reasoning that pays attention to the significant role of recognition struggles can help to historically and theoretically

explain the violence that accompanies moral claims to disobey institutional authority, to found new institutions, and to turn to war and terror under the banner of
justice, human rights, or liberation.

Just war theory falls down when it turns to an abstract practice of moral reasoning that is disconnected from the violence of ethics. When a theory does not, or
cannot, explain how the bearer of the sword got the sword, and whether it got the
sword by use of the sword, then it is not in a strong position to dictate to others
the moral conditions under which a particular act of violence should or should not
take place.

For a theory to express a claim that it provides a valid form of moral reasoning
whereby we can, in different concrete cases, delineate legitimate from illegitimate
violence, then one might expect that such a theory would be able to provide some
coherent account of the nature of the relationship between violence and legitimacy,
that is, the relationship between violence and ethics more generally. Yet the tradition
as a whole probably does not ever venture very close to producing such an account;
and its tendency to separate moral reasoning from the practice of violence, as if
they were wholly distinct forms of human action, renders it deficient. If just war
theory, as a form of moral reflection, were to build itself upon an account of social
and political life that paid attention to the relation between violence and ethics,
then such a theory might hold a little more merit. Such an approach would pay
more attention to the similarities between emperors and pirates.

NOTES

1. Augustine, *City of God against the Pagans*, ed. R. W. Dyson (Cambridge: Cambridge
University Press, 1998), 147–48.

2. For a general discussion of these criteria, see J. T. Johnson, *Morality and Contemporary
Warfare* (New Haven, CT: Yale University Press, 1999), 27.

3. M. Walzer, *Arguing about War* (New Haven, CT: Yale University Press, 2004). For
differing discussions of the notion of the "triumph" of just war theory, see chapters 15 and
16 in this volume by, respectively, John Kelsay and Nicholas Rengger.

4. M. Hardt, and A. Negri, *Empire* (Cambridge, MA: Harvard University Press, 2001).

5. See, e.g., chapter 2 in this volume by Chris Brown.

6. My argument stands in disagreement with the position taken by James Turner Johnson
in chapter 1 of this volume. Johnson's position presents an interpretation of the just war
tradition which privileges a premodern modern conception of sovereignty. His account contains little means of conceptualizing the important role of violence within social change and
offers a static and sometimes "authoritarian" interpretation of "legitimate authority."

7. I. Kant, "Perpetual Peace: A Philosophical Sketch," in *Political Writings*, ed. H. I. Reiss
(Cambridge: Cambridge University Press, 1991), 103.

8. For a contemporary account of the use and abuse of the concept of hospitality, see D.
Bulley, *Ethics as Foreign Policy* (London: Routledge, 2009). For a contemporary critique of
international law in terms of the concept of "sorry comforters," see M. Koskenniemi, "Miserable Comforters: International Relations as the New Natural Law," *European Journal of International Relations* 15 (2009): 395.

9. F. Vitoria, *Political Writings*, ed. A. Padgen and J. Lawrance (Cambridge: Cambridge University Press, 1991).

10. Ibid., 239.

11. Ibid., 240–46, 250–51.

12. Ibid., 250.

13. For a more general account of the European construction of the non-European other in relation to America, see D. F. Silva, *Toward a Global Idea of Race* (Minneapolis: University of Minnesota Press, 2007); E. Dussel, *Beyond Philosophy*, ed. E. Mendieta (Lanham, MD: Rowman & Littlefield, 2003); and W. Mignolo, *The Idea of Latin America* (New York: Blackwell, 2005).

14. See, e.g., J. B. Scott, *The Spanish Origins of International Law: Francisco De Vitoria and His Law of Nations* (Oxford: Clarendon Press, 1934).

15. F. Vitoria, *Political Writings*, 278.

16. Ibid., 279–80.

17. Ibid., 282.

18. Ibid., 285.

19. Ibid., 288.

20. See, more generally, C. Schmitt, *The* Nomos *of the Earth*, trans. G. L. Ulmen (New York: Telos Press 2003); R. Tuck, *The Rights of War and Peace: Political Thought and the International Order from Grotius to Kant* (Oxford: Oxford University Press, 1999); and A. Padgen, *The Fall of Natural Man: The American Indian and the Origins of Comparative Ethnology* (Cambridge: Cambridge University Press, 1982).

21. See M. Somos, *Secularisation and the Leiden Circle* (Leiden: Brill, 2011).

22. H. Grotius, *The Rights of War and Peace*, ed. R. Tuck (Indianapolis: Liberty Fund, 2005), 89.

23. See, more generally, R. Tuck, *Philosophy and Government 1572–1651* (Cambridge: Cambridge University Press, 1993); and B. Tierney, *The Idea of Natural Rights* (Grand Rapids: William B. Eerdmans, 2001).

24. M. Weber, "Politics as a Vocation" in *From Max Weber: Essays in Sociology*, ed. H. H. Gerth and C. W. Mills (New York: Oxford University Press, 1958), 78.

25. On the role of property within this branch of the natural law tradition, see I. Hont, *Jealousy of Trade* (Cambridge, MA: Harvard University Press, 2005); and P. Garnsey, *Thinking about Property* (Cambridge: Cambridge University Press, 2007).

26. H. Grotius, *Rights of War and Peace*, 1021–23.

27. Ibid., 1021–23.

28. Ibid., 1024.

29. Tuck, *Rights of War and Peace*, 103.

30. On the colonial nature of modern international law, see A. Anghie, *Imperialism, Sovereignty and the Making of International Law* (Cambridge: Cambridge University Press, 2005).

31. See, generally, C. Brown, "From Humanised War to Humanitarian Intervention: Carl Schmitt's Critique of the "Just War Tradition," in *The International Political Thought of Carl Schmitt: Terror, Liberal War and the Crisis of Global Order*, ed. L. Odysseos and F. Petito (London: Routledge, 2007).

32. For an approach which reads political theory in this way, see Q. Skinner, *The Foundations of Modern Political Thought* (Cambridge: Cambridge University Press, 1978).

33. On the ways in which "legitimate authority" cannot simply be equated with state sovereignty, see the introduction to this volume.

34. I. Kant, "Perpetual Peace." On the role of the great powers in the construction of international law, see G. Simpson, *Great Powers and Outlaw States* (Cambridge: Cambridge University Press, 2004); and D. Zolo, *Victor's Justice* (London: Verso, 2009).

35. On the Grotian aspect of modern international society, see H. Bull, *The Anarchical Society* (London: Macmillan, 1977).

36. UN Charter (1945), Art. 39.

37. Ibid., Art. 51.

38. Ibid., Art. 2 (3) & (4). For a consideration of these positions, see C. Gray, *International Law and the Use of Force* (Oxford: Oxford University Press, 2008).

39. For a discussion of this, see D. McGoldrick, *From 9–11 to the Iraq War: International Law in an Age of Complexity* (Oxford: Hart, 2004).

40. On the role of rhetoric in international law, see M. Koskenniemi, *From Apology to Utopia: The Structure of International Legal Argument* (Cambridge: Cambridge University Press, 2006).

41. For a general discussion of this, see C. Douzinas, *The End of Human Rights* (Oxford: Hart, 2000); and J. Donnelly, *Universal Human Rights in Theory and Practice* (Ithaca, NY: Cornell University Press, 2002).

42. See "Responsibility to Protect," Report of the International Commission on Intervention and State Sovereignty, 2001, www.iciss.ca/pdf/Commission-Report.pdf. Consider the language of United Nations Development Program, *Human Development Report 1994: New Dimensions of Human Security* (New York: United Nations, 1994), http://hdr.undp.org/en/reports/global/hdr1994.

43. "A More Secure World: Our Shared Responsibility," Report of the High-Level Panel on Threats, Challenges, and Change, 2004, 66, www.un.org/secureworld/report2.pdf.

44. For a critical discussion of humanitarian intervention, see A. Orford, *Reading Humanitarian Intervention: Human Rights and the Use of Force in International Law* (Cambridge: Cambridge University Press, 2007).

45. Koskenniemi, "Miserable Comforters."

46. A. Orford, *International Authority and the Responsibility to Protect* (Cambridge: Cambridge University Press, 2011).

47. E.g., consider the theory of just war articulated by Michael Walzer, which places human rights at the center. Michael Walzer, *Just and Unjust Wars* (New York: Basic Books, 2000). We can think about this in the terms of Raymond Geuss's notion of the "partisan" nature of moral and political theory. Raymond Guess, *Philosophy and Real Politics* (Princeton, NJ: Princeton University Press, 2008).

48. Consider, e.g., United Nations, *Universal Declaration of Human Rights* (1948), Art. 29 (2) & (3).

49. J. Locke, *Two Treatises of Government*, ed. P. Laslett (Cambridge: Cambridge University Press, 2005), 278, 412. See also U. Steinhoff, *On the Ethics of War and Terrorism* (Oxford: Oxford University Press, 2007).

50. UN Charter, Art. 1 (2); 1970 UN Declaration on the Principles of International Law Concerning Friendly Relations and Co-operation among States.

51. See, generally, A. Cassese, *Self-Determination of Peoples: A Legal Reappraisal* (Cambridge: Cambridge University Press, 1995); and J. Crawford, *The Creation of States in International Law* (Oxford: Clarendon Press, 1988).

52. See, generally, B. Saul, *Defining Terrorism in International Law* (Oxford: Oxford University Press, 2008).

53. Universal Declaration of Human Rights (1948), Preamble: "Whereas it is essential, if man is not to be compelled to have recourse, as a last resort, to rebellion against tyranny and oppression, that human rights should be protected by the rule of law. . . ."

54. E. Bloch, *Natural Law and Human Dignity*, trans. D. J. Schmidt (Cambridge, MA: MIT Press, 1996), xxx.

55. B. Santos, *Toward a New Legal Common Sense: Law, Globalisation, Emancipation* (London: Butterworths, 2002), 458.

56. K. Marx, "Toward a Critique of Hegel's Philosophy of Right: Introduction," trans. L. D. Easton and K. H. Guddat, in *Karl Marx Selected Writings*, ed. L. H. Simon (Indianapolis: Hacket, 1994), 32.

57. Consider V. I. Lenin, "The Military Programme of the Proletarian Revolution," in *Collected Works*, by V. I. Lenin, vol. 23, ed. M. S. Levin (London: Lawrence and Wishart, 1974).

58. E. Bloch, *The Spirit of Utopia*, trans. A. Nassar (Stanford, CA: Stanford University Press, 2000), 242.

59. My reading of the natural law tradition draws heavily on that given by Ernst Bloch.

60. Aquinas, *St. Thomas Aquinas on Politics and Ethics*, ed. P. Sigmund (New York: W. W. Norton, 1988), 64–65.

61. J. W. Goethe, *Faust*, tr. D. Constantine (London: Penguin, 2005).

62. A list might include Machiavelli, Hegel, Marx, Lenin, Carl Schmitt, Walter Benjamin, Jacques Derrida, Bernard Williams, and Raymond Geuss.

63. On the concept of the "wrong of law," see V. Kerruish, "But What's It Got to Do with Law?" *Dillemata* 4 (2009): 81–124.

64. On Kant's advice that the people should not inquire into the origin of the authority to which they are subject, see I. Kant, *The Metaphysics of Morals*, ed. M. Gregor (Cambridge: Cambridge University Press, 1996), 96.

65. J. Derrida, *On Cosmopolitanism and Forgiveness*, tr. M. Dooley and M. Hughes (London: Routledge, 2001), 57.

66. On the disconnection, see, e.g., John Rawls, *The Law of Peoples* (Cambridge, MA: Harvard University Press, 2001). On those who follow this error in thought, see, e.g., Jean Bethke Elshtain, *Just War against Terror* (New York: Basic Books, 2003).

67. For different interpretations of the role of recognition, see A. Honneth, *The Struggle for Recognition: The Moral Grammar of Social Conflicts*, tr. J. Anderson (Cambridge: Polity Press, 1995); G. Rose, *Hegel Contra Sociology* (London: Athlone, 1981); C. Taylor, *Multiculturalism and the Politics of Recognition* (Princeton, NJ: Princeton University Press, 1992); and Robert Pippin, *Hegel's Practical Philosophy* (Cambridge: Cambridge University Press, 2008). See also T. Kochi, *The Other's War: Recognition and the Violence of Ethics* (Abingdon, UK: Birkbeck Law Press, 2009).

CHAPTER 8

Narrative Authority

Anthony F. Lang Jr.

How can citizens of democratic states engage in moral deliberation about war? Public discourses about war in democratic states tend toward the nationalistic or even jingoistic. This tendency is exacerbated in such states by the assumption that democracies only use force for good purposes and never resort to war for self-interested reasons. That is, any judgments about war tend to be ones that reinforce the right and good of war-making by democracies rather than critical moral debate about just or unjust wars.

This chapter proposes one way to make possible a more critical moral debate. I begin with the assumption that the just war tradition is the best means by which to deliberate about war in democratic states. But if it is to be used by a wider civil society and not just by philosophers, it needs to be recast in terms of narrative rather than rules. This alternative conception of the tradition retains its conceptual categories but employs them as a structure whereby a narrative about war can be structured and then judged. Furthermore, to ensure that narratives about war do not become nationalistic histories that celebrate every military action undertaken by democracies, and to ensure that there is a wider deliberation about war than just among elite political and military leaders, I propose that such deliberations take place in religious institutions. Using the analogy of a pastoral encounter, I suggest that these institutions provide the space where narratives about war can be constructed through a process of active listening by clerics or lay leaders who can guide citizens through a critical dialogue about war that draws on the just war categories as framing devices rather than as applied rules.

The bulk of the chapter focuses on why narrative rather than rules is the preferred way to employ the just war tradition. It does so by exploring the use of narrative in history, moral philosophy, and political theory. The just war tradition tends to be understood through a rule-based framework, one that begins with a set of principles from which are generated a series of rules governing the proper conduct of warfare. Although such a method provides rigor and logical coherence to moral inquiry, such inquiry does not always find purchase in wider debates about war. Rather than logical analyses of right and wrong, everyday citizens tell stories about war.

Instead of these rule-based styles of reasoning, I suggest in this chapter that a narrative approach makes the just war tradition more accessible to civil society. In any society or polity, stories about its past and present uses of force appear in multiple guises—as popular histories, in the news media, as fiction, as entertainment, and in public education. These narratives will conflict and contest each other, but over time polities develop stories of their role in the world that are often related to stories of how they use military force. This largely narrative account of war and its justification is thus one that already exists in society, and so it is one into which citizens can be invited to participate in a more active way.

But one of the dangers of narratives of war is that they can easily become nationalistic or jingoistic accounts of a nation's wars. How, then, is it possible to both deploy the narrative mode and also provide some discipline in making judgments about war? Put differently, and more in line with the focus on authority in this volume, how can narratives about just war be constructed that have some authority for the political community in which they take place? I suggest that one way to avoid nationalist accounts of war is to turn toward institutions in civil society as formal structures within which narratives of war can be best articulated. I point to how religious institutions can serve this function, especially if they employ a pastoral model in how war is discussed, debated, and eventually narrated.

The first section of the chapter fleshes out the concept of narrative through an engagement with history, social science, moral philosophy, and political theory. Throughout, I connect these different conceptions of narrative with the just war tradition. The next section points to how a narrative approach might be utilized in a pastoral context to make judgments about war. Concretely, it proposes the use of religious institutions as a place where such pastoral contexts can take place. It suggests how the just war tradition provides a frame for developing narratives about war rather than seeing it as a set of rules to apply in judging war.

NARRATIVES OF WAR

A narrative is the representation of events that creates a boundary around them in order to provide meaning. Although narratives tend to be fiction in literature, in this chapter I am interested in narratives that are historical. This is not to judge the truth or falsity of narratives, for historical narratives can be false in important ways and fictional narratives can provide access to important truths.[1]

In my definition, meaning is a central element of narrative. Rather than truth, meaning is the goal of narrative. This meaning corresponds to the idea of *Verstehen*, or understanding, in the human sciences.[2] History gives us one way of providing this meaning. Historians, however, tend not to make judgments in their character-izations of the past. But in providing an explanation or giving greater meaning to a set of political events, their construction of the meaning of events results in the making of implicit moral judgments. The classic case of this is A. J. P. Taylor's study of the origins of World War II, where he argued that the war did not result from the agency of Hitler or anyone else in particular but arose from a set of structural conditions in both Europe and more widely.[3] This argument raised a widespread controversy because of the implication that a horrific war resulted from no one person, which meant that no one could be held legally or morally responsible for it. Taylor denied that he made moral judgments, but instead was simply reporting the facts.

Other historians integrate moral judgment more directly into their narratives. In *Moral Combat* Michael Burleigh explores some of the more contested terrain of moral choice that faced those fighting in World War II.[4] He does not shy away from making judgments, arguing that the German and Japanese leaders were morally depraved, though decisions made by American and British leaders were more com-mendable. His account does raise some moral complications for those actors, such as in his chapter about the decision to carpet bomb Germany. At the same time, his overarching moral judgment is that the war was won by the morally just side.

A very different set of normative judgments appear in a recent study of the Vietnam War. Bernd Greiner argues that the atrocities committed by American forces in Vietnam, culminating in the My Lai massacre, were not aberrations but resulted from a conscious decision-making process that demonized the enemy and placed the success of the war above any other consideration, especially moral or legal ones.[5] Greiner's approach is not a single narrative, but a series of overlapping studies of events in the war. In his construction of responsibility, he creates a causal story that relies upon narrative to make sense.

These historical accounts raise important questions about responsibility, causal-ity, and narrative structure. Such themes have been explored in recent years by Hidemi Suganami. Suganami argues that the distinction between explanation and understanding in social science theory, and particularly in international relations (IR), fails to account for the fact that narratives are just as explanatory as covering law accounts.[6] He critiques the distinction made famous in IR by Martin Hollis and Steve Smith, arguing that they helped to perpetuate a false dichotomy in positing explanation versus understanding.[7] Instead, Suganami points to how historians of necessity explain the world around them, even allowing for generalizations across different eras and places. Moreover, he highlights how historians employ causality in their narratives, as the examples of Taylor, Burleigh, and Greiner demonstrate.

Of particular importance for the argument I am making here, though, Suganami extends this discussion of narrative and causality to the question of moral judgments. Building upon the controversy surrounding Taylor's judgment about Hitler noted above, Suganami cites the work of the philosopher W. H. Dray, who highlighted the fact that Taylor's explicit refusal to make a moral judgment about Hitler was simply illogical.[8] Whereas Dray, as an analytic philosopher, uses these debates to clarify the concept of causation, Suganami explores how Dray ended up making a moral judgment of his own. Suganami argues from a pragmatic perspective that causation may well lead to morality: "The reason why, in some cases, our moral judgments seep through to our causal explanations is that some questions, presented as causal questions, turn out to be, or may plausibly be interpreted as asking for our moral views."[9] In other words, though not all causal accounts will lead to moral judgments, many of which are of interest to scholars in IR do indeed lead to such judgments, and not only in narratives about Hitler. As Suganami so clearly demonstrates, causal accounts within narratives of international affairs will oftentimes lead us to the necessity of making judgments.

Other scholars in IR have also sought to understand how narratives can be used to understand a state's foreign and security policies. Jennifer Mitzen and Brent Steele have proposed the idea of "ontological security" as a way to understand international affairs.[10] In the construction of narratives about themselves, states seek to secure not only their physical presence but also their identity and honor. For instance, Steele develops this point in relation to the construction of narratives about torture, arguing that the challenge to American identity arising from the stories of its use of torture creates unsettling dissonances for many.[11] Of particular importance, the construction of this ontological security occurs through the narratives that states tell about their participation in world politics. These accounts provide a clearer understanding of how history plays a central role in the construction of security.

Although these works within IR have advanced our understanding of how narrative can be used to better understand the practices of international affairs, they fail to provide a perspective from which to make *judgments* about war. And though Suganami's account points to the ways in which causality leads to claims about responsibility, his analysis does not suggest a means whereby those accounts might be disciplined by moral judgment. Mitzen and Steele position their accounts in terms of the construction of security for a state, which is not the same as assessing whether or not the pursuit of security is just. Of course, these theorists, or those who draw on them, might well use these concepts to make moral judgments. But their own analyses do not point to how judgments might be made.

This failure to turn a narrative into moral judgment may be why traditions like just war become rule oriented. By creating a rule-like structure against which practices can be compared, just war theorists make moral judgments easier. Narratives do not naturally lead to judgments; though they might lead to causal accounts and some conception of responsibility, they also allow individuals and states to justify their practices in terms of wider contexts. Although a rule might clearly state that something is immoral, a narrative can allow agents to make excuses for their behavior by piling up numerous reasons for action. This exculpatory potential within narratives makes them liable to being amoral accounts in which no one can be held responsible.

NARRATIVE IN MORAL PHILOSOPHY

There are theorists within moral philosophy and political theory who draw on narrative to enable judgment. Alasdair MacIntyre's use of the idea of a tradition of inquiry provides one such method. MacIntyre's overarching claim throughout his work is that morality no longer makes sense because it relies on a false set of assumptions about rationality and ethics. Specifically, morality cannot be understood when disconnected from an understanding of what it means to be a human person. For MacIntyre, this means morality can only really function within an Aristotelian framework, the teleological conception that defines persons in particular ways in order to understand what it means to be a good person. He argues that a way to return to this understanding is to revive the virtues, for the Greek concept of virtue (*arête*, or excellence) assumes that there exists a standard by which a human life can be judged. In *After Virtue*, he argues that in various times and places, there did exist a coherent conception of what is good for the human person.[12] This meant not only knowing what is good to do if you are in a particular profession—that is, a soldier—but also how that practice connected to the larger question of what it meant to be a good person. In *Whose Justice? Which Rationality?* MacIntyre continues with this line of argument, exploring the link between various conceptions of human life and their associated claims about justice and reason. In this book he argues that there is no rational standpoint from which one can make judgments about which form of human life is to be preferred, which has led some critics to argue that MacIntyre is a radical historical relativist.[13]

In *Three Rival Versions of Moral Inquiry* MacIntyre responds to these concerns in his comparison of the encyclopedic, the genealogical, and the Thomistic or "tradition" approach to moral inquiry. Unlike the previous two books, in this text MacIntyre argues that there is indeed a vantage point from which judgments about the human person can be made. This vantage point is that of Thomism, where Thomas Aquinas's account of what it means to engage in moral inquiry is explicitly dialogic, as reflected in the peculiar form of the medieval *Summa Theologia*. In this text, Aquinas (and others in the medieval world of philosophy and theology) acknowledges that some texts are authoritative. These texts are the necessary beginning point for any inquiry. Although such texts provide a starting point, they are put in dialogue with divergent accounts of the moral and political life. In this dialogue, the authoritative texts may return to place limits on inquiry; but, of particular importance, there are also assumptions about what it means to be a human person that provide those limits. In fact those limits, which arise from an understanding of the human person, really establish how moral inquiry can proceed. For Aquinas, the human person was defined by a combination of Aristotelian assumptions about rationality and group life and the Christian conception of a life oriented toward union with God.

The narrative element of MacIntyre's philosophy gives detail to how one learns about morality and the nature of the human person. As MacIntyre explains, in order to engage in moral inquiry, an individual needs to accept that some texts are more authoritative than others. This recognition of those texts, and modes of interpreting those texts, results from being part of a particular community of inquiry. Of particular importance, this places the person in a grander narrative structure in which not only the history of the world and the generic human person is to be found but the specific person who is undertaking this form of analysis can understand himself or herself: "By accepting authority, . . . one acquires a teacher who both introduces one to certain texts and educates one into becoming the sort of person capable of reading those texts with understanding, texts in which such a person discovers the story of him or herself, including the story of how he or she was transformed into a reader of these texts. The story of oneself is embedded in the history of the world, an overall narrative within which all other narratives find their place."[14]

It is not only the acceptance of authority, however, that necessitates a narrative approach. Learning to be a good person is the same as learning a craft, which corresponds to the Greek notion of virtue. And to learn a craft, one recognizes that one is part of a tradition. To be a good marine means learning the history of using a rifle, storming beaches, and operating computer-guided munitions. To be a good person means learning a much more complicated and diverse history, but a history nonetheless: "A craft in good order has to be embodied in a tradition in good order."[15]

One reason why MacIntyre has been seen as relativistic is that he argues in his earlier works that "being a good person" only makes sense within specific cultural traditions. This means that there is no single, universal tradition or narrative that makes sense for all human persons. But of course, for the two most important moral philosophers from MacIntyre's perspective—Aristotle and Thomas Aquinas—there is a single human condition within which one can make judgments about the human person. For Aristotle, this condition is not narrative but biological; that is, the human person is understood as an animal that both reasons and lives in community. These essential characteristics construct the person as one who lives in community and seeks to know.[16] But for Aquinas, the condition does result from a story about the human person in which the interjections of God into human history change the world radically. To understand the human condition, then, means accepting the Christian narrative about the world, one in which the stories of ancient Israel and the particular story of Jesus create a narrative of the fall of humanity and its redemption.[17]

So whereas MacIntyre develops this narrative account of tradition and morality in these texts, the bases upon which he is drawing in recent years—that is, Christianity—is not a relativist narrative one. He develops a more universal understanding of the human person in his 1999 book, *Dependent Rational Animals*. In this work, he begins with an Aristotelian mode by linking the human person to the animal world and making important distinctions within the animal world in terms of communication and vulnerability. Rather than Aristotle's focus on communication as the defining feature of humanity, MacIntyre proposes the idea of vulnerability as that feature, or more specifically, how the human person treats vulnerable others such as children and the disabled. Through this exercise, he seems to move away from the narrative account so prominent in *Three Rival Versions of Moral Inquiry*, ending up with a very naturalistic, Aristotelian account of what defines human persons. This account of vulnerability is then linked to an account of giving and receiving, traits that allow the human person to live and thrive in community. He does not, however, leave his focus on Thomas, for giving, receiving, and caring for the vulnerable become Christian virtues.

MacIntyre, then, is not entirely comfortable accepting a purely narrative account of morality and politics. For to accept such an account either means accepting one single narrative within which all human persons fit, such as the Christian one, or becoming a relativist who accepts multiple narratives and ways of being good. MacIntyre, it would seem, wants to have both by constructing the Thomistic account as one that both has a master Christian narrative yet also invites dialogue with other narratives through the disputational mode of moral inquiry.

Before turning to an alternative account that might help modify some of the problems in MacIntyre, let me return to the just war tradition. This tradition fits in well with MacIntyre's conception of a tradition of inquiry. It rests upon a craft, that of using military force. It is shaped by the normative goal of ensuring that force is only used in the pursuit of justice and attempting to lessen the use of force if at all possible. It relies upon "authorities," which include the Christian scriptures, medieval theology and philosophy, theoretical works on just war, and the practical manuals of militaries around the world. Most important, it arises from a narrative about war, one that is not specific to any one nationality, but seeks to take in the developments over time of a wide range of wars from various locales. In point of fact, the tradition draws heavily on European and North American experiences of warfare, although it also has come to include a wider range of military practices and traditions in recent years. Not all theorists of just war, however, see the tradition as important; indeed, not all contributors to this book see just war through the lens of tradition. But when seen through the lens of an authoritative tradition, just war can be seen as part of a larger discourse of political and moral reflection on the use of military force.

Just war could, then, fit well into MacIntyre's conception of how a tradition functions as a source of authority. But just war may suffer from exactly the problem that I have hinted at in MacIntyre's work. As noted above, he begins with a radical historical relativism, arguing that to understand morality requires understanding what defines a good person. In *Whose Justice? Which Rationality*, he argues that this can vary across different cultural contexts. As he moves toward the Aristotelian/Thomistic account, however, he comes closer to a universal conception of human nature, one based in biology and, eventually, Christianity. In the same way, the just war tradition might be understood as culturally bound; it arises for some with the Ancient Greeks and Romans and then is fundamentally transformed by the Christian tradition, especially throughout the medieval era. In recent years, efforts have been made to find "just war" in other religious and cultural traditions. Are these efforts a way to find a "universal" human nature that includes all persons? For those who see just war through the lens of natural law, this is undoubtedly what is happening. And clearly it is possible to find analogues to the just war tradition in the legalism of Islam,[18] or in broadly defined Asian contexts.[19] And yet there remain tensions in finding this universal narrative, especially as uses of force arise from drastically different contexts. Even within the "Western" tradition, there are anomalous uses that do not fit well within just war; the crusades, for instance, hardly correspond to the just war tradition.[20]

The just war tradition, then, falls victim to some of the problems that bedevil MacIntyre. It has an inherent narrative feature to it, but it is a narrative that is brought back to a single authoritative conception of the human person. This conception, one that parallels accounts in natural law, relies heavily on a Classical and Christian conception of the human person. The diversity and plurality of the modern world, however, prevents such an account from functioning properly and leaves out not only divergent practices of warfare but also divergent conceptions of what it means to live a good life.

NARRATIVE IN POLITICAL THEORY

Can the idea of narrative be saved from this universalizing process? Hannah Arendt provides an alternative way to draw on the idea of narrative in articulating a conception of politics. Her work links narrative more closely to the idea of judgment, a concept through which she avoids the relativism that can arise from simple "story-telling" but that also grounds political analysis in the richness of narrative accounts. Arendt is a difficult figure to capture in any single account both because of the range of her thought and the eclecticism of her theoretical orientation. As such, this chapter does not present her thought as a whole, but highlights those elements that are specifically oriented toward the question under consideration here. She is certainly not a theorist of just war, but her work on narrative and political authority makes her directly relevant to the concerns that are raised in this book more widely and to the practices of war in the twenty-first century.

Arendt became well known for *The Origins of Totalitarianism*, a work published in 1951.[21] This work was categorized by some as part of the larger Cold War debate, but was really about the ways in which the modern nation-state and nationalism played a role in some of the worst excesses of the twentieth century. Her next popular book, *Eichmann in Jerusalem*, made her infamous to some, particularly those in the American Jewish community. The book introduced the idea of the banality of evil in describing the role of Adolph Eichmann, the Nazi bureaucrat whose moral blindness to the consequences of "following orders" epitomized how bureaucratic governance and rule following can lead to horrific results. The book also highlighted how the Jewish Councils in Europe facilitated the Holocaust by enabling the Nazi bureaucracy in its task of moving Jews from their home countries to concentration camps. In placing part of the responsibility for the Holocaust on the Jews themselves, the book became part of a polemical debate about Arendt's identity as a Jew.[22]

Along with these two more popular books, Arendt published an important study of the "political" in *The Human Condition*, a work in which she drew heavily on the Classical heritage of the Greeks, particularly Aristotle, in arguing that political action was a good in and of itself.[23] Her ideas about political action were made concrete in her study of the French and American revolutions, in which she celebrated the creation of small political groups, councils, in political contexts around the world.[24] Her essays and reviews cover a wide range of issues and subjects, from violence to history to education.

These works form the core of Arendt's political theory, one that focuses on political action. But for the purposes of this chapter, I am highlighting some less-well-known elements of her oeuvre. The first is a study of a Rahel Varnhagen, a Jewish woman from the late eighteenth and early nineteenth centuries.[25] In what can only be described as a "political biography," Arendt explores how this woman helped to create the "salon culture" of Europe through her role as a hostess and intellectual during a time when being a Jew and a woman would have normally prevented such things. In this work Arendt explores the role of the Jew as both parvenu and pariah, categories that allowed her to develop ideas about politics, the public realm, and plurality (themes not articulated as such in this text, but developed more fully in her later works). Both Richard Bernstein and Seyla Benhabib identify this work as central for understanding the development of Arendt's thought.[26] The work demonstrates how a narrative reconstruction of a life helps to reveal wider dynamics of the political condition of a people. This is not a simple metonymic account in which Varnhagen becomes a representative of the "Jew"; indeed, Arendt's emphasis on plurality and resistance to such totalizing categories would not allow such a move. Instead, the narrative of Varnhagen's life reveals the complexities, both moral and political, that faced Jews and women in Europe during this period. Nor does it necessarily celebrate Varnhagen as a hero; rather, her struggles to assimilate into European culture, and especially the efforts of her husband to retell her story in such a way that her Jewish identity was downplayed, demonstrates the difficulties in constructing a narrative of one's own life.

Benhabib brings out of this text an important point about Arendt's understanding of political life. In her more mature work, *The Human Condition*, she argues for a politics that is about public action, modeled on the Greek polis, where citizens stand up and reveal themselves in their actions and words. This formal political sphere is the one that she believed needed to be protected and cultivated in the face of the increasing pressures from social systems that would normalize life. Benhabib contrasts this later work with Arendt's earlier study of Rahel Varnhagen, in which a private sphere, the salon, becomes a constructed space in which politics of a sort can take place. Arendt is critical of the space that she describes in this work, but she also celebrates it as a place where stories could be told and give life to a particular kind of politics. Benhabib notes that the space Varnhagen created is one in which difference and plurality were allowed to flourish, and she wonders why Arendt abandons this "social" space for the more formal politics of the polis.[27]

For the purposes of this chapter, I do not need to resolve this question. Instead, the biography of Varnhagen reveals a method that Arendt continued to use in her mature political works, particularly *The Origins of Totalitarianism* and *On Revolution*, the narrative method. The importance of this narrative element in creating political action becomes even more evident in her book *The Human Condition*, where she turns away from the social space of her biography of Varnhagen to the larger political sphere in which public political action occurs. In this work she draws upon the classical Greek understanding of politics to argue that it is public deeds that must be protected and encouraged. Of particular importance for the purposes of this chapter, such deeds only become political once stories about them are told. In acting we reveal ourselves, but action is so intangible and ephemeral that it must be made concrete through a story told about it—that is, a history. Crucially, this story cannot just be told by the agent but must be told by others. As Arendt notes, "Although everybody started his life by inserting himself in the human world through action and speech, nobody is the author or producer of his own life story.

In other words, the stories, the results of action and speech, reveal an agent, but this agent is not an author or producer. Somebody began it and is its subject in the twofold sense of the word, namely, its actor and sufferer, but nobody is the author."[28]

One might think, according to this Arendtian conception of political action, that war would be the perfect instance of storytelling that reveals the glory of the human person. Indeed, at times, Arendt's conception of the political seems almost Homeric, one in which glory comes from political action on the battlefield, which is then glorified in great tales.

But to make this argument would fail to appreciate how Arendt understood war and violence. In 1970 she wrote a review piece in *The New York Review of Books* in response to the events of the Vietnam War. In that work, now known as *On Violence*, she argues that violence is no longer heroic—if it ever was.[29] She claims that violence is distinctly nonpolitical, for it silences voices and does not allow a narrative to emerge. In the essay Arendt poses violence against power, arguing that violence is an instrumental use of tools to advance ends that need some further justification, whereas the exercise of power is in the very nature of what political communities do. Unlike most accounts of power, Arendt argues that power is acting in concert, a way in which individual actions can become part of the political realm. Political action, through the exercise of power, creates new political orders and spaces. Arendt calls this ability to create anew "natality," and it is at the core of her conception of politics.[30] To act together in the political realm is to create new beginnings and new potentials. Violence can do this; but, as Arendt notes, "the practice of violence, like all action, changes the world, but the most probable change is to a more violent world."[31]

Two other essays by Arendt are worth mentioning before bringing the discussion here back to the question of just war. In these two essays Arendt more directly explores the question of narrative and history. In "Understanding and Politics" she links historical narrative with the practice of judgment.[32] To understand human events, she argues, we need to see not only their beginning—that idea of natality— but also their end. Complete understanding only comes with the finality of death for a person. Hence, a full biography only comes when one has died. But political action is not like this. Its impact is never ending, in a sense. It continues to extend beyond itself. Unlike a single violent act, which achieves a short-term end, true political action results in consequences that continue to recreate the world around us. Arendt uses this as a way to critique social scientific efforts—rule-based, in the terms identified earlier in this chapter—as never able to fully capture political life because such approaches must assume an end, an end that never comes. Instead, she argues, we can understand politics only barely, but through the construction of narratives. The reason for understanding is not to forgive or explain away, but rather to allow us to be "at home in the world," or to be reconciled to our place within it. That is, understanding is never comprehensive, in the scientific sense of the term, but is always tentative and uncertain.

Yet even if it is tentative, understanding is what allows us to make judgments about the world around us. Arendt makes clear and considered judgments about events—judgments that are not based on a foundation in natural law or human rights but on this narrative construction of the world around us.[33] As Jerome Kohn, who has edited and republished much of Arendt's work in the last ten years, puts it: "The depth of her appreciation of politics can be glimpsed in her contention that the only standards of judgment with any degree of dependability are in no sense handed down from above but emerge from human plurality, the condition of politics. Political judgment is not a matter of knowledge, pseudoknowledge, or speculative thought. It does not eliminate risk but affirms human freedom and the world that free people share with one another. Or rather, it establishes the reality of human freedom in a common world."[34] And it is only through the telling of stories, through the narration of the multiplicity of the political realm, that true judgments become possible.

The final essay from Arendt I wish to highlight here brings us to the question of responsibility and judgment as it relates to communities. From what I have argued thus far, it would seem that Arendt's work leaves us without standards by which to make judgments. And, indeed, she was wary, as Kohn notes, of judgments that come from "on high." But she does indeed see judgments as possible and necessary. In her essay "Collective Responsibility," she argues that it is possible to hold not just individuals to account but communities as well. Of course, she does not dismiss individual responsibility, as her study of Eichmann demonstrates. Rather, the point of the essay is to say that such a thing as collective responsibility does make sense and it is an important way to understand what it means to be a member of a community. When an action is undertaken in my name that has consequences— that is, all actions that states undertake—I share responsibility for that act. Without that conception of collective responsibility, our political lives would be impoverished: "This vicarious responsibility for things we have not done, this taking upon ourselves the consequences for things we are entirely innocent of, is the price we pay for the fact that we live our lives not by ourselves but among our fellow men, that the faculty of action which, after all, is the political faculty par excellence, can be actualized only in one of the many and manifold forms of human community."[35]

Nowhere is collective responsibility more important than in how states undertake war, and how they narrate those wars. As John Williams explores in chapter 4 of this volume, the claim that a war has been undertaken by a democracy but "not in my name" suggests the complexities of collective responsibility. Indeed, the story of protests against the 2003 war are on the one hand demonstrations of political action in an Arendtian sense, but on the other hand simultaneously a caution about what such actions are capable of achieving.

Let me bring these Arendtian themes now to the question of just war. Arendt's account emphasizes that we must make judgments about politics, and such judgments are part of the political realm. But rather than judgments based on preexisting codes, such judgments must result from the stories we tell of the political actions we undertake as a community. And, crucially, we can make judgments about our collective responsibility, judgments that reinstate the political realm as a place of public action and plurality. Through Arendt's lens, then, we can see the just war tradition in a new light. The tradition is not based on knowledge or rules, but its deployment becomes part of the process of understanding the use of violence as a political community. Arendt was not a pacifist, so even though she critiqued the use of violence at times, she understood that "politics is not a nursery."[36] But her work reminds us that to make judgments, we must create narratives that highlight all the dimensions of the use of force, resulting in an understanding of politics that can be richer and more demanding.

But where can such forms of judgment take place? How can communities narrate their political lives, particularly their wars, in such a way that it enacts the kind of judgments that Arendt suggests are necessary? Of particular importance, are there spaces in modern polities where communities might even make judgments about themselves, judgments of collective responsibility? It is to these questions that the final section turns.

JUST WAR, NARRATIVES, AND CHURCHES

In the introduction to this volume, Cian O'Driscoll and I suggest that the just war can manifest itself in four different modes: political, prophetic, pastoral, and philosophical.[37] The political function is when the tradition speaks directly to policymakers about the judgments they make in using violence. The prophetic is the use of the tradition to critique policymakers by holding them up to a standard of behavior that will force them to confront the moral dilemmas that they are generating with their use of force. The philosophical is the exploration of dilemmas and problems that arise from within the tradition without necessarily directing it toward a specific policy outcome.

The pastoral model, the one I want to develop here, is the use of the tradition as a guide for those who must confront the dilemmas raised by modern warfare, usually soldiers. I describe this function as follows:

> A third way to approach the tradition can be called the pastoral. Those drawing on the just war tradition also answer specific moral dilemmas facing individuals who have to use force. Here attention would be more specifically focused on the *in bello* side of the tradition and would be oriented toward individual combatants. This might manifest itself as education for military

officers, which would focus more on developing their ability to make judgments in cases where the law or military manuals do not provide clear guidance. Indeed, in the US military establishment, just war has long played an important role in the education of the officer corps (as I would imagine it has in a number of other military officer traditions). This approach eschews larger questions about the justice of wars and instead helps those who must follow orders from policy makers develop their ability to confront difficult moral dilemmas.[38]

The emphasis here is on the tradition as a tool for members of the military to use as a way to make judgments. I would like to develop this idea a bit more fully, and take it from the realm of the military officer out to the wider civil society. Rather than taking place in military academies, I want to suggest that this pastoral function might be a possible avenue for the churches to be more directly engaged in the use of the just war tradition.

Before explaining how the just war tradition can be used in this way, let me expand briefly on the pastoral role in a clerical setting. In pastoral contexts, clerics are trained above all to listen. Members of their community who find themselves in morally challenged positions will often approach a cleric looking for answers to their problems. Rather than mechanically apply a set of moral rules or even make the judgment for the person, clerics allow individuals to tell their stories, to narrate the problem through the concrete details of the situation. Throughout this process, the cleric's role is to ask questions that arise from within the religious tradition so that the person can place his or her dilemma into a context that will resonate with the tradition itself. It is this process of telling stories, guided by incisive and morally penetrating questions, that allows individuals to make judgments that are both morally informed but sensitive to their own situations.

What arises from these pastoral settings is a narrative that is informed by a set of moral standards. The narrative, however, is not completely controlled by the individual or even controlled by the moral standards, but is framed by the questions brought to bear by the pastor or cleric. The presence of the pastor prevents the story from being a completely self-affirming one; the cleric ensures that individuals tell stories that acknowledge the moral responsibility of all.

This idealized process of pastoral interaction is not the same as a relativist or situational ethics approach. Clerics counsel individuals from within clearly defined religious traditions with moral standards found in sacred texts and historical practice. Nor are clerics always acting in this pastoral context; preaching and public advocacy would require using prophetic voices in which listening is less important than pronouncing the truth. But in the pastoral context, the role of the cleric is to guide individuals toward an understanding of their own moral dilemmas and, hopefully, a resolution of some sort.

The just war tradition provides exactly the kind of framework that could guide the question-and-answer process of a pastoral interaction. Rather than a set of rules that the population demands the military or political elites to follow, the just war tradition could serve as a framework through which an entire society can narrate the moral dilemmas of war. Such an understanding of the pastoral role of the tradition also mirrors, at least in part, the Arendtian conception identified above. Of course, as Arendt emphasizes, to impose a moral standard from a particular tradition on the political realm would violate some of her core understandings of politics. Here I diverge from Arendt to some degree, for I do not think we can understand the political realm deprived of some foundations in texts, traditions, and standards. Rather, the pastoral mode I propose here comes close to Arendt's account by creating the space where judgments, including collective judgments, can arise in the process of telling the story of a war. The judgment about the war is not made by referring to a passage from a key text in the tradition in a final, definitive way; rather, the judgment is made by forcing communities to tell their stories through an institutional framework. When combined with the categories provided by the just war tradition, this pastoral mode can result in judgments about war that rely upon narrative accounts of war.

But where can such idealized pastoral interactions take place? In the remainder of this chapter, I want to propose religious institutions as the setting for such interactions. Why churches? To begin with, the just war tradition has its origins in the Christian tradition, and in chapter 3 of this volume Nigel Biggar demonstrates how a Christian theological approach can inform the tradition even in a largely secular political order. Certainly, as we suggest in the introduction, Christianity is not the authoritative source for the tradition for all. Indeed, many of the best-known accounts of the tradition today avoid its Christian heritage, preferring to see it as part of the common morality of Western efforts to understand war in the modern world.[39] And yet its categories arise from Christianity, sometimes in ways that are not immediately obvious to those who deploy them. For instance, Larry May's recent efforts to draw upon the tradition focus on the idea of mercy through an engagement with Hugo Grotius's work. Mercy as a political concept is most intimately connected to Christianity, suggesting that its use here makes most sense when drawing upon the Christian tradition.[40]

Second, the tradition continues to be a touchstone for churches that wish to speak on matters of war and peace. For instance, in the United States and United Kingdom, churches of all denominations have found in the just war tradition a means by which to frame their public statements on war and peace. Although the ways in which the churches have drawn upon the tradition have been contested by some, they continue to serve as a framing device for many churches.[41] Moreover, in their deployment of the tradition, churches have helped to adapt it to the modern world. As suggested below, the way the American Catholic Church used the tradition to critique US nuclear policy in the 1980s not only made an important statement about the tradition but also shaped the tradition in important ways.[42]

Third, and more in accordance with the argument of this chapter, religious institutions provide the kind of institutional framework that allows the pastoral purpose to function. There are numerous other institutions within civil society that can serve as places where debate about war and peace might take place. A town hall meeting, a nongovernmental organization, a political party, or even a neighborhood gathering might be a place where a war can be debated. But churches serve the function identified here better, for three reasons. First, they are infused with a master narrative, the story of the Christian tradition. This master narrative provides a backdrop for the articulation of a meaningful life, one that links moral and ethical concerns with practical life in important ways. Second, clerics are trained to use pastoral methods in daily life. Their training allows them to serve as active listeners, who can connect that master narrative to the specific stories of war that face a country. Third, and most important, churches are not linked to the state in the way that other civil society organizations are. They stand outside the concerns of the nation and the government. As such, they are not bound by the "official" narratives of war that are so often presented in media accounts. They can bring a morally critical perspective on how wars are narrated, forcing communities to confront their collective responsibility for war-making.

Of course, this last point does not function similarly in all societies. For instance, in the United States, where a clear separation of church and state exists, churches would seem ideally situated to play this role of critics of the state. And yet for anyone familiar with the discourse of church and state today in the United States, there are many churches in which American nationalism is not only prominent but is linked directly to the Christian story. Efforts to argue for America as a "Christian nation" are rife throughout the political discourse of the United States. As such, this idealized picture of how churches might provide a critical, pastoral space for the narratives of a nation's wars might remain largely that—an ideal rather than a reality.

In the United Kingdom, other problems arise. For one, the church is officially linked to the state, although this has not prevented the church from playing a critical role at key moments. Another problem is that of sectarianism, which often plays itself out in terms of the Catholic Church's relationship with the dominant Anglican or Presbyterian churches. Such tensions mean that the ability of any single church to play the role of a pastoral institution framing the space for emerging narratives of war might be more problematic.

In both contexts, of course, membership in churches has declined radically over the last fifty years, meaning that the ability of the church to serve as an authoritative voice has become even more problematic. So, for instance, the ability of the church to connect its master narrative to the specifics of the nation and its wars will be highly problematic for many. The growing number of immigrants from Muslim countries in the United Kingdom further complicates this picture.

I would argue that the general claim I am making here—that religious institutions are important sites in civil society where narratives about war can be employed—can be developed in non-Christian contexts. For instance, the role of the mosque in Islamic traditions as a site of not only worship but also community life and scholarship might provide a similar framework within which narratives can be constructed. Moreover, as religious preaching and dialogue develops through a globalized media, there will be more interactive and international ways in which such narratives might arise.[43] Christian traditions as well have moved out of specific church contexts and into global spaces through the internet and other media. As such, the specifics of how a narrative can be constructed in a global political space are much more complicated than the picture I paint here.

This is not the place to resolve these problems. Rather, my point here is to identify one institutional framework that is not tied to the state that can provide a pastoral space in which narratives of war can be developed and judgments can be made about those wars. In order to clarify how this might work, let me compare this idea to one famous example in which an American church did undertake a national conversation that drew upon the just war tradition. In 1983 the American Catholic bishops published a pastoral letter that addressed the morality of nuclear weapons. The letter drew upon the just war tradition, although there is some debate about how much the bishops may have altered some of the core elements in their portrayal of it. The letter resulted from a consultation process that included theologians, philosophers, political scientists, policymakers, and other elements of civil society. The letter then became a point of discussion among Catholics throughout the United States. It served as a focus of discussion groups that were held in parishes, led by both lay people and clerics.

The model I have proposed here is different in some important ways. The pastoral letter concerned an issue rather than a war. As a result, it did not lend itself to a narrative style. Rather, it articulated a set of rules whereby the bishops formulated judgments about the appropriateness of a nuclear deterrent posture for the United States. The letter was quite nuanced and drew upon both just war and pacifism, which the bishops identified as the frameworks most in alignment with Catholic social teaching. At the same time, it did not seek to articulate a new narrative about how the United States came to the doctrine of nuclear deterrence, a narrative that might well have drawn upon the fact that the United States is the only power that has ever used a nuclear weapon, and the immense numbers of civilians who were killed by it.

My proposal here is that rather than a set of rules that would be used to evaluate an issue or war, the tradition could be used to guide a discussion about particular wars. There is always hesitancy among just war theorists to examine particular wars in too much detail, as this can either lead to a moralistic criticism or an equally moralistic celebration of the virtues of one's own side. To avoid this, the pastoral model I have briefly outlined may allow the tradition to guide the questions that might be asked in the service of constructing a new narrative about various wars.

For instance, a just war question sheet could be produced by an inter-Christian or wider interfaith group and distributed to a wide range of churches. Taking this sheet, churches could investigate various wars in which the United States has been engaged in order to construct new stories of those wars. This might take place in small group discussions led by clerics who have been trained in pastoral listening, supplemented by individuals with some background in just war theorizing.

Of particular importance, however, the groups would be for members of church communities, allowing them to place their histories, or their understandings of the histories, of various wars into a moral context. In so doing, new stories might emerge concerning the wars in which the United States and United Kingdom have been engaged, stories that would not locate responsibility for war in others, either foreign or domestic, but would force a confrontation with how individual citizens understand their participation in the larger social and political context that justifies and makes possible American wars.

This is a very vague proposal, at best. What I want to point to here is how an approach that draws upon the pastoral model of listening, constructing narratives, and infusing those narratives with judgments seems to be a way in which churches can draw upon the just war tradition and provide a service to the wider civil society. Narratives are powerful social and political ideas that can be used in various moral debates. The just war tradition can play a key role in shaping the narrative contexts through which American wars are framed, interpreted, critiqued, and, perhaps, fought.

NOTES

Thanks to Patrick Hayden, Cian O'Driscoll, Brent Steele, Karin Fierke, and John Williams for insightful comments on this chapter. And, thanks to the participants in the workshop sponsored by the US Institute of Peace, where a very early version of this chapter was first presented.

1. For a discussion of various elements of narrative, primarily from the perspective of literary theory, see H. Porter Abbott, *The Cambridge Introduction to Narrative*, 2nd ed. (Cambridge: Cambridge University Press, 2008).

2. For an overview of this idea, see Fred Dallmayr and Thomas McCarthy, eds., *Understanding and Social Inquiry* (Notre Dame, IN: University of Notre Dame Press, 1977).

3. A. J. P. Taylor, *The Origins of the Second World War* (London: Hamilton, 1961).

4. Michael Burleigh, *Moral Combat: A History of World War II* (London: Harper Press, 2010).

5. Bernd Greiner, *War without Fronts: The USA in Vietnam* (New York: Vintage, 2010).

6. Hidemi Suganami, "Narrative Explanation and International Relations: Back to Basics" *Millennium* 37, 2 (2008): 327–56.

7. Martin Hollis and Steve Smith, *Explaining and Understanding International Relations* (Oxford: Clarendon Press,1990).

8. Hidemi Suganami, "Causal Explanation and Moral Judgment: Undividing a Division," *Millennium* 39, no. 3 (2011): 717–34. For the material from Dray on which Suganami draws, see W. H. Dray, "Concepts of Causation in A. J. P. Taylor's Accounts of the Origins of the Second World War," *History and Theory* 17 (1978): 149–74; and W. H. Dray, "A Controversy over Causes: A. J. P. Taylor and the Origins of the Second World War," in *Perspectives on History*, by W. H. Dray (London: Routledge, 1980), 69–96.

9. Suganami, "Causal Explanation," 730.

10. Jennifer Mitzen, "Ontological Security in World Politics: State Identity and Security Dilemma," *European Journal of International Relations* 12, no. 3 (2006): 341–70; Brent Steele, *Ontological Security in International Relations* (London: Routledge, 2008).

11. Brent J. Steele, "Ideals That Were Never Really in Our Possession: Torture, Honour and US Identity," *International Relations* 22, no. 2 (2008): 243–61.

12. Alasdair MacIntyre, *After Virtue: A Study in Moral Theory* (London: Duckworth, 1981).

13. Alasdair MacIntyre, *Whose Justice? Which Rationality?* (Notre Dame, IN: University of Notre Dame Press, 1989).

14. Alasdair MacIntyre, *Three Rival Versions of Moral Inquiry: Encyclopaedia, Genealogy, and Tradition—Being Gifford Lectures Delivered in the University of Edinburgh in 1988* (Notre Dame, IN: University of Notre Dame Press, 1990), 92.

15. Ibid., 128.

16. Aristotle, *The Politics*, Book I, 1253a1–18.

17. For an explanation of how this narrative of Christianity works in terms of morality, see Alexander Lucie-Smith, *Narrative Theology and Moral Theology: The Infinite Horizon* (Burlington, VT: Ashgate, 2007).

18. John Kelsay has so ably demonstrated this over time; see John Kelsay, *Islam and Just War: A Study in Comparative Ethics* (Louisville: Westminster John Knox Press, 1993); and John Kelsay, *Arguing the Just War in Islam* (Cambridge, MA: Harvard University Press, 2007).

19. Howard Hensel, ed., T*he Prism of Just War: Asian and Western Perspectives on the Legitimate Use of Military Force* (Burlington, VT: Ashgate, 2010).

20. James Turner Johnson has argued that crusading constitutes an alternative tradition within the Western approach; see James Turner Johnson, *The Holy War Idea in Western and Islamic Traditions* (University Park: Pennsylvania State University Press, 1997).

21. Hannah Arendt, *The Origins of Totalitarianism* (New York: Harcourt Brace, 1951).

22. Hannah Arendt, *Eichmann in Jerusalem: A Study in the Banality of Evil,* 2nd ed. (New York: Viking Press, 1965).

23. Hannah Arendt, *The Human Condition* (Chicago: University of Chicago Press, 1958).

24. Hannah Arendt, *On Revolution* (New York: Viking Press, 1965).

25. Hannah Arendt, *Rahel Varnhagen: The Life of a Jewish Woman*, rev. ed., trans. Richard and Clara Winston (New York: Harcourt Brace Jovanovich, 1974; orig. pub. 1957).

26. Richard Bernstein, *Hannah Arendt and the Jewish Question* (Cambridge: Polity Press, 1996); Selya Benhabib, *The Reluctant Modernism of Hannah Arendt* (Thousand Oaks, CA: Sage, 1996).

27. Benhabib, *Reluctant Modernism*, 29–30.

28. Arendt, *Human Condition*, 184.

29. Hannah Arendt, *On Violence*, reprinted in *Crises of the Republic* (San Diego: Harcourt Brace Jovanovich, 1972), 103–98.

30. Arendt articulates the theoretical idea of natality most clearly in *The Human Condition*, 175–88. In *On Violence*, she draws upon the idea as well; see 176–84.

31. Arendt, *On Violence*, 177. For an elaboration and exploration of Arendt's views on war and violence, see Patricia Owens, *Between Politics and War: International Relations and the Thought of Hannah Arendt* (Oxford: Oxford University Press, 2007).

32. Reprinted in *Essays in Understanding, 1930–1954*, ed. Jerome Kohn (New York: Schocken Books, 2005), 307–27.

33. For a nonfoundational account of Arendt's thought as it applies to international affairs, see Patrick Hayden, *Political Evil in a Global Age: Hannah Arendt and International Theory* (London: Palgrave, 2009).

34. Jerome Kohn, "Introduction," in *The Promise of Politics*, by Hannah Arendt, ed. Jerome Kohn (New York: Schocken Books, 2003), x–xi.

35. Hannah Arendt, "Collective Responsibility," in *Responsibility and Judgment*, by Hannah Arendt, ed. Jerome Kohn (New York: Schocken Books, 2003; orig. pub. 1968), 157–58.

36. Arendt supported a Jewish armed force in the context of World War II as a way to give the Jewish people a political existence more meaningful than that which they had previously. See her essays in Hannah Arendt, *The Jewish Writings*, ed. Jerome Kohn and Ron H. Feldman (New York: Schocken Books, 2007).

37. Categories I first introduced in Anthony F. Lang Jr., "The Just War Tradition and the Question of Authority," *Journal of Military Ethics* 8, no. 3 (2009): 202–16.

38. Ibid., 206.

39. The most obvious example of this move is by Michael Walzer, *Just and Unjust Wars* (New York: Basic Books, 1977). The reputation of Walzer as a leading theorist of the tradition has only reinforced the view for many that just war no longer needs a religious foundation to make sense.

40. May has drawn on both the law and the tradition in a recent series of books. The work in which mercy plays the most prominent role is Larry May, *War Crimes and Just War* (Cambridge: Cambridge University Press, 2007).

41. There are numerous examples of how Christian churches draw upon the tradition. For an overview of British and American uses of the tradition, see Charles Reed and David Ryall, eds., *The Price of Peace: Just War in the 21st Century* (Cambridge: Cambridge University Press, 2007). The chapters in that volume by Nigel Biggar on the British churches and James Turner Johnson on the American churches provide critical overviews of how the tradition has been used by a wide array of denominations.

42. For an argument that the Church's use of the tradition here should be seen as more authoritative than some have argued, see Lang, "Just War Tradition." For an opposing view, see James Turner Johnson, "The Broken Tradition," *The National Interest* 45 (1996): 27–37.

43. For a discussion of a globalized Islamic discourse, see Peter Mandaville, *Global Political Islam* (London: Routledge, 2007).

PART II

~

Authority in Practice

CHAPTER 9

Culpability and Punishment in Classical Theories of Just War

Gregory M. Reichberg

"JUST WARS ARE USUALLY DEFINED as those which have for their end the avenging of injuries [*ulciscuntur iniurias*]." This phrase from Augustine, cited in Gratian's *Decretum*, was repeated approvingly by successive generations of canon lawyers and theologians.[1] For these early authors in the just war tradition, punishment was intimately connected with the issue of legitimate authority. Most assumed that waging war to punish wrongdoers fell within the exclusive jurisdiction of the supreme authority in each country. By the same token, legitimate authority was posited as a strict requirement of just war only when such force was exercised in view of punishment. Purely defensive measures, by contrast, did not *de jure* require the authorization of a specially designated superior, and could therefore fall within the prerogative of lower princes and even private individuals. Defense was taken to be the inherent right of any individual or community that had been unjustly attacked. But these private individuals or groups that applied force in self-defense were not allowed to seek redress for past wrongs or to punish offenders. Jurisdiction was required whenever war was undertaken to right a wrong. The classical discourse on just war was mainly about the exercise of this corrective function. Consequently, this doctrine was typically framed under the heading of "offensive war" (*bellum offensivum* or *aggressium*). The theory of legitimate defense was accorded a subordinate place and on some accounts was not even treated under the label of "just war."[2]

Despite its importance within the classical doctrine, the place occupied by punishment was often ambiguous. Sometimes punishment was presented as the underlying rationale of just war. On this understanding, the right to wage war was

157

premised on the culpable fault of one's wrongful adversary. War had an essentially penal character. As such, it could licitly be initiated only as a response to a prior culpable offense. At other times punishment was presented as an aim that might be pursued in some wars only; thus the term *bellum punitivum* was introduced to contrast this aim with other rationales for resorting to armed force. Apart from the obvious case of immediate defense, it was recognized that wars could also be undertaken for security against future harm, recuperation of stolen property, or to exact payment of debts. Vis-à-vis these rationales for offensive war, which Wolff later categorized under the heading of *bellum vindicativum*, there was no presupposition of culpability—*mens rea*—on the part of the adversary.[3] Material wrongdoing, if sufficiently damaging, would warrant resort to armed force if the wrong could not be righted by other means.

The ambiguous place of punishment in just war theory is visible in the formative account given by Thomas Aquinas. This will be our starting point. Afterward I examine how his successors dealt with this issue.

Thomas Aquinas (ca. 1224–74) famously described just cause in terms that suggest a punitive rationale for waging war: "Those who are attacked," he wrote, "should be attacked because they merit it on account of some fault."[4] Commentators have generally assumed that Aquinas's intent in uttering this phrase was to conceive of just cause in terms of desert. The fullest expression of this viewpoint may be found in the *Summula* of Thomas de Vio (1468–1534), an Italian Dominican better known by the moniker Cajetan.[5] An alternative reading (anticipated in some measure by Vitoria) was, however, proposed by Luis de Molina (1535–1600). Drawing a distinction between material and formal wrongdoing in his treatise *On Justice and Law* (ca. 1593), the Spanish Jesuit articulated a liability-based theory of just cause.[6]

Aquinas's conception of just cause has been discussed by Jeff McMahan.[7] Working under the assumption that Aquinas's formulation was deliberately focused on desert, McMahan raises a twofold objection. On the one hand, he faults this formulation for being overly narrow, as on this construal a just war could be waged *only* against a party that had *culpably* engaged in wrongdoing. Thereby excluded from legitimate attack would be objective (material) wrongdoing for which the perpetrator can be considered free of guilt on subjective grounds (e.g., by reason of ignorance or duress). An example would be the Native Americans discussed by Vitoria in the *De Indis*. Despite their condition of invincible ignorance, Vitoria nonetheless considered them to be a legitimate target of defensive attack by the Spaniards. On the other hand, McMahan takes Aquinas's definition of just cause to be overly expansive insofar as it would appear to posit retribution as a valid motive of just war. Thus understood, "those who deserve to be attacked" are made the target of attack precisely in order to punish them for their prior wrongdoing. This punishment is an end in itself; on McMahan's reading it will be implemented "even when harming [the unjust belligerent] is unnecessary for the achievement of any other aim—for example, when harming him would not prevent, deter, or rectify any other harm or wrong."[8] But "in this sense" it is generally recognized today that "people seldom, if ever deserve to be warred upon"; McMahan takes for granted that this punitive rationale should be stricken from the list of just causes for war.[9]

In place of the desert-based conception of just cause, McMahan advances a theory organized around the concept of liability. Developed at some length in his recent book, *Killing in War*, liability to attack, as he understands it, is premised on moral responsibility for objective wrongdoing.[10] A person is "morally responsible" in this way "when he engage[es] in some form of voluntary action that ha[s] some reasonably foreseeable risk of creating a wrongful threat."[11] This responsibility for positing a wrongful threat—in war and in other conflict settings—encompasses a broad range of harm-causing acts for which agents may be deemed responsible, regardless of their personal culpability, which in fact may be minimal or null.

McMahan's proximate aim in writing *Killing in War* is to elucidate how liability to attack in war is conditioned inherently upon the injustice of the cause for which one is fighting. Warriors who wage war on behalf of an unjust cause are *de iure* liable to attack, even if they bear little or no moral blame for postulating this wrongful threat (a blame that vests primarily with their leaders who have initiated the unjust war). However, these rank-and-file warriors cannot legitimately appeal to self-defense in killing enemy combatants, because, as the adage goes, "there is no defense against legitimate defense." The modern supposition that impunity for killing in war can be determined in isolation from the reasons, good or bad, that states may have for engaging in armed conflict cannot be sustained, he argues. Consequently, the related idea that warriors confront each other on the battlefield as moral equals, irrespective of the justice of their cause, must also be denied. In this twin refutation, McMahan finds himself in continuity—accurately, in my opinion—with the older approach to just war found in the works of the classical theorists.[12] The overriding aim of the book is to promote less resort to unjust war. If rank-and-file warriors can be led to understand that they are justifiably liable to attack because they are in some measure responsible for the unjust war (if only in the minimal sense that they, by not refusing to fight, are accomplices in the commission of a grave injustice), then, in light of the patent fact that most wars are unjust, they will be encouraged by this understanding to withhold their consent more often than has hitherto been the case. If enough warriors refuse to fight in unjust wars, it will become harder for leaders to initiate such wars, resulting in a less war-prone world.

The classical theorists would not have encouraged selective conscientious objection to nearly the same degree, given that they operated with a considerably more robust conception of obedience than has been advanced by McMahan. His liability account of licit killing in war nonetheless provides a more systematic reiteration of the positions staked out in the sixteenth and seventeenth centuries by Vitoria, Molina, and Grotius. Like McMahan, these classical theorists sought to carve out a middle ground between two opposing views. On the one hand, they took for granted that only the just belligerent was entitled to employ lethal force on the battlefield. Warriors on the opposing side enjoyed no such right, in any strong moral sense of the term.[13] On the other hand, these same theorists denied that all licit killing in war should be premised on the moral culpability of those attacked. Nor, by the same token, did they concede that this killing should have the character of a punishment due. Rather they maintained that the commission of objective wrongdoing—even when unaccompanied by wrongful intention and other components of subjective guilt—could justly permit the agents of such wrongdoing to be targeted with lethal harm in war. In this chapter my principal concern is to elucidate how some classical theorists sought to disentangle just war from the postulation of an essential link with culpability and punishment. How they distanced themselves from the other extreme (the "independence thesis" and its corollary the "moral equality of soldiers"), has already been dealt with elsewhere in my work, and thus I largely set it aside here.[14]

JUST CAUSE IN AQUINAS: CONTRASTING ASSESSMENTS

During the last hundred years or so, the scholarly treatments of just cause in Aquinas have tended toward two quite different assessments. One assessment criticizes his purported identification of culpability as the raison d'être of just cause. On the basis of this identification, it is assumed that Aquinas himself took punishment as the chief aim of just war. This take on just cause is then unfavorably compared with the modern, international law approach, which rejects punitive measures within the context of war. Thus, in a theological work on the Decalogue command "Thou shalt not kill," the author comments that "we can no longer see the soldier as one going out, armed with divine authority to kill enemy soldiers, as though they were so many criminals, an idea clearly reflected in St. Thomas. . . . The idea of a punitive war is completely unreal and outdated."[15] A similar inference is implied, although not stated outright, by John Finnis, who, after noting that Aquinas's "discussion of just war highlights the analogy with punishment—capital punishment—and downplays, without eliminating, the analogy with private defense of self and others," goes on to conclude that because capital punishment is no longer morally acceptable, neither is intentional killing in war.[16] Apparently assuming that any intentional killing will be punitive in character, Finnis argues that to be in conformity with contemporary Catholic morality, killing in war must be unintentional. The intention of warriors must be to stop the enemy's attack; whatever killing takes place should solely have the character of foreseeable side-effect harm. Ethical killing in contemporary war is accordingly modeled on (Finnis's reading of) Aquinas's treatment of private self-defense in ST II-II, q. 64, a. 7.[17] In a manner similar to McMahan, Finnis maintains that killing in war is not a sphere apart; it should obey the same logic as killing in other areas of human life. But whereas McMahan concedes that private individuals may intentionally kill in self-defense, under the condition that this is necessary and proportionate to the threat,[18] Finnis, as we have just seen, adopts the opposing position.

The other assessment was advanced by the French Catholic peace activist Alfred Vanderpol (1854–1915). In a work published posthumously, Vanderpol maintained that the original purity of the just war idea, as it had been articulated by Augustine, the canon lawyers, and especially Aquinas, was deformed by the "probabilism" that had been introduced into the doctrine by Vitoria's theory of simultaneous ostensible justice.[19] Molina, in particular, was singled out for special criticism, as having argued that material injustice, apart from any inner culpability (formal injustice), was sufficient to warrant a response of just war. The Jesuit scholastic thus opened the door to the idea, later to be taken up in nineteenth-century international law, that states were entitled to resort to war as a means of resolving their grievances. Just war, on Molina's logic as understood by Vanderpol, was akin to a civil lawsuit undertaken by parties who were juridically equal. The moral barrier to war was thereby lowered to the point whereby it could be viewed as a normal procedure for resolving conflicts in the international sphere. Far more preferable, Vanderpol thought, was the older approach, whereby just war was premised on a grave, culpable offense. Modeled on the procedures of criminal justice, the classical standard of just cause was extremely stringent. In this standard Vanderpol accordingly found a principle of restraint that could provide a theoretical foundation, guaranteed by the weight of long-standing tradition, for his pacifist internationalism.[20]

In a manner similar to McMahan, the articulation of just cause in terms of high standards of accountability was meant to promote less resort to war, but with this difference: Whereas Vanderpol was concerned chiefly with placing limitations directly on the decision making of political leaders, McMahan's interest is in achieving this goal by restraining the cooperation of lower military personnel in the unjustifiable war initiatives of their superiors. Note how both projects revolve around the *jus ad bellum*; in this respect they stand in contrast to the opposing orientation of those, like Finnis, who resist speaking of unjust combatants in terms of moral guilt so as to promote restraint *in bello*.[21] If warriors engaged in battle do not view each other as morally responsible for this state of affairs, they will engage in the fight with less ferocity, that is, with little or no desire to punish each other for complicity in an unjust cause. Rousseau famously voiced this viewpoint when he wrote that "war is . . . not a relationship between one man and another, but a relationship between one state and another, in which individuals are enemies only by accident, not as men, nor even as citizens, but as soldiers; not as members of the fatherland, but as its defenders."[22]

AQUINAS'S FORMULATION OF JUST CAUSE

In his entire corpus, Aquinas sought to define just cause only once, where it appears as the second of three requirements that must be met if a war is to be deemed just.[23] Here is a literal translation of the passage: "In order for a war to be just . . . in second place a just cause [*causa justa*] is required, so that those who are attacked [*impugnantur*], deserve [*mereantur*] this attack [*impugnationem*] by reason of [*propter*] some fault [*culpam*]."[24]

Aquinas's statement highlights two key elements that together constitute just cause. The first is the *target* of an attack. In Aristotelian terminology, this is the "material cause" of the just war, the "mobile" or "passive belligerent."[25] This target is described by Aquinas in the plural: "Those who are attacked." This is in line with the general thrust of medieval just war doctrine, which spontaneously conceived of war as directed at determinate individuals. Alien to this conception was the ancient Roman understanding, revived in modernity by classical international law and reflected in authors such as Rousseau, whereby the enemy had the character of a moral person, a collective whole, in which the composing individuals were united by formal bonds of affiliation.

The second key element is the *reason* motivating the attack: "some fault." A wrong has been committed that calls for a determinate response, namely, an attack to be carried out by the just belligerent (the efficient cause of just war). Those who have thus made themselves subject to a just war (the passive belligerents, or the material cause of this war) have done so by reason of their prior personal fault (the efficient pole of the material cause[26]). This fault would rest first and foremost with the political and military leadership, but on the standard medieval understanding it would extend in some measure to rank-and-file warriors and even to those civilians who by giving their support to the unjust military effort are complicit in perpetuating the unjust state of affairs (for a summation of this implication, see the discussion of Cajetan below). Within this context, the term *culpa* suggests not merely objective wrongdoing (*actus reas*) but also the inner subjective state of the agent, namely, some degree of sinful choice (*mens rea*). Aquinas often speaks of *malum culpae* (the evil of fault) as an equivalent for sin or moral evil.[27] Likewise, his employment of the verb *merere* ("to merit") in the passive voice to designate those who deserve to be warred upon seems intended to designate the punishment that is due in justice for the culpable performance of wrongful deeds.[28]

The retributionist tonality of Aquinas's statement on just cause seems further reinforced by the passage on legitimate authority that precedes it. To explain why princes alone may wield the sword of war against external enemies, Aquinas draws a parallel with the exclusive authority possessed by princes within the commonweal, an authority that they exercise, inter alia, by "punishing criminals" (*malefactores puniunt*), according to the famous words of St. Paul in Romans 13:4: "He [the prince] beareth not the sword in vain: For he is God's minister, an avenger to execute wrath upon him that doth evil."

On the basis of the terms chosen and the passages cited, it would seem patently obvious that for Aquinas the *attack* described in his account of just cause is undertaken by the agent in question (soldiers acting under the command of a prince) precisely in order to *punish* the *culpable offense* of the passive belligerent. To be the target of a just war is to suffer an evil of punishment (*malum poenae*) in retribution for the commission of an evil of sin (*malum culpae*). Just war is thus punitive in its essence; retribution is the end to which it is specifically ordered.

Is there any reason to cast doubt on the retributionist reading of the passage from Aquinas quoted above (q. 40, a. 1)? Though this has indeed been the dominant interpretation of the text, an alternative, liabilist reading has nonetheless been voiced by some authors, discretely at first by Vitoria and then very directly by Molina. What possible basis could Aquinas's text offer to the liability interpretation?

This issue is taken up textually by Peter Haggenmacher, who draws on the earlier work of the Dutch Jesuit Robert Regout.[29] The main lines of Haggenmacher's argument are as follows.

In Aquinas's *Quaestio de bello*, a. 1, the terminology of retribution appears most often in citations from St. Paul and St. Augustine. When speaking in his own voice Aquinas himself is very sparing in this usage. Here I might add that on the sole occasion in article 1 when he employs the term "punish" of his own accord (albeit by allusion to Rom 13:4) to designate a basis for using armed force, it refers to the administration of criminal penalties *within* a commonwealth; he does not expressly apply this verb when he speaks of the military force that civil authorities apply against *external* enemies.[30] Moreover, Aquinas's use of citations from St. Paul and others similar to them from St. Augustine should not be interpreted at face value or simply by reference to the underlying thought of the authors in question (where a strong retributionist viewpoint may well have been intended); rather, these citations should be interpreted in light of Aquinas's own thought, because it was in view of a particular purpose that he made use of these passages. In this connection, it should not be assumed that he employed these passages expressly to highlight the theme of punishment.[31] For instance, when Aquinas quoted Augustine's statement that "just wars are usually defined as those which have for their end the avenging of injuries," his attention seems to have been directed not to this clause but to the one that immediately follows, which enumerates two offenses that could give rise to just cause.[32] In other words, Aquinas's purpose was to provide a short list (by no means exhaustive) of what sort of wrongs could justify resort to arms, so as to bring specification to the notion of just cause. In other words, the "avenging of wrongs," which Augustine mentioned in the sentence's first clause, and which was paramount in his mind, was cited by Aquinas simply in order to make available the second clause.

Similarly, when Aquinas observed (q. 40, a. 1) how within the civil sphere princes employ the sword to "punish malefactors," it is by no means clear that his usage of the domestic analogy to elucidate the notion of legitimate war-making authority was directed precisely to the issue of punitive justice. Though this was indeed how some later authors (Cajetan, in particular, as we shall see below) read the passage in question, with the implication that just as princes are empowered to punish criminals within their jurisdiction, so too are they authorized to avenge themselves against external enemies. In all exactitude, however, it must be said that punishment was here mentioned by Aquinas only as an illustration or instantiation (presumably one among several) of the forcible actions that could be exercised by the prince *ad intra*. In fact, when he draws the analogy *ad extra*, to the prince's use of the sword against other polities, no reference is made to punishment; the emphasis is rather on protective action, "rescuing the poor" and "delivering the needy."[33]

A related point can be made regarding Aquinas's use of the verb "merere" (to merit), which seems to have been lifted directly from the *Summa theologica* of Alexander of Hales (1185–1245), where it appears in the form of a noun (*meritum*) as one of six criteria of a just war.[34] Indeed, Alexander's thought on this topic appears in a section of his *Summa theologica* that is devoted to the laws of punishment ("De legibus punitionis"). In keeping with the *Decretum* gloss *Quid culpatur* (ca. 11), Alexander viewed just war first and foremost as a kind of punishment. Aquinas's reference to "desert" (and others like it) in his famous statement on just cause may reflect his desire to build on the work of an eminent predecessor, thereby utilizing his terminology, rather than a personal and deliberate selection of the conceptual apparatus best suited to the issue at hand.[35]

The term "*impugnatio*" (attack or assault), which Aquinas employs to designate the action of the just belligerent, is surprisingly neutral. If Aquinas had really wanted to make the point that just war is a sanction, a form of punishment, why did he not speak instead of *vindicta, punitio,* or *poena*?

After discussing just war in q. 40 of ST II-II, Aquinas subsequently took up the theme of punishment in q. 108 (on the virtue "of vengeance"). Although he duly quotes Romans 13:4, just war receives no mention in this *quaestio*. If the connection between just punishment and just war is as tight as has been alleged, why did Aquinas not even hint at it in when offered a clear opening in q. 108?[36] I can add that this silence is particularly salient in light of the fact that Aquinas took care to discuss just war in two other questions that appear subsequent to q. 40—namely, q. 50, a. 4 on military prudence, and then q. 123, a. 5 on battlefield courage.

Aquinas did not carve out a special mode of justice that pertains specifically to the administration of penalties for wrongdoing. The exercise of punishment by legitimate authority he subsumed under the broader category of commutative justice. Some of Aquinas's exponents in early modernity (Cajetan and Suarez in particular) did, however, adopt a specialized category of corrective justice (the exercise of which would be the exclusive preserve of legitimate authority), and this move facilitated a reading of Aquinas wherein just war would naturally seem to be an extension of this form of justice.[37]

For these reasons Haggemacher concludes that Aquinas's theory of just cause does not hinge specifically on the dual concepts of culpability and desert.[38] The hinge is rather the idea of injustice or injury done (*iniuria*). The underlying or primary aim of just war is to efface an injury, to reestablish a right. Aquinas makes allusion to this aim when he writes (apropos the requirement of legitimate authority) that "it is not the business of a private individual to declare war, because he can pursue his right [*jus suum prosequi*] before the tribunal of his superior."[39] This statement carries the implicit supposition that a prince, having no superior, may licitly pursue redress of his violated right by resorting to war. Vindicating such a right is the specific aim of just war. At this juncture Aquinas seems to be assuming that harm can justifiably be inflicted as the result of a carefully orchestrated project only when it is premised on the prior fault of the one targeted. In other words, the notion of a violated right is at the foreground of his analysis, whereas culpability plays a background or supporting role. To drive home this point, Regout explains how the center of gravity in Aquinas's doctrine of just cause consists not so much "in the culpability of an injustice," as it does "in an injustice which is culpable."[40]

Haggenmacher maintains, furthermore, that the ambiguity in Aquinas's formulation of just cause results from the extreme brevity of his account.[41] War in the overall scheme of the Angelic Doctor's writings did after all represent a very peripheral topic. Had he paused to concentrate on this theme at greater length, he likely would have disentangled the various strands which are merged in his short account in q. 40, a. 1. In fact, one of Aquinas's contemporaries, his confrère Ulrich of Strasbourg, did provide a more detailed analysis of just cause. Though using much the same vocabulary as Aquinas, he nonetheless framed his argument around the notion of *noxia* (harm) rather than *culpa*. And though not excluding *culpa* or *meritum*, it nonetheless with greater precision designated the injury, the action opposed to *jus*, which calls forth the violent response of the just belligerent.[42]

Finally, I can point to two additional reasons that attenuate the retributionist tonality of Aquinas's statement about just cause. First of all, though he clearly believes that punishment is strictly due for every culpable misdeed—thereby rebalancing the violated order of justice—the exact correlation between fault and punishment will be effected by God only in the afterlife. Now, by contrast, punishment functions more as a "remedy" (e.g., deterring future threats or prompting the moral betterment of the criminal) than as an operator of strict justice.[43] The retributivism that McMahan and others have read into the text, and that they rightly deem unacceptable in today's context, is a glove that does not snugly fit Aquinas's hand. Moreover, if the side effects to emerge from the punishment of wrongdoing are anticipated to be worse than the original fault, Aquinas emphasizes how a wise ruler will set this punishment aside, because its remedial function will no longer obtain. Thus, though he maintains that punishment is always premised on prior guilt, with respect to the temporal order, he resists a strict equation between culpability and punishment. Not all wrongs are punishable under human law, and among those that are, punishment should sometimes be waived in the interest say of civic peace.[44]

Second, Aquinas shows some flexibility in the use of the word *culpa* (fault). Most often it signifies a fault for which the agent bears subjective guilt (*mens rea*); but occasions may be found where Aquinas employs this term to describe objective wrongdoing that has been voluntarily carried out, yet not necessarily with the awareness, and thus the intention, to do what is wrong.[45]

CAJETAN: JUST WAR AS VINDICATIVE JUSTICE

Cajetan is a pivotal figure in the development of scholastic just war theory. He was frequently cited by Vitoria, Molina, Suarez, and Grotius. Cajetan's influence is largely due to his Commentary on the *Summa theologiae* of Thomas Aquinas, which circulated widely and even achieved something of an official status when, under the authority of Pope Leo XIII, it was published alongside the *Summa theologiae* in the standard ("Leonine") edition of Aquinas's works. In this commentary, Cajetan offered a detailed treatment of legitimate war-making authority, the first of the famous three requirements of a just war set out by Aquinas in article 1 of question 40, "De bello."

Central to Cajetan's account was the distinction (not explicitly formulated by Aquinas) between two kinds of war: defensive and offensive. Defensive war required no special appeal to legitimate authority; political leaders of lower status, or even private individuals, were permitted by natural law to resort to such force in case of urgent need. Offensive war, by contrast, was more a matter of choice than of necessity. This mode of warfare Cajetan equated with the administration of punitive justice. No political community could be deemed self-sufficient (a "perfect commonwealth") if it did not possess the power to exact just retribution against its internal and external foes. The authority to wage war against *external* wrongdoers, in particular, he viewed as the distinctive mark of a fully independent commonwealth.

Cajetan provided further elucidation on the idea of just war in a later work, the *Summula*. This, as its name suggests, was a compendium of brief discussions, written especially for the use of confessors, on selected topics in canon law. In a section titled "When War Should Be Called Just or Unjust, Licit or Illicit," Cajetan considers the case of an unjust belligerent (in the *ad bellum* sense) who makes his just opponent a last-minute offer of reparation; until what point in time is the latter obligated to accept the offer? Clearly, Cajetan argues, if armed hostilities have not yet commenced, under the principle of necessity (i.e., that war should only be a last resort) the aggrieved party does indeed have an obligation to accept such an offer. By contrast, once hostilities have begun, the juridical situation is no longer the same. At this stage no offer of reparation, however complete, need be accepted by the just belligerent. To elucidate this point, Cajetan describes offensive war as a criminal proceeding, in which the just belligerent assumes the office of both prosecutor and judge. Though they are ordinarily equals, one sovereign indeed can come to have authority over another by reason of the latter's fault. On this account, just war is first and foremost an exercise in "vindicative justice" (*justitia vindicativa*).

As should be manifest from this summary, Cajetan views just war as akin to the administration of a penal sanction against a condemned criminal. That just war is an expression of criminal justice is clear to him from the fact that it involves the deliberate killing of persons and destruction of goods, none of which would be permitted were it not for the prior fault of the target. And as in a criminal prosecution, before the judge enunciates his decision, all manner of plea bargaining is admissible, but afterward, the judge has no obligation whatsoever to lighten or remove then sentence based on the condemned criminal's offers of restitution, sincere confessions of guilt, and so forth. Similarly, "he who has a just war embodies a judge of proceedings in vindicative justice against foreign disturbers of the commonwealth. [Once the war is under way] he has already become the master [*dominus*] of the case. The vindicative proceedings being no longer in their initial state, he can continue the war and enforce vindicative justice with the sword of war (unless he chooses to exercise mercy)."[46]

Notice how on this conception war is a punishment that is brought to bear on the guilty. The aim of the just belligerent is precisely to exact satisfaction from a culpable party who was unwilling to offer it up voluntarily by the payment of restitution, damages, and so on. To describe the satisfaction that has thus been imposed, Cajetan coins the neologism "satispassion." Finally, he explains how *satispassion* can extend well beyond the leaders immediately responsible for the offense:

> Concerning the harm inflicted by war, [it] should be understood . . . that all of the losses resulting from a just war, not only for the soldiers, but also for any member of the commonwealth against which there is a just war are devoid of sin [on the part of the just belligerent] and entail no duty of restitution, . . . even if by accident innocents should happen to be injured. . . . The sentence pronouncing the justice of the war need not distinguish whether some part of the enemy state is innocent, since it is presumed to be entirely

hostile, the whole of it being considered as enemy, and therefore it is entirely condemned and pillaged.[47]

Summing up Cajetan's argument for just war as a criminal proceeding, Haggenmacher maintains that it commits the fallacy of begging the question (*petitio principii*): Having asserted in the opening premise that, by reason of their severity, the effects of an offensive war can only be justified as a penal sanction, it proceeds in the second premise to hold that every penal sanction presupposes (1) on the part of its enforcer an authority to carry out vindicative justice, and (2) on the part of its recipient the commission of a grave injustice. Then in the conclusion it is said that as offensive war is by definition an act of vindicative justice, it can permissibly be applied only against grave criminal infractions. But this conclusion was already implicit in the major premise. Moreover, this premise is not self-evident; it requires demonstration.

SUÁREZ: PUNISHMENT, LEGITIMATE AUTHORITY, AND *AD BELLUM* RESTRAINT

Picking up where Cajetan left off, Francisco Suárez (1548–1617) underscored how his own treatment in the *Disputation on War* was chiefly about offensive war with the corollary that legitimate authority would be a condition indispensable to its exercise.[48] A resort to force is considered *offensive* when it aims to counter an injustice that is past and done (*facta iam sit*). A *defensive* resort, by contrast, is put up in opposition to an injustice that is in some measure still under way (*in fieri*).[49] With respect to the latter, the agent's purpose is accordingly to resist harm (to his person or his property), whereas vis-à-vis the former, the goal is to obtain a remedy (satisfaction) for the injury suffered. Because harm is especially to be resisted when it occurs in the heat of the moment, under this urgent immediacy there is no requirement to wait for an intervention of civil authorities (the police) before resorting to force in self-defense. Conversely, when satisfaction is sought for past wrongs, urgency cannot be alleged, and private persons have no entitlement to take this form of justice into their own hands. A civil authority alone is empowered to administer penalties for wrongdoing, especially when these involve the imposition of physical harm. Taking for granted that "the punishment inflicted through war is of the severest kind," Suárez concludes that "it ought to be inflicted with the utmost restraint," and not by just anyone in a position of authority, but solely under the order of a supreme prince.[50] Here we see emerging the modern view developed by Vanderpol that the close linkage of *bellum justum* with punishment functions to limit the allowable scope of resort to war.

VITORIA: LIABILITY FOR WRONGDOING
AS THE BASIS OF JUST CAUSE

Although taking Aquinas's treatment of just cause (q. 40, a. 1) as the framework for his own analysis, Francisco de Vitoria (ca. 1492–1546) moved the doctrine in a direction that had the effect of prioritizing liability over culpability as the basis for just cause. The contrast between the two forms of responsibility was not developed by him explicitly, although by his choice of vocabulary and his various comments he nonetheless provided an impetus for the later work of Molina.

Most notably, where Aquinas had seemingly premised just cause on a culpable offense (*culpa*), Vitoria discreetly substituted a different term—injury (*iniuria*)—to describe this same state of affairs.[51] This shift in vocabulary is not accompanied by the slightest hint of criticism for Aquinas's earlier usage. This rephrasing seems intended instead to render more visible the argument effectively at work in the master's own text. The careful selection of this term opened up a space—apparently in Vitoria's eyes consistent with Aquinas's formulation—for the differentiation of two kinds of adversaries against whom war may rightly be waged. On the one hand, there are those who have shown malice in doing what is wrong. In light of their manifest culpability and hardness of will, against them the full "rights of war" (*jura belli*) may be applied."[52] On the other hand, some adversaries do what is wrong out of ignorance. In this connection Vitoria famously cites the example of the Native Americans who, upon encountering the Spanish newcomers, "were understandably fearful of men whose customs seemed so strange, and who they can see are armed and much stronger than themselves."[53] Due to their "invincible ignorance," Vitoria reasons that these "barbarians" understandably, but nonetheless voluntarily and wrongly, attacked the Spaniards who (at least initially) wished them no harm. Being wronged in this fashion, the Spaniards had just cause to wage war against their assailants. But because the initial attack resulted from a condition of excusable ignorance, in responding with force the Spaniards were obligated to show the utmost restraint possible, staying wholly within the bounds of proportionate self-defense. That the just belligerent's mode of conducting the war should be proportionate to the adversary's degree of responsibility for the commission of wrongdoing was summed up by Vitoria when he wrote that "the rights of war (*jura belli*) against really harmful and offensive enemies are quite different from those against innocent or ignorant ones."[54] This insight is usefully developed in some detail by McMahan, who explains how "the extent to which a person is excused for posing a threat of wrongful harm affects the degree of his moral liability to defensive harm, which in turn affects the stringency of the proportionality restriction on defensive force."[55] In so doing McMahan establishes a typology of wrongful threats—innocent, excused, partially excused, and culpable—that are liable to defensive attack.[56] The proportionality gradation from one kind of threat to another becomes particularly relevant when it is a matter of deciding how much risk just combatants should be willing to place on themselves or on innocent victims in order to minimize harm to their assailants. In other words the order of presumptions (e.g., should I aim at killing the assailant or incapacitating him?) varies from one case to another. Confronted with a patently culpable threat, "it may be permissible," McMahan argues, "to kill him *rather than* incapacitate him at the cost of suffering a substantial injury, for example a broken arm."[57] By contrast, if it seems clear that the assailant "has a partial excuse, it may be wrong for you to kill him—that is, you may be required to suffer the broken arm in order to avoid killing him."[58] In sum, then, "the harmfulness of the defensive action to which [a threat] is liable varies with the degree of his culpability."[59]

Returning now to Vitoria's analysis: Even in a circumstance where the wrongful intent of the adversary is clearly manifest, such that the entire range of sanctions could be directed against him, these punitive measures—deposition of enemy rulers, execution of the guilty, destruction of enemy fortresses as a precaution against future harm, enslavement of captives, and so on—are understood by Vitoria to be chiefly applicable in the period *post bellum*.[60] In this manner, Vitoria distances himself from the idea, advanced as we have seen by Cajetan, that offensive war is a retributive sanction that is directed against the enemy *in bello*.

MOLINA: JUST OFFENSIVE WAR IS NOT COEXTENSIVE WITH PUNISHMENT

Molina opens his discussion of just cause with a reference to Vitoria's *De jure belli*. Commenting on what above I termed "the efficient pole of the material cause," Vitoria had designated this aspect of just cause as an "injury done" (*iniuria*). Molina, like Vitoria before him, viewed this new term as consistent with Aquinas employment of "*culpa*," as both Spanish scholastics cited him in this connection without any indication that their new terminology represented an innovation. The shift of vocabulary did nonetheless set the discussion of the material cause of war on a new trajectory. Immediately after citing Vitoria's assertion that only *iniuria* can provide a basis for just cause, Molina adds that this injury can give rise to a threefold response on the part of the just belligerent: (1) hindering the injury, (2) redressing the injury, or (3) avenging the injury.[61] Having established this distinction, the inquiry then moves to an examination of the latter two categories, both of which come under the heading of "offensive war" (which Molina takes to be the concern of ST II-II, q. 40, a. 1, and for this reason defensive war is left outside the ambit of his discussion).

In the analysis that ensues, Molina is intent on showing how redress and punishment (responses 2 and 3 above) are separable aims. Redress can be sought without also seeking to punish the offender, precisely when the party from whom redress is sought does not bear culpability for the injury he has done. "Notice," Molina writes, "it is sometimes sufficient for a just war that there be injury [committed] materially [*materialiter*] which involves no sin [*absque peccato*]." To illustrate this point, he cites Deuteronomy 1:7, where God granted to the Israelites the land of Canaan, and by virtue of this gift he concomitantly permits the Israelites the right to expel by war those inhabitants who resisted them. But because these inhabitants (Canaanites and Amorites) were wholly ignorant of God's gift to the Israelites, they were "without blame in resisting and trying to retain these lands; and therefore they inflicted only a material injury upon the children of Israel."

Subsequently applying this teaching on invincible ignorance to the issue of redress, Molina envisions two different forms of material injury, one of which could justify a reaction of offensive war and the other not. In the first case injury is blamelessly inflicted and the doer benefits thereby; say, he takes possession of land that is de facto another's. Should he refuse to return this property, sincerely believing it to be his, the party that has suffered this loss (presupposing, of course, that the loss is sufficiently grave) can seek redress of his claim by dint of force. War thus becomes the remedy for a violated right, for, seeing as this property is really his, objectively "on the part of the thing itself" (*ex parte ipsius rei*), his opponent has a strict obligation (*obligatio*) to hand it over. The fact that the unjust possessor is unable, by no fault of his own, to grasp this obligation in no way changes this state of affairs. Using force to compel return of the property may thus be perfectly justified, even though it would entail the deliberate infliction of death on enemy combatants who are in fact subjectively innocent. Molina is quick to add, however, that when the unjust belligerent is invincibly ignorant of his wrongdoing, a higher degree of restraint is required than would ordinarily be the case. Because no punishment whatsoever is involved, the just belligerent in bringing harm upon his adversary must limit himself to doing only what is "necessary to wrest from their power what they have unjustly withheld materially." And should this measure be exceeded, the just belligerent will be obligated to make restitution. This is an early formulation of what is now termed "military necessity."

If, conversely (the second case), the party (also in a condition of invincible ignorance) that has done injury to another retains no benefit from this injury, the injured party cannot take up arms against him because there is nothing to get back. In the absence of any possible redress and in the face of the offender's invincible ignorance, no punishment will be apposite. Armed action is thereby strictly excluded. This distinction underscores for Molina how redress is (in principle) an aim entirely separable from punishment.

Molina does not deny that punishment can sometimes be taken as a legitimate aim of war, under the condition, of course, that there is not only material but also formal wrongdoing. Clearly the unjust seizure of property—knowingly or out of culpable ignorance—could merit an armed reaction in view of punishing the offenders. Such a war would accordingly combine the two aims of redress and punishment. Wars undertaken for other aims (redress or defense) do not per se stand in need of this requirement. In other words, Molina takes neither Augustine nor Aquinas as having advanced an underlying (primary) punitive aim for just war.

By explicitly distinguishing several possible modes of offensive war, Molina made an important contribution to the development of just war thinking. No longer would punishment be viewed as the proximate goal of waging war. Military acts were henceforth conceived as directed first and foremost to the defeat of the enemy. This proximate goal would itself be sought by reference to several possible final goals: defense, the recovery of property, or the punishment of wrongdoing. And even in this last case, the punishment in question would be meted out not during the war but only afterward, once the enemy was defeated. In other words, war should never be conducted as though it were itself a form of punishment. This removal of punishment from the sphere of war represented an important advance that paved the way for the codification of rules of war regarding the humane treatment of enemy combatants (e.g., The Hague rules).

GROTIUS: SYSTEMATIZING THE PATH MARKED OUT BY VITORIA AND MOLINA

Hugo Grotius (1583–1645) discussed the links between war, liability, culpability, and punishment at least twice in his career. The first account appears in his youthful work *De jure praedae* (*On the Law of Prize and Booty*, written 1604–6).[62] After noting that a just war can have its basis in four causes—the defense of self or property, the recovery of property, the exaction of debts, and the punishment of wrongdoing—he proceeds to explain that such a war is necessarily unilateral: "When it is evident that the belligerent waging a just war is acting with rightful force, it follows that the enemy agent against whom the just war is waged must necessarily be disposed in the opposite fashion."[63] Because "the opposite of a right is a wrong [*iniuriam*]," that party rightly becomes the passive subject of the said war, who does a wrong [*iniuraim facit*]."[64] To elucidate this "material cause" of war, Grotius embarks on an investigation into the meaning of the key term *iniuria*, which underlies his discourse about the target of a just war.

Iniuria (which may be translated as a "wrong" or an "injury") can have three distinct but related meanings. In the first and broadest sense, it designates the wrongful thing done (*opus*), that is, some action that, taken in itself, is unrighteous or unjust. Thus understood, even nonrational animals can engage in wrongful action, as when a dog bites a man, or by extension, when one who is insane (*non compos mentis*) commits what is (objectively speaking) a crime against another. In the second sense, *iniuria* can designate an action (*actio*) that is wrongful, in the minimal sense that it is carried out by an agent who, knowingly and voluntarily, performs what he does. Finally, in the third and narrowest sense, an action can be said to be injurious when it proceeds from a depraved will (*affectio*).[65]

Having articulated this threefold distinction (injury as *opus*, *actio*, or *affectio*), Grotius concludes that each of these modes of wrongdoing can underlie a resort to just war; but depending on the case, the war's consequences and severity of will differ.[66] Most restrictive will be a resort to force against wrongs situated in the first category. Thus, should someone threaten me with harm while he is insane or when he is dreaming, "I may rightly repel force with force, even to the point of slaying that person if no other way of ensuring my safety is left open," but my violent response must remain strictly within the bounds of proportionate self-defense.[67] Less restrictive will be the force used against soldiers who serve in an unjust war, for by their deliberate action they perpetrate a wrong.[68] But because they do so under obedience to their superiors, in support of a cause that is not (from their limited vantage) patently wrong, and though they may be rightly targeted with lethal harm, their lack of personal fault (as they are merely acting instrumentally under the initiative of a higher authority and thus are not to be deemed guilty of murder when they wrongly kill) renders them fit for the special protections that the Romans accorded under the heading of "just enemies."[69] Finally, the severest measures are reserved for those who knowingly "have transgressed with unjust intent."[70] Their culpability deserves punishment, for according to the fifth law of nature (enunciated in the Prolegomena to the work), "evil deeds must be corrected."[71] Thus liable to punishment are robbers and other malefactors who use force without proper authority, instigators of rebellion, leaders who command their subordinates into unjust wars, soldiers who are aware of this injustice but obey regardless, and individuals who have committed (or commanded) atrocities in wartime ("been carried away, so to speak, by the impetus of war").[72] This punishment will be meted out, not by virtue of the war action itself, but only afterward, once the just side is victorious, and in conformity with due measure and proper legal procedure.[73]

Grotius returned to the theme of war and punishment in his mature work, *De jure belli ac pacis* (*On the Law of War and Peace*, published 1625). In laying out the architecture of its second part (book II) on just cause for war, he distinguished three scenarios in which resort to force can legitimately be employed: First, there is defense from an ongoing or imminent attack; second, there is action to repair wrongs (*iniuria*) already done; and third, there is the punishment of those responsible for some (but not all) of these wrongs.[74]

By relating punishment to a restricted subset of actionable wrongs, Grotius effectively prioritized a liability-based approach to the question of just cause. Punishment is rightly due for wrongdoing only when it proceeds from some evil intent (*malitia*). He acknowledges, by contrast, that the scope of liability for the commission of wrong is much wider, as even persons who have not intended wrongs can be compelled to make restitution, or can be forcibly restrained from persisting in harmful action, as in the case of nonresponsible or innocent threats.[75] He thus organizes his treatment of just cause for war around the broad category of *delictum*, rather than under the more restricted heading of *maleficium* (causing harm with wrongful intent).[76] Thus, while admitting how de facto "wars are usually begun for the purpose of exacting punishment," it is still the case de jure that wars can also be undertaken simply "to make good a loss."[77] Wars of the latter sort are of a different nature than those initiated with the former motive in mind. To sum this up, Grotius significantly reverts to a similarly broad usage of the term *culpa*, using it as an equivalent for *delictum*, when he writes that "any sort of fault [*qualiscumque culpa*] may frequently be sufficient to give rise to a liability [*obligatio*] for damages inflicted."[78] This usage of *culpa is* similar to what Vitoria had earlier termed *iniuria*. In so doing, Grotius discretely emphasized the continuity between Aquinas's seminal treatment of just cause and the approach articulated afterward by Molina, in contradistinction to the retributionist line of Cajetan.

Specifically on wars that are carried out for the end of punishment, Grotius did, however, mark out a more robust position than his predecessors Vitoria and Molina. Although they had denied that violations of the law of nature could furnish a *casus belli*—an issue much discussed at the time when it had been advanced by some Spanish publicists as a rationale for attacking the Indians of the New World— Grotius argued in favor of the affirmative view. In so doing, he seems mainly to have been motivated by a subsidiary issue, namely, Vitoria's contention that Christian princes were possessed of no special jurisdiction over the Native Americans and thus were not entitled to punish overt violations of the natural law (sodomy, idolatry, etc.). This served Grotius with a useful occasion to develop his view that the right to punish (*jus puniendi*) did not derive first and foremost from civil authority. Far from being an "effect of civil jurisdiction," he maintained that by the law of nature it attached originally to individuals and only later, by delegation as it were, came to be vested in temporal authorities.[79] This in turn enabled Grotius to explain how one prince could exercise the sword of war against another, even in the absence of any special jurisdiction, thus overcoming the paradox, previously discussed by Suárez (who nonetheless remained unnamed), that if two belligerents are each sovereign, with by definition no superior to judge over them, and furthermore if resort to war for redress of a grievance is indeed the exercise of a jurisdiction, this would seem to imply that even the just belligerent cannot legitimately sanction the wrongdoing of his opponent, thus undermining the very basis of just war.[80]

In thus justifying the exercise of war for punitive ends, in *De jure belli ac pacis* Grotius left open the question of whether the said punishment should be administered *in bello* (in which case the war itself could have a punitive character) or whether this would become an appropriate measure solely in the period *post bellum*. In one passage he makes passing reference "to this right [of inflicting punishment] which is confirmed also by the usage of all nations, not only after the conclusion of a war but also while the war is still going on," yet without specifying whether this usage was in accord with his own reasoned view.

CONCLUSION

This chapter has explored the place of punishment in classical theories of just war. Dependency on a few citations from Augustine, most especially the famous passage *ulciscuntur iniurias* in his *Questions on the Heptateuch*, led early authors to define just cause as the response to a culpable offense. Just war was accordingly about the avenging of wrongs; it was conceptualized around the theme of desert. This understanding of just war received its most systematic articulation in the sixteenth century, by the pen of Cajetan. Soon after, a competing theory was advanced, first discretely by Vitoria but later more explicitly by Molina and Grotius, which posited liability for wrongdoing, rather than culpability, as the foundation of just cause. Retribution lost the central position it had previously occupied. No longer was war taken to be a penal sanction that would be directed against enemy combatants. This shift away from desert opened up a space for the emergence of modern laws of armed conflict, wherein punishment, if due, is relegated chiefly to the period *post bellum*. Warfare has the purpose of opposing unjust enemy aggression; but only as much force should be used as is necessary to achieve this purpose.

In this story, the just war doctrine of Thomas Aquinas occupies an ambiguous position. His famous definition of just cause, with its terminology of culpability and desert, seems consistent with the penal conception. Yet, on closer reading, it remains uncertain whether he intended to ascribe so central a position to punishment, or whether this is a distortion created by Cajetan's later systematization. Other elements in Aquinas's thought lend themselves to the liabilist reading, and this is in fact how his doctrine was later read by Vitoria, Molina, and Grotius.

NOTES

1. Causa 23, q. 2, canon 2; reproduced by Gregory M. Reichberg, Henrik Syse, and Endre Begby, eds., *The Ethics of War: Classic and Contemporary Readings* (Oxford: Blackwell, 2006), 113, citing Augustine, *Questions on the Heptateuch*, bk. VI, chap. 10.

2. This can be seen most notably in the influential writings of Pope Innocent IV (ca. 1180–1254), who contrasted "defense" with "war"; see "On the Restitution of Spoils" in *The Ethics of War*, 150–51. This was later summed up by Cajetan, who wrote that "in order to ascertain the authority needed to wage war, it should be understood that this is not a discussion of defensive war, namely when someone makes a war in defense against a war made on himself; for any people has a natural right to do this. But here the concern is with declaring war: what authority is required for this?" Cajetan, Commentary to *Summa Theologiae* II-II, q. 40, a. 1; translation taken from Reichberg, Syse, and Begby, *Ethics of War*, 242. Aquinas

himself seems to have staked out a middle ground regarding the status of defensive war. On the one hand, he dealt with war and self-defense in two different *questions* of the second part of the *Summa Theologiae*—the first in q. 40, and the second in q. 64, a. 7—thereby suggesting that the two are subject to quite different assessments. On the other hand, in his famous treatment of legitimate authority in q. 40, a. 1, he emphasized how such authority is needed even for defensive war, as it is the special task of the prince to assemble "the multitude" (i.e., an army) so as to protect his polity against the attack of external enemies. This indicates how Aquinas took care not to conflate public and private defense into a single category.

3. Christian Wolff contrasted punitive and vindicative war in his *Jus gentium methodo scientifica pertractatum*, §639, translation in *The Classics of International Law* (Oxford: Clarendon Press, 1934), no. 13, 327–28.

4. *Summa Theologiae* II-II, q. 40, a. 1; trans. by Reichberg, Syse, and Begby, *Ethics of War*, 176–78). Other authors—e.g., Cajetan—used *vindicativum* as a synonym for *punativum*.

5. Cajetan, "When War Should Be Called Just or Unjust, Licit or Illicit," in *Summula* (Lyon: A. de Harsy, 1581), 32–39; trans. by Reichberg, Syse, and Begby, *Ethics of War*, 245–50.

6. Molina, *De Iustitia et Iure*, II, 102, 2; trans. by Reichberg, Syse, and Begby, *Ethics of War*, 334–38.

7. Jeff McMahan, "Just Cause for War," *Ethics and International Affairs* 19, no. 3 (2005): 1–21.

8. Ibid., 7.

9. Ibid.

10. Jeff McMahan, *Killing in War* (Oxford: Oxford University Press, 2009), esp. chap. 4; Jeff McMahan, "Liability and the Limits of Self-Defense," 155–202.

11. Ibid., 177.

12. Ibid., 238n26.

13. However, Grotius conceded, based on an appeal to the lesser evil, that they might nonetheless be accorded impunity for battlefield killing by a special dispensation of the law of nations. See *De jure belli ac pacis* III.iv.4; trans. Francis W. Kelsey, in *The Classics of International Law*, no. 3, vol. 2 (Oxford: Clarendon Press, 1925); reproduced with an emended translation by Reichberg, Syse, and Begby, *Ethics of War*, 426.

14. Gregory M. Reichberg, "Just War and Regular War: Competing Paradigms," in *Just and Unjust Warriors: The Moral and Legal Status of Soldiers*, ed. David Rodin and Henry Shue (Oxford: Oxford University Press, 2008), 193–213.

15. Augustine Regan, *Thou Shalt Not Kill* (Dublin: Mercier Press, 1979), 77.

16. John Finnis, *Aquinas: Moral, Political, and Legal Theory* (Oxford: Oxford University Press, 1998), 285–89.

17. Gregory M. Reichberg, "Aquinas on Defensive Killing: A Case of Double-Effect?" *The Thomist* 69 (July 2005): 341–70; this article argues against the view (advanced by Finnis and many others) that on Aquinas's account intentional killing in private self-defense is per se illicit.

18. McMahan, *Killing in War*, 159.

19. Alfred Vanderpol, *La doctrine scholastique du droit de guerre* (Paris: Pedone, 1919); on "probabilism," see 171–88.

20. Peter Haggenmacher, *Grotius et la doctrine de la guerre juste* (Paris: Presses Universitaires de France, 1983), 417–26, the section "La guerre juste des scholastiques est-elle nécessairement vindicative? Les theses de Molina à la lumière des conceptions anatgonistes de Cajetan et de Vitoria"; Peter Haggenmacher explains how Vanderpol's reading of Molina is

anachronistic in that it projects onto the thought of the seventeenth-century Jesuit a perspective (the freedom of states to undertake war at their own discretion) that emerged only later during the period of classical international law. In so doing, Haggenmacher presents an excellent overview of the historical debates on the link between culpability and punishment. This chapter has benefited from his penetrating analysis.

21. "Unjust combatants" is here intended to signify warriors who fight on behalf of an unjust cause. The *in bello* meaning, whereby the term designates combatants who violate the norms of war, is set aside in the present essay.

22. J. J. Rousseau, *The Social Contract*, book I, chap. 4, § 9, in *The Social Contract and Other Later Political Writings*, ed. and trans. Victor Gourevitch (Cambridge: Cambridge University Press, 1997), 46–47.

23. Passing reference is however made to just cause in *Summa Theologiae* I-II, q. 105, a. 3, where Aquinas notes that the Old Law contained suitable precepts "regarding hostile relations with foreigners," for instance the commandment that "war should be declared for a just cause."

24. *Summa Theologiae*, II-II, q. 40, a. 1.

25. The Aristotelian terminology of material and efficient causality is borrowed from Grotius, who applies it to just war in his *De jure praedae*, VII, 6.

26. See Haggenmacher's discussion of material and efficient causality in the context of just cause: Haggenmacher, *Grotius et la doctrine de la guerre juste*, 148–54.

27. See Gregory M. Reichberg, "Beyond Privation: Moral Evil in Aquinas's *De malo*," *Review of Metaphysics* 55 (June 2002): 731–64.

28. See *Summa contra Gentiles* III, chap. 140.

29. Haggenmacher, *Grotius et la doctrine de la guerre juste*, 417–19; Robert Regout, *La doctrine de la guerre juste de saint Augustin à nos jours d'après les théologiens et les canonists catholiques* (Paris: A. Pedone, 1935), 25–35, 144–46, 184–85.

30. "And just as it is permissible [for princes] to have recourse to the material sword in defending the common weal against internal disturbances, as when they punish malefactors, according to the words of the Apostle [Romans 13:4]: 'he beareth not the sword in vain: for he is God's minister, an avenger to execute wrath upon him who does evil'; so too, it is their business to have recourse to the sword of war in protecting the common weal against external enemies"; translation, here emended, by Reichberg, Syse, and Begby, *Ethics of War*, 177.

31. Haggenmacher, 419, footnote 2063.

32. "when it is necessary by war to constrain a nation or city which has either neglected to sanction (*vindicare*) an infraction committed by one of its citizens, or to restore what has been taken injuriously."

33. Thus, after saying that it is the business of princes "to have recourse to the sword of war in protecting the common weal against external enemies," Aquinas observes how those who are in authority are enjoined (Ps. 81:4) to 'Rescue the poor: and deliver the needy out of the hand of the sinner . . . " trans. by Reichberg, Syse, and Begby, *Ethics of War*, 177.

34. Alexander of Hales, *Summa theologica* III, n. 466; trans. by Reichberg, Syse, and Begby, *Ethics of War*, 157–59. In fact, Aquinas rarely uses the term "meritum" to describe a punishment due for sinful acts; he typically speaks of merit as the reward due for goods acts.

35. For a translation of this canon, see Reichberg, Syse, and Begby, *Ethics of War*, 112. The canon is taken from Augustine's treatise against the Manichees; in this passage he states that "good men undertake wars . . . to inflict punishment. . . . "

36. A similar silence is visible in Aquinas's earlier work, the *Summa contra Gentiles*. In book III, chap. 146, on the infliction of punishment by civil authorities, and quoting Rom

13:4, Aquinas emphasizes how peace ("the ordered concord of citizens") is assured, inter alia, by the timely administration of sanctions for wrongdoing. Though capital punishment is abundantly referred to, nowhere does he mention the special case of war.

37. See Haggenmacher, *Grotius et la doctrine de la guerre juste*, 409–16.

38. Ibid., 419–26.

39. Aquinas, *Summa theologiae* II-II, q. 40, a. 1.

40. Regout, *La doctrine*, 146; cited by Haggenmacher, *Grotius et la doctrine de la guerre juste*, 418.

41. Haggenmacher, *Grotius et la doctrine de la guerre juste*, 166–67.

42. See ibid., 166, for the relevant reference.

43. *Disputed Questions on Evil* (*De Malo*), q. 2, a. 10, ad 4.

44. See the *Commentary on Aristotle's* Nicomachean Ethics (in VIII *Ethic*, 1), where Aquinas approves the practice of legislators who "have greater zeal for maintaining friendship among citizens than even justice itself which is sometimes omitted, for example, in the infliction of punishment, lest dissention be stirred up"; trans. C. I. Litzinger (Notre Dame, IN: Dumb Ox Books, 1993), 477.

45. See, e.g., *De Malo*, q. 5, a. 5, ad 6.

46. Reichberg, Syse, and Begby, *Ethics of War*, 248.

47. Ibid., 249. At this point Cajetan seems to be describing not killing, but the confiscation of goods. He does allow that not all members of the enemy side should be deemed complicit in the wrongs perpetrated by its leaders: among these "innocents" he mentions (citing a famous decretal *De pace et treuga*—taken from the early medieval "Peace of God" movement) priests, monks, converts, pilgrims, merchants, farmers traveling and returning, and animals as they plow, as "exempted from harm brought about by war." But while recognizing the wisdom of this positive law, he questions whether it has in fact "been abolished through frequent violation."

48. "Bellum aggressivum." See *Disputatio de bello* 1.6; trans. by Reichberg, Syse, and Begby, *Ethics of War*, 342.

49. Ibid.

50. *Disputatio de bello*, 6. 4; trans. by Reichberg, Syse, and Begby, *Ethics of War*, 362. For a more detailed elucidation on Suárez's thought concerning these matters, see Gregory M. Reichberg, "Suárez on Just War," in *Interpreting Suárez: Critical Essays*, ed. Daniel Schwartz (Cambridge: Cambridge University Press, 2011), 185–204.

51. *De jure belli* (On the Laws of War), 1.3, §10, fourth point, "the sole and only just cause for waging war is when harm (*iniuria*) has been committed (quoting from the translation by Francisco de Vitoria, *Political Writings*, ed. Anthony Pagden and Jeremy Lawrance [Cambridge: Cambridge University Press, 1991], 303). This translation obscures Vitoria's subtle shift in vocabulary, when several lines later it renders the same term, *iniuria*, as "culpable offense."

52. *De Indis* (On the American Indians) 3.1, § 8; trans. by Vitoria, *Political Writings*, 283.

53. Ibid., 282.

54. Ibid (where I amend the translation by substituting "rights" for "laws").

55. McMahan, *Killing in War*, 156.

56. Ibid., 159–67. Nonresponsible threats are excluded by McMahan from this typology, as on his account these are reducible to the status of innocent bystanders, and thus may not be taken as the target of legitimate defensive action (167–73).

57. Ibid., 161.

58. Ibid.

59. Ibid.

60. Some of these measures are mentioned *De Indis*, ibid. A more elaborate list of these measures may be found in *De iure belli*, 3.1, §§42–59 (*Political Writings*, 318–26).

61. At this juncture Molina quotes from the passage in Augustine that Aquinas had earlier used to illustrate the sort of wrongs (refusing to make amends for the wrongs committed by subjects, etc.) that could justify armed action in response.

62. English translation: *Commentary on the Law of Prize and Booty*, trans. Gwladys L. Williams, in *The Classics of International Law* (Clarendon Press: Oxford, 1950).

63. Ibid., 70.

64. Ibid.; translation modified.

65. McMahan makes use of substantially the same tripartite division when he refers to three kinds of threats, (1) nonresponsible, (2) innocent or excused (partially or wholly), and (3) culpable. He is more restrictive than Grotius in denying that nonresponsible threats may be a legitimate target of lethal defensive action. But on this score McMahan shows an affinity with the moral rigor of St. Augustine. E.g., in *De serm. Dom.* I, 19, 57, he lauds the example of a caregiver who voluntarily refrains from using force in self-protection upon receiving blows from an insane person in his charge. Augustine emphasizes how charitable concern for the assailant, wishing what is good for him, entails the voluntary assumption of harm upon oneself.

66. "Those persons who bring about injury in any way whatsoever are liable to prosecution in war"; *Commentary on the Law of Prize and Booty*, 74

67. Ibid., 73. Grotius justifies this use of force against nonresponsible threats by appealing to the first law of nature: "It shall be permissible to defend [one's own] life and to shun that which threatens to prove injurious"; ibid., 10.

68. "For he who resists a just execution (whether knowingly or ignorantly) causes an injury, since he either keeps back that which belongs to another or fails to do that which he is under an obligation to do, and since, moreover, he is also offending one whom he ought not to offend"; ibid., 74.

69. Ibid., 82–84.

70. Ibid., 111.

71. Ibid., 14.

72. Ibid., 111.

73. Ibid., 111–12.

74. *De jure belli ac pacis* II.i.2; trans. by Reichberg, Syse, and Begby, *Ethics of War*, 401–2. In chapter 1 of the present volume, James Turner Johnson maintains that Grotius posited self-defense as the foundation of the other rationales for waging just war. However, I do not see any basis for this claim in either the *De jure belli ac pacis* or the *De jure praedae*. In both texts, defense, punishment, etc., are presented as independent just causes of war.

75. Ibid., II.i.3: "Wherefore, even if the assailant be blameless, as for instance a soldier acting in good faith, or one who mistakes me for someone else, or one who is rendered irresponsible by madness or by sleeplessness—this, we read, has actually happened to some— the right to protect oneself (*jus se tuendi*) is not thereby taken away; it is enough that I am not under obligation to suffer what such an assailant attempts, any more than I should be if attacked by an animal belonging to another"; trans. by Reichberg, Syse, and Begby, *Ethics of War*, 402. In subsequent passages, he qualifies this assertion by adding that (1) "even under such circumstances the person who is attacked ought to prefer to do anything to frighten away or weaken the assailant, rather than cause his death," II.i.4; trans. by Reichberg, Syse, and Begby, *Ethics of War*, 402) and (2) it is impermissible to deliberately harm innocent bystanders so as to protect oneself, II.i.3; ibid.

76. See ibid., II.xxi.1, in *Classics of International Law*, 522; also II.xvii.1, ibid., 430.

77. Ibid., II.xx.38; trans. by Reichberg, Syse, and Begby, *Ethics of War*, 402.

78. Ibid., II.xxi.1, in *Classics of International Law*, 522.

79. Ibid., II.xx.40; trans. by Reichberg, Syse, and Begby, *Ethics of War*, 407–8.

80. Suarez exited this dilemma by arguing that it is precisely by reason of his fault that the otherwise sovereign (but wrongful) belligerent falls under the jurisdiction of his righteous opponent (*subjectio ex ratione delicti*); see Gregory M. Reichberg, "Suarez on Just War," in *Interpreting Suárez: Critical Essays*, ed. Daniel Schwartz (Cambridge: Cambridge University Press, 2011), 185–204.

CHAPTER 10

The Necessity of "Right Intent" for Justifiably Waging War

Joseph Boyle

Tʜᴇ ᴍᴀɪɴsᴛʀᴇᴀᴍ ᴡᴇsᴛᴇʀɴ ᴄʜʀɪsᴛɪᴀɴ ᴛᴇᴀᴄʜɪɴɢ about just war, as it had developed up to the 1270s, was succinctly summarized by Thomas Aquinas. His summary included three conditions for justifiably waging war.[1] In referring to waging war or war-making ("*bellare*" in Latin), Aquinas appears to be discussing the complex social act of a group of people. His initial moral concern was about whether and under what conditions that action is morally permissible. His attention was on the grounds for rightly undertaking war in the first place and for rightly carrying it on. Thus, Aquinas was not primarily concerned with the particular actions by which a war, even a just war, is conducted.[2] Aquinas holds that each of these conditions is necessary for the moral justification of making war and by implication that they jointly are sufficient. Although succinctly formulated and explained, these conditions—proper authority, just cause, and right intent—are not elements in an easily applied moral algorithm. They are general norms of public morality that require interpretation and reflective application in the dynamic conditions of international life.[3]

This volume is especially concerned with the continuing importance and complexities of the condition of proper authority as invoked in an international environment increasingly dominated by actors other than sovereign nations. The volume also addresses questions about the authority of the just war as a tradition of inquiry and about what counts as authoritative within that tradition. This chapter indirectly addresses these questions about authority by focusing on the complexities raised by the decreasing profile of the condition of right intent in just war discourse.

This condition for justified war-making is tightly connected in the moral logic of the Augustinian tradition with the conditions of proper authority and just cause. Within this logic, right intention is morally necessary because its object is the ultimate purpose—just peace—toward which public authorities undertaking war should direct their efforts, including the war goals they pursue. Right intention is also connected to the authority of and within the just war tradition, and for a similar reason: It points to the fundamental human value that should shape decisions to make war. My specific concern is with right intention as a moral condition for making war.

JUST CAUSE AND PROPER AUTHORITY: NOT SUFFICIENT FOR MORAL WAR-MAKING

Two of the conditions—proper authority and just cause—are based on common moral sentiments and remain salient elements of religious and secular, ethical and legal just war doctrine. The commonsense moral judgments underlying even the simplest versions of these conditions explain this salience: Not any objective for going to war can morally justify it. One polity's interest in the assets of another polity, or its will to dominate or destroy another polity, is obviously incapable of contributing to the moral justification of a war. Similarly, not anyone can rightly undertake war, only those with requisite public authority. Just as the legitimate use of violence within a polity is generally limited to those having appropriate public authority, so also the use of violence against outsiders is limited to those in authority, in this case the authority over the polity as a whole.

Aquinas gives some precision to the common sense judgments supporting the just cause condition. His precision of the notion of just cause is that those attacked should deserve it because of some fault. A quotation from St. Augustine spells this out: "A just cause must avenge a wrong." This quotation provides some examples of relevant wrongs: a polity's failure to make amends for its subjects' misdeeds, and its refusal to restore what was wrongly seized.[4]

Aquinas also provided a rationale for the condition of proper authority, and in so doing highlighted the role and responsibility of those who have the authority to go to war. He explicitly understood the condition as excluding justifiable war-making by private persons. He provided two reasons for the exclusion. First, private persons can seek redress for injuries by appealing to higher authorities; and second, private persons cannot call together the community, which is required for war-making.

Less explicitly, Aquinas identified the authority whose actions are required for justifiable war-making. That is the authority of the person (or perhaps group) who bears final responsibility for the common good of the polity. Quoting St. Paul's endorsement of the use of violence by political authorities within a polity (Rom 13:4), Aquinas drew the Augustinian analogy from this use of authority to its use to protect the society from external enemies. Quoting St. Augustine, he made plain that the relevant authorities are those that have the final say, sovereign power.[5] In short, war is an action in which the role of the person or persons who decide to do it is essential for its moral quality. Only those with responsibility for the common good of a polity may rightly go to war; others, such as expert advisers or academics as such, lack that responsibility. Citizens in a democracy may have some say insofar as their Constitution gives them one. It is a person's responsibilities, and particularly his or her final responsibility for the welfare of a polity, that pick out the proper authority.

Given these compelling moral judgments, it is not surprising that these conditions remain salient in just war thinking.[6] An example of this salience is provided in recent Catholic just war doctrine: The definition of just cause appears to have been narrowed to defense, but thus restricted remains necessary for justified warmaking. The authority of political leaders is also held necessary, even if it is recognized that some of that authority can and ideally should be transferred by treaty to international bodies. The right of the leaders of a polity to act in defense of the polity when attacked is explicitly recognized.[7]

The United Nations Charter also reflects this salience. It restricts the rights of nations to make war, and it allows only the Security Council legally to undertake war-making. But it also includes a provision for a nation to legally undertake needed and immediate self-defense. Defense against aggression remains a just cause, and although the authority to wage war is deemed generally to exist only at the international level, a residue is recognized to exist in national authorities.[8]

In spite of their evident foundational importance for just war thought, these two conditions clearly are not sufficient for morally justified war-making.[9] A polity might make war for a just, defensive objective, with proper respect for the relevant treaties and fully in accord with its procedures for the exercise of its sovereign power, and yet it might still fail to be morally justified. For example, there are cases in which warfare is not the only practical option for defending legitimate interests, and cases in which where the rights defended by actions, although legitimate if considered abstractly, are disproportionate to the harm predicted by the military action. There are obviously also cases in which the just cause exists but is the merest pretext for making war. Some further condition (or conditions), therefore, is required for the moral justification of making war.

RIGHT INTENT: THE IDEA AND ITS APPLICATION
TO THE ACTION OF MAKING WAR

Aquinas's third condition, right intent, is a candidate to fill this lacuna. Indeed, he explained the insufficiency of the first two conditions in terms of the possibility that waging war meeting these conditions might be wrong because of a "perverse intention."

Like Aquinas's other conditions, right intent represents the main lines of the Augustinian moral tradition of Western Christianity. Although the vocabulary of "right intent" presupposes a conception of intention relatively new in the thirteenth century, the underlying idea of this condition surely exists in the tradition going back to St. Augustine. It is sometimes formulated as a mental condition, in which a will toward hatred and destruction is excluded (and the contrary will toward justice and peace in the relationships among political societies is mandated).[10]

Aquinas began his discussion of this condition by stating that those making war should aim to promote what is good and to avoid evil. This very general formula, verbally close to a standard natural law formulation of general moral principle, might be understood as enjoining the consideration of any other aspect of just and authorized actions of war-making, taken broadly as including all its circumstances and consequences, from the perspective of ethical principle. Thus perhaps the additional requirement of right intent does not address a specific aspect of the action of making war, but rather a more global moral consideration requiring, in addition to any specific moral consideration about war-making, an "all-things-considered" moral assessment of the action in its widest context.

Aquinas certainly believed that the moral assessment of war includes considerations in addition to those directly relevant to the question of whether the action of war-making is morally justified. Some people can have responsibilities that either generally or in some conditions make it wrong for them to go to war. Aquinas believed that the role-specific responsibilities of clerics, for example, prevent them from participating in war (ST 2–2, 40, 2). One can easily think of similar responsibilities that are not common to an easily defined group such as the clergy, but are nevertheless capable of creating such a moral limit on a given person's engaging in warfare. Similarly, other circumstances of warfare, such as its timing, might become morally significant by custom or legislation (ST 2–2, 40, 4). Finally, there are moral limits to what can be done in making war, which if violated make one's conduct of the war immoral. Aquinas's example is that of lying, which he believed always to be wrong, and which is, therefore, excluded from the deceptions one can employ against enemies (ST 2–2, 40, 3). No doubt he believed that the absolute prohibition against killing innocents (ST 2–2, 64, 6) provided another such constraint on bellicose actions.

In a word, the immediate context of Aquinas's discussion of the conditions for just war-making strongly suggests that requirement of right intent is far more focused than the thought that one's overall will in doing this should be in conformity with morality; his concerns about the circumstances that might flaw a given act of war-making, at least for some persons at some times or by some actions, are addressed in separate articles of the question about war. Aquinas clearly understood the role of right intent, like that of just cause and proper authority, to be an element in evaluating the act of making war, considered independently of such circumstances.

Moreover, this "all-things-considered" account of Aquinas's addition to the conditions of just cause and proper authority has other difficulties, not simply interpretative implausibility. For this account seems incapable of distinguishing the moral failures of the person or group deciding to make war from the moral properties of the common public act of making war.

Aquinas provided this more specific focus on the action of making war by way of the gloss he used to explicate his generally stated requirement that belligerents should intend to promote the good and avoid the evil. According to the gloss, a quotation taken to be from St. Augustine, the general statement refers to those wars known among true worshipers of God as peacemaking.[11] The assumption is that these wars alone are morally justified. They are characterized as carried out not with desire or cruelty but with zeal for peace, in order that evildoers be restrained (*coerceantur*) and good people relieved (*subleventur*).

A second text from St. Augustine provides further indication of this focus. Aquinas cites it to confirm his claim that just cause and proper authority are alone insufficient for the moral acceptability of making war: "The passion for inflicting harm, the cruel thirst for vengeance, an unpacific and relentless spirit, the fever of revolt, the lust of power, and such like things, all these are rightly condemned in war."[12]

The list exemplifying things rightly condemned in war is presented as a list of motivations, not of actions: passion, thirst, spirit, fever, and lust.[13] Similarly, in the shorter list, contrasted with the zeal for peace in the first text Aquinas uses, are cupidity and cruelty. Aquinas does not explain how these motivations are related to intentions, nor for that matter does he tell us how they are related to morality, except insofar as he endorsed St. Augustine's judgment that they are widely condemned. These motivations might in some cases be desires or feelings that arise unbidden because of the circumstances in which a person must cope: One can hardly think of a community at war whose members do not experience some such desires. Sometimes these feelings are unwelcome and are effectively removed from a person's set of potential motivations. Sometimes, in spite of such efforts, they remain as irritants and outliers within the set of motivations with which a person wishes to identify and on which they act. But such motivations can be more than temptations or irritants; they can be endorsed and made practical as intentions.

Intentions are effective motivations, which are rationally articulable, not simply felt inclinations, toward goals judged good or useful, which one believes one can achieve or foster by acts within one's power. On Aquinas's account of intention, it is an act of willing bearing on the end insofar as it can be achieved by means (ST 1–2, 12, 1). Willing is understood to be "rational appetite," that is, motivation based on the propositional judgment that something is good. To intend, therefore, is to will effectively, not simply to have an interest in or a wish for some goal.

Thus, although it does not make sense morally to condemn feelings, however negative, insofar as they are simply given and not directly under one's control, it does make sense morally to prohibit forming intentions to make the objects of those feelings real.[14] For in intending a goal, one chooses a means and this choice is free. In this way, the motivations listed by St. Augustine are morally relevant, and this relevance does not depend simply on the performance of the immoral actions that are the objects of these motivations. The effective will toward dominating enemies and treating them vengefully will structure one's war-making, even if no acts are performed that are not properly authorized and in the service of the just cause. Opportunities for reconciliation and mercy, for example, are likely to be unmotivated, and the relationship to one's enemies after the war is concluded will remain hostile, unless these motivations are repudiated.

The moral significance of the motivations in question, at least insofar as they are listed by St. Augustine, appears, however, to be personal, not public and common. For communities are not literally capable of desire or passion. The lusts and avarice that arise in war are the motivations of members of a community. Therefore, the motivations of groups, to the extent that it makes sense to think of such things, must somehow be a function of the motivations of the individuals who constitute the group. Because Aquinas is plainly assuming that the action of making war that demands moral assessment is the common, public action coordinated by the authority of the leader of a polity, the right intention that is a condition for the moral permissibility of war-making must be the intention involved in that action, and not directly the likely variable motivations of the participants. How individual motivations and intentions contribute to constituting the intention of a common action is obscure at best.

The common acts of communities, such as making war, do seem to have something of the intentional structure of individual actions. In these acts, goals are pursued by the coordinated actions of many individuals. The choice of the many actors of various performances is undertaken by each as a contribution to the common goal. As coordinated by the relevant actions of the leaders, these performances are the means to the common goal. Consequently, the combination of the coordination by the political authority and the performances of those cooperating function in the same way as a chosen means in individual action. As in individual action, there is no choice of means without an intention of a goal for the sake of which the means are chosen.

The intentions involved in the common action necessarily are primarily those of the authorities in doing their part in achieving the common goal, namely, coordinating the actions of the others involved. The actions coordinated by those actions of the authorities also involve that intention to the extent that those undertaking them understand them practically as contributing to the common effort.[15]

Therefore, groups having an authority structure capable of organizing individual actions for common goals can make choices and intend goals. Because the structure of authority includes much that is based on a community's prior decisions, the exercise of the coordinating function in a polity having a developed legal structure can be complex, involving actions by legislatures, the executive authority, and the judiciary. The complexity of the coordinating activities, however, does not suppress the function of the authority, and does not remove the need for pursuing common goals as the basis for common action.[16]

Other motivations of members of a community that are not incorporated in these features of common action are not common but are the motivations of individuals, related to common actions in the ways individual interests and desires are related to individual intentions. In other words the motivations, morally good or bad, of the authorities and those obeying them are not relevant to the intentions of public actions such as war-making as long as they are not part of the actions taken with the intention of the common goal. Thus, soldiers motivated to violate the rights of civilians and others are not engaged in the common action of the community unless those motivations are commanded, encouraged or not carefully monitored, and limited with due diligence. Similarly, the personal aspirations of leaders remain personal as long as the goals toward which they direct the actions of community members are not set by reference to these personal aspirations. A political leader who harbors hateful feelings toward his enemies but resists making them effective in the public acts by which he generates cooperation in making war is not acting out of hatred. Of course, the existence of the hatred blocks the full reality of peace, because the presence of that motivation tempts toward hateful acts. Moreover, the presence of such hatred is hard to conceal. If not, if it is expressed in public speech, for example, the presumption that it is purely private and not instead structuring the public acts a leader undertakes is weakened.

In a word, the language of the Augustinian tradition suggests that the motivations excluded by the condition of right intent are the base motivations of individuals—soldiers, citizens, and leaders. However, right intent seems to have been proposed, by Aquinas at least, as a moral consideration of the common act of a community. This use of intention to apply to the common act of a community is not incoherent, because the view that feelings like hatred are acts of groups, not individuals, might well be.

The right intention of a public act necessarily shares some of the publicity of the action itself. Coordinating the actions of others requires that they have some idea of what they are being commanded to do and why. Leaders are perhaps not willing or able to reveal the details of the final goals they seek in exercising their function. However, they must make clear a good deal about intermediary goals if others are to play their part in the common effort. Moreover, communicating intermediate goals invites a process of practical reflection that makes more final and even ultimate goals clear. Suppose that only actions for just causes are commanded, and the war aims announced are to realize the state of affairs in which the just cause is satisfied. But suppose also that the general plan of war and statement of war aims exclude discretion about such things as how vigorously to pursue the various aspects of the war, or to what degrees less violent undertakings might be preferred to making war. In such a case, the goal intended in the common action seems to be something beyond the condition in which the just cause is realized. This can be ascertained by the sort of questioning commonly used to expose intentions that are obscure: What does our refusal to consider again how vigorously to pursue war aims actually contribute to what we say we seek—satisfying the just cause? What value is in doing that? And so on.

Neither Aquinas nor his sources explicitly explain what unifies the list of motivations rightly condemned in war. However, these do have some obvious unity: Although they emerge not only in war or similar situations of violent conflict, they do all emerge in contexts of interpersonal conflict, sometimes as its cause, for example, in envy or avarice, but often as a response to the conflict. Right intention is the ethical refusal to allow such motivations to be the intentions for which one fights in a just war. More positively, right intention is the ethical requirement that in making war one should aim for a goal in which the conflict between communities is resolved in such a way that the wrongs constituting a just cause are rectified. This resolution of conflict is a matter of a union of the wills of the people in conflict in agreement or concord. Concord concerning the rectification of the wrongs constituting a just cause requires rejecting the motivations toward those wrongs. For those making war justly, motivations of the sort listed by Augustine should be rejected, because they motivate unjustifiable actions. Eliminating such motivations establishes a motivational integrity in an agent or community that makes its union with others as stable and friendly as its own actions can secure. This positive objective of the condition of right intent is suggested by the characterization of the wars regarded as peacemaking: These are waged out of the zeal for peace that allows evildoers to be coerced and good people to be upheld.

The peace that is intended in a war fought with right intent is necessarily morally defined. That is supposed by Aquinas's view that peace is a proper act of the virtue of charity (ST 2–2, 29, 4). He held that peace is not a disposition to act in the way a virtue is, but is an action. This seems counterintuitive, but is perhaps less jarring upon reflection. Peace is essentially a union of the wills of discrete persons that includes the union of the motivations within each of the parties united. This union is itself an act of willing, not a disposition, but an act of will that can be developed or rejected as it is maintained over time. Moreover, the fact that the peace one seeks in any particular relationship is a goal and not simply a means is explained by the fact that peace is a final good, sought for its own sake; in such cases the goal is the same individual event as the action chosen and instantiates the good in question.

If peace is otherwise defined, for example, as the simple cessation of hostilities, there could be agreement among the parties, but this agreement could well be forced on one or both sides. The desires conflicting with the settlement remain, and they are likely to include motivations toward continuing hostility. By contrast, settlements based on the prospect of a just peace need not be coerced if the parties embrace a commitment toward mutual cooperation and respect and a serious effort to undo motivations pushing toward further conflict.

The need for an additional condition of right intent arises because the act of making war carried out for the sake of satisfying morally unacceptable motivations —such as the lust to dominate, or the desire for vengeance—can be done with proper authority to realize a just cause yet nevertheless be wrong because of the perverse intent these motivations involve. This possibility exists because properly authorized war-making aimed at realizing goals that satisfy the just cause can be motivated more fundamentally by these desires than by the genuine goods to be realized when the war goals established by a just cause are achieved and when authority genuinely but too narrowly serves the common good of the community defended because the role within this good of just peace is set aside.

One can act on these inappropriate motivations and still perform no action that is not authorized and no action that does not contribute to the just war goals. But in so acting one conforms only materially to these conditions; one acts on authority, but not for the sake of what justifies the authority's war-making, namely, concern for the polity's common good. Similarly, one acts for a just cause, not because it is a just cause but because achieving a just goal also serves vengeance, dominance, or other improper goals. The just cause is a pretext.

In sum, on this account the action of war-making can be morally flawed even when all acts of war-making are consistent with the conditions of just cause and proper authority but are primarily motivated not by them but instead by interests incompatible with the moral grounds for just cause and proper authority. This sort of failing is a failing of the action of war-making, not a failing due to the circum-stances of some who should not engage in such acts or who make use of actions prohibited irrespective of their inclusion in war-making.

GROTIUS'S VIEW OF RIGHT INTENT: A FAULT FROM THE DISPOSITION OF THE AGENT

Grotius seems to have disagreed with Aquinas on whether right intention is a requirement for the justification of war-making or a failure of those undertaking a war for a just cause. He recognized in wars fought for a just cause the effective presence of motivations from the "Disposition of the Agent." Grotius distinguished those that are morally acceptable, such as desire for honor, from those that are base, such as delighting in another's misfortune. He accepted that the latter "are crimi-nal," but he denied that such intentions render unjust a war fought for a just cause.

No restitution is required for such wrongfully fought but just wars.[17] The implication is that the moral failure is on the part of the agent, not in the action of making war.

As suggested above, Aquinas and the tradition he represents allowed that there are moral flaws in making war that could be distinguished from the morality of the act of making war itself. But this tradition would reject the idea that the objects of the commitments motivating the war-making are not part of the action being evaluated. For Aquinas morality directs the exercise of human freedom in choosing and intending. One's goals therefore are morally primary, because one's freedom is exercised by endorsing and pursuing some of them and not others. This version of traditional morality certainly allows that the moral assessment of actions includes considering them abstractly, that is, without taking note of circumstances, including the further intentions for which one performs an intentional action. But that abstract consideration of an action described is only a partial assessment of the exercise of freedom one assesses in moral evaluation (ST 1–2, 18, 2–7). Thus, war made for the glory of victory might be materially just, but it is not a work of justice but of self-glorification—unless, of course, the glory sought is that of a just and peacemaking victor. Moreover, the flawed choice of making war for glory seems precisely a choice to make war. This is not a separable moral failing of a leader.

Grotius's position on this matter seems remarkably modern. The idea that we can adequately morally assess the intentional actions of individuals and groups in abstraction from what these actors mean to achieve by those actions is now widely accepted. Matters of intention belong not to the evaluation of action but to the assessment of character; and obviously, people acting on bad motives can perform good actions.

This raises the question of whether the difference here is not a matter of substantive moral assessment but of moral classification. For Grotius agrees with the medieval thinkers that there is a moral flaw; he simply locates it differently than they do.

However, the difference may be significant at the level of the conduct of warfare. The medieval position appears to be more stringent than the Grotian position. Wars failing to meet the condition of right intention are impermissible; that constraint does not exist on Grotius's view. Morally, one may fight, and perhaps must fight, some wars having a just cause, even if the dispositions of the agents are morally flawed, because changing these personal dispositions is a distinct moral project from that of undertaking a just war by actions justified by a just cause. The additional stringency of the medieval view is significant in cases where the just cause is merely a pretext for making war and not a central reason for it. But even in cases where the requirements of the just cause are carefully respected because of its standing in positive law, acting consistently with the just cause remains at best a side constraint on actions undertaken for nonpacific reasons.

More theoretically, a just cause cannot be such unless its claim to justice is grounded; an injury must be repelled or an injustice vindicated, and doing that must be morally good. This grounding is plausibly found in the condition of just peace or ordered tranquillity, which is the object of right intention. To the extent that one pursues a just cause simply because it serves other goals, one abandons that justifying condition as the ground for the moral importance of just cause. The moral flaw in cases of bad intention is perhaps also a flaw of some individuals involved in the action, but it is substantially a flaw of the action of war-making itself. In cases where there is some moral concern for the just cause but some willingness to act for goals inconsistent with the grounds for that condition, the sort of internal conflict in the war-making party that Aquinas regards as incompatible with peace remains.

To develop this line of reasoning, let us consider another unworthy motivation Aquinas mentions: avarice for an enemy's goods. Avarice would not motivate going to war if the goods had been stolen by the enemy and their just return sought in war. That is a commonly accepted just cause. But avarice remains a possible motive for making war, as is revealed by many cases of plundering an enemy's territory. Aquinas's argument requires that there be cases in which warfare involving a failure of right intent is properly authorized for the sake of a just cause. In these cases the actions motivated by avarice, considered independently of that motivation, will be permissible.

What the avaricious motivation adds seems to be a horizon, beyond the war aims defined by the just cause, in which one's effective will continues to be directed against the interests of the enemy, even if the considerations justifying war-making are removed by success in war. Thus, even if just causes are fully satisfied, to the extent that avarice remains an effective motive, the avaricious will of the victor cannot be united with that of the defeated enemy but remains in conflict with it. This is not peace but continuing hostility.

To intend this peace is to set it as a goal, a goal that comprehends over time the entire relationship a polity maintains with a former enemy.[18] Ongoing and effective motivations, such as intending to possess the benefits of the enemy's goods, clearly destabilizes the goal of peace. For example, avarice for the enemy's goods as such neither supports and vindicates people unfairly harmed by war, nor suppresses the actions of evildoers; this avarice, even if constrained in practice by authorized actions for the sake of a just cause, has its own decidedly unpacific agenda.

PARTIAL SUBSTITUTES FOR RIGHT INTENT?

In spite of the plausibility of the thesis that just cause and proper authority are not sufficient for the permissibility of the public act of making war, it certainly appears that Aquinas has not succeeded in persuading others that his condition of right intent provides the needed addition to just cause and proper authority. The absence of this condition from many subsequent formulations of the conditions for justified war-making, including many by moralists within the Catholic tradition, strongly suggests that just war theorists generally do not accept that this condition really is necessary and important for a complete just war doctrine. Indeed, the condition of right intent appears to have largely disappeared from just war discourse.

For example, the treatment of just war in the *Catechism of the Catholic Church* makes no reference to right intent. This summary of current Catholic teaching includes conditions besides just cause and proper authority. The *Catechism* (2309) lists four such conditions: the damage against which one defends must be lasting, grave, and certain; other means of stopping aggression must be ineffective or impractical; there must be a serious prospect of success; and warfare must not produce evils greater than those opposed by it.

These conditions are intuitively plausible and are more focused than the condition of right intent. Part of this plausibility lies in the fact that, like the condition of right intent, they address the act of war-making, not the personal failures of those making war. Another source of their intuitive plausibility is that instead of directing moral attention to the objects intended in the action of making war, they address more specific concerns about the goals of this action, for example, the seriousness of the aggression to which one responds or the likelihood of the success of the warfare carried out in resisting it.

However, the normative basis for the plausibility of these conditions appears to lie in their connection with right intent. Last resort requires exhausting the possibilities of less violent ways of responding to aggression. In cases where there exists a just cause and proper authorization, this condition adds a pacific constraint that excludes not only using the presence of a just cause as a pretext for war made for other reasons but also warfare motivated by the just cause as such when it is reasonably avoidable. Willingness to fight when other avenues are available for settling disagreements belies a readiness to inflict the evils of warfare when they and the hostility they provoke are avoidable; this readiness is neither just nor friendly. Likewise, when warfare is carried on without hope of success, one might fight for a just cause but satisfying this cause brings on oneself and one's enemies only the evils of war. Similar considerations apply to the other, more specific conditions that have become the dominant contenders for the additional necessary conditions for just war.

In short, these conditions are plausible precisely because of their reliance on the considerations highlighted in the condition of right intent. It seems that each of these conditions is implied by right intent but not equivalent to it. If the leaders of a polity make decisions about war-making in the light of a resolve to realize just peace, then they will not go to war if it is avoidable, will not organize a violent response to aggression that is not serious, will not inflict harms unjustified by the response to aggression, and will not make war if there is little chance of success. If right intent is understood to require a commitment to establishing just and potentially friendly human relationships with a polity's enemy within the polity's very acts of war-making, then such conditions appear to capture parts of what the condition of right intent was meant to require.

If understood as implications of right intention, these conditions are useful articulations of at least some of what is involved in right intent. If it is correct to see them as implications of that condition, then the elaboration of what is involved in right intention, by using concepts related to but distinct from the central concept of just peace, provides an advantage for those wishing to think clearly and fully about the morality of a war. However, no one of these conditions exhausts the idea of right intent, and taken together they can fail to capture some features of the act of making war, in particular, those suggested by the rich Augustinian language of right intent: that wars fought for the sake of vengeance and domination, out of implacable hatred and a desire to dominate, are unjustifiable. Those flaws might be excluded by one or another of the conditions formulating implications of right intention, but that is not guaranteed. It seems, therefore, that the modern preference for conditions such as those listed in the *Catechism of the Catholic Church* is not justified. As elaborating right intent, such conditions do real moral work; as replacing right intent, their relationship to what grounds their moral force is severed; and even taken as a package, they fail to provide the further sufficient condition for just war-making.

The specificity of these conditions in comparison with that of right intention may create the appearance that they are capable of functioning practically in a just war doctrine that is clear enough to be applied by statesmen and soldiers. This specificity appears to allow for greater confidence that the condition has been fulfilled or not; for example, although it is often quite difficult to know that one's choice to go to war is a last resort, that appears much easier to ascertain than whether the choice is made with a right intention. Sometimes, of course, it will be clear that other possibilities exist for resisting aggression. In such cases, where the more specific, operational conditions are met, it will generally remain unsettled whether one's intention is for a well-ordered peace. When they are not met, presumably right intention is not met either, supposing it implies them. In these cases it seems that the more specific conditions, not right intent, are doing the ethical work.

The greater specificity of these conditions, however, provides rather little of the obvious advantage it seems to promise. One must acknowledge the difficulties in knowing, before one undertakes war, whether the aggression is serious enough to fight about; whether the harms likely to be inflicted by resistance are or are not proportionate to those expected from the aggression; whether one's defense is likely to succeed; and whether one has tried everything reasonable to settle the matter without making war. All these actions require reflection and information, neither of which settles the issue except in the easy cases. The decision these considerations are to inform generally requires practical wisdom if it is to be morally good. That is the mature practical knowledge that presupposes that the overarching human good or value to be served in a decision to make war or to refrain is practically in place; this basic value is the object of right intent.[19] To the extent that the preference for modern conditions is based on a desire to avoid the need for this sort of moral reflection, which is not codified but accessible to honest reflection, the preference is ill founded. There is no advantage to be had on that front.

It follows that if the appeal of the specificity of the modern replacement conditions for right intention is based on rendering them into rules that can be applied without difficulty and care, that appeal must be illusory. Perhaps people can be tempted to believe that the conditions of just cause and proper authority can be handled as easily applied rules, but neither right intention nor its implications are plausibly so understood. Moral reflection on this aspect of the justification of war-making escapes construction in the clear terms of decision theory or of a deontological rule book.

If the replacement conditions for right intent were to be understood as clear rules in such a book, they could hardly be implications of right intention, although they might be cited as rules that have been followed. For example, the last resort might get an operational definition in terms of the options articulated and debated, a time frame, and a number of offers to the offending party. By such specifications, the condition of last resort would be readily judged as met or not, but only in such a way as to sever its connection to right intent. One could follow the book on last resort and still fail to make war only so as to promote a just peace: "We have offered the enemy several alternatives, given them some time to respond, and no response. At last they will get their comeuppance—every bit they owe."[20] Here no action is taken that does not contribute to just war aims; the other conditions are all met, and, nevertheless, it remains true that not peace but dominance or destruction is intended. This possibility is what renders the right intent criterion necessary. That is not to say that it will always be easy to determine that it has been met or violated. But it can come to light that military action taken or anticipated, although abstractly justifiable, points toward a different goal than peace.

To sum up: It seems possible that a belligerent's properly authorized actions contribute to war aims satisfying just causes, and that even so the act of making war is impermissible. Modern just war theorists favor a list of intuitively plausible conditions, each of which seems necessary for a war to be permissible. However, the combination of these conditions, and their addition to just cause and proper authority, do not constitute a sufficient condition for the permissibility of war-making. Actions meeting these conditions, as well as the conditions of right intent and proper authority, can be flawed morally by failures of right intent that are not captured by these favored conditions. Right intention is necessary for the moral goodness of making war.

The hankering to reduce the standards for the moral rightness of war-making to rules that can be more or less automatically applied belies an unjustifiable desire for clarity and an oversimplification of the conditions for communicating about morality and the limits morality sets. Morality is focally about the goodness or badness of choices, individual and communal; the truth about the status of any choice emerges in a conscience formed and tested by reflection and conversation in the light of moral principle, not by ticking off items on a checklist.

NOTES

1. *Summa Theologiae*, second part of the second part, question 40, article 1 (ordinarily abbreviated as ST 2–2, q. 40, a. 1). This is the standard way to refer to this work and allows precise reference to any translation or edition.

2. ST 2–2, 40, 3, deals with one issue concerning the "*in bello*" standards for the conduct of war—the issue of deception and laying ambushes. Aquinas allowed this but not lying, which he held to be always wrong. Other absolute prohibitions, such as that prohibiting intentional killing of the innocent, would seem, pari passu, to apply.

3. In chapter 2 of this book, Chris Brown provides a good statement of what thinking about moral reasoning as an algorithm amounts to. Though I agree with Brown that the moral evaluation of warfare is not a moral algorithm, I believe it is capable of resulting in firm judgments by leaders and citizens that a war should or not be undertaken, and that similar judgments, even by outsiders, are possible after the war. Thus, on my account just war thinking can guide and so also constrain the decisions of authorities. I suspect this marks a substantive difference from Brown's view. He would probably regard my view as an abandonment of the older conception of just war as a moral praxis in favor of a more legalistic conception. I cannot here directly engage Brown's reasoning on this apparent disagreement; my analysis here of Aquinas's discussion of the morality of war would be a major part of the historical element of my response.

4. In chapter 9 of this book, Gregory Reichberg provides a wonderful survey of the issues involved in understanding Aquinas's conception of just cause, in particular the extent to which the conception includes a retributive element that supposes moral culpability on the part of those whose wrongful action can generate a just cause. Aquinas's conception of a just cause as involving responses to wrongdoing excludes some reasons for going to war, but it does not answer all questions raised by the idea of wrongdoing.

5. In chapter 1 of this book, James Turner Johnson provides a more developed account of this condition, along with useful context.

6. This claim does not contest Johnson's objection in chapter 1 of this book to the deemphasizing, especially in recent years, of the condition of proper authority in ways that, in effect, remove or displace to "experts" the judgment of those responsible for a polity.

7. *Catechism of the Catholic Church with Modifications from the Editio Typica* (New York: Doubleday, 1997), 615–17. Like many official Catholic documents, this is cited by paragraph numbers—here, 2307–17: The endorsement of just cause and proper authority is a quotation from Vatican II: "However, 'as long as the danger of war persists and there is no international authority with the necessary competence and power, governments cannot be denied the right of lawful self-defense, once all peace efforts have failed'" (2308).

8. United Nations Charter, Article 2, nos. 3 and 4; Article 42; Article 51.

9. This thesis seems consistent with the priority of proper authority emphasized by Johnson in chapter 1 of this book. It would not be if Johnson maintained that one or both of the other conditions are not necessary. However, he endorses the necessity of right intention,

and his thesis that the political authority, and not others, must judge whether or not a just cause exists does not (by itself) imply that the presence of a just cause is not necessary.

10. See Gratian, *Decretum*, part ii, Causa 23, question ii, quoting Isidore. Here it is held that war can be unjust in five ways: Two of these are failures of just cause or proper authority; another is a failure of the state of mind, as when one makes war for the sake of revenge.

11. The source is apparently Gratian's *Decretum*, question 1, although Thomas mistakenly identifies it as Augustinian.

12. This translation of Augustine is from St. Thomas Aquinas, *Summa Theologica*, trans. Dominican Fathers of the English Province (New York: Benzinger Bros., 1947), vol. 2, 1360.

13. For a helpful explication of some of the items on the Augustinian list and their relevance to right intention, see Anthony Coates, "Culture, the Enemy and the Moral Restraint of War," in *The Ethics of War: Shared Problems in Different Traditions* (Aldershot: Ashgate, 2005), 215–17.

14. Coates regards right intention as a moral disposition; ibid., 215–16. But an obligation to make war only if one has right intent would sometimes oblige the impossible if the intention were a disposition beyond the immediate power of an agent to create. Volitions have some of the features of dispositions; e.g., they can exist over time, but they are actualities in a way dispositions are not.

15. The importance of public authority in coordinating the actions of war-making and so in determining the intentions involved in a war is a point of convergence of my analysis on Johnson's analysis focused on proper authority. See chapter 1 of this book, especially Johnson's brief discussion of right intent.

16. For a discussion of the complexity of the public action that was the maintenance of the American nuclear deterrent, see John Finnis, Joseph Boyle, and Germain Grisez, *Nuclear Deterrence, Morality and Realism* (Oxford: Oxford University Press, 1987), 188–20, 343–51.

17. Hugo Grotius, *The Rights of War and Peace*, book ii, chapter 22, number xvii, ed. Richard Tuck (Indianapolis: Liberty Fund, 2005), 1113–14.

18. See ST 2–2, 29, 1, for Aquinas's definition of peace. It is a kind of concord among people, a union of their wills. It is specified by the union within each party of their diverse motivations. For a short account of peace and its role in Aquinas's understanding of right intent, see John Finnis, "The Ethics of War and Peace in the Catholic Natural Law Tradition," in *The Ethics of War and Peace: Religious and Secular Perspectives*, ed. T. Nardin (Princeton, NJ: Princeton University Press, 1996), 15–20.

19. Practical wisdom is one of the cardinal virtues ("*prudential,*" in Aquinas's translation of Aristotle). In chapter 2 of this book, Brown presents a useful account of Aristotle's conception of practical wisdom. I suspect that Brown and I would have some disagreement about how practical wisdom functions in Aquinas's development of Aristotle. I believe that in Aquinas's account of moral decision making, general moral considerations, such as not lying in conducting war and not intentionally killing innocents, are among the general considerations that shape moral deliberation, and can exclude acts of those kinds prior to an all-things-considered judgment about the action as a particular. Like all virtue, practical wisdom is a disposition. Though a leader lacking this virtue could apply the right intent condition correctly, that would be difficult. Therefore, Coates's reflections on the importance of morally defined dispositions for the conduct of just war seem to me to be sound and helpful, my earlier dissent notwithstanding. See Coates, "Culture."

20. In chapter 2 of this book, Brown ably criticizes last resort, likelihood of success, and proportionality in ways that support my contention that they are not very useful as standalone conditions independent of right intent. His criticism of right intent seems to be of a somewhat different idea than mine, i.e., the intention of a specific war aim.

CHAPTER 11

Revenge, Affect, and Just War

Brent J. Steele

There's something fundamentally odd about celebrating a death, but that fact is certainly not stopping anybody right now.

> "10 Celebrations of Osama bin Laden's Death from around the Country."

Revenge is an unfashionable word among post-imperial Europeans, who feel more comfortable with notions of justice, preferably after due legal process. Gleeful Americans, who chanted "USA, USA!" outside the White House after Barack Obama announced the killing of Osama bin Laden, show fewer inhibitions.

> "Osama bin Laden: The Americans Got Him in
> True John Wayne Style," Michael White.

Did you hear about the new bin Laden drink? Two shots and a splash of water.

> Dark humor popular following bin Laden's killing.

IN THE LATE HOURS OF May 1, 2011, city streets around the United States filled with people celebrating the announcement by the US media, and the president of the United States, that al-Qaeda leader Osama bin Laden had been killed in a targeted operation in Abbottabad, Pakistan, by a team of Navy SEALS. The quotations given above capture some of the confusion over these celebrations. One more quotation in particular, by the *US News & World Report* foreign affairs writer Susan Milligan, shows the real discomfort felt by some in the United States over these celebrations: "So while all of us were glad to see bin Laden gone, there is still something distasteful about the jubilant cries of 'USA! USA!' at gatherings to celebrate bin Laden's demise. It looked as though the demonstrators had just witnessed the winning of the World Cup. Their fists pumped in the air, with understandable happiness and some relief, to be sure. But the image also looked creepily like some of the crazed anti-American demonstrations that have occurred around the world."[1]

Revenge is a part of being human, and so it would seem intuitive that revenge is also part of global politics, based as the latter is upon *human* action, interaction, practice, and organization. This chapter seeks a place for revenge in debates surrounding just war. It does so, however, in a somewhat unconventional manner. Rather than assuming that revenge is only a *motivating* factor for war, it instead sees revenge as (1) an affective apparatus and (2) a practice within conflict. It defends this social understanding of revenge with special reference to authority, and it further seeks to recover revenge's relationship with popular, even traditional (if not timeless), referents deployed in just war discussions, including reprisals, retribution, proportionality, and, generally, punishment. It then problematizes the prevailing temporal (i.e., knee-jerk nature) and spatiocultural ("uncivilized") assumptions about revenge (some of which are captured, I think, in the Milligan quotation above), and concludes by way of assessing how revenge in an era of war against ill-defined actors might undermine the notion of just war.

AUTHORITY, ACTION, AND REVENGE

The debates that surrounded bin Laden's death, the celebrations that followed it, and even the decision by the Obama administration to *not* release visual evidence of a dead bin Laden to the US public and world at large—debates to which I allude throughout this chapter—can lead us to revisit some of the connections between authority, agency, and revenge. Authority is not only an enabling stipulation to act, it is social status, a condition of a particular social identity that burdens an actor with a *requirement* to publicly act when it is challenged. The United States, as a "great power," exemplifies the notion that its authority "confirms and validates [its] self-identification . . . by revealing that significant others share this view."[2] To reinforce that view, however, requires action to reinscribe this authority. Such "action" is not limited to the use of deadly force—but extends through *justifying* and contextualizing that use of force. Further, such authority is not only providing a response when it is challenged; it is enabled by a group to speak on their behalf. As Harry Gould discusses via a description of the Hobbesian contract: "When one person acts on behalf of another, the former is the actor, and the latter is the author—the author of the representative's actions. Acting on behalf of the author is to act with authority. Because the people have authorised the artificial person, the sovereign, to act on their behalf, they are the *authors* of the sovereign's acts and bear responsibility for them regardless of whether the 'author' ordered, consented to, or willed them."[3]

This authority becomes more complex in a representative government, as a challenge like bin Laden's damaged the United States' great power authority (both directly and indirectly) and thus its corporate identity of the "self" merely by the fact that he was alive and publicizing his security in the form of video communiqués for years after the September, 11, 2001, terrorist attacks.[4] Thus, though some in the United States felt merely that "justice" was served in killing bin Laden, others expressed dissatisfaction that his body was treated with any dignity at all in the United States' burial at sea.[5] Far from counseling restraint in a mode of punishment, democratic politics in this vein seems to validate the concerns of Hans Morgenthau and other classical realists from decades ago: "The popular mind, unaware of the fine distinctions of the statesman's thinking, reasons more often than not in the simple moralistic and legalist terms of absolute good and absolute evil. . . . The Popular mind wants quick results; it will sacrifice tomorrow's real benefit for today's apparent advantage."[6]

Thus the central argument pursued in this chapter—authority in global politics, when it is challenged, leads to not only a motive of revenge but also an expectation that such revenge must occur in a public setting. Such authority—and a notion of "just cause"—is built into the *jus ad bellum* plank of the just war tradition. Yet revenge as a public action is in great tension with the central *jus in bello* prescription of proportionality. The squaring of the circle between the two—revenge and just war principles—occurs because revenge gets transformed into "authoritative punishment" or "justice" when it is linked to rules.

Recent works seeking to rehabilitate punishment in a more modern context exhibit a similar argument to that which I am advancing here. Chapter 9 by Gregory Reichberg in the current volume provides an impressive engagement with the nuanced treatment of punishment in several just war philosophers such as Suarez and Vitoria. And in the need to "relate political ideals to a population," Keally McBride argues that punishment serves to remind citizens and subjects about the ideals of a political order. McBride's opening pages are telling here—we get so used to most forms of state punishment that "we forget about the awesome power [of the state] until we are *forced to confront it through a shocking revelation*" (emphasis added).[7] And yet works like McBride's, as well as that of Anthony F. Lang, see a risk in punishment, in that it can be a "problem for political regimes" because some "over-the-top" punishment generates political resistance.[8] What maintains in the distinction between revenge and punishment is authority. For Lang an institutional order or set of rules can, "if we relax our assumptions about the type of authority necessary" for punishment, prove to be *the* deciding factor on whether a punitive action is retribution or revenge.[9] Such institutional structures seem to be, in Lang's view, more formal, although one might surmise, as I do here, that just war principles could be considered informal institutional categories for retributive action, action that otherwise (separated discursively or legally from institutional orders) may "appear" to very much *be* revenge-filled. The point that both McBride and Lang assume, and one which they provide compelling evidence to support, is that violence that *appears* to be capricious or otherwise disproportionate or "passionate" can serve to delegitimize the authority of the political actor that carries such punishment out. I return to the important arguments of Lang and McBride below.[10]

Such observations about legitimacy, authority, and revenge lead us to investigate how revenge has been handled in just war theory writ large. In the few instances revenge emerges within discussions of just war, it is considered, and then dismissed, as an "unjust cause" for war.[11] If just war is meant to limit war and right a wrong through a constrained use of violence, revenge as a motive can prove problematic, leading to cycles of violence. Here one can note two (what I call) "tiptoe" engagements with revenge. First, in Neta Crawford's 2004 *Perspectives* piece on just war and the US counterterrorism war, a quotation from Ed Koch, the former mayor of New York, appears that also bears upon the bin Laden celebrations referenced in other sections of this chapter. Shortly after 9/11, Koch stated that "some call our reprisals 'revenge,' which they denounce even more heatedly, because revenge conveys a feeling of satisfaction. Some shy away from the use of the word 'vengeance.' I say what's wrong with avenging our innocent dead?"[12] Crawford rightfully notes the problems with this—and the same can be said about revenge more generally—that it creates a cycle of violence with little to no end in sight.[13]

Another sustained discussion of revenge vis-à-vis "just war" is found in Jean Bethke Elshtain's *Just War against Terror*.[14] She discusses how revenge was *not* at work in the United States–led "War on Terror." She makes, further, a key distinction between justice and revenge—that the two of them are in tension with one another and, presumably, if justice is part of just war, that revenge has no place in either. Of course, other treatments of just war are aware of revenge—that if certain actions go too far, they may "appear" to signal revenge. We see this with reprisals, where revenge is also implicated with authority, and punishment. I return to all these just below.

For now, my goal here is to suggest broadly that just war, revenge (and, below, authority) all are loosely related in that they are *social*, intersubjective phenomena. One study that I use to begin a conceptualization of revenge is a *Security Studies* article by Oded Lowenheim and Gadi Heimann. These two authors, defining revenge as "negative reciprocity," note that in conceptualizing revenge, we might think of goals, means, and behavior: "*Goals of Revenge*: (1) include it being past-oriented, to inflict suffering; (2) it's an inward-looking practice, focusing on recouping the disrespected Self. *Means*: (3) disproportionality; (4) symbolism. *Behavior*: (5) explicitness; (6) low sensitivity to material costs; (7) longevity."[15]

Rather than assuming that revenge is only a *motivating* factor for war, we can rebuild revenge as (1) an affective apparatus and (2) a practice in global politics. This vision of revenge assumes that it is a social, intersubjective process that, though not "objectively real," can be grasped or understood (if not condoned) by political communities and even international society writ large. Rather than assuming, put another way, that revenge is (only) "natural," this is a social, and even social-psychological, conception of revenge. Although we may see revenge as a motive, and though cursory definitions include this aspect—"to avenge oneself," they also clarify this definition as a practice, as an *action*, "by retaliating in kind or degree," or "to inflict injury in return for."[16]

REVENGE AS AN AFFECTIVE APPARATUS

Revenge seems at first blush to be in great tension with just war principles from both *jus ad bellum* (just cause, proportionality), and *jus in bello* (proportionality, discrimination). Indeed, it implicates the latter by being disproportionate and collective.[17] But revenge can also be considered an affective apparatus—as many of the opening quotations above regarding Osama bin Laden's death suggest, and an urge for which even just wars might satisfy.

A basic insight from research on revenge is that it can be emotionally satisfying, in that revengers feel better the more pain they inflict.[18] Thus, a revenge-as-affective apparatus take on revenge/just war implicates some of its conditions in several ways. First, it demonstrates that proportionality is much more difficult to accomplish. Revenge might only serve as an effective affective apparatus when it is manifested through an *overwhelming* use of force. Like reprisals that are "meant" to "teach a lesson" to an opponent to provide a proper deterrent function, revenge may have an "educative" function for two, and perhaps even three audiences: (1) the party being attacked; (2) the society at large; (3) the attacker, who in making an example of a target "actually communicates with itself, thus reaffirming its own psychological world."[19] It is this third possible audience—the political community seeking revenge through force—which is social-psychologically satisfied (theoretically) in a revenge event. So though revenge may be thought of by Lowenheim and Heimann as an inward-related process, it is only through the self's engagement with an other that this satisfaction (fleeting though it may be) obtains.

Although this educative and psychological function obviously implicates the proportionality condition of *jus in bello* (and *jus ad bellum* as well), it also can have dire consequences for the notion of combatants and noncombatants, as well as confounding the euphemistically titled phrases of "unintended consequences" or "collateral damage" when it comes to uses of force. Again, in the 2006 July War, Lowenheim and Heimann point out that in contrast to the "nominal" restraint that Israel "showed" in the operation, other indications demonstrated that "Israel considered many of the civilians remaining in South Lebanon and the Shiite neighborhoods of Beirut to be associated with or sympathetic to Hezbollah and that such sympathy was at times seen by Israel as a legitimate cause for *targeting noncombatants.*"[20] Such actions seem to echo the problematic consequences stemming from collective punishment writ large. Here, the motive of revenge, and even the intent for actions that can be linked to the motive, are both pushed aside in favor of the public spectacle of violence, which serves and satisfies a collective emotional need.

Again, authority intersects with the question of *whose* affect is being served by revenge, and through what means this affect can be served. The social satisfaction an authority such as the nation-state allows for is not only to the individual to have their vengeance fulfilled against an abstract other—although it does that indeed, it provides two other psychological potentialities as well. First, it allows even a "moral man" with his "own lust for power and prestige thwarted" by his "limitations," to instead "project his *ego* upon his nation and indulge his anarchic lusts vicariously."[21] Much like the satisfaction served in the "emotional rush" of so-called forward panic—panic that results not in paralysis but springing action—the exercise of this national power "comes out in an emotional rush." Unlike that panic, however, the emotions are served in this sense by at-a-distance contact—virtual contact—with an enemy by visualizing, or viewing, the deployment of national force against that enemy.[22] Second, it also "sluices" (to borrow another Niebuhrian phrase) individual revenge into an orderly, albeit violent, channel of state military force: "the nation is a corporate unity, held together much more by force and emotion, than by mind."[23] The result of these two psychological manifestations is that "the nation is at one and the same time a check upon, and a final vent for, the expression of individual egoism."[24]

The "proper authority" condition of just war, like the authority to seek revenge, is a condition privileged to satisfy the value of order. A nation-state, and even more specifically national governments, are "proper authorities" that can not only legitimately deploy violence but also *speak for* and justify its use to an international community. So authority is important here (so far) in that it organizes violence in an internationally palatable, but also nationally and emotionally and individually satisfying, manner.

Put another way, Niebuhr's argument reconfigures the classical, Hegelian conceptualization of revenge. As summarized in McBride's study, Hegel saw "the right of revenge [as being] pursued out of a position of particularity; it has a personal dimension, which then reasserts the rights of the particular person who has been wronged at the expense of the universal. When punishment is levied in court, however, particularity of revenge is replaced by the universality of injured right. . . . The reassertion of the power of universality over the particularity of injury or crime establishes the rule of law again."[25]

Yet Niebuhr's point above is that though a nation might act as an authority in a universal manner (even outside its borders), its public display of force nevertheless satisfies a *particular and personal* "anarchically lustful" urge in the individual citizen *precisely because the nation is carrying out that violence.*[26]

"REVENGE-AS-PRACTICE" (AND PUNISHMENT)

Although Lowenheim and Heimann see revenge as an *inward*-related phenomena (and though I do not disagree with this conceptualization), the discussion above regarding authority suggests that venge-ish behavior in the context of war is, at the same time, inherently social. What I call here "revenge-as-practice" is then an outward-oriented process, in several respects. In an obvious sense, revenge is interactive, focusing both on the action itself and also on the pain inflicted on an other. Further, it is also relational, directed toward the "in-between" space of the two protagonists—their past histories and rivalries—but also circumscribed by the environment within which revenge takes on a "meaning."[27] When revenge is a practice, it becomes much more difficult to claim that there is only, for instance, "one purpose" (e.g., retribution or restoration), or "just cause" (e.g., deterrence or defense) served in a particular violent action.[28] Thus, and as I intimated above, actions such as war are not mere "events" but also fluid processes producing a multitude of meanings for those "watching" these processes unfold. In this way, organized violence can seem to be *both* a just cause upholding certain principles of order *and* a set of actions emotionally satisfying to the "viewer."

Additionally, though we see just war as a set of institutionalized principles (or implicit norms) that can be *invoked* by an actor to justify their violent acts, Lowenheim and Heimann remind us of two more possibilities regarding such "environmental settings" and revenge: that such settings might *facilitate* the "negative reciprocity" at the heart of revenge, while at the same time limiting the actions allowed in such an action. They argue that if a victim is supported by a society, the "less vindictive the injured party becomes." Scaling this to international society, Lowenheim and Heimann assert that "societal empathy, identification, and solidarity represent a form of deep recognition that helps the victim maintain dignity thereby reducing the negative emotions that arise from the harm suffered."[29] So just war, as a set of implicit institutional principles or islands of debate, can at least provide the means through which revenge-as-affect is diminished but also, paradoxically, satisfied one and the same.

ANALYZING REVENGE

As mentioned above, the notion of authority is important in just war doctrine (the "proper authority" condition of *jus ad bellum*), but the authority I wish to examine here is the authority "in here," in our scholarly community and its deliberations over just war. This turn to authority shifts our focus from the authority to fight a just war toward the authority to (1) determine which acts are just versus which acts are revenge, and (2) the authority to claim that certain "types" of populations are more prone toward revenge than others.

What analytically "counts" as revenge-as-affect or practice? A very loose interpretation would be that revenge colors all actions in international politics, at least all violent ones (which include the use of force but also sanctions, which can be violent as well). That is, revenge could be the base from which actors then serve to intersubjectively "make sense" of their past, current, and even future actions through discourses that link to institutionalized principles, to *legitimate* otherwise vengeful actions.

We might notice two other quasi-strategies. The first can be seen in Elshtain's book, which uses the words of leaders (at face value) to assess the amount of "revenge" in a just war. In a subsection titled "Justice, Not Revenge," Elshtain refers to US president George W. Bush's September 20, 2001, address to the nation, which she asserts contained "not a word, a phrase or a paragraph that could be reasonably characterized as a call for revenge. He distinguished carefully between Islam as a great world religion and terrorists who are 'trying, in effect, to hijack Islam itself.'" Elshtain continues by reference to how revenge works on the small group level: "The distinction between revenge and justice is as clear as the distinction between the actions of a lynch mob and a conviction by a jury in a first-degree murder case arrived at after a fair trial and hours of careful deliberation . . . an open and fair verdict rendered under the best judgment of fellow citizens cannot be equated to a group of inflamed persons running amok and stringing someone up without a trial. With this distinction in mind, *I find that there is no justification for calling President Bush's speech a cry for revenge*" (emphasis added).[30]

Of course, there are some obvious problems with this conclusion, its construction, and the terms which Elshtain uses to distinguish "justice" from "revenge," but I mostly relegate those to a note.[31] The analytical distinction Elshtain's example provides us is that revenge "does not involve deliberation or care, and it often recognizes no limits; . . . justice, by contrast, is measured."[32] That is the "what" we should use for evidence (or not) of revenge, but what about the "where"? For Elshtain, we investigate revenge with reference to the deliberation found in the words of leaders. This also has implications for the notion of authority—and its persuasiveness as an analytical strategy comes from the recognition that elites, not the masses (to borrow a rather outdated distinction), deploy violence.

But let us return to the Koch quotation noted above in discussing Crawford's article. I think that is a very telling quotation, as is its use in Crawford's piece, for several reasons. First, it suggests something that we all intuitively grasped in those minutes, but also days and weeks after 9/11: that vengeance was a primary condition after 9/11, discussed out in the open, circulating and being used especially by officials, serving the public's emotional needs. Take, for instance, the iconic "bullhorn moment" that helped to define George W. Bush's aggressive tone following 9/11. Standing on the rubble of the Twin Towers on September 14, 2001, surrounded by rescue/relief workers, and with his arm around one of them, Bush responded to one person who yelled "I can't hear you," by saying in turn "I can hear you! I can hear you! The rest of world hears you! And the people—and the people who knocked these buildings down will hear all of us soon!"[33] The crowd cheered, and then responded with chants of "USA!"[34]

Second, though Crawford is surely correct that "Koch does not suggest how a cycle of revenge might end," when Operation Enduring Freedom began, people like Koch were no doubt very much in favor of the operation. Even if, as Elshtain above suggests, that war was a "just one," the operation could have helped satisfy revenge as an affect. The two—justice and revenge—coexisted for some time in the United States. So instead of one overzealously shading over into the other, they run parallel to one another.

Third, the quotation brings us back to where I began this chapter—with the public and social celebrations following the bin Laden killing. Susan Milligan, whose article on how the celebrations went "too far" has been referenced in several portions of this chapter, still honestly expressed *her* reaction to the news of bin Laden's death:

> I was thrilled to learn of bin Laden's death. As soon as I felt that emotion, I half expected to feel a backlash of shame, of some guilt over feeling so overjoyed at someone's brutal demise. But I didn't. I don't like violence. I don't even like to see violent movies . . . I hadn't, before bin Laden, understood that I was capable of feeling nothing but pure happiness over the violent death of another human being. Most likely, that is because I find it hard to see bin Laden as a human being, since he could not be to me anything other than a vessel for hate and destruction and death. Moreover, I was especially pleased that bin Laden was killed by a bullet to the head. Had he been killed by an explosion or aerial attack, the result would have been the same. But I am especially satisfied that the last thing bin Laden likely saw was a U.S. soldier with an American flag on his uniform, pointing his gun at the face of evil.

What distinguishes Milligan's reaction is that, though perhaps vengeful, it was largely *private*. Many other Americans who did not head straight out into the streets that Sunday evening surely had the same reaction as Milligan—but again, privately, in their own living rooms and at most sharing that reaction with their families.

Revenge on this personal, private level again accords with Hegel's understanding of revenge noted above by McBride. However, others took to the streets to experience the exhilaration of bin Laden's death with *fellow Americans* presumably because it was an act of US military force that brought him down, and it was bin Laden's (political) organization that was responsible for the 9/11 attacks.[35]

In light of this—and that revenge might obtain in different settings of a political community (both public and private)—Lowenheim and Heimann provide us with a more fruitful analytical possibility. For them, we might view the reactions or lack thereof of the political communities engaging in the action. They, too, entertain in their examination of the 2006 July War the justifications Israeli leaders provided for the use of force against Hezbollah and more generally in Lebanon. One of the most important justifications for the general bombing of the southern areas of Lebanon was to weaken Hezbollah's military capacity. The authors note that "by February 2007, IDF [Israeli Defense Forces] intelligence estimated that Hezbollah had recovered from most of the harm it suffered and perhaps even acquired more capabilities than it had before. *The fact that this estimation did not generate public debate in Israel attests to the fact that few in Israel were surprised to hear it*; . . . quite amazingly, no indication exists in the extensive Winograd material or in any other *open source* that any thought was given during the war to Hezbollah's postwar recovery" (emphasis added).[36]

We might consider the differences between these two strategies: Where Elshtain focuses on revenge-as-motive, Lowenheim and Heimann's analysis engages both revenge as a motive and also as a public practice. In order to get to the public practice of revenge, the latter strategy also engages how war, and ostensibly even just wars, might serve the emotional needs of a political community, and thus our domain for potential revenge-as-practice evidence extends past the elite level and into the field of democratic politics especially.

As mentioned in the introduction, revenge is often portrayed by analysts as knee-jerk, exemplified by a lack of deliberation, or as a reflexive, hyperreactive set of actions. This is Elshtain's conclusion noted above—that deliberation, as illustrated by the United States after 9/11, is different than an angry, quick-to-react mob. Others see it as less knee-jerk but still more "expressive, and mostly uncoordinated" compared, for instance, with reprisals.[37]

For one, revenge is often at the same time likened as an "age-old cycle of violence" between salient-identity groups, and that it can fester for decades and even centuries, and if this is so, then revenge is therefore subject to conditioning, to being culturally shaped, formed and re-formed, through time. A second related conceptualization of revenge is that certain populations are more prone to revenge than others. Some of the work on the ethnic conflicts of the late 1980s and 1990s inadvertently (or not) assumed this, but as others have pointed out, even conflicts considered "tribal" or "ancient" in nature were at their core politically stimulated.[38] The connection between these two conceptualizations is quite clear: The types of groups that are assumed to be prone to revenge are those who seem to be stuck in premodernity, namely, those found in the postcolonial developing world. The Milligan quotation referenced in the opening pages of this chapter foregrounds this concern regarding the bin Laden death celebrations in the United States—"But the image also looked creepily like some of the crazed anti-American demonstrations that have occurred around the world."[39]

Yet if we see revenge as a social practice meant to reinscribe authority, it can both be a "quick," less deliberate (re)action and yet still serve an important function. Stated alternatively, one reason revenge appears this way is that the revenging party is conditioned to exact revenge by its authoritative status—globally, politically, and domestically. But to the extent that revenge is an *affective* apparatus, there can be in a vengeful action a fine line between authority and going "too far." The problem—as the varied reactions to the bin Laden killing demonstrate—is that in the public and diverse realm of global politics, some will see actions going too far, though others will see them as not going far enough. And *both* sets of judgments will hold the authority doing the "acting" responsible. In this respect, a good example of wanting vengeance to go further comes from the former US vice presidential candidate and now political celebrity Sarah Palin, who, following the news that the Obama administration would not release the photograph of the "headshot" of a dead bin Laden, tweeted on her Facebook page to "show photo as warning to others seeking America's destruction. No pussy-footing around, no politicking, no drama; it's part of the mission."[40]

CONCLUSION

Revenge is not always knee-jerk, willy-nilly, and out of control; rather, it can be socialized, constructed, shaped, formed and re-formed, and *politicized* over time. Just war can either help stem or, in other times, facilitate this socialization. In his conclusion to this volume Cian O'Driscoll helpfully engages the different ways the book's contributors situate authority in the just war tradition. In this chapter I have tried to delineate the constitutive relationship between authority and action. This connection can be further developed as an even more problematic condition in an era where the former, authority, gets challenged by deterritorialized *actors* such as al-Qaeda. As Oded Lowenheim and I have observed, and as Anthony Lang has asserted in more detail, punishment can be a necessary condition for both realizing the rules of an international order and maintaining the meaning of an order's rules and norms.[41] Yet without a defined territory to act upon, but still maintaining the *need* for thinking about action in terms of "war," and more immediately requiring *some kind of action*, period, a set of forceful responses against a rather abstract enemy can serve, rather, to unravel the fabric of the rules of international order, as Mendelsohn averred an actor such as al-Qaeda could bring about by "provoking an overreaction by the hegemon that leads to the breakdown of the accepted code of conduct for states' behaviour in general and for the hegemon's in particular. This can be done by magnifying the conflict between the hegemon's dual roles as systemic leader and great power, provoking it to act in accordance with the latter at the expense of the former."[42]

If revenge is socially expected, or at least minimally anticipated out of hegemonic authorities, and helps to satiate a democratic polity's sensibilities, such overreaction against an ill-defined enemy will be both more likely, and probably more deleterious on the principles of international society. In this way, the bin Laden killing demonstrates both a troubling and an inadvertently beneficial possibility with regard to the "order" of international society that the just war tradition is claimed to uphold.

The troubling possibility stems from the fact that the raid occurred without the permission of the Pakistanis. Obama so much as admitted this in an interview shortly after the raid:

> At the end of the day, this was still a 55/45 situation. I mean, we could not say definitively that bin Laden was there. Had he not been there, then there would have been significant consequences. Obviously, we're going into the sovereign territory of another country and landing helicopters and conducting a military operation. And so if it turns out that it's a wealthy, you know, prince from Dubai who's in this compound, and, you know, we've sent Special Forces in—we've got problems. So there were risks involved geopolitically in making the decision.[43]

Steve Croft, the CBS television interviewer, failed to point out to the president that even though no wealthy prince from Dubai was in the compound, the raid was *still* conducted on Pakistan's sovereign territory without prior notification or approval.[44] The problem that comes into focus is not only al-Qaeda or the nature of any nonstate actors in general but also the notion that using *war* to combat such organizations is the most effective option.

An emerging concern in the recently developed *jus post bellum* plank of the just war tradition is the notion of a "just termination" of war. In that sense the inadvertently beneficial development coming out of bin Laden's killing is that it is the closest "USS *Missouri*" moment one can hope for in the so-called "long war" against terrorism. What we should take from all of this is that our just war tradition is useful as long as it does not blind us to the more immediate possibility that behind all our referents and language and analysis lies a more parsimonious intuition about a postmodernity of warfare that has made it both distant and entertaining—that in the safety of our homes, revenge can only be served by disproportionality. In such a case, the notion not only of war, but especially of "just war," is merely an academic exercise.

NOTES

1. Susan Milligan, "Celebrations after Bin Laden's Death Went Too Far," *US News & World Report*, May 3, 2011, www.usnews.com/opinion/blogs/susan-milligan/2011/05/03/cele brations-after-bin-ladens-death-went-too-far.

2. Oded Lowenheim, *Predators and Parasites: Persistent Agents of Transnational Harm and Great Power Authority* (Ann Arbor: University of Michigan Press, 2007), 29–30.

3. Harry Gould, "International Criminal Bodies," *Review of International Studies* 35, no. 3 (2009): 701–21, at 710.

4. On the damage to the United States' great power authority, see, especially, Barak Mendelsohn, "Sovereignty under Attack: International Society Meets the Al Qaeda Network," *Review of International Studies* 31 (2005): 45–68, at 68—a point to which I return in my conclusion. I reconstructed bin Laden's late October 2004 communiqué, released in the

days leading up to the US presidential election, as a form of "cynic parrhesia" meant to incite the United States in a provocative manner. As I characterized it, "Bin Laden's mere visual presence, three years after the 9/11 attacks, [was] enough to enrage" the US populace into a reaction. In that case, I made the qualified conclusion that this reaction manifested in a higher likelihood for a George W. Bush reelection. Brent J. Steele, *Defacing Power: The Aesthetics of Insecurity in Global Politics* (Ann Arbor: University of Michigan Press, 2010), 116.

5. One commentator, Robert Spencer of *Human Events*, asked rhetorically: "Can you envision FDR ordering that [Hitler] be given a dignified funeral and burial? Of course he would not have, for to have done so would have been to suggest some legitimacy to this genocidal monster's actions, his life, and his legacy. And in saying (counterfactually) that Osama bin Laden was 'not a Muslim leader,' Obama seems to have been trying to deny the al-Qaeda chief exactly that. So why then turn around and force American troops to endure the rites of the very religion that inspired bin Laden to commit mass murder in the first place? It was no less absurd and insulting than the Americans' burying Hitler with a Nazi flag draped over his coffin would have been in 1945. Obama owes the American people an apology." "Obama's Abominable 'Respect' for Bin Laden Burial Rites," May 10, 2011, www.humanevents.com/article.php?id=43404.

6. Hans Morgenthau, *American Foreign Policy: A Critical Examination* (London: Methuen, 1952), 223, also quoted by Piki Ish-Shalom, "The Triptych of Realism, Elitism, and Conservatism," *International Studies Review* 8, no. 3 (2006): 441–68, at 443. Ish-Shalom comments on this quotation: "Democratic politics can lead to imprudent and inefficient foreign policy when the wise statesman makes decisions with the specter of re-election in mind."

7. Keally McBride, *Punishment and Political Order* (Ann Arbor: University of Michigan Press, 2007), 1–2.

8. Anthony F. Lang Jr., *Punishment, Justice and International Relations: Ethics and Order after the Cold War* (London: Routledge, 2008).

9. Ibid., 26, 64–65.

10. "The failure to link that action to an institution makes such actions *appear closer to revenge than to retribution*" (emphasis added); ibid., 64. McBride discusses the importance of law as a way to make punishment "dispassionate." McBride, *Punishment*, 8.

11. Neta Crawford, "Just War Theory and the US Counterterror War," *Perspectives on Politics* 1 (2003): 5–25, at 7; Eric A. Heinze, "Private Military Companies, Just War, and Humanitarian Intervention," in *Ethics, Authority, and War: Non-State Actors and the Just War Tradition*, ed. Eric A. Heinze and Brent J. Steele (London: Palgrave, 2009).

12. Crawford, "Just War Theory," 19.

13. And, of course, the killing of bin Laden led to quick, *and public*, pronouncements by al-Qaeda and its affiliates that it would seek "revenge" for bin Laden's death. "Al Qaida Seeks Revenge for Bin Laden's Death," May 6, 2011, www.msnbc.msn.com/id/42928874/ns/world_news-death_of_bin_laden/t/al-qa ida-vows-revenge-bin-ladens-death/.

14. Jean Bethke Elshtain, *Just War against Terror* (New York: Basic Books, 2003), 23–25.

15. Oded Lowenheim and Gadi Heiman, "Revenge in International Politics," *Security Studies* 17, no. 4 (2008): 685–724. Several other definitions see it as past oriented. Michael Boyle articulates revenge as "acts of expressive violence against a member of a targeted group with the intention of punishing them for a previous act of violence." Michael J. Boyle, "Revenge and Reprisal Violence in Kosovo," *Conflict, Security & Development* 10, no. 2 (2010): 189–216, at 191. Jon Elster defines revenge as "the attempt, at some risk of cost to oneself, to impose suffering on those who have made one suffer, because they have made one suffer." Jon Elster, "Norms of Revenge," *Ethics* 100, no. 4 (1990): 862–85, at 862.

16. Eric Heinze sees revenge this way while discussing the "right intention" condition of just war, that revenge is one of several "ulterior motives," before helpfully and sharply distinguishing intentions from motives, which somewhat echoes or reinforces my argument below, that revenge can be satisfied by actions even deemed to be "just." The definition of "revenge" is from *Merriam-Webster's Eleventh Collegiate Dictionary Online*, www.merriam-webster.com/dictionary/revenge.

17. It may have implications for the emerging work on *jus post bellum*—for a review, see Melissa Labonte, "*Jus Post Bellum*, Peacebuilding, and Non-State Actors: Lessons from Afghanistan," in *Ethics*, ed. Heinze and Steele, 205–38—in that the possibility of revenge impacts punishment or the adjudication of retributional rights, and especially the prospects for peace building and reconciliation. As Michael J. Boyle claims, revenge and its "mirror image" reprisals are one of the "most common forms of violence in post-conflict states." Boyle, "Revenge," 190.

18. Ibid., 191.

19. Harry D. Gould, "What Happened to Punishment in the Just War Tradition?" in *Ethics*, ed. Heinze and Steele, 73–100, at 91; Lowenheim and Heimann, "Revenge," 696.

20. Reinhold Niebuhr, *Moral Man, Immoral Society* (New York: Charles Scribner's Sons, 1932).

22. Randall Collins, *Violence: A Micro-Sociological Theory* (Princeton, NJ: Princeton University Press, 2008), 85.

23. Niebuhr, *Moral Man,* 88.

24. Ibid., 93.

25. McBride, *Punishment,* 7.

26. This is Lang's distinction with Hobbes's notion of authority and punishment. Lang, *Punishment,* 30.

27. On relationalism, see Patrick Thaddeus Jackson and Daniel Nexon, "Relations before States: Substance, Process and the Study of World Politics," *European Journal of International Relations* 5, no. 3 (1999): 291–332.

28. Lang leaves the door open on what I would term this "multivalent" potentiality of war when distinguishing his different "types" of punitive actions with reference to "sovereign intentions": "There need not be a single intention articulated by a sovereign authority in order to describe these actions as punishments. Moreover, the intentions (and there are *always more than one intention when states use military force*) can include self-defence or the pursuit of national self-interest; indeed, punishment can be self-interested in part." Lang, *Punishment,* 64 (emphasis added).

29. Lowenheim and Heimann, "Revenge," 699–700.

30. Elshtain, *Just War,* 23–24.

31. Cian O'Driscoll made one of the strongest (not to mention stylish) critiques on one of these problems, that "from an Augustinian perspective, then, we need to guard against sanguinely accepting the pious nostrums of those who proclaim themselves to be agents of the good as they go about their business waging war. To borrow a term favored by social ethicists, we need a 'hermeneutics of suspicion.'" See Cian O'Driscoll, "Elshtain's *Just War against Terror,* a Tale of Two Cities," *International Relations* 21, no. 4 (2007): 88. Elshtain's assessment, further, ignores some of Bush's, and other US opinion leaders', proclamations issued elsewhere.

32. Ibid.

33. The text of the speech, as well as audio and video files, can be viewed/heard at www2.bakersfieldcollege.edu/jgiertz/Bush%20Bullhorn%20speech.htm.

34. What is interesting here is twofold. First, the literal meaning of doing something to be "heard" by the people who "knocked these buildings down," made no sense as those people were in fact lying dead along with all the victims in the rubble. Yet the purpose served here is a declaration that *some* action would follow against *somebody*. Further, one can notice the important aesthetic setting, the spectacle of the speech and the promise of revenge for the terrorist acts against the rather amorphous enemy of al-Qaeda.

35. Others still were already in public settings—e.g., those attending the Major League baseball game in Philadelphia between the New York Mets and Philadelphia Phillies, where by the ninth inning especially chants of "USA! USA!" broke out in a collective rhythm—see http://www.youtube.com/watch?v = 35pfllMiLag.

36. Lowenheim and Heimann, "Revenge," 706–7.

37. Boyle, "Revenge," 191.

38. While making the point that the Kosovo conflict was politically conditioned, Tim Judah also fell into this practice, even subtitling his book on Kosovo "War and Revenge." Tim Judah, *Kosovo: War and Revenge* (New Haven, CT: Yale University Press, 2000). See also Robert D. Kaplan, *Balkan Ghosts: A Journey through History* (New York: St. Martin's Press, 1993). Nicholas Wheeler writes in his Rwanda paper of *Saving Strangers*: "It is comforting for those of us who live in the West to think that what happened in Rwanda was the result of ancient tribal hatreds; that the orgy of violence that consumed Rwanda is an African phenomenon that we could do very little about. However, this image, replete with Conradian overtones of Africa as *The Heart of Darkness*, is simply wrong . . . [rather] the genocide was the produce of deliberate political design" Nicholas Wheeler, *Saving Strangers: Humanitarian Intervention in International Society* (Oxford: Oxford University Press, 2000), 209.

39. Susan Milligan, "Celebrations after bin Laden's Death Went Too Far—Comments," May 5, 2011, *US News & World Report Online*, www.usnews.com/opinion/blogs/susan-milli gan/2011/05/03/celebrations-after-bin-ladens-death-went-too-far/comments.

40. Obama seemed to recognize, in his decision, the restraint necessary in not seeming to go "too far," justifying his decision by saying that "we don't need to spike the football." Brian Montopoli, "Obama: I Won't Release Bin Laden Death Photos," May 4, 2011, www.cbs news.com/8301–503544_162–20059739–503544.html. In this way, Obama indeed seems to have been wary of the appearance of revenge. David A. Patten, "Palin: Don't 'Pussyfoot' on Releasing Photos Obama," May 4, 2011, www.newsmax.com/InsideCover/palin-pussy-footing-bin/2011/05/04/id/395190.

41. Oded Lowenheim and Brent J. Steele, "Institutions of Violence, Great Power Authority, and the War on Terror," *International Political Science Review* 31, no. 1 (2012); Lang, *Punishment*, 25.

42. Mendelsohn, "Sovereignty under Attack," 68.

43. "Obama on Bin Laden: The Full *60 Minutes* Interview," CBS News, May 8, 2011, www.cbsnews.com/8301–504803_162–20060530–10391709.html.

44. However, there could be a case that Pakistan had already given its approval in previous agreements regarding US forces in "hot pursuit" of al-Qaeda suspects. See "US, Pak Agree to 'Quiet' Hot Pursuit," *Indian Express*, January 7, 2003, www.indianexpress.com/oldStory/16206/.

CHAPTER 12

Just War and Guerilla War

Michael L. Gross

ALTHOUGH IT IS CRUCIAL TO ASK how state armies should fight nonstate guerrilla organizations justly, it is equally important to ask whether guerrillas can wage just war. It is often thought that they cannot—that guerrilla armies violate the principles of just war in the most egregious way and leave state armies to wring their hands in frustration and debate the price of violating the same principles that their adversaries mockingly ignore.

Although this dismal perspective dominates the thinking of state actors, it is decidedly narrow and, ultimately, unconvincing. Some, though not all, nonstate actors that dominate armed conflict today have legitimate recourse to the force of arms when accompanied by just cause and legitimate authority. Just cause reaches beyond traditional notions of territorial self-defense to embrace a range of threats that undermine fundamental human rights that sometimes, but not always, include the right of national self-determination. Similarly, the *ad bellum* principle of legitimate authority—or who, exactly, may authorize the use of armed force—requires greater nuance and elasticity in the context of guerrilla warfare. Among nonstate actors liberation movements, self-governing political organizations, and, often, rival political groups replace the sovereign governments of nation-states. Deprived of just cause and legitimate authority, guerrilla organizations indeed face charges of criminal behavior. Armed with just cause and legitimate authority, however, these same organizations enjoy the right to fight, combatant status, and, in some cases, the right to aid from the international community. In the sections that follow, I give a brief overview of the state of guerrilla warfare today, lay the ground for guidelines to describe just guerrilla war, and consider the implications for war-fighting itself.

GUERRILLA WARFARE AND NONSTATE
ACTORS TODAY: A BRIEF OVERVIEW

Observers are mightily confused about the state of the world today, the status of the nation-state, and the role of the great powers. For some, the state remains pre-eminent, whether it is the United States serving out its tenure as the reigning hegemon or China and Russia slowly gaining control over their respective regions and nipping at the heels of the United States. For others, the state is in decline whether by design in Europe or by violence and accident in the Middle East and Africa. Regardless of the scenario the world, as usual, is pockmarked with conflict. Hot spots today are not ignited by rivalry among nation-states but by many nonstate groups challenging failed states and emerging hegemonic powers alike.

These conflicts take many forms. For the purposes of assessing the justice of guerrilla warfare, here I focus on nationalist conflicts for independence and self-determination, and proxy wars. Transnational agendas, such as those al-Qaeda and other radical Islamic organizations espouse, are more difficult to evaluate. On one hand, there is nothing inherently incoherent or illegitimate about organizations striving to establish an *umma* or Islamic religious transnation that stretches beyond traditional national boundaries. On the other hand, these transnational movements are about subjugation, not freedom. They thrive on discord and disruption and seem to seek nothing more than the ruin of Western interests rather than the betterment of those they claim to represent. This immediately undercuts any appeal to just cause (see below) that may justify the use of armed force. Although this does not exclude transnational movements whose goals promote human rights and welfare at the expense of state sovereignty, such organizations are saddled with the burden of proof. They must show that their agenda does not dispense with the state system without offering an alternative to sustain the international order. Transnational Islamic movements do not do this. Although nationalist movements also challenge state sovereignty, they ultimately seek accommodation and recognition within the international order.

Nationalist conflicts of the last quarter century are the extension of colonial guerrilla war. Some are secessionist: Chechnya, Kosovo, Sri Lanka, and Southern Sudan, for example. Others fight battles against foreign occupation: Afghanistan, East Timor, Western Sahara, Northern Ireland, and the Palestinians of Gaza and the West Bank. Proxy guerrilla wars occur as state actors enlist the aid of nonstate proxy agents to initiate conflict in their stead. In the 2006 Lebanon War, for example, Syria and Iran enlisted Hezbollah in their fight against the United States and Israel. In each of these cases there may be some semblance of *casus belli*. Nationalist guerrillas fight for independence, self-determination, and/or the protection of human rights, whereas proxy guerrillas and their patron states use armed force to deter, distract, or weaken their enemies.

Unlike nonstate actors, states (and their proxies) generally find it easy to ignore questions of just cause. *Ad bellum* principles of war have never been very popular among nation-states. States recognize their supreme moral status in the international order and have never contested one another's right to wage war when necessitated by national interest. Legitimate and just *casus belli* embraces anything short of bald aggression and allows states recourse to armed force in nearly any situation as long as they act in self-defense. As a practical matter, the international community has rarely condemned a member state for aggression. It is not surprising, then, that international humanitarian law and the law of armed conflict—strict legal regimes dedicated to mitigating the destruction of modern war—generally eschew anything having to do with just war. For Jean Pictet, the eminent jurist and midwife of post–World War II humanitarian law, the very idea of *just* war represents nothing less than a "malignant doctrine" that "hampered humanitarian progress for centuries."[1] By offering one side (or both!) the moral anchor of justice, just war theory relegated a nation's adversary, its soldiers and civilians alike, to criminal status. With right on one's side, conquering an unjust foe permitted and even demanded the unrestrained use of armed force, thereby stripping unjust soldiers of their rights and just soldiers of their duties.

These prospects warranted the wrath of legal scholars who understood that any successful attempt to introduce restraint into armed conflict would require each side to uncouple *ad bellum* from *in bello* justice, bracket the justice of their cause, and confer rights and privileges on enemy soldiers and civilians as if they were moral equals and untainted by criminality. And, in fact, this is what they did. Putting *ad bellum* principles aside, jurists and philosophers directed their attention to the just and legitimate conduct of war—*jus in bello*. But if *ad bellum* principles were of scant concern when states fought one another, they stand front and center when states fight nonstate rivals. In asymmetric war, just cause and legitimate authority are everything. Without them, nonstate actors—guerrillas, insurgents, rebels and/or freedom fighters—are without standing, deprived of combatant rights and treated as criminals. With just cause and just authority, these same nonstate actors regain their standing and privileged status as combatants. Only then is it possible to evaluate the *in bello* provisions of asymmetric war. The rules of just guerrilla warfare will prove vexing enough as the norms are tweaked to make room for human shields, improvised explosive devices, direct attacks on civilians, and hostage taking. Preceding this discussion, however, is necessarily one about just cause and authority. Bridging *ad bellum* and *in bello* principles is what I term "the right to a fighting chance."

THE RIGHT TO A FIGHTING CHANCE

In just war theory and positive law, nations have a right to defend themselves from armed attack. The right is not controversial but is usually subject to several other conditions, including last resort and success. Diplomacy, sanctions, and other less-harmful means than armed conflict must precede a decision to go to war, and likewise the prospect of prevailing by force of arms must be reasonably assured. Assurance, for the most part, comes from the material and diplomatic resources available to a nation defending itself from aggression. But assurance may also come in the form of noninterference so that the world community does not impede a nation's efforts to exercise its right to self-defense. One form of interference is legal. Commenting on the Additional Protocol I provision that allows guerrillas the right to shed uniforms under certain conditions, Charles Chaumont writes: "In order to remain objective and credible, humanitarian law must allow every party an equal chance in combat. If a norm of this body of law is incompatible with this principle and makes it impossible from the outset for one of the parties to have any prospect of victory, it is better not to draft such a norm at all."[2]

Stated in this way Chaumont's comments are provocative. At the very least, they suggest that guerrillas may disregard the rules of war when it suits them. It is also not clear what chance of victory parties deserve. An equal chance is untenable, for it might demand that third-party actors are somehow obligated to provide belligerents with the men and matériel they need to wage war. But some minimal prospect of victory is more reasonable. This only demands that a state or group going to war have the resources necessary for some reasonable chance of victory and that other states do not interfere as they exercise their right of self-defense. For nonstate actors it is also particularly important to emphasize the role of just cause, with which states rarely have to contend in practice.

To clarify these points, I would define the right to a fighting chance as follows: When fighting for a just cause, nonstate actors representing a people (i.e., enjoying legitimate authority) have a right to pursue their claims by force of arms as a (1) last resort, (2) when success is possible, and (3) by means that are effective and necessary and (4) do not violate the basic rights and protections afforded combatants and noncombatants.

Under these conditions, the law of armed conflict cannot abrogate the right to a fight by making its exercise impossible. The right to fight demands and guarantees a chance of success when the cause is just. States, therefore, have a duty not to impede or interfere with the exercise of this right and may have a positive duty to aid some nonstate actors fighting for a just cause.

Conditions 1 through 4 are common enough stipulations of just war theory. War, as noted above, is only justified when other, less violent and destructive avenues of conflict resolution fail. Some prospect of success is essential to exercising the right to go to war. The chance of success is related to the nature of the threat a nation faces. Generally, the greater the threat, the lower prospect of success a nation is willing to tolerate. A nation fighting against genocide will go to war when the prospect of success might be very low, whereas a nation fighting with its neighbor over border demarcations will only risk war if the prospect of success is very high and the cost is very low. Effectiveness and necessity are the hallmarks of the tactics a group chooses to fight. Effectiveness demands that the means of war accomplish their goal while the benefits of action outweigh the costs. But effectiveness is not enough. There are many effective tactics, but not all are necessary. Offered an array of tactics, the principle of necessity gives preference to the least destructive one. The fourth stipulation further limits the reach of effectiveness and necessity. War and the tactics it employs may be effective but nonetheless unduly destructive. Deliberate attacks on civilians may be an effective and necessary means of winning a war but impermissible because they egregiously violate the rights of noncombatants and upend their immunity from direct, unnecessary, and disproportionate harm.

If these four conditions apply equally to states and nonstates, the other stipulations—just cause and legitimate authority—are more problematic for nonstate actors. For states, just cause is the rule. Except in extreme circumstances, the international community assumes that all parties to a conflict have legitimate cause. For nonstates, however, just cause is the exception. Here, the international community generally assumes that nonstate groups have no right to fight. Moreover, nonstates are rarely fighting *against* something, such as an armed attack. Instead they are usually fighting *for* something, such as national liberation or secession. Just cause is much easier to articulate in terms of self-defense than in terms of self-determination. Legitimate authority is equally vexing. With few exceptions, sovereign nation-states enjoy legitimate authority as a matter of course. Nonstate actors do not, and must they prove they represent or benefit a people or some other recognized entity or cause. Just cause and legitimate authority are necessary to establish the right to a fighting chance. With this in hand, we can now discuss the international community's duties of noninterference and/or active aid to nonstate actors.

JUST CAUSE

Because nonstate actors do not carry the inherent legitimacy of nation-states during war, it is crucial to think about the conditions necessary for them to bring their grievances to the battlefield. For states, self-defense turns on a state's right to resort to armed force to protect itself from armed attack and aggression. Aggression, as construed by the International Criminal Court, refers specifically to the use of armed force against the sovereignty, territorial integrity, or political independence of another state.[3] Nonstates, however, cannot be responding to any infringement of sovereignty or political independence. Territorial infringements may, of course, excite nonstate actors that control some territorial enclave, but the idea of territorial *integrity* remains the domain of states laying claim to internationally recognized borders. Nonstate actors must therefore settle for something less than armed attacks against their sovereign borders. This "something less" ultimately determines their right to go to war. In some cases, nonstates may be defending themselves against genocide—the "intent to destroy, in whole or in part, a national, ethnical, racial or religious group,"—or crimes against humanity, that is, "widespread or systematic attack directed against any civilian population."[4] In other cases, the abuses may be more systemic, reflecting long-term discrimination and the denial of basic rights of representation or equal access to resources. In still other cases, nonstate actors may simply desire a greater level of control and autonomy than membership in the state where they currently reside affords. An armed response to any of these situations can be construed as self-defense, but not in terms typical of an armed attack that triggers this same right among nation-states. In all these cases nonstate groups are fighting for some form of self-determination.

Writing in 1919, Woodrow Wilson defined self-determination as the "right of every people to choose the sovereign under which they live." This has been under-stood as both an individual and collective right. Article 27 of the Covenant on Civil and Political Rights emphasizes an individual right: "In those States in which ethnic, religious or linguistic minorities exist, persons belonging to such minorities shall not be denied the right, in community with the other members of their group, to enjoy their own culture, to profess and practice their own religion, or to use their own language." Two points are immediately important. First, this article reflects an individual, not a group right; and second, it does not entail political, economic, or social autonomy, much less independence. The right to self-determination only requires that minority group *members* receive the means necessary to maintain their unique identity.[5] This may simply require individual equality before the law, while saying nothing about a group right to special territorial or legal privileges. There are, however, also collective implications, because the right of self-determination only applies to members of what Margalit and Raz term "encompassing" cultural groups that exhibit a "pervasive" culture that is characterized by a unique identity, history, and language and that is "of great importance for the well-being of individ-uals."[6] Moreover, international instruments declared the right of certain groups, those listed in "trust or non-self-governing territories," to self-determination—regardless of any human rights abuses their members may suffer. These were mostly colonies and territories of the United States and European states, and most received independence by 2002. Finally, Additional Protocol I recognizes the rights of "peo-ples fighting against colonial domination and alien occupation and against racist régimes in the exercise of their right of self-determination."[7] Although there is gen-eral agreement that the terms "colonial domination," "alien occupation," and "rac-ist regime" were tailored solely to grant combatant status to guerrillas fighting, respectively, against Portugal, Israel, and apartheid-era South Africa in the early 1970s, the gross injustice associated with "alien occupation" continues to resonate as *casus belli* today among guerrillas fighting in Gaza and the West Bank, Chechnya,

Afghanistan, the Western Sahara, Turkey, and elsewhere. Protocol I not only recognized the right of self-determination; it also recognizes the right to fight in its pursuit. These rights reflect both individual and collective rights to self-determination.

Self-determination is a claim right: People, however defined, have a claim against the nations of the world to choose their ruler and live without the threat of genocide or systematic murder or abuse. Self-determination is not only about representation but also about a people's right to establish a sovereign of their choice. They might choose to remain part of an existing sovereign nation or establish their own. A nation, such as a colonial or occupying country, and/or international body that fails to answer this claim loses immunity and may be attacked. This affords the attacker—representing a people denied primary human rights, political rights, and/or rights to cultural identity—the right or license to fight under the conditions outline above.[8]

Demands for human, political, or cultural rights are distinct moral claims that generate obligations on the part of the international community and ground the right to fight when all other means to achieve self-determination fail. Referring to the "remedial" right of self-determination, Allen Buchanan justifies political secession and/or regime change only when individuals are subject to egregious *human* rights violations.[9] Under these conditions, any persecuted group—and not necessarily a cultural, ethnic, or religious people—may pursue its right of self-determination against an oppressor state. A just war of secession, as just war theory stipulates, is a last resort when other measures fail. Nor is national self-determination necessarily the optimal political arrangement if other avenues of political organization are available or if the resulting division of sovereignty makes the persecuted people less well off. Secession and war must both meet conditions of last resort, necessity, and effectiveness before undertaken by an oppressed group. Demands for human rights are the weightiest of just cause conditions, stripping an oppressor of any claim to self-defense and, as I suggest below, obligating the international community to provide a people fighting for self-determination with humanitarian aid, military support, and/or armed intervention. Demands for political rights, representation, and cultural autonomy, conversely, are less weighty, set a higher bar for going to war, justify less than independence, and only obligate third-party states not to interfere.

When civil rights are at stake, the claim of certain groups to national self-determination weakens, as do the obligations of the international community. Appeals to a nation's judicial, executive, and legislative branches, not war, are the first avenue of recourse to rectify such civil rights violations, inadequate representation, job discrimination, or an unequal distribution of resources. The same is true of demands for special minority rights, such as cultural or religious autonomy. In each of these cases war is rarely a legitimate option because nonviolent political measures remain available and effective. And if they are not readily available or effective, the cost of war may often exceed the political or cultural benefits it might confer. Absent recourse to war, it may just be that discriminated groups must work slowly to attain their ends. As I suggest below, groups going to war to satisfy political grievances also generate bystander duties. These do not necessarily involve active aid but may require other nations to refrain from interfering as groups form political movements and employ armed force to press their claims.

Finally, consider the just causes that proxy guerrilla groups embrace. Lacking sovereign territory of their own, guerrilla organizations may throw in with sovereign states that, if attacked, may provide guerrillas with *casus belli*. Guerrillas gain just cause by proxy. Proxy wars are nothing new. Often, they describe client states that wage war from different sides of an ideological and geopolitical divide, indirectly supporting the interests of the larger states that support them. For instance, during the 1960s and 1970s the American-Soviet Cold War rivalry played out in the Middle East Arab-Israeli wars as the Soviets heavily supported Egypt and Syria while Israel received massive military aid from the United States. Often, proxy actors embrace nonstate actors. Continuing a postwar pattern that began during the Greek civil war, the United States and the USSR interfered to influence the outcome in civil wars and wars of independence in such venues as Angola and Mozambique.

The role played by Hezbollah during the 2006 Lebanon War represents a marked change from these Cold War conflicts. Hezbollah itself was not fighting a civil war or war of independence nor, previous to the fighting, was it a significant party to a regional conflict. Instead the organization provided strategic services to its benefactor states, Iran and Syria, in their respective confrontations with the United States and Israel in the Middle East. The 2006 war was precipitated by a border incident and fueled by Iran and Syria's desire to strengthen Hezbollah's place in the political constellation of Lebanon, weaken Israeli forces, and draw attention to Israel's vulnerability should the United States contemplate using armed force against Iran. As in many conventional conflicts, just cause was simply not on the table. All the parties involved—Israel, Hezbollah, Lebanon, Syria, and Iran—were sufficiently concerned about their geopolitical interests to establish a reasonable presumption of just cause as they resorted to armed force. In response, other states will interfere, participate, aid, desist, sanction, embargo, and so on as they see fit and in accord with their national interests, treaty obligations, and international law.

Just cause, then, takes several forms. Many groups—particularly individuals bound together by cultural, racial, or religious ties—are defending themselves against a range of threats against their life, liberty, or lifestyle. Legitimate responses vary with the intensity and immediacy of the danger that each group faces. For proxy groups, just cause is anchored in the more traditional concepts of self-defense and the protection of national interests. For both groups, the weight of their claims varies and as the physical or existential threat wanes the right to wage war weakens. Just cause is, as just war theory often suggests, only a necessary condition of war.

Equally as important for nonstate actors are the legitimacy and standing of the entity that decides on war or any other political measure. For states, this is a sovereign government; for nonstates, the identity of legitimate authority is considerably more obscure.

LEGITIMATE AUTHORITY

Although the idea of legitimate authority is central to classical just war theory, it is generally of little concern in conventional war. By law and custom, internationally recognized, sovereign states and members of the United Nations enjoy the authority necessary to wage war. Although this excludes unrecognized states such as Taliban Afghanistan, it does not appreciably affect rogue or criminal regimes, a list that includes or has recently included such countries as Sudan, Syria, Myanmar, and Libya. These states do not lose their standing in the world community or United Nations, although they may find their sovereignty curtailed and their regimes subject to military intervention by other states when they commit or threaten to commit genocide or crimes against humanity. Still, should one or another go to war in defense of legitimate political interests and in accordance with international law, the legitimate authority of these regimes would not be questioned.

Nonstate actors do not enjoy such forbearance. Even with just cause on their side, it remains unclear who, exactly, enjoys the right to go to war. The right to fight belongs to the "people"—of which, we have seen, there are many and may include ethnic, religious, geographical, linguistic, cultural, and just plain persecuted groups. To wage war, however, these groups require a military organization. Ideally, this would be a military organization that mirrors a state military organization, one that is hierarchically centralized and under the control of legitimate and hopefully representative political organizations. Cassese, for example, is explicit: "Racial groups are entitled to claim self-determination and vindicate their rights only if there is a representative organization capable of acting on behalf of the entire group."[10]

Cassese demands two conditions: representation and capability. Others, who are less sanguine about the possibility of representation, only demand capability. Fabre, for example, grants legitimate authority to those "best placed to put a stop to the wrongdoings which provide agents with a just cause for war."[11] The test, then, is not one of representation but efficacy. Any agent "best placed" to stop the wrongdoings or secure the right of self-determination acquires legitimate authority.

As John Williams and Nahed Artoul Zehr note, respectively, in chapters 4 and 6 of this volume, Fabre's claim turns on a rejection of the traditional idea that only states have legitimate authority to wage war. From Fabre's cosmopolitan perspective, any person or persons whose basic rights are threatened may turn to force, assuming their actions meet the other condition of just war: just cause, necessity, effectiveness, proportionality, and so on. And though Fabre uses this argument to extend legitimate authority to guerrilla organizations (and indeed, any organization or individual capable of fighting unjust aggression effectively), her claim may push things too far. Just as Zehr describes, unchecked violence in the hands of organizations like al-Qaeda may ensue in the wake of decentralized authority.

Decentralized authority may also encourage factionalism. Although it may make sense to confer authority on the organization that can best confront the threat that a people faces, granting license to any group that thinks it is effective seems to be a recipe for chaos, confusion, and, at worst, fratricide among those vying for the role of "best placed." A single force seems to be a much more effective alternative, and if efficacy is Fabre's principal requirement, it might easily stipulate that at one point a persecuted people must coalesce around a single military and political organization. Otherwise, no one is best placed to end the wrongdoing.

But must this organization be representative in any particular way? The world community, after all, does not demand representative government from its member nations. The link between legitimacy and representation deserves closer scrutiny among nonstate actors. For state actors, legitimacy comes with sovereignty, beneficence, and effectiveness but not necessarily with representation. A legitimate government is a sovereign government that sees to the needs of its people and that thus provides stability and security, social welfare, law, order, and justice.[12] In doing so, its institutions command respect and it thereby garners recognition and authority. An illegitimate government is criminal, terrorizes and persecutes all or some of its people, wages war without cause, and offers none of the benefits that legitimate governments strive to provide. Only a few governments are illegitimate in this sense. Most governments, then, even the most unrepresentative, carry legitimate authority, recognized by their people and the international community alike.

What, then, of nonstate actors? Absent a procedural mechanism or well-ordered institutions to bestow authority upon guerrilla leaders, legitimate authority is closely tied to a "background of shared beliefs" that the editors of this volume attribute to theoretical authority (as discussed in the introduction). These shared beliefs are theoretical only in the sense that they are pre-political, for they define the community or people waging an armed struggle for political recognition against a common enemy. Among a people, authority often attaches to charismatic, religious, or patrimonial leaders. The genesis of authority varies greatly among guerrilla movements. South American guerrillas began by trying to impose a revolutionary ideology to advance what they perceived as their people's social and economic interests. Divorced from the community, most of these groups failed to secure authority and eventually collapsed. More successful groups build upon preexisting patterns of authority, which are most often anchored in the tight social networks of clans and tribes. Guerrillas managing to bring local leaders over to their cause could then build upon their authority to recruit the fighters necessary to wage war. Guerrilla organizations as culturally disparate as the Kosovo Liberation Army, the Free Aceh Movement (Indonesia), and the Taliban (Pakistan) relied heavily on existing social networks and family ties to recruit soldiers and civilian supporters.[13] As recruitment increased, legitimacy and authority strengthened. Slowly, and with the ability to show moderate success, guerrilla organizations gain momentum.

To maintain legitimacy, guerrillas need to provide essential social services and human security, eventually open up their organization to some degree of representation and gain international support. Satisfying these conditions—effectiveness, domestic acceptance, representation, and international recognition—is not easy. Some organizations will be effective and enjoy domestic recognition, and even representation, but not international recognition. For instance, when it was first elected to office in Gaza in 2005, Hamas had everything but international recognition because it was perceived as an organization bent on terror and not national self-determination. The Palestinian Authority, conversely, met all these conditions for a period of time but, like Hamas, soon became a nonrepresentative movement when it failed to hold scheduled elections. Similarly, national movements in Ireland, Kosovo, and Chechnya held periodic but not regular elections.[14] East Timorese guerrillas, in contrast, elected their leaders by delegates.[15] At the same time, all these organizations were also able to provide essential social services to varying degrees. These two factors—a modicum of representation and the capability to improve the lot of their people—formed the basis for legitimate authority.

Each national liberation movement has a different history. In some cases, representative pre-state organizations grew under the auspices of a colonial or mandatory power (as in mandatory Palestine). Often, however, the institutions of government (whether representative or not) could come only *after* a liberation movement had achieved some of its goals, thereby leaving incipient guerrilla movements and their political and military organizations falling short of representation and international recognition. In the early stages of resistance, guerrilla groups often compete for effectiveness and loyalty. Only when one or more have crossed some threshold of loyalty, ad hoc representation, and effectiveness do they gain some measure of authority. Until then, their authority is precarious in the eyes of their compatriots and in the eyes of the state army they fight. Both may regard them as criminals until they prove themselves and gain a following. Unlike state army combatants, guerrillas do not have legitimate authority from the get-go. They must earn it and make the transition from criminal or warlord to guerrilla or privileged combatant over time. In Uganda, for example, the National Resistance Army slowly built support as it fought Uganda's repressive regime. This army modeled itself on FRELIMO's successful efforts to build popular support in their war against the Portuguese in Mozambique by tapping into local leadership to establish voluntary clandestine committees to supply guerrillas. As guerrilla strength grew, they were able to provide human security through safe zones that also offered administrative services and representative political organizations.[16]

Those movements that failed to heed popular demands saw their authority deteriorate before taking remedial action. For example, after waning support amid accusations of unresponsive leadership and human rights abuses, the Sudan People's Liberation Army convened its first national convention in 1994. The outcome was to clearly define its objectives in terms of national self-determination; democratize the movement; separate the military from the civilian authorities; create legislative, executive, and judicial branches of government; and strengthen the local courts. Thereafter, notes Metelits, "the SPLA experienced little difficulty marshaling support for its cause."[17] These dynamics hold true for proxy guerrilla groups as well. Hezbollah, for example, grew from an association of religious and social welfare bodies to a well-oiled political and military organization as it first confronted Israeli presence in Southern Lebanon and later forged alliances with Syria and Iran, before joining the Lebanese parliament as a full-fledged political party.

Unlike states, then, nonstate guerrilla organizations must constantly struggle to gain legitimate authority. The sources of authority are as varied as the circumstances surrounding national liberation. They are also fluid. Movements start off with the barest of authority, if any, to wage war on behalf of their people. Authority begins with the exercise of power but only acquires legitimacy if married to an ideology of just cause that gains the support of local religious, tribal, or community leaders. Rarely do liberation movements come to exercise legitimate authority without attaching themselves to preexisting loci of power. In time, they may turn in several directions; some may push toward democratization or other forms of representation and popular participation and, thereby, gain a measure of authority not far from a state, though other movements may descend into warlordism and a predatory war economy and thereby lose their popular support and the authority that goes along with it.[18]

BYSTANDER DUTIES IN JUST GUERRILLA WARFARE

Taken together, just cause and legitimate authority provide guerrilla organizations with the right to fight. Because the right to fight is a license to wage war against a state that has lost its right not to be attacked, it also generates obligations on the part of the international community to either refrain from interference or to provide proactive aid to ensure some chance of success. The chance of success they must assure varies with the moral gravity of a nonstate group's grievance against the state it fights. When fighting for basic human rights, the claim rights of a nonstate actor are strongest, but these rights weaken as states fight for political representation and equality and weaken further still when they are fighting for cultural or religious autonomy. As claim rights weaken, the duty to provide active aid similarly attenuates to the point where all bystander states owe guerrilla groups is a duty of noninterference, itself no mean concession during asymmetric war.

Bystander Duties in the Face of Human Rights Violations

When states violate the human rights of a group of citizens under their protection, they lose their immunity from armed attack. Faced with genocide or crimes against humanity, persecuted groups have the right to defend themselves with armed force when other means fail. Chaumont suggests that international law cannot make the chance of victory impossible. Although this is true when just cause is less weighty than prevention of genocide or crimes against humanity, there is a more positive, proactive obligation on the part of the world community to guarantee success when basic human rights are at stake. Noninterference is not enough; military intervention may be necessary to ensure that a persecuted people successfully defends itself against abusive states.

The duty of humanitarian aid stems from the claim right that oppressed groups have against the international community and bystander nations to ensure the extension of human rights to all people and to prevent genocide or crimes against humanity when the cost to bystander nations is reasonable.[19] Human rights and justice are pivotal for justifying humanitarian intervention. "If we deny the moral duty and legal right to [intervene]," writes Fernando Tesón, "we deny not only the centrality of justice in political affairs, but also the common humanity that binds us all.[20] Of course, humanitarian intervention takes many forms, of which resort to military force is the most extreme. Less violent means include economic sanctions, diplomatic isolation, embargoes, the protection and transporting of refugees, nonmilitary aid to guerrillas, and the provision of weapons and supplies to guerrilla forces. All these measures fall short of putting foreign military forces on the ground. None of these measures guarantee guerrilla success but offer a greater probability of success than noninterference in a guerrilla war. Noninterference, however, is the minimal duty of the international community when guerrillas fight for a just cause under the auspices of legitimate authority.

Bystander Duties in the Face of Civil Rights Violations or Minority Aspirations

Although Buchanan affords the right of secession only to those persecuted groups fighting against the threat of grave human rights violations, other scenarios dictate different circumstances. When groups are denied basic civil rights they may, at least in a democracy, resort to civil disobedience. This was the characteristic of the US civil rights struggle in the 1960s as African Americans strove for civil, social, and political equality. Often, however, disaffected groups also aim for special, minority privileges in the form of cultural, educational, or territorial autonomy and/or independence. Basque, Namibian, Quebec, and Irish Republican Army separatists, for example, did not face any immediate threat of genocide or crimes against humanity but sought instead to fulfill national political aspirations through secession.

Resorting to war to fulfill these aspirations and achieve civil liberties is a far more difficult decision to justify than going to war to remedy human rights abuses. An aggrieved group may exhaust all its nonviolent and political remedies, and still find that war is not justified at all. There are some political grievances that may never justify armed conflict but will demand instead relentless judicial, legislative, and electoral confrontation. If, however, a group's situation deteriorates significantly to the point of systemic discrimination, economic hardship, gross political inequality, and a severe lack of political representation, the group may justifiably resort to armed violence if no other means prove helpful. Until basic human rights are endangered, however, the international community owes no other obligation than to refrain from interfering as a group exercises its right to self-determination.[21]

Noninterference takes two forms: material and legal. Bystanders have a duty to respect a group's right to resort to armed force to press political claims. When these claims are weighty but fall short of human rights abuses and when the conditions of last resort, necessity, and effectiveness are met, aggrieved groups may choose force of arms. Noninterference is also the minimal obligation of bystanders when a people faces human rights abuses. Material noninterference demands that bystander nations not provide an oppressor nation with military support or impose sanctions or blockades or arms embargoes against an oppressed people. Legal noninterference goes to the heart of Chaumont's remarks. The international community cannot promulgate laws or treaties that make it impossible for the oppressed people fighting for their human or political rights to wage war. Legal impediments are just as restrictive as material impediments. Both unduly and unjustifiably restrict, if not abrogate, an aggrieved people's right to fight. This was the impetus for removing one of the most basic restrictions placed upon combatants: the obligation to wear uniforms and distinguish oneself from combatants. Recognizing that the requirement to wear uniforms makes it extremely difficult if not impossible for guerrillas to wage war in an occupied territory, the international community allows nonstate combatants to shed their identifying insignia during battle. This was a huge concession to guerrilla groups fighting for national liberation but is consistent with their right to a fighting chance.

It must be remembered, however, that the laws of armed conflict and international humanitarian law restrict the rights of belligerents for a good reason: to protect noncombatants. Because the protection of the innocent remains the primary purpose of any law of armed conflict, no law may be abrogated or modified to protect the right to fight if it impinges on the rights of noncombatants. Combatants have both rights and duties. Their rights protect them from unnecessary suffering and superfluous injury, and their duties require them to protect the welfare of noncombatants even when this involves risk to the soldiers themselves. Noncombatants, conversely, have only rights and no duties as long as they do not participate in the fighting. Their right to protection from unnecessary, direct, and disproportionate harm is absolute and superior to the rights of combatants, military necessity, and the right to a fighting chance. Thus Chaumont's stipulation is necessarily self-limiting. The international community cannot enact laws that make fighting for nonstate actors vying for national self-determination impossible unless these laws are necessary to protect the rights of noncombatants. This is an important caveat that demands that lawmakers balance the rights of aggrieved groups with the rights of all noncombatants. Its purpose is to make room for tactics and strategies that facilitate a group's right to fight while continuing to protect noncombatants. Framed in this way, *jus ad bellum* is of crucial importance, for oppressed people enjoy certain rights that affect the implementation of the laws of armed conflict. For example, not all groups merit the right to shed their uniforms—only those whose right to wage war is just. No longer can one consider the law of armed conflict in the absence of just cause or without accounting for the identity of the parties.

CONCLUSION

Just guerrilla warfare demands just cause and legitimate authority. These two demands differ significantly from those attached to just conventional warfare. Instead of self-defense against imminent armed attack, guerrillas have a right to defend themselves against gross human rights abuses, lack of political liberties, and infringements of cultural autonomy. This right also guarantees a chance of success during war and, to varying degrees, obligates the international community to either assist guerrillas to vastly improve the likelihood of their success or refrain from material and legal interference so that success is not impossible. The right to a fighting chance does not allow guerrillas a free hand but constrains their actions so that they do not infringe upon the rights of noncombatants.

Although restrained, the right to a fighting chance has important implications for the laws of armed conflict. Born of the need to allow guerrillas a reasonable chance of victory in wars of national liberation, nonstate combatants were accorded the right to shed their uniforms and assimilate among noncombatants when fighting in occupied territory. Such a concession immediately undermines a long-standing ban on using human shields. Guerrillas fight without uniforms to hide from occupying forces by disguising themselves as civilians. Occupying forces pursuing guerrillas without uniforms will find themselves stymied as guerrillas intermingle with and hide behind noncombatants, who effectively become human shields. As such, any attempt to relax the requirement to wear uniforms also relaxes the ban on human shields. Other traditional practices of war may also require modification to meet the legitimate demands of those who enjoy a right to a fighting chance. This may allow guerrillas to directly target civilians with nonlethal weapons, employ improvised explosive devices and cyberweapons, and hold prisoners of war incommunicado to create leverage for lopsided prisoner exchanges. The underlying principles at stake here—proportionality, noncombatant immunity, distinction, neutrality, and the rights of prisoners of war—have a long but checkered history as basic norms of war. The right to a fighting chance, however, may compel us to rethink or modify these principles to allow guerrillas fighting for a just cause and endowed with legitimate authority a reasonable chance of victory in armed conflict.

NOTES

1. J. Pictet, *Development and Principles of International Humanitarian Law* (Leiden: Martinus Nijhoff, 1985), 13–14.

2. "Additional Protocol I," Commentary, C. Chaumont, 1977, Article 44, p. 519, n. 40.

3. Resolution RC/Res.6, The Crime of Aggression, June 11, 2010, www.icc-cpi.int/icc docs/asp_docs/Resolutions/RC-Res.6-ENG.pdf.

4. Rome Statute of the International Criminal Court, Part II, Articles 6, 7.

5. Antonio Cassese, *Self-Determination of Peoples: A Legal Reappraisal* (Cambridge: Cambridge University Press, 1995), 61.

6. Avishai Margalit and Joseph Raz, "National Self-Determination," *Journal of Philosophy* 87, no. 9 (1990): 439–61, at 443–44.

7. "Additional Protocol I," Article 1, 4.

8. On the legal right to fight, see also Cassese, *Self-Determination*, 154.

9. Allan Buchanan, "Theories of Secession," *Philosophy and Public Affairs* 26, no. 1 (1997): 31–61. For a more extensive discussion of the right of secession and a people's right of self-determination, see Margaret Moore, ed., *National Self-Determination and Secession* (Oxford: Oxford University Press, 1998); and Percy B. Lehning, ed., *Theories of Secession* (London: Routledge, 1998).

10. Cassese, *Self-Determination*, 147.

11. Cecile Fabre, *Cosmopolitan War* (Oxford: Oxford University Press, 2012), 142.

12. On the relationship between sovereignty and legitimacy, see the introduction in the present volume and also chapter 4 by John Williams, "'Not in My Name'? Legitimate Authority and Liberal Just War Theory."

13. Shehzad H. Qazi, "Rebels of the Frontier: Origins, Organization, and Recruitment of the Pakistani Taliban," *Small Wars & Insurgencies* 22, no. 4 (2011): 574–602; Macartan Humphreys and Jeremy M. Weinstein, "Who Fights? The Determinants of Participation in Civil War," *American Journal of Political Science* 52, no. 2 (2008): 436–55; Kirsten Schulze, *The Free Aceh Movement (GAM): Anatomy of a Separatist Organization,* Policy Studies, no. 2 (Washington, DC: East-West Center, 2004); Garentina Kraja, "Recruitment Practices of Europe's Last Guerrilla: Ethnic Mobilization, Violence and Networks in the Recruitment Strategy of the Kosovo Liberation Army" (senior thesis, Yale University, 2011); Kimberly Marten, "Patronage versus Professionalism in New Security Institutions," *Prism* 2, no. 4 (2012): 83–98.

14. Christopher Finlay, "Legitimacy and Non-State Political Violence," *Journal of Political Philosophy*, 18, no. 3 (2010): 287–312; Armend Bekaj, *The KLA and the Kosovo War: From Intra-State Conflict to Independent Country,* Berghof Transitions Series 8 09/2010, www.berghof-conflictresearch.org/documents/publications/transitio ns8_kosovo.pdf; James Hughes, *Chechnya: From Nationalism to Jihad* (Philadelphia: University of Pennsylvania Press, 2007).

15. Chisako M. Fukuda, "Peace through Nonviolent Action: The East Timorese Resistance Movement's Strategy for Engagement," *Pacifica Review: Peace, Security & Global Change* 12, no. 1 (2000): 17–31.

16. Nelson Kasfir, "Guerrillas and Civilian Participation: The National Resistance Army in Uganda, 1981–86," *Journal of Modern African Studies* 43, no. 2 (June 2005): 271–96.

17. Claire Metelits, "Reformed Rebels? Democratization, Global Norms, and the Sudan People's Liberation Army," *Africa Today* 51, no. 1 (2004): 65–82, at 71. See also Douglas H. Johnson, "The Sudan People's Liberation and the Problem of Factionalism," in *African Guerrillas*, ed. Christopher Clapham (Bloomington: Indiana University Press, 1998), 53–72.

18. Rune Henriksen and Anthony Vinci, "Combat Motivation in Non-State Armed Groups," *Terrorism and Political Violence* 20, no. 1 (2007): 87–109.

19. Michael L. Gross, *Moral Dilemmas of Modern War: Torture, Assassination, and Blackmail in an Age of Asymmetric Conflict* (Cambridge: Cambridge University Press, 2010), 205–29.

20. Fernando R. Tesón, "The Liberal Case for Humanitarian Intervention," in *Humanitarian Intervention: Ethical, Legal and Political Dilemmas*, ed. J. L. Holzgrefe and Robert O. Keohane (Cambridge: Cambridge University Press, 2003), 93–129, at 129. See also Chris Brown, "Selective Humanitarianism: In Defense of Inconsistency," in *Ethics and Foreign Intervention*, ed. Deen K. Chatterjee and Don. E Scheid (Cambridge: Cambridge University Press, 2003), 31–52.

21. Margalit and Raz, "National Self-Determination."

CHAPTER 13

Bugsplat

US Standing Rules of Engagement, International Humanitarian Law, Military Necessity, and Noncombatant Immunity

Neta C. Crawford

War is thus an act of force to compel our enemy to do our will. . . . Attached to force are certain self-imposed, imperceptible limitations hardly worth mentioning, known as international law and custom, but they scarcely weaken it [emphasis added]. *On War,* Carl von Clausewitz

These ROEs [rules of engagement] might sound fine to academics gathering at some esoteric seminar on how to avoid civilian casualties in a war zone. But they do absolutely nothing to protect our combat troops who have to respond in an instant to a life-or-death situation. "Untie Military Hands," James A. Lyons Jr.

THE *JUS IN BELLO* GUIDELINES of the just war tradition—discrimination and proportionality—infuse international humanitarian law and the contemporary US understanding of ethical conduct in war. There is nothing new in that: The rhetoric of the US military since the middle of the nineteenth century has reflected both the just war tradition's articulation of the justice of going to war and its articulation of limits on conduct in war. The US operational and legal rhetoric—as articulated in US rules of engagement and military law—also reflect and amplify the long-standing tensions within the just war tradition between the normative values of military necessity and noncombatant immunity. Specifically, there is a tension between the consequentialist logic of military necessity and a deontological prohibition on harming noncombatants. Consequentialist reasoning, which is exemplified in the just war notion of proportionality and in the US military's interpretation of the notion of "military necessity," dominates the rhetoric and shapes the practice of US war-making. The result is that many civilian deaths may be both anticipated and forgiven, a phenomenon I have elsewhere described as "systemic collateral damage."[1]

Both just war theory and a particular interpretation of international law have become the dominant organizational frame of the US military with respect to noncombatant immunity and civilian protection. The concept of "organizational frames," a term coined by the sociologist Lynn Eden, points to how certain beliefs become the taken for granted, the "organizational 'common sense'" that structures subsequent understanding and practices.[2] The just war framework is institutionalized in US rules of engagement, and the technical procedures of US targeting and operations. The lacunae in just war theory and international law concern the balance between the norms of military necessity, force protection, and noncombatant immunity: The consequentialist frame of military necessity often overrides noncombatant immunity. The weaknesses of the just war framework, as reproduced in international law, are thus reified in US war-making practices. So Clausewitz is wrong on the one hand—law does make a difference in the conduct of war. But Clausewitz is right on the other hand, that difference in conduct may have a minimal effect on the consequences of war on noncombatants. Moreover, the fact that just war theory and the humanitarian laws of war are institutionalized in US law and conduct suggests that moral responsibility for foreseeable noncombatant killing rests with both individual actors and collective agents.

AUTHORITY

The questions of authority in war—what it is and who has it—are highlighted in the practices of military targeting. In other words, one might think that issues of authority are primarily about who is legitimately able, and by what criteria, to consider *jus ad bellum* criteria and to authorize the use of force—to make decisions about the justice of the cause, whether military force is necessary, whether and when last resort has been reached, and so on. But authority is also at stake in decisions about the use of military force once war has begun. Whose advice about the conduct of war shall be listened to as authoritative in deliberations about proportionality and discrimination? What criteria are legitimate in these decisions?

In the United States at least, it has gradually become the norm that deliberations about and supervision of the conduct of war are almost entirely under the purview of the military. Within the military, deliberations about the ethics of conduct have also become centralized and compartmentalized. Authorizations for the use of force, when there are questions of discrimination or proportionality, are often passed through the legitimating authority of military lawyers, who rely on both international law as a source of authoritative guidance and technical expertise. The technical expertise is necessary, of course, because contemporary battle and weapons effects are complex. In evaluating proportionality and discrimination, both the lawyers and targeters involved increasingly rely on decision-making tools—rules of thumb and algorithms. One important tool is the collection of computer programs used to calculate the incidental killing of civilians, "collateral damage." So decisions about the use of force in any particular instance—whether to drop a bomb, and of what size, at what specific time of day—are reasoned through the framework of both international law (itself deeply infused with just war reasoning) and technical analysis. The technical analysis is used to help decision makers stay within the law, but it may also serve to excuse decisions that we might otherwise believe were wrong and to defuse moral responsibility for actions. The moral tensions between military necessity and discrimination and proportionality are not eliminated, but they are smoothed by the use of technical analysis. In a sense, some amount of authority over *jus in bello* that was ceded to the military, then to military lawyers, is then ceded to technical analysis and a form of computer-assisted expertise.

JUS IN BELLO AS ORGANIZATIONAL FRAME

The relevant US military field manuals and legal documents refer to the Geneva Conventions as a source of US military law.[3] The US Law of Land Warfare of 1956 is clear that the purpose of the law is "to diminish the evils of war by (a) protecting both combatants and noncombatants from unnecessary suffering; (b) safeguarding certain fundamental human rights of persons."[4] As with the earlier Lieber Code (General Orders 100 of 1863), the aim is to avoid "unnecessary" suffering, but military necessity does not vitiate the force of international law. The question obviously becomes what is militarily "necessary" and what is unnecessary suffering? The *jus in bello* criterion of proportionality implies an evaluation of military necessity. International humanitarian law articulates an ambiguous understanding of military necessity in the context of the use of force that is descendent from both the Lieber Code tradition and the just war tradition. Indeed, the same provisions in the laws of war can be read in three different ways. Military necessity can be understood as an indispensable use of force, as a license to override prohibitions on the use of force, or as a limit on the use of force.

The first interpretation of military necessity is that force is required; it is, as the General Orders 100 suggest, "those measures which are *indispensable* for securing the ends of war" (emphasis added).[5] The second interpretation of necessity is as a license or provision to override prohibitions; an action considered militarily necessary can excuse a breach in the law of war. The Hague Convention of 1899 articulates this understanding of necessity in the preamble: The provisions of the treaty were "inspired by the desire to diminish the evils of war so far as military necessities permit."[6] Similarly, as noted above, the 1899 and 1907 Hague Conventions forbid belligerents to "destroy or seize the enemy's property, unless such destruction or seizure be imperatively demanded by the necessities of war."[7] The third interpretation of military necessity is as limit or ceiling to guard against excessive or unnecessary uses of force. Larry May takes this interpretation: "Only that use of force that can accomplish the military objective is justified."[8] Article 15 of the Lieber Code can be read this way, as can the 1907 Hague Convention, which explicitly forbids armed forces to "employ arms, projectiles, or material calculated to cause unnecessary suffering."[9]

Before the Vietnam War, the US military deliberately targeted noncombatants (nominally targeting their "morale" or labor in support of war), on the view that it was militarily advantageous. US nuclear policy still puts noncombatants at deliberate risk. In the Vietnam War the calculus of military necessity versus noncombatant immunity was fluid, depending on the political calculations of the president. Following Vietnam, greater emphasis was placed on protecting civilians, and this emphasis was institutionalized in the Law of War program and in rules of engagement and targeting guidelines. In the first days of the 2003 war against Iraq, the US military and civilian planners set a ceiling of thirty anticipated noncombatant deaths before permission must be sought and given by the secretary of defense or the president. The ceiling did not mean that the strike would not occur, only that permission must be sought and given. In the cases where significant loss of civilian life was anticipated, more often than not, the targeting was changed so as to reduce the risk to civilians—for example, the strike would be made at a time when fewer civilians might be harmed or the size of the weapon was reduced. I say more about the methods used to estimate and minimize civilian casualties below.

In this respect, and also as when the United States modified its bombing tactics in Bosnia and Kosovo to minimize harm to civilians, the US military has taken "due care."[10] In exercising due care, according to Michael Walzer, the strategist has attempted to reduce the risk to noncombatants or has forgone the attack altogether. But of course to reduce the risk to noncombatants, or to wait, may mean that the risk to one's own soldiers has been increased.[11] Walzer emphasizes "leeway" in military judgment in these calculations. He argues that "strategists and planners will for reasons of their own weigh the importance of their target against the importance of their soldiers' lives. But even if the target is very important, and the number of innocent people threatened relatively small, they must risk soldiers before they kill civilians."[12]

Once the idea of noncombatant immunity was gradually institutionalized, the prohibition on killing civilians and the exceptions created by military necessity and double effect create a tension that has not been resolved. The US Air Force historian W. Hayes Parks argues that during the "Rolling Thunder" bombing campaign of the Vietnam War, the United States misread the balance between military necessity and concern for noncombatants. Parks argues that the United States chose its targets with an eye toward minimizing casualties, which led to denying targets that the civilian and military leadership thought could lead to too many civilian casualties. In Parks's view, the United States paid too much attention to the potential for collateral damage and thus ignored the fact that the law of war recognizes that civilian casualties will occur and that what is prohibited is excessive collateral damage.[13] In the 1976 US Air Force guide to the law of war and combat operations, the tensions are resolved by arguing that everything not forbidden is acceptable if it is needed for victory: "measures of regulated force not forbidden by international law which are indispensable for securing the prompt submission of the enemy, with the least possible expenditures of economic and human resources."[14]

Francis Lieber's mid-nineteenth-century language and reasoning—specifically the notion that killing is "incidental" and inevitable—is echoed in a 1990 US military guidance for targeting where an effort is made to avoid civilian killing: "In spite of precautions, such incidental casualties are inevitable during armed conflict."[15] Similarly, the 1998 Air Force targeting guide says:

> Collateral damage is generally defined as unintentional or incidental damage that occurs as a result of an attack but affects facilities, equipment, or personnel that are not militarily acceptable targets. Since this kind of damage is often the focal point for national and international scrutiny, the type and level of force applied against a target must be carefully selected to avoid excessive collateral damage. International law does not prohibit attacks against military objectives even though they may cause collateral damage since incidental damage is inevitable during armed conflict; but this damage should not be excessive in relation to the military advantage anticipated.[16]

OPERATIONALIZING NECESSITY AND NONCOMBATANT IMMUNITY IN US SROE

The US "Standing Rules of Engagement" (SROE)—articulated by the head of the uniformed military, the chairman of the Joint Chiefs of Staff, and approved by the secretary of defense—outline the general guidelines for the use of force. The concept of necessity appears in the January 2000 US SROE, which articulate the conditions under which commanders and individual soldiers are authorized to use force. Necessity "exists when a hostile act occurs or when a force or terrorist(s) exhibits hostile intent." Necessity is understood as permission to override legal and moral limits on the use of force. The understanding of military necessity in current US SROE is less a limit than a license or a threshold for permission to use force. Under the United States' SROE, "necessity" is not a condition where the use of force is a last resort or the *only effective* way to defend oneself. Nor is there a sense that the threat must be significant. Proportionality is also required for self-defense under the January 2000 SROE. The definition of proportionality is: "Force used to counter a hostile act or demonstrated hostile intent must be reasonable in intensity, duration, and magnitude to the perceived or demonstrated threat based on all facts known to the commander at the time."[17] In this context, proportionality functions as a potential limit on the use of force even as it can be used to override limits.

The United States has been consistent in its interpretation of military necessity and double effect: The military should do what is required or necessary to win its military objectives and it should strive to "avoid *excessive* collateral damage." Judge advocates advise soldiers in the field before the fact of target selection and weapons use, and after the fact to determine whether the laws of war have been observed. These lawyers' understanding of the intersection between the laws of war (LOW) and operations, "operational law," can be inferred from their *Operational Law Handbook*. In 2009 the handbook for US military lawyers interpreted military necessity as *not* vitiating the rights of noncombatants to protection. Further, the US view of the LOW contains a concept of due care: Civilians can never be deliberately targeted, and care must be taken should action inadvertently but knowingly harm civilians: "The principle of military necessity authorizes that use of force required to accomplish the mission. Military necessity does not authorize acts otherwise prohibited by the LOW. This principle must be applied in conjunction with other LOW principles discussed in this chapter, as well as other, more specific legal constraints set forth in LOW treaties to which the United States is a party."[18]

US military lawyers say that, "under the principle of distinction, the civilian population as such, as well as individual civilians, may not be made the object of attack."[19] Conversely, collateral damage, called "incidental damage," is understood as within the LOW under the principle of proportionality: "Incidental damage consists of unavoidable and unintentional damage to civilian personnel and property incurred while attacking a military objective. Incidental damage is *not* a violation of international law. While no LOW treaty defines this concept, its inherent lawfulness is implicit in treaties referencing the concept. As stated above, [the Geneva Convention] AP I, Art. 51 (5) describes indiscriminate attacks as those causing '*incidental loss of civilian life . . . excessive . . . to . . . the military advantage anticipated*'" (emphasis in the original).[20] The *Operational Law Handbook* uses an instance from the 1991 Gulf War as an example of how to understand the laws of war in the case of "incidental" inadvertent killing of civilians:

> There may be situations where, because of incomplete intelligence or the failure of the enemy to abide by the LOW, civilian casualties occur. Example: Al Firdus Bunker. During the first Persian Gulf War (1991), US military planners identified this Baghdad bunker as an Iraqi military command and control center. Barbed wire surrounded the complex, it was camouflaged, armed sentries guarded its entrance and exit points, and electronic intelligence identified its activation. Unknown to coalition planners, however, some Iraqi civilians

used upper levels of the facility as nighttime sleeping quarters. The bunker was bombed, allegedly resulting in 300 civilian casualties. Was there a violation of the LOW? No, at least not by the US forces (there was, however, a clear violation of the principle of distinction and discrimination (discussed *infra*) by Iraqi forces). Based upon information gathered by Coalition planners, the commander made an assessment that the target was a military objective. Although the attack may have resulted in unfortunate civilian deaths, there was no LOW violation because the attackers acted in good faith based upon the information reasonably available at the time the decision to attack was made.[21]

The issue thus becomes a balancing act, conceived within a utilitarian framework, where the "anticipated" and sufficiently compelling ends may justify the "incidental" or "inevitable" consequences of the means used. In this way, the prohibition on killing civilians, either intentionally or inadvertently, is seriously eroded by a utilitarian logic, which we can find stated rather baldly in the words of the philosopher R. B. Brandt: "Substantial destruction of lives and property of enemy civilians is permissible only when there is good evidence that it will significantly enhance the prospect of victory."[22] In this respect, the American military is like all other militaries that put "necessity" and efficiency above protection of noncombatants. The Germans called this *kriegsraison*, or reason of war; when particular means were understood as necessary to achieve victory, they were justified.[23] The trouble in applying the doctrine of double effect and military necessity comes—as it did during World War II and the Vietnam War—when the distinction between combatants and noncombatants is lost or denied or when military necessity is defined to include deliberate or at least a high tolerance for inadvertent harm to civilians.

The SROE repeatedly emphasize that soldiers have an "inherent right of self-defense": "US forces always retain the right to use necessary and proportional force for unit and individual self-defense in response to a hostile act or demonstrated hostile intent."[24] The SROE then go on to define these terms, and give the authority and obligation to commanders to use "all necessary means" for self-defense:

> a. *Inherent Right of Self-Defense.* A commander has the authority and obligation to use all necessary means available and to take all appropriate actions to defend that commander's unit and other US forces in the vicinity from a hostile act or demonstration of hostile intent. Neither these rules, nor the supplemental measures activated to augment these rules, limit this inherent right and obligation. At all times, the requirements of necessity and proportionality, as amplified in these SROE, will form the basis for the judgment of the on-scene commander (OSC) or individual as to what constitutes an appropriate response to a particular hostile act or demonstration of hostile intent.[25]

The SROE appear to limit collective and unit self-defense to "an observed hostile act or demonstrated hostile intent." A hostile act is "an attack or other use of force against the United States, US forces, and, in certain circumstances, US nationals, their property, US commercial assets, and/or other designated non-US forces, foreign nationals and their property. It is also force used directly to preclude or impede the mission and/or duties of US forces, including the recovery of US personnel and vital US government property." Hostile intent is understood as the "threat of imminent use of force against the United States, US forces, and in certain circumstances, US nationals, their property, US commercial assets, and/or other designated non-US forces, foreign nationals and their property. Also, the threat of force to preclude or impede the mission and/or duties of US forces, including the recovery of US personnel or vital US government property."[26]

But demonstrated hostile acts and hostile intent may not be required in some instances. National self-defense "may be exercised by designated authority declaring a foreign force or terrorist(s) hostile [in this case, individual US units do not need to observe a hostile act or determine hostile intent before engaging that force or terrorist(s)]."[27] Specifically, "once a force is declared hostile by appropriate authority, US units need not observe a hostile act or a demonstration of hostile intent before engaging that force."[28] The definition of hostile force includes civilians: "Any civilian, paramilitary, or military force or terrorist(s), with or without national designation, that has committed a hostile act, exhibited hostile intent, or has been declared hostile by appropriate US authority."[29]

The soldier is concerned with their individual right to self-defense. The definition of individual self-defense is "the inherent right to use all necessary means available and to take all appropriate actions to defend oneself and US forces in one's vicinity from a hostile act or demonstrated hostile intent is a unit of self-defense."[30] The SROE further define two "elements of self-defense":

1. Necessity: Exists when a hostile act occurs or when a force or terrorist(s) exhibits hostile intent.
2. Proportionality: Force used to counter a hostile act or demonstrated hostile intent must be reasonable in intensity, duration, and magnitude to the perceived or demonstrated threat based on all facts known to the commander at the time.[31]

The duties of US military commanders at every level are made explicit in the SROE and in officer training. Commanders must tell their subordinates when the use of force is authorized. Force protection and military necessity are given equal weight in the SROE: "The SROE differentiate between the use of force for self-defense and for mission accomplishment." Self-defense is an absolute right in the SROE and is defined in a way that makes self-defense a military necessity: "Commanders have the inherent authority and obligation to use all necessary means available and to take all appropriate actions in the self-defense of their unit and other

US forces in the vicinity. ROE supplemental measures apply only to the use of force for mission accomplishment and do not limit a commander's use of force in self-defense"[32] It is the commander's responsibility to ensure that soldiers understand the rules of engagement: "Commanders have the obligation to ensure that individuals within their respective units understand and are trained on when and how to use force in self-defense.[33]

These rules are reiterated and specified in each conflict. Every soldier is told by their commander the conditions under which they may use deadly force, the ROE that apply to their particular mission. These rules are given orally and often summarized on the equivalent of a 3-by-5 card that a soldier may carry with them that outlines when it is permissible to use deadly force and when it is not. The question of when it is legitimate to use force has long been a source of tension in Iraq and Afghanistan. First Lieutenant Wade Zirkle described the problem clearly: "You got a guy trying to kill me but he's firing from houses . . . with civilians around him, women and children. You know, what do you do? You don't want to risk shooting at him and shooting children at the same time. But at the same time, you don't want to die either."[34]

A summary of the US military's ROE for Iraq, given to all US Army and Marine personnel by the US Central Command in 2003, read, in part: 1. "(c) Do not target or strike any of the following except in self-defense to protect yourself, your unit, friendly forces, and designated persons or property under your control: —civilians—Hospitals, mosques, national monuments, and any other historical and cultural sites. (d) Do not fire into civilian populated areas or buildings unless the enemy is using them for military purposes or if necessary for your self-defense. Minimize collateral damage."

In January 2007 James A. Lyons, a retired navy admiral, described the then-current ROE for Baghdad as too restrictive: "The current ROEs for Baghdad—including Sadr City, home of the Mahdi Army—have seven incremental steps that must be satisfied before our troops can take the gloves off and engage the enemy with appropriate violence of action":

1. You must feel a direct threat to you or your team.
2. You must clearly see a threat.
3. That threat must be identified.
4. The team leader must concur that there is an identified threat.
5. The team leader must feel that the situation is one of life or death.
6. There must be minimal or no collateral risk.
7. Only then can the team leader clear the engagement.

These ROEs might sound fine to academics gathering at some esoteric seminar on how to avoid civilian casualties in a war zone. But they do absolutely nothing to protect our combat troops who have to respond in an instant to a life-or-death situation.

> If our soldiers or Marines see someone about to level an AK-47 in their direction or start to are [*sic*] receive hostile fire from a rooftop or mosque, there is no time to go through a seven-point checklist before reacting. Indeed, the very fact that they see a weapon, or begin to receive hostile fire should be sufficient justification to respond with deadly force.

Lyons argued that Iraqi insurgents used the United States "restrictive" ROE to "to their advantage" by deliberately putting civilians in the way and targeting civilians themselves. Lyons said this showed that the enemy has "no regard for human life." Protecting civilians was thus unrealistic: "We cannot, therefore, afford to keep our combat troops shackled by a naive, legalistic disadvantage that takes no note of the real world, or the real battlefield."[35]

But because of the greater emphasis on civilian protection that was at the core of the new counterinsurgency strategy, US rules of engagement became more restrictive. The United States changed its ROE in Afghanistan in mid-2009 to emphasize restraint. The "tactical directive" issued by General Stanley McChrystal read in part:

> I recognize that the carefully controlled and disciplined employment of force entails risks to our troops—and we must work to mitigate that risk wherever possible. But excessive use of force resulting in an alienated population will produce far greater risks. We must understand this reality at every level in our force.
>
> I expect leaders at all levels to scrutinize and limit the use of force like close air support (CAS) against residential compounds and other locations likely to produce civilian casualties in accordance with this guidance. Commanders must weigh the gain of using CAS against the cost of civilian casualties, which in the long run make mission success more difficult and turn the Afghan people against us.
>
> I cannot prescribe the appropriate use of force for every condition that a complex battlefield will produce, so I expect our force to internalize and operate in accordance with my intent. Following this intent requires a cultural shift within our forces—and complete understanding at every level—down to the most junior soldiers. I expect leaders to ensure this is clearly communicated and continually reinforced.
>
> The use of air-to-ground munitions and indirect fire against residential compounds is only authorized under very limited and prescribed conditions (specific conditions deleted due to operational security).[36]

US troops in Afghanistan complained that the ROE were too restrictive, and indeed, the number of US soldiers killed in Afghanistan increased after the directive was operationalized. The most striking number is that in Afghanistan in 2009, the number of fatalities among US and UK forces more than doubled at the same time that progovernment killing of noncombatants declined by a third. During the first five months of 2009, the number of US military fatalities averaged 12.2 per month in Afghanistan; from June through December 2009, the incidence of US military fatalities averaged 36.6 per month.

In his June 2010 Senate confirmation hearings to become the US commander in Afghanistan, replacing General McChrystal, General David Petraeus was asked if the rules were too restrictive and might be rethought. Petraeus responded by talking in terms of protecting troops as a "moral imperative." He said: "I want to assure the mothers and fathers of those fighting in Afghanistan that I see it as a moral imperative to bring all assets to bear to protect our men and women in uniform and the Afghan security forces with whom ISAF [International Security Assistance Force] troopers are fighting shoulder-to-shoulder. Those on the ground must have all the support they need when they are in a tough situation."[37] He acknowledged these tensions when he said: "I am keenly aware of concerns by some of our troopers on the ground about the application of our rules of engagement and the [2009] tactical directive. They should know that I will look very hard at this issue."[38]

OPERATIONALIZING *JUS IN BELLO*: ALGORITHMS AND OPERATIONS

I have only space here to outline the ways that the US military operationalizes *jus in bello* precepts. I suggest that this organizational frame is deeply institutionalized in operations research/systems analysis techniques to estimate and minimize collateral damage. Operations research and systems analysis (mathematical analysis of weapons effects against targets) have long been in use by the US military and perhaps reached their peak or nadir during the US–Soviet nuclear arms race.[39] Of course one of the main emphases of US strategic bombing and targeting during the world wars, the Korean War, the Vietnam War, and the Cold War was to either deliberately target civilians or to threaten to put civilians at risk.[40] The institutionalization and operationalization of noncombatant immunity were ad hoc and occurred gradually after Vietnam.

The United States made an effort to minimize collateral damage in the 1991 Persian Gulf War, specifically by increasing the proportion of precision-guided munitions, and after the Al Firdos bunker incident, refraining from attacks on Baghdad. During the US air strikes against Serbian forces in Bosnia in 1995, the general in charge of the operations, Michael Ryan, took tight control of operations in order to minimize collateral damage while at the same time destroying Serbian military: "The concepts of proportionality, military necessity, and collateral damage dominated the thought process surrounding the development and execution of ROE for each air strike. The single most defining element of every planning and

execution decision was the overriding need to avoid collateral damage and escala-
tory force."[41] General Ryan was personally involved in selecting every target in the
Bosnia air campaign, and within that, every aim point (desired mean point of
impact). Ryan was also engaged in selection of weapons and battle damage assessment. He interpreted the operational orders' emphasis on minimizing collateral
damage to require the selection of precision-guided munitions, and he also prohibited the use of cluster bombs (an indiscriminate weapon).[42] There were relatively
few civilian deaths as a result of US bombing in Kosovo, though some errors—such
as bombing the Chinese Embassy in Belgrade—were spectacular. The 1999 US air
campaign in Kosovo, which lasted longer and was more intense, yielded about five
hundred civilian casualties.

During the first Gulf War, which was known as Operation Desert Storm, collateral damage estimates were computed "using engineering estimates developed independently for each appropriate target in a very lengthy process."[43] The Conventional
Casualty Estimation Tool and the Collateral Damage Estimation Tool (CDET) were
used during the 1999 Kosovo air war to estimate, respectively, casualties and collateral damage for more than four hundred targets. CDET utilizes three-dimensional
modeling for "high fidelity assessment" of collateral damage. Again, the evaluation
of each target could take several hours. The US chairman of the Joint Chiefs of Staff
issued a directive in September 2002 that combatant commanders must estimate,
evaluate, and mitigate potential collateral damage.[44] According to the directive, several algorithms, which were either already in use or had been newly developed for
use by the services, were utilized for estimating both casualties and collateral damage and were to be used to evaluate targets.

During the early part of the war in Afghanistan, the United States used the older
CDET but for the first time also used the Fast Assessment Strike Tool—Collateral
Damage (FAST-CD), which had earlier been known as "BugSplat," to "vet" about
four hundred targets.[45] During Afghanistan, the CDET process was considered too
slow because it requires modeling and analysis of both natural and human-made
features of the target area. FAST-CD, which was developed from the CDET to be
much faster, uses two-dimensional images. Brigadier General Kelvin Coppock,
director of intelligence for the Air Combat Command, told a reporter before the
United States attacked Iraq that BugSplat was "a significant advance": "It will allow
us to target those facilities that we want to target with confidence that we're not
going to cause collateral damage."[46] FAST-CD became the tool of choice for estimating collateral damage for "time-sensitive targets" in both Afghanistan and Iraq
because it could take as little as five minutes to run the program.

FAST-CD and other programs are part of a command and control process where
targets are selected and then evaluated. A Department of Defense briefing before the
launch of the 2003 war against Iraq included a description of the process. Assuming
they have identified a valid military target, they assess likely collateral damage caused
by a particular weapon which has an "effective area" of destruction: "A Hellfire missile

has only about a 40-pound warhead. So the circle that it might cause damage is relatively small: 60 or 70 feet. Conversely, a 2,000-pound bomb will create about 90 percent of its effect out to about 600 feet of the target."[47] If the circle of damage includes civilians or civilian infrastructure, analysts will attempt to minimize the damage to civilians by using a number of techniques. They might change the weapon to one that causes less damage, or use the same weapon but mitigate its potential damage by changing how the weapon is employed. The bomb might be fused differently: "For example, if you use a bomb with an air burst, meaning it explodes some number of feet above the ground, there's nothing that absorbs the fragmentation of that bomb, so it travels farther. If you use a delay fuse that goes a millisecond or two milliseconds under the ground, in fact the explosive—the fragmentation doesn't go very far at all, and the explosive damage is created mostly straight up, as opposed to out from the target. So you can reduce the area that's affected."

Or the aim point on a target might be changed to decrease collateral damage. Or the angle of attack (azimuth) might be changed by having the pilot come from a different direction so that the effects of a bomb are directed away from civilians. And the timing of an attack is sometimes shifted to avoid times when civilians might be congregating in the area.

The collateral damage mitigation techniques for bombing appear to work well for fixed targets that are not time sensitive. Both CDET and FAST-CD software and procedures have also been modified and improved so that they are now, respectively, known as Advanced CDET and FAST-CD 2.0. But there are still spectacular failures of collateral damage assessment and little effort appears to go into the evaluation of failures.

In other cases it appears that the decision is made that the chance of killing insurgents is worth the costs in civilian lives. But clearly estimates must be compared with actual effects. Yet the effects of a strike may themselves be quite controversial and contested.

For example, the United States began a program of targeted killing in Pakistan in 2004 using remotely piloted vehicles. The idea was to target and kill al-Qaeda leaders and also leaders of the Taliban. These strikes are semicovert, and one must thus rely on public sources to assess their effects. By all accounts, though most sources agree that few leaders have been killed, they also agree that about two thousand people had been killed by the drone strikes between 2004 and mid-2011. Where observers disagree is about the number of civilians killed by the strikes. Figure 13.1 shows different estimates of the ratio of civilians to insurgents killed during the United States' remotely piloted vehicle, or "drone," strikes in Pakistan from 2004 to mid-2011. But these public sources of casualty estimates—given by the *Long War Journal*, the *New America Foundation*, and *Pakistan Body Count*—have made different assessments of the identities of the victims of US drone strikes.

These are widely varying estimates of who is being counted as a member of al-Qaeda, the Taliban, and so on, and who is a civilian. Because Pakistan keeps reporters

Figure 13.1   Counts and Percentages of Civilians Killed in US Drone Strikes from 2004 to June 2011

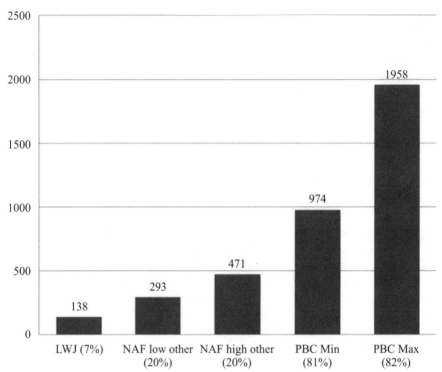

Sources: LWJ, *Long War Journal*; NAF, New America Foundation, PBC, Pakistan Body Count websites, June 2011.

away from the area of the US drone strikes, it is hard to know what is happening there with any sense of certainty. This example of counting who has been killed by US drone strikes highlights not only the questions of discrimination and proportionality raised by the use of "drone" strikes for "targeted" killing but also the issue of authority in estimating and evaluating the results of the strikes in terms of discrimination and proportionality. Who do we trust to make evaluations of those killed, to assign them to the category of insurgent/terrorist leader or ordinary combatant or civilian? Which authorities should be held to account for the killing of noncombatants in these instances?

CONCLUSION: GROUND TRUTH

Soldiers call what actually happens in combat the "ground truth." I have said nothing about many other aspects of the current wars: firefights, checkpoints, night raids. But the ground truth admits much more noncombatant killing that is both deliberate and "incidental." It is the consequence of fatigue, racialized hatred, trauma, and training. It is also sometimes truly accidental. I write about these elements of civilian killing in my forthcoming book on *Collateral Damage*.[48] My focus in this chapter has been at the organizational level. My argument is that processes at the organizational level make much of the ground truth the way it is—these processes that occur before and far from the ground encounters constrain and enable.

I have gone to great effort here—some might call it overkill (pun intended)—to show how the *jus in bello* considerations of discrimination and proportionality are important components of the US military organizational frame and are institutionalized in rules of engagement and standard operating procedures. I have also argued that the logic of military necessity—understood as permission to override *jus in bello* restraints on harm to noncombatants—may lead to foreseeable, albeit incidental and/or unintended, harm to civilians. Indeed, as the US military argues, it generally abides by international law in its efforts to minimize collateral damage. The fact that large numbers of civilians may be legally killed is a result of the fact that military necessity, which is implicit in the just war criteria of proportionality, is generally understood to trump noncombatant immunity.

The kinds of collective action and collective intention that might make organizations or institutions subject to claims of moral responsibility are those organized for coordinated action. Complex collectives, organizations and institutions, can be said to be more than a collection of individuals independently moving in the same direction for private reasons to the extent that their members communicate and coordinate their actions to achieve specific outcomes. No single individual could achieve the goal of a complex organization, nor could a single individual decide to reorient the institution without the consent of the other members. Complex organizations have emergent properties that make them more than the sum of their individual parts; and those emergent properties shape, enable, and constrain the options of individual actors and likewise shape, enable, and limit both the intended and unintended effects of organizational actions.

Complex organizations are imperfect moral agents to the extent that they have at least five characteristics. First, members have articulated shared intentions or common purpose. Second, the entity has a persistent organization; individual members may come and go, but the institution remains functional over time. Individual members' behavior is prescribed by rules and roles, and the organization has the ability to enforce the role performance of members. Role violators may be reeducated, removed from their position, or potentially face legal sanctions. Third, decision-making procedures have been institutionalized; the organization has knowledge resources, the ability to process information, decision-making rules and roles, and deliberative capacity.[49] Fourth, the organization has the capacity to act.

To act, the organization has mobilized the coordinated efforts of its members and has also mobilized and deployed preexisting or new resources. The actions in complex organizations are often based on routines, standard operating procedures, and scripted responses to expected scenarios. Organizational frames shape all these aspects—purpose, persistent roles, decision-making resources and procedures, and the capacity to act—of the organization. Fifth, the organization should have the capacity to reflect or evaluate its purposes, the organization of its rules and roles, its knowledge-production and decision-making procedures, and the quality of its actions and their consequences. Such evaluations may lead to revisions of the intentions, structure, or rules of the organization, although the openness of the organization to reflection and revision is again often a function of the content of its organizational frames.[50]

Organizations must be held to account for acts of commission or omission because organizations have capacities that are emergent from the aggregation, coordination, and institutionalization of the behavior of individual actors. Further, organizations not only enable individual beliefs and behaviors; they also constrain them, even to the point where individuals and the collective may have intentions that are opposed to the actions of the organization, but they are nevertheless compelled to act in ways that produce the outcome. We can often explain unintended consequences by looking at the systemic or structural features of decision and action that are conditioned by organizational frames, resources, and standard operating procedures. Even if organizations are imperfect moral agents, we have much to gain by acting as if they are moral agents.

For institutions or collectives to operate as *effective* moral agents, they must be able to critically reflect on their normative beliefs and the consequences of their beliefs, decisions, and actions. With regard to intended and unintended harm, this means that each collective must have the potential to foresee the consequences of its actions and the ways the causal chains that link its beliefs and actions produce outcomes. This is prospective or "forward-looking" moral responsibility.[51] The mechanisms for discerning harmful or counterproductive consequences and assuming backward-looking or retrospective responsibility will vary for each collective actor. Many individuals and institutions do not have an incentive to analyze how it is they knowingly or unintentionally harm others or even group members. Few seek out information that may provoke feelings of guilt or shame or raise questions of legal liability. Further, collective actors will be unable to exercise either prospective or retrospective responsibility unless there are venues and mechanisms for reflecting and arguing about what is happening. Some professions and institutions have such mechanisms, such as review boards for understanding the causes of mortality in hospitals. Finally, because some organizations lack adequate mechanisms for exercising prospective or retrospective responsibility, there must be a mechanism for each collective to encourage the other collectives to be responsible.

I have shown—by reconstructing some of the ways that decision making occurs and is institutionalized in SROE, in ROE, and in modeling collateral damage—that the US military is acting as an imperfect moral agent. It bears collective moral responsibility for noncombatant killing, even though its efforts show that it has taken due care and obeys the laws of war. This collective moral responsibility is shared with other moral agents—namely, individual commanders, along with the US institutions that are obligated to oversee the US military, and the US public.[52] The use of computerized algorithms and the resort to interpretations of international law can both assist moral agents in decision making and displace agency and authority. The authority devolves from the political realm to the realm of experts acting as military technical authorities.

NOTES

The name "BugSplat" was originally chosen because munitions have a fragmentation footprint in two dimensions that resembles the impact of an insect on a moving vehicle's windshield. Douglas D. Martin and Steven C. "Flash" Gordon, "Collateral Damage Estimation: Transforming Time-Sensitive Command and Control," paper 1768 delivered at Interservice/Industry Training, Simulation, and Education Conference, 2004.

1. Neta C. Crawford, *Accountability for Killing: Moral Responsibility for Collateral Damage in America's Post-9/11 Wars* (Oxford: Oxford University Press, 2013).

2. Lynn Eden, *Whole World on Fire: Organizations, Knowledge, and Nuclear Weapons Devastation* (Ithaca, NY: Cornell University Press, 2004), 50–51.

3. See "The Uniform Code of Military Justice," preamble on the sources of military jurisdiction, A21–3.

4. US Army Field Manual (27–10), *The Law of Land Warfare* of 1956, revised in 1976, paragraph 2. Also see Department of Defense Directives regarding the Law of War Program: 5100.7, July 1979, 5100.77, December 1998; and 2311.01E, May 2006.

5. US Government, *Laws of War: General Orders 100*, Article 14.

6. Hague Convention with Respect to the Laws and Customs of War on Land (Hague II), July 29, 1899, preamble.

7. Hague Convention with Respect to the Laws and Customs of War on Land (Hague IV), October 18, 1907, Article 23.

8. Larry May, *War Crimes and Just War* (Cambridge: Cambridge University Press, 2007), 21.

9. Hague Convention with Respect to the Laws and Customs of War on Land (Hague IV), Article 23.

10. See Michael Walzer, *Just and Unjust Wars: A Moral Argument with Historical Illustrations* (New York: Basic Books, 1977), 156.

11. Ibid., 157.

12. Ibid.

13. W. Hayes Parks, "Rolling Thunder and the Law of War," *Air University Review* 33, no. 2 (January–February 1982): 2–21.

14. US Air Force, *International Law: The Conduct of Armed Conflict and Air Operations*, Pamphlet 110–31, 1976, paragraph 1–3a (1).

15. US Air Force, *Target Intelligence Handbook: Unclassified Targeting Principles*, Pamphlet 200–18, vol. 1, October 1990, 97.

16. US Air Force, *Intelligence Targeting Guide*, Pamphlet 14–210 Intelligence, February 1998, 52.

17. US Chairman of the Joint Chiefs of Staff Instruction, "Standing Rules of Engagement for US Forces," CJCSI 3121.01A, January 15, 2000, enclosure A, para. 5f, A-4.

18. International and Operational Law Department, *Operational Law Handbook 2009* (Charlottesville, VA: Judge Advocate General's Legal Center and School, 2009), 10.

19. International and Operational Law Department, *Operational Law Handbook 2009*, 12.

20. Ibid.

21. Ibid., 11.

22. R. B. Brandt, "Utilitarianism and the Rules of War," *Philosophy and Public Affairs* 1 (1972): 156, quoted by Richard Norman, *Ethics, Killing, and War* (Cambridge: Cambridge University Press, 1995), 165.

23. See Mika Nishmura Hayashi, "The Martens Clause and Military Necessity," in *The Legitimate Use of Military Force: The Just War Tradition and the Customary Law of Armed Conflict*, ed. Howard M. Hensel (Aldershot, UK: Ashgate Publishing 2008), 135–59; and Walzer, *Just and Unjust Wars*, 144.

24. US Chairman of the Joint Chiefs of Staff Instruction, "Standing Rules," enclosure A, para. 1c (1), A-1.

25. Ibid., para. 5a, A-3.

26. Ibid., paras. 5 g and h.

27. Ibid., para. 5b, A-4.

28. Ibid., para. 6, A-5. The rest of the paragraph reads: "The responsibility for exercising the right and obligation of national self-defense and as necessary declaring a force hostile is a matter of the utmost importance. All available intelligence, the status of international relationships, the requirements of international law, an appreciation of the political situation, and the potential consequences for the United States must be carefully weighed. The exercise of the right and obligation of national self-defense by competent authority is separate from and in no way limits the commander's right and obligation to exercise unit self-defense."

29. Ibid., para. 5i, A-5.

30. Ibid., para. 5e, A-4.

31. Ibid., para. 5f, A-4.

32. Ibid.

33. Ibid., para. 5e, A-4.

34. Zirkle, quoted by Chris Hedges and Laila Al-Arian, *Collateral Damage: America's War Against Iraqi Civilians* (New York: Nation Books, 2008), 25–26.

35. James A. Lyons Jr., "Untie Military Hands," *Washington Times*, January 25, 2007, www.washingtontimes.com/news/2007/jan/25/20070125–091730–8692r/.

36. Declassified excerpt from NATO Tactical Directive, July 2, 2009, released by NATO ISAF Headquarters, July 6, 2009.

37. General David Petraeus, "Opening Statement," Confirmation Hearing, Commander, ISAF/US Forces, Afghanistan, June 29, 2010.

38. Ibid.

39. For an overview and explanation, see Neta C. Crawford, "Policy Modeling," in *Oxford Handbook of Public Policy*, ed. Martin Rein, Michael Moran, and Robert Goodin (Oxford: Oxford University Press, 2006), 769–803.

40. See Neta C. Crawford, "Ordinary Atrocity and Collateral Damage," unpublished paper; and Sahr Conway-Lanz, *Collateral Damage: Americans, Non-Combatant Immunity and Atrocity after World War II* (New York: Routledge, 2006).

41. Ronald M. Reed, "Chariots of Fire: Rules of Engagement in Operation Deliberate Force," in *Deliberate Force: A Case Study in Effective Air Campaigning*, ed. Robert C. Owen (Maxwell Air Force Base, AL: Air University Press, 2000), 381–429, at 405.

42. I do not have space here to elaborate on the idea of "discriminate" and "indiscriminate" weapons. All weapons (besides knives) are potentially indiscriminate in their effects. The question is how the weapon is used. I argue, however, that cluster bombs, because they are both inaccurate and have relatively high dud rates, are more indiscriminate than the precision weapons used in Bosnia.

43. Martin and Gordon, "Collateral Damage Estimation"

44. Office of the Chairman of the Joint Chiefs of Staff, "Joint Methodology for Estimating Collateral Damage and Casualties for Conventional Weapons: Precision, Unguided and Cluster (U)," Manual (CJCSM) 3160.01, September 20, 2002.

45. Senior defense official, "Background Briefing on Targeting," March 5, 2003, www.defense.gov/transcripts/transcript.aspx?transcriptid = 2007.

46. Bradley Graham, "'Bugsplat' Computer Program Aims to Limit Civilian Deaths at Targets," *Washington Post*, February 22, 2003.

47. Senior defense official, "Background Briefing."

48. Crawford, *Accountability for Killing.*

49. Peter French calls this a "corporate internal decision structure." See Peter A. French, "The Corporation as a Moral Person," *American Philosophical Quarterly* 16, no. 3 (1979): 207–15.

50. See Kay Mathiesen, "We're All in This Together: Responsibility of Collective Agents and Their Members," in *Midwest Studies in Philosophy, Volume XXX: Shared Intentions and Collective Responsibility*, ed. Peter A. French and Howard K. Wettstein (Boston: Blackwell, 2006), 240–55, at 244–45; and Paul Sheehy, "Holding Them Responsible," in ibid., 74–93, at 85, 92.

51. Margaret Gilbert uses the terms forward-looking moral responsibility about one's obligations and backward-looking moral responsibility about one's causal responsibility for what one has done. Margaret Gilbert, "Who Is to Blame? Collective Moral Responsibility and Its Implications for Group Members," in *Midwest Studies in Philosophy*, ed. French and Wettstein, 94–114, at 94–95.

52. There is a large literature on collective and shared responsibility that I have no space to cite here. For introductions, see Larry May and Stacy Hoffman, eds., *Collective Responsibility: Five Decades of Debate in Theoretical and Applied Ethics* (New York: Rowman & Littlefield, 1991); Larry May, *Sharing Responsibility* (Chicago: University of Chicago Press, 1992); and Larry May, *War Crimes and Just War* (Cambridge: Cambridge University Press, 2007).

CHAPTER 14

Just War and Military Education and Training

Martin L. Cook

COMBATING TERRORISM AND counterinsurgency warfare pose novel challenges to the system of professional military education and training. Indeed, the many dimensions of the changing nature of war is a theme that unites many of the chapters in this volume. Further, because, as the editors point out in their introduction to this volume, so much of just war theory in recent centuries has been formed in the context of state-centric ideas of authority, necessarily existing legal regimes fit the nature of some of these challenges poorly, if at all. Such changes will require the evolution and development of agreed-upon legal principles and approaches to military training as nations attempt to cope with somewhat novel challenges. Finally, procurement programs and policies (and the acquisition of new weapons systems, for that matter) will in all probability adopt significantly different trajectories from those they had been on when the guiding planning paradigm was large interstate and combined arms conflict.

The Law of Armed Conflict (LOAC) is integrated into military training and education in a number of ways at every level. As required by Geneva treaty obligations, annual training in the basic elements of LOAC is given to every member of the US military. All precommissioning military education programs (ROTC, the military academies, Officer Candidate School) integrate some education regarding the just war tradition into their curricula—both as training in the legal framework of LOAC and almost always in a philosophy course that includes just war as a central element. Some lectures and elective courses dealing with the just war tradition are a part of every level of professional military education in all the military services (command

and staff college for officers at the rank of O-3, and war colleges at the rank of O-4 and O-5). In theater, military lawyers (judge advocates general) assist commanders in ensuring compliance with provisions of LOAC through crafting of Rules of Engagement that make LOAC as concrete and specific to the environment as possible. Finally, in traditional combat environments, it is the special responsibility of the officers and noncommissioned officers (NCOs) to discipline and monitor the conduct of their units to ensure that their actions are within the bounds of LOAC.

The kinds of conflicts in which the United States is now finding itself pose some real challenges to these models for ensuring LOAC compliance—both because of the size and nature of the operational units most typically employed and because of the nature of the environment of counterinsurgency war. Unlike conventional warfare conducted by platoons and companies under the direct supervision of officers and NCOs in clear force-on-force combat situations, counterterrorist strikes and counterinsurgency operations require different types of forces and different tactics and operational concepts. For the kinds of small unit engagements typical of counterinsurgency and counterterrorism warfare, the responsibility for that discipline devolves to lower and lower ranks, which poses additional challenges for military training and education.

Direct action against terrorist leaders and cells will most typically be conducted covertly by small special forces units. Unlike a conventional force-on-force firefight, such units are inserted covertly and hope to kill or capture their targets and withdraw as quietly as possible and without detection. They attack their targets either by direct action by the unit itself or by the Joint Terminal Attack Controller's (JTAC's) orchestration of various air assets to strike the target. Direct action by the members of the unit necessarily requires each operator on the team to make split-second decisions and to exercise fire discipline if discrimination and proportionality are to be respected. Because such actions are inherently unpredictable and require each member of the team to react quickly and appropriately, the challenge of ensuring adherence to just war principles is far more subtle and complex than traditional military operations. Each operator has to deeply understand the principles and have the training, discipline, and ability to act accordingly under extreme stress and danger.

In the case of attack from the air, the ground unit will observe the target in the attempt to ensure that only legitimate military targets are struck. Their embedded JTAC may augment their eyes-on intelligence with his Remotely Operated Video Enhanced Receiver (ROVER) unit, which can see video feed from Predator, Reaper, and Global Hawk remotely piloted vehicles and Advanced Targeting Forward Looking Infrared pods on human piloted strike fighter aircraft. Those feeds, and the JTACs' ability to direct surveillance where he needs it for proper target identification, greatly assist the ground unit in trying its best to ensure correct targeting. Once identified, the JTAC can direct the strike either by designating coordinates or by lasing the target for laser-guided munitions. In chapter 13 of this volume, Neta Crawford very thoughtfully analyzes the tensions inherent in the use of airpower in such engagements. Determining how much collateral damage to civilians and civilian objects is tolerable without fundamentally undermining larger mission accomplishment is a vexed topic indeed. As Crawford points out, the standard of "military necessity" is more elastic and unclear than it might initially seem.

The challenges are similar, but perhaps even more demanding, on more conventional units engaged in counterinsurgency warfare. Because gaining the trust and confidence of the local population is the essence of successful counterinsurgency, the requirements for discrimination and proportionality far exceed the "military necessity" standard of more conventional fighting. Necessarily, this means that soldiers will need to accept a much higher degree of risk and even actual casualties if they are to conduct effective operations. Inevitably and understandably, soldiers and units under attack or threat will experience frustration and anger at the restrictive rules of engagement they may perceive as depriving them of legitimate permission to defend themselves.[1]

For such self-restraint to be completely effective, it seems obvious that soldiers' training, education, and formation must go considerably deeper than traditional training supplemented by carefully crafted rules of engagement. Although it is a demanding requirement, a maximally effective counterinsurgency must, down to the lowest ranks, inculcate a deep understanding and embrace of the nature of the mission and the unique and challenging requirements that places on soldiers. In other words, it is not enough to define the mission and train for the Rules of Engagement. Soldiers need to incorporate an understanding of their purpose and mission in a way that becomes integral to their self-understanding. More challenging still is the requirement that they maintain and sustain that self-understanding over extended periods of time and repeated deployments in which they experience frustration and losses of their friends and comrades. Brigadier General H. R. McMaster has written eloquently of the need for leaders to make the maintenance of appropriate attitudes and behaviors a fundamental focus.[2]

Clearly, these requirements set a truly daunting task. This task requires inculcating a deep professional self-understanding not merely (as has historically been required) in the officer and NCO corps; it also requires individual enlisted personnel to understand and embrace the nature of the counterinsurgency mission to a degree that Plato described in the training of the Auxiliaries in the *Republic*: "Courage is a certain kind of preserving . . . the preserving of the opinion produced by law through education about what . . . is terrible. . . . [The soldiers] should receive the laws from us in the finest possible way like a dye . . . so that their opinion about what's terrible . . . would be colorfast . . . and their dye could not be washed out by pleasure . . . and pain, fear and desire" (*Republic*, 429d–430b).

Is this possible? Clearly, it will require superbly disciplined and morally self-aware soldiers to be self-possessed in the extreme in their dealings with the local populace. Further, the perceptions of the locals are not really in the span of control of US forces—they are influenced by inputs besides their direct perception of the conduct and attitudes of US troops. As General David Petraeus testified during his confirmation, the "human terrain" is where the struggle in a place like Afghanistan will be won or lost. In other words, the central issue is not a traditional military victory but to effectively persuade a large segment of the population that they can and should cooperate with coalition forces and that they can eventually (and fairly quickly) take control of their environment themselves. If that is not achievable, then protracted counterinsurgency is not a winnable conflict.

These considerations also point to the pastoral role of the just war tradition, as discussed by the editors in the introduction. Individual military personnel need to make moral sense of what they have done and experienced. There is considerable evidence that the kinds of deployments ground forces have experienced in Afghanistan and Iraq are especially demanding in this regard for a number of reasons. In many cases, individuals experience very high levels of stress for long periods of time, relatively unrelieved by "down time" or time in known safe areas. They are in close and constant proximity to a local population whose language and culture they do not well understand, and among whom are individuals actively planning to harm them. All these elements continually threaten an erosion of the discipline and respect for the other at the foundation of *jus in bello* requirements of just war. The pastoral role will be critical in helping individuals maintain a clear sense of their moral identity in theater, and to the restorative process necessary to cope with their return to civilian life and to work through the posttraumatic stress and moral injury they may have experienced.

JUST WAR AND THE DEVELOPMENT
OF LEGAL REGIMES

Another challenging area for the application of just war theory in current conflicts concerns the inadequacy of existing legal regimes to frame and guide conduct. The state-centric model of international law, which privileges sovereignty above all else, is inadequate and even unhelpful for coping with al-Qaeda-like threats to individuals, states, and the international system. Conversely, as the editors discuss thoroughly in the introduction, it is very much the essential frame of the international system as it exists.[3]

Thinking of the international system as a system of sovereign states generates a number of baseline assumptions about the use of force. It bifurcates the use of force into two fundamentally different types: conflicts internal to states, and interstate conflict. Hoping to minimize causes for the legitimate use of military force, it places great importance on the sovereignty of states, and attempts to define legitimate causes of war to self-defense, ever-increasingly narrowly conceived as clear military attack by one nation upon another. These trends peaked in the Kellogg-Briand Pact of 1928, which made all nondefensive war illegal (and which served as the basis for prosecution for Crimes against Peace at Nuremberg) and in the UN Charter's restriction of legitimate use of force to only two types: clear-cut self-defense and Security Council–authorized collective self-defense. This whole discussion points to the centrality of the question of legitimate authority for the authorization of the use of force, discussed thoroughly in the introduction to this volume.

Although this state-centric trajectory, supplemented with collective security, was the main evolutionary course of the international system throughout the period from the sixteenth to the twentieth centuries, there was always a competing cosmopolitan strand that questioned the sanctity of state sovereignty in the name of the rights and protection of human individuals. This was an issue even at the inception of Westphalia because the rights and even lives of religious minorities were set aside in favor of the hoped-for stability the sovereign state system promised. But as the enormity of the dangers of an exclusive focus on state sovereignty culminated in the Holocaust, there emerged a steady evolution of another (largely incompatible) legal regime that attempted to protect individuals, at least in extreme cases, from the actions or failures of their states. Beginning with the Genocide Convention of 1949, and culminating in the recent codification of the responsibility to protect, in theory state sovereignty has become more porous. Of course, that theoretical porosity has rarely been acted on in practice—for reasons having to do with the nature of national self-interest; the political, moral, and economic costs associated with using military forces of independent sovereign states for purposes not narrowly linked to their interests; and the deep desire of all states to maintain the maximum amount of sovereignty whenever possible.

How does this tension between Westphalian sovereignty and the cosmopolitan/human rights impulses of the international system bear on the question before us? Most obviously, the threats posed to states and their citizens by al-Qaeda and other international terrorist groups are not states and therefore do not fit the Westphalian paradigm at all. Conversely, they necessarily exist inside the territory of traditional Westphalian states (or, in many cases, in failed or weak versions of those states). The consequence of these facts is that resting on a high regard for national borders and sovereignty would allow nonstate terrorist groups safely to shelter behind those borders, unless the individual state where they were located was willing and able to act against them or invited others to do so.

In recognition of these legal realities, the George W. Bush administration attempted in its 2002 *National Security Strategy* to redefine the existing legal permission for "anticipatory self-defense" in broader terms than existing law recognized. The details are well known and too complex for detailed recounting here, but in essence the *National Security Strategy* made a bid to allow the United States to legitimately use military force against capabilities wherever it might detect them, even in the absence of clear evidence of a specific plan imminently to use them. The argument was as follows:

> For centuries, international law recognized that nations need not suffer an attack before they can lawfully take action to defend themselves against forces that present an *imminent danger of attack*. Legal scholars and international jurists *often conditioned the legitimacy of preemption on the existence of an imminent threat*—most often a visible mobilization of armies, navies, and air forces preparing to attack. We must *adapt the concept of imminent threat* to the capabilities and objectives of today's adversaries. . . . The *greater the threat*, the *greater is the risk of inaction*—and the more compelling the case for taking anticipatory action to defend ourselves, *even if uncertainty remains as to the time and place of the enemy's attack. To forestall or prevent such hostile acts by our adversaries, the United States will, if necessary, act preemptively.* (emphasis added)[4]

Clearly, this *National Security Strategy* is an attempt to widen the existing permission in international law for legitimate "anticipatory self-defense." The restriction on legitimate use of military force to obvious after-attack self-defense and UN Security Council–authorized collective security actions always had a small and somewhat grudging place for legitimate actions that anticipated attack. But because of great concern to maintain the stability of the international system and to avoid balance-of-power wars, that permission was conceived of as narrowly as possible.[5] The Bush administration was making the not entirely unreasonable claim that a nonstate actor might be able to function covertly to deliver weapons of mass destruction in ways that would not be detected until after they were successfully delivered. In the face of that threat, the argument was for attempting to remove capabilities, even in the absence of specific knowledge of a plan to use those capabilities.

It fairly quickly became obvious that the "Bush Doctrine" articulated in the 2002 *National Security Strategy* was not a basis for a commonly accepted new understanding of the international system. Any attempt to generalize the unilateralism articulated in it as a generally acceptable basis for legitimate state action by all states would quickly destroy the limited restraints in place on states justifying the use of military force. Consequently, even by the time of the issuance of the second Bush *National Security Strategy*, the language of unilateralism (if not always the practice of it) had been significantly toned down, and it has disappeared entirely from the Obama administration's rhetoric.

That said, nonstate terrorist groups do pose genuinely novel challenges to the international system that mere respect for the sovereign state will do little to resolve. What, after all, should a state do if it is certain that a nonstate group sheltering within the borders of a sovereign state is actively planning an attack? Obviously, if it is possible to share intelligence information regarding such plans, and the state containing the terrorist group is willing either to remove the threat or allow others to do so, there is no serious problem with respecting sovereignty and acting effectively. But what if the state in question cannot or will not take effective action to protect against the terrorist threat to a third party?

Clearly, there is a need to work diplomatically to develop a new legal regime flexible enough to deal with challenges of this nature. NATO's decision to invoke the chapter 5 mutual defense clause in the case of Afghanistan in the aftermath of the September, 11, 2001, terrorist attacks is, perhaps, one such example of a direction in which things may need to evolve. This is the case because, the reader will recall, the attack on the United States was not directly attributable in the least to the actions of the de facto government of Afghanistan, but rather of a non-Afghan Arab group—al-Qaeda—residing and training inside the territory of Afghanistan. Another similar example is the ongoing operations of weapons-launching remotely piloted vehicles against al-Qaeda and the Afghan Taliban inside the sovereign airspace of Pakistan, sometimes with at least the tacit permission of the government and military of Pakistan.[6]

The fact that al-Qaeda and its affiliates have not restricted attacks to the United States (or even to the United States and its NATO allies) has one perversely salutary effect. It should be possible in light of this reality to make the case that the threat posed to the entire international system is a general one. That is to say, freedom from the kinds of attacks perpetrated in India, Indonesia, Spain, Scotland, and so on is a general good for the international system. This would seem to point to the need for creating modifications to the international system that limit the extent to which sovereign borders will protect such groups. Conversely, the proclaimed right of the United States (or any other power, for that matter) to act wholly unilaterally seems to threaten anarchy in the international system if that were to become de facto the sole means of responding to such threats—not to mention the danger if, as the 2002 *National Security Strategy* seemed to imply, this were proposed as a de jure legitimization for such responses.

These considerations point to a need for developing new legal regimes that are robust enough to deal with the genuine threat of nonstate actors inside sovereign states and failed states that cannot or will not take effective action against them. It is possible that this can be left to emerging patterns of state practice that will, over time, develop customary international law in this area. But it seems risky and too slow to entrust these questions to that process. It is risky because states (perhaps especially the United States) are likely to act too aggressively and further erode the international trust and confidence necessary to evolve that process. It is, possibly, too slow because the threats are emergent and are rapidly spreading to new places and thus are generating new requirements for effective action.[7] Nevertheless, clearly there is an authority of practice aspect to the current situation. By this I mean that states will engage in a variety of activities in an effort to cope with the threats posed by terrorism. Other states and perhaps international bodies will assess the legitimacy of these actions. As this process unfolds, a somewhat stable body of acceptable practice will emerge that will form the core of novel customary international law in advance of or even in lieu of more deliberate interstate actions such as the formation of new treaties and new structures for international cooperation and decision making.

The realities of the situation ought to be sufficient to drive more explicit and deliberate modification of the relevant legal regimes. These realities are the following.

1. The threat posed by violent nonstate actors like al-Qaeda is not fundamentally a threat to individual sovereign states, but rather to the stability of the globalized international system of travel, trade, and so on, as well as notionally universal concepts of human rights. These are public goods of the international system. Therefore, all states have a common interest in their defense.

2. A system that privileges state sovereignty too highly makes it impossible to deal effectively with such threats. This is because al-Qaeda and similar groups can always find someplace within a state to train and gather. Sometimes this will be a state sympathetic to their aims. Sometimes it will be a failed or near-failed state or an ungoverned part of the territory of a state. In any case, it is imperative to deprive these groups of such sanctuaries.

3. It is far too destabilizing to any system of international law to allow individual states to act unilaterally to attempt to eliminate such threats. For one thing, the intelligence necessary to correctly identify such groups and sanctuaries will be hard to obtain. It will also be in error. Therefore, collective international determinations will be more likely to be accurate, and mistakes more excusable, than any pattern of unilateral action.

4. In sum, it would be in the interests of all states that have a stake in the international system that now exists to cooperate in creating mechanisms to vet and authorize interventions into states reasonably and collectively believed to be harboring terrorist groups.

One realizes, of course, that historically the existing international mechanisms of collective security have worked erratically at best. But in retrospect it seems obvious that the kind of collective security envisioned in the original UN Charter was based on the somewhat naive expectation that the permanent members of the UN Security Council would see threats and interests in a similar way over a long period of time. That was not realistic for routine interstate conflicts, where the interests of the various powers would not usually line up in the same direction.

The threats posed by international terrorism are of a fundamentally different sort. They really are threats to the shared international system, and therefore have a greater probability of being seen as such if the diplomacy necessary to evolve that perception is the priority. Further, the options we have at present are clearly unacceptable. These options are either failing to deal effectively with the threat at all because of respect for sovereignty, or involve acting unilaterally and destabilizing the system of international law and diminishing the international trust necessary to advance cooperation. If that is the case, as Sherlock Holmes once said, "When you have eliminated the impossible, whatever remains, however improbable, must be the truth."[8] In this case, the improbable but true idea is that the system of international law needs to evolve in a direction that will allow it to deal effectively with these threats, wherever they may be located, and that state sovereignty cannot be the fig leaf behind which terrorism hides.

Fortunately, evolution in this direction has been evident ever since World War II—albeit from a different direction. Since the 1949 Genocide Convention, there has been a steady trajectory in international law to diminish the threshold of sovereignty in favor of the weight of other important concerns. Human rights considerations have been the primary driver of these developments, culminating in the 2005 World Summit's adoption of the norm of responsibility to protect individuals and groups from genocide, war crimes, crimes against humanity, and ethnic cleansing.

Needless to say, these developments of legal regimes in tension with the Westphalian system of sovereignty have been largely on paper, and have been honored in the breach as much as in the observance. Still, the persistence of cumulative developments along these lines over decades manifests a genuine dissatisfaction with relying exclusively on sovereign states to define the global legal regime. By no means am I suggesting that the path is clear to squaring the circle of sovereignty with such considerations. But I am suggesting that the need for evolving legal regimes to deal effectively with terrorist organizations in the international system is the obverse of the problem with which the international system has already been dealing for more than half a century: the need to make sovereignty more porous and to create permissions and perhaps even obligations to reach through sovereign borders in the name of other considerations of great weight. The concern with the fundamental human rights of individuals (which rights are not to be trumped by the screen of state sovereignty, at least in the most extreme cases) is what drives the evolution of international concepts from the Genocide Convention through the responsibility to protect and beyond. The fact that the stated ideals of such movements are rarely matched with effective and truly cooperative international action points, of course, to the tremendous mismatch between ideals and the military and political cooperation that would be necessary to instantiate them. The threats of international terrorism are an even more direct affront to the public goods of the international order, which are goods of a similarly universal sort. It is therefore perhaps even more likely that states will be motivated to find the political will to work cooperatively in sharing intelligence, law enforcement, and military power in service of these common international goods.

Counterfactual history is in many respects a fool's errand. But it is tempting nonetheless to speculate: If the United States had worked with the near-universal goodwill and sympathy it experienced after 9/11 to advance the international conversation along these lines, might it not have been in a position to make considerable progress? But if that is correct, even though America's unilateral actions in the interim obviously have diminished considerably that universal sympathy and goodwill, they did not change the objective realities on the ground. Those realities regarding the nature of the threat of international terrorism to the international system are as true today as they were then. Consequently, though the atmospherics may have changed, the objective requirements to evolve the system to deal with these threats effectively have not.

JUST WAR AND WEAPONS
PROCUREMENT POLICIES

Another challenge arising from the kinds of conflicts in which the United States engaged in Afghanistan and Iraq is weapons procurement. For decades, the United States has optimized its forces for large-scale conventional combined arms conflicts (such as would have been expected at the Fulda Gap in Germany in a war with the Soviet Union). America's weapons systems and its training centers prepared US forces for that conflict.

Having experienced the conflicts in Iraq and Afghanistan, the military services have come to see the need for weapons systems not in their inventories at the conflicts' outsets. For example, as ground forces realized they would be fighting insurgent groups in urban environments, the need for ever-great precision has emerged as a critical need, because avoiding civilian casualties clearly became the central issue for counterinsurgency war. Consequently, there was a rush program to deploy a Global Positioning System–guided artillery round. The US Air Force responded to these operational requirements by acquisition of precision weapons with reduced blast effects—the "small-diameter" bomb of 250 pounds explosive yield and even precision concrete warheads with only direct kinetic effect and no explosives.

Because persistent observation of a building, a group of people, or an area was critical to accurately determining legitimate targets, that requirement has driven an enormous expansion of acquisition of long-loiter intelligence, surveillance, and reconnaissance platforms. That meant that the secretary of defense had to override considerable air force cultural resistance to provide ever-larger numbers of remotely piloted vehicles (RPVs).

Another example of acquisition adaptation was generated by the realization that the threats of rocket-propelled grenades and improvised explosive devices (IEDs) buried in roadways rendered the standard Humvee very vulnerable and required a rush acquisition of mine-resistant ambush-protected (MRAP) vehicles if ground units were to be able to have motorized transportation that was relatively safe.

Again, in the face of service culture resistance, the air force has begun acquisition of new platforms to address the capability gap between long-loiter RPVs and jet fighter-bombers, which require very frequent refueling and cannot operate efficiently at low altitudes, by acquiring humanly piloted vehicles. The light attack and armed reconnaissance aircraft and the light mobility airlifter acquisition programs are advancing in fits and starts as the air force considers propeller-driven long-loiter aircraft capable of operating out of unimproved and austere landing surfaces to support counterinsurgency warfare.[9] Even in these programs, however, such is the cultural resistance in the air force to acquiring and operating such platforms that some continue to argue that their sole purpose is for the "capability building" of allied air forces rather than for the US Air Force to operate them themselves.

All these adaptations are, one might argue, slower in coming than one might ideally like. Conversely, unless one assumes that counterterrorism and counterinsurgency are the kinds of wars in which the United States will be engaged in the future, to the exclusion of other kinds, all the military services must necessarily engage in spirited debate about balancing maximal adaptation to the current wars with also preparing, training, and procuring weapons for other kinds of conflicts. As the deployments in Afghanistan and Iraq wind down, intense debate is under way in all the services to determine what realistic training should look like with a view to future engagements. For instance, should they continue to train for counterinsurgency and counterterrorism, or return to training optimized for large combined force combat? Should they train different units to different contingencies, and if so, which? On the procurement and equipment side of the discussion, should equipment acquired for the specific operational requirements of Iraq be retained in the inventory? An example of the latter is that the MRAPs acquired to cope with the IED threat in Iraq are not in the table of organization and equipment of any army units. Should they be retained? If so, by what kinds of units? Should additional similar acquisitions be made?

Similar issues arise in training regimes as well. Between Vietnam and the Iraq war, the crucible for US Army training was provided by the national training centers—at Fort Irwin, California, for heavy and mechanized units, and at Fort Polk, Louisiana, for light forces. Training there prepared the army superbly for combined arms combat against similar armies (e.g., Iraq's). And obviously the army performed magnificently when that was the fight it was in—against conventional Iraqi forces.

But that training did practically nothing to prepare army units for the complexity of the counterinsurgency and counterterrorism "battlefield," where civilians and civilian objects are jumbled together with, and often almost indistinguishable from, combatants. Further, very little training integrated airpower into the close air support mission, which resulted in army commanders who had to learn on the fly from their JTAC (who was an air force officer or NCO) about the limits and proper use of air assets.

Close air support has not traditionally been a "prestige" mission for the air force, either. The best platforms to perform the mission—A-10 "Warthogs" and C-130 "Jolly Green Giant" gunships—are not, in air force culture, prestige platforms. What the air force "prefers" is a deliberative planning process that generates a theater-wide air tasking order for all airframes in the airspace—a process that normally takes at least 72 hours from target nomination through dispatch of a mission. That yields an "orthodox" mission of a carefully coordinated air campaign against "centers of gravity," which cumulatively will demolish (for example) an air defense system.

None of these preferred ways of operating work well or at all in an environment with furtive and mobile targets and high-value individuals. Here the premium is on surveillance, identification, ensuring protections against damage to noncombatants, and prompt response. As Crawford points out in chapter 13, the tension between the protection of civilians and the "utilitarian" calculus of military urgency often allows the utilitarian calculation to dominate. The system of embedded JTACs coordinating between ground units and air assets is an ever-improving and effective means of addressing this objective requirement. But until the environment required it, this was not the prestige end of what the air force trained for, and it was (and is) not the "prestige" end of the service. The measures of prestige, of course, can be found in promotions to the highest ranks of the service from within each job specialty. Only over time, as the objective demands placed on the service indicate what the real "pointy end of the spear" is—that is, where the capabilities of the service prove most relevant to the military engagement before us—do those patterns of prestige and promotion shift.

CONCLUSION

The kinds of conflicts in which the United States is currently engaged, and in which it seems likely to continue to be engaged for the near future, have indeed placed strain and required adaptation in the areas of military training, understanding of the law and ethical principles undergirding the legitimate use of military power, and the acquisition of more relevant weapons systems. As then–secretary of defense Donald Rumsfeld famously remarked in response to a soldier's question about inadequate armor in Iraq, "You go to war with the army you have—and not the army you might want or wish to have a later time."[10]

One might generalize Rumsfeld's point. The United States went to war with the training, law, weapons systems, and service cultural biases it had. At some point, the weaknesses and inadequacies of aspects of all of those characteristics became apparent in the conflicts in which it is presently engaged. Over time the recursive interaction of these realities with the structures of law, the kinds of training required to best prepare US forces for the environment in which they will find themselves, and the equipment and platforms best adapted for success emerge. This process is now (admittedly somewhat more slowly than would have been optimal) working its way through the system.

All the US military services clearly state their goal of preparing senior officers who are prepared to be flexible and adaptive so that they are able to make the kinds of adjustments required by the objective demands of a fluid strategic environment. Clearly, it took longer than it should have for the services to make adaptations so as to be maximally effective in Iraq and Afghanistan. But as budgets shrink (and military forces structures shrink in parallel), the environment of the next decade and beyond will require very intelligent choices to acquire the right equipment and design the right training so as to be as relevant as possible to the emerging security requirements of the United States and the world. In the days of large budgets, one might have been able to afford to develop multiple tracks, capabilities, and platforms. But the current environment of budget cutbacks will only permit a narrower range of options. And this will require extremely clear strategic thinking to ensure that the services design that smaller force as intelligently as possible. The ability to make such calculations is, of course, completely dependent on the ability to accurately predict the nature and scale of future conflicts that this force will face—an inherently uncertain and difficult prediction. If there is any single lesson learned from the years of conflict since 2001, it is that whatever force the services design and train will almost certainly need to adapt and learn quickly as it finds itself facing requirements not anticipated in its training.

NOTES

A variant of this chapter will appear in an edited volume of Martin L. Cook's previously published essays, *Issues in Military Ethics* (Albany: State University of New York Press, in press). ©Martin L. Cook.

1. For examples of this tension as manifested in Afghanistan, see Spencer Ackerman, "Petraeus: I'll Change Afghanistan's Rules of War," *Wired Online*, June 29. 2010, www.wired.com/dangerroom/2010/06/petraeus-ill-change-the-rules-of-war-in-afghanistan/.

2. General H. R. McMaster offered these remarks at the Spring 2010 Ethics Conference at the US Naval War College. They have been published in the *Journal of Military Ethics* 9, no. 3 (2010): 183–94; and the *Naval War College Review*, Winter 2011, 7–19.

3. See "At White House, Weighing Limits of Terror Fight," *New York Times*, September 16, 2011.

4. US National Security Council, *National Security Strategy of the United States of America 2002*, http://ics.leeds.ac.uk/papers/pmt/exhibits/378/NSS.pdf.

5. The clearest articulation of this extreme narrowing of the legitimate causes of war is found in Michael Walzer's "legalist paradigm" in *Just and Unjust Wars*, where the pivotal principle is "nothing but aggression can justify war." See Michael Walzer, *Just and Unjust*

Wars: A Moral Argument with Historical Illustrations, 2nd ed. (New York: Basic Books: 1977), 62.

6. Just to be clear, I am not necessarily endorsing this policy as effective. Clearly, there are serious risks of undermining the Pakistani government's legitimacy in the eyes of its own people with these operations. Furthermore, the fact that the aircraft are largely being operated by the Central Intelligence Agency rather than by the US military seems to me a serious break of LOAC—although having the US military operate them would be difficult, too, because that would constitute an armed attack on the territory of Pakistan by the US military—an act of war, in fact, under international law.

7. See, e.g., the dangers posed by current US operations in Yemen, where a very weak government in a very unstable country is forced to manage US unilateral strikes—as reported by Scott Shane, Mark Mazzetti, and Robert F. Worth, "Secret Assault on Terrorism Widens on Two Continents," *New York Times*, August 14, 2010, www.nytimes.com/2010/08/15/world/15shadowwar.html?_r = 1&hp.

8. Arthur Conan Doyle, *The Sign of Four*, chap. 6.

9. See *Wikipedia*, http://en.wikipedia.org/wiki/Light_Attack/Armed_Reconnaissance.

10. Fred Kaplan, "Rumsfeld vs. the American Soldier: What Rummy's Survival Says about Bush's Plans for His Second Term," *Slate*, December 8, 2004, www.slate.com/id/2110818/.

PART III

~

The Triumph of Just War?

CHAPTER 15

The Triumph of Just War Theory and Imperial Overstretch

John Kelsay

I BEGIN WITH SOME COMMENTS on this chapter's title. As many will recognize, the first words are borrowed from Michael Walzer's 2004 essay, *The Triumph of Just War (and the Dangers of Success)*.[1] Walzer's concern is shared by all those engaged in interpreting the just war idea. If we do our work well, the vocabulary of *jus ad bellum* and *jus in bello* becomes better known. More people refer to the idea, and many of them do so in ways that are—well, unreflective, or at least not very well informed. So Walzer mentions the way President George H. W. Bush invoked the notion on the eve of Operation Desert Storm. As Walzer has it, the president got it partly right. He did understand that just wars require that soldiers fight with soldiers, so that noncombatants are protected. But the president also showed an unfortunate tendency to moralize, so that the rhetoric of justice tended to slide in the direction of a righteous crusade.

One can multiply examples of the invocation of just war notions in recent public discourse. President George W. Bush employed just war vocabulary in speaking about the "War on Terror," though Walzer (among others) thought the younger Bush also tended to conflate the language of justice with that of the crusade. By contrast, former president Jimmy Carter's March 2003 *New York Times* op-ed arguing that a war to oust Saddam Hussein would fail to fulfill the criteria associated with just war reasoning moved in a different direction. Given Carter's interest in opposing this particular war, it is perhaps not surprising that he emphasized the *jus ad bellum* criterion of last resort. No crusading mentality here; however, Carter's statement that this criterion would be satisfied only when "all nonviolent options [have been] exhausted" did not match the standard presentation of scholars. Indeed, many interpreters would argue that such an understanding would turn the just war idea into a type of pacifism.[2] Further points of interest in Carter's argument included the statement that the *jus in bello* requirement of discrimination would be violated by foreseen collateral damage. On Carter's account, legitimate authority would be assigned to the UN—a good argument if one is thinking about international law, though more controversial in just war discourse. And of the remaining criteria, the only one to which Carter referred was a version of aim of peace: "The peace [the war] establishes must be a clear improvement over what exists." Not quite right, though certainly interesting.[3]

More recently, President Obama's much-acclaimed Nobel Peace Prize address referred to the notion of just war, albeit in a truncated version. Placing the idea in the context of a developmental account of humanity's experience with armed force, the president explained the concept as requiring that certain conditions be met; these serve to distinguish between just and unjust fighting. A just war would be one "waged as a last resort or in self-defense"; in which "the force used is proportional"; and where, "whenever possible, civilians are spared from violence."[4] The *New York Times* took note of the reference, and carefully following the White House's example placed the phrase "just war" in scare quotes in the days following the speech. Interestingly, the *Times* articles read as though the reporters had never heard of the idea. Given this, one might wonder whether we should even worry about the "triumph" of just war theory or the "dangers of success."

And indeed, that is the point I wish to stress.[5] Given the ways presidents make decisions about foreign policy, it is certainly noteworthy that three of the last four (and, in Carter's case, a former president still interested in influencing public policy) made reference to "just war." One may judge their presentations as more or less articulate or acute. In all cases, however, the real point seems to be that the "theory" or "tradition" has found a particular niche in contemporary discourse. In this, its competitors—or sometimes, fellow travelers—are international law, conceptions of national interest, and especially strategic doctrines like those associated with Secretary of Defense Caspar Weinberger in the 1980s, General Colin Powell in the 1990s, and these days with counterinsurgency (known by the acronym COIN). In the current setting, as always, we are at a teachable moment, when advocates of the just war notion have an opportunity to speak, to write, and to forge alliances with others in discussions of policy. There is no "triumph" of just war theory, in the usual sense of the term. Advocates of the idea have secured a place at the table of public discourse, where they now strive with others in the giving and taking of reasons for action.

This is Walzer's point as well, or at least that is how I read his essay. If the "dangers of success" have to do with public figures putting the just war framework to less-than-desirable uses, or articulating piecemeal versions of it, then the proper response is to produce more and hopefully better just war discourse. Walzer does not propose retreat, and neither should we.

In that sense, there are (as always) a number of questions one can ask about the current state of just war discourse. The mention of "imperial overstretch" in the second part of my title is associated with two such questions.[6] One type of question I shall call "epistemological." As will be clear, the issue involves the nature of just war discourse, particularly in relation to other frameworks that human beings have developed for purposes of distinguishing legitimate from illegitimate uses of military power. Here I am particularly interested in the Muslim tradition of "the judgments pertaining to armed struggle." How far should one go in describing this as the Muslim equivalent of or analogue to the just war tradition? A second type of question is more oriented toward practice. Here I am interested in the usefulness of just war reasoning in statecraft, with particular reference to discussions of the NATO effort in Afghanistan.

COMPARATIVE ETHICS AND JUST WAR DISCOURSE

If we track the discussion of just war since World War II, one of the more striking developments has been the growing interest in historical studies. James Turner Johnson is the best-known contributor in this vein, though Frederick Russell, LeRoy Walters, and others deserve mention. Indeed, the notion that contemporary just war thinking rests on or refers to a longer history has become standard in the literature.

Comparative studies are of more recent vintage. When Johnson and I first proposed a study of the ways resort to and conduct of war were construed in the "Western" and "Islamic" cultural traditions, we did not have much in the way of models.[7] We simply took questions we considered standard: What were the sources of thinking about resort to and conduct of war in the two traditions? What did these sources say about right authority, just cause, and the other criteria familiar to students of the just war framework? What was the relationship between just war, holy war, and pacifism in each case? And so on.

Although many colleagues expressed appreciation for this effort, it did not take long for a number of objections to emerge. In my view the most important of these had to do with the possibility that comparative inquiry suppresses the particularity of traditions.

In a recent essay I argued that this objection is not particularly apt; or to put it another way, I suggested that worries about particularity are no more appropriate with respect to comparison than with respect to more generally historical work.[8] In one sense, Cicero, Ambrose and Augustine, Thomas Aquinas, and the other heroes of the just war tradition are participants in an ongoing discussion. In another, they are authors whose work is located in particular places and times, so that to speak too easily of a "just war tradition" runs the risk of hiding important differences from view. Nevertheless, contemporary authors continue to speak about the importance of this tradition, and the reason seems clear. We are not the first to worry about issues of resort to and conduct of war, and as Ernst Troeltsch said on more than one occasion, those who would think about such matters do well to "think with the dead, for their thoughts are many."[9]

This is even truer in matters involving inquiry across cultures. In a time when the lines suggested by the very use of a phrase like "cross-cultural inquiry" are blurred by immigration and global trade networks, we do well to expand the scope of just war inquiry. In doing so, it is of course possible that we will make mistakes. So long as we understand scholarly discourse as an ongoing conversation, we may have hope of correction, however. In an important sense, the ongoing activity of comparative studies of ethics and war is a testimony to Donald Davidson's claim that translation is a fundamental aspect of rationality.[10] We are always running up against people whose way of speaking is different from our own. It may be that one day we will come upon a vocabulary for which translation is not possible—indeed, we often find that there are some thoughts difficult to express when we attempt to move back and forth between cultural traditions. For the time being, however, we do well to act on the faith that "nothing human is foreign" to us, or to put it in a more Davidsonian way, on the assumption that there is no good reason to think that we will not be able to understand what other people are saying—for example, when they make claims regarding the justice or injustice of particular instances of war.

When it comes to studies of just war and jihad, one of the more interesting criticisms advanced focuses on the mode of reasoning by which the two traditions proceed. Commenting on the comparative project, a number of authors familiar with Islam note that *ahkam al-jihad* proceeds by means of questions and answers, rather than by means of an application of principles. Leaving aside for now the issue of philosophical and other modes of writing whereby Muslims have and do address questions about the morality of war, any reader of texts like al-Shaybani's *Siyar* or the treatises of al-Mawardi, Ibn Taymiyya, and others will quickly recognize what is at stake.[11] These authors participate in an ongoing conversation in which texts are treated as precedents, which are to be related to questions raised by believers asking for guidance. Suppose that the Muslims hold a city under siege, and that the inhabitants of the city try to deter Muslim archers by tying children to the city walls? Or what happens when women on the enemy side take up arms? What should Muslims do?

The first task of a jurist in responding to such questions is to make plain the background against which they make sense. Muhammad, the Prophet of God, said that those fighting in God's path do not kill women, children, and others who do not bear arms. The texts reporting this declaration are precedents that inform the conscience of those aiming at active submission to the will of God.

The second task is to relate such precedents to new situations. In doing so, the jurist will ask "how new" is the problem? That is, responsibility involves a search for other prophetic dicta that may be relevant, or for judgments set forth in the Qur'an or in previous rulings by jurists that have attained the status associated with a "consensus," in order to ascertain whether precedents do in fact exist. Assuming there is something new in the case at hand, however, the jurist's responsibility involves a kind of analogical reasoning whereby established precedent is extended in ways that may—assuming that other jurists ultimately concur—provide apt guidance for dealing with changing circumstances. The pattern of reasoning is historical, broadly speaking; in this, it acknowledges that discussions of justice did not begin with the question at hand. One ought not blindly imitate the past, but one should "think with the dead, for their thoughts are many."

Now, the point of such observations seems plain, with respect to comparative studies of just war and jihad. The latter tradition develops case by case, in response to particular questions of practice. To speak of jihad criteria in the mode of contemporary just war discourse requires us to make generalizations. Further, to speak about the principles of justice or defense of rights, as contemporary just war advocates often do, involves abstractions that are somewhat removed from the concrete discourse of Muslim jurists.

This raises an important point, however. Many contemporary interpreters speak in terms of just war "theory" rather than "tradition." The former has a lot going for it, especially if we are thinking of recent analyses by Jeff McMahan, David Rodin, and others. McMahan says quite explicitly that he has no particular loyalty to the notion of just war as a "tradition," but is rather more interested in examining the logic of conventional assumptions allowing killing in war—what principles are at stake, and how can we strengthen and refine them, given issues people face today?[12] Similarly, the US Conference of Catholic Bishops issues statements pronouncing that the baseline of just war reasoning has to do with a presumption against war, so that the logic of just war criteria has to do with determining when the burden of proof suggested by such a presumption has been met.[13] Much contemporary writing about just war does seem to involve a kind of principles-rules model of ethics rather different from that of the jurists whose particular judgments make up *ahkam al-jihad.*

If we think of just war "tradition," however, a rather different picture emerges. Recall the point made above, to the effect that almost every major contribution to contemporary discussions of just war acknowledges the importance of a historical sensibility, and thus in some sense seeks to claim the mantle of tradition. Consistency and continuity with reference to significant precedents, depth of knowledge about the various contexts in which "just war" has been an important idea—these are at least a part of the way rationality is construed, even in a society more obviously governed by appeals to cost-benefit analysis and personal autonomy. In just war discourse, no one has made this point more often or more powerfully than James Turner Johnson. Consider his discussion of the work of canonists in medieval Christendom. These drew on precedents from Roman law, biblical theology, and Germanic military traditions in order to compile a set of judgments by which just and unjust wars might be distinguished. They did so with particular reference to the political and military institutions of their day. Perhaps most importantly, they arrived at a way of assigning authority for war to some political leaders and not to others. In a time when rulers at all levels of society saw themselves in competition for power, this was no small matter.[14]

More recently, Johnson has argued (1) that the listing of right authority as the first criterion of just war in historical works establishes an important precedent; (2) that historical just war authors did not share the modern penchant for "limiting" just wars to those which might be construed as "defensive"; and (3) that contemporary just war thinking will benefit from attending to these precedents. I will not go into all these arguments at this point. Rather, I simply observe that if we follow the example of Johnson, we have evidence that runs counter to the characterization of just war reasoning as a type of principles-rules approach. Instead, we have something that bears a closer—not exact, but closer—resemblance to the form of *ahkam al-jihad*. Although this does not free comparativists from worries about the ways their categories may obscure particularity, it does suggest a way forward with respect to just war and *jihad*. The point needs further study, but in my judgment, it is useful to consider the ways that both traditions exemplify the form of rationality Robert Brandom terms "historical," in the sense that rationality consists in "a certain kind of reconstruction of a tradition," or in which people "find a way forward by reconstruing the path that brought us to our present situation."[15]

JUST WAR TRADITION AND THE PRACTICE OF STATECRAFT

Above I noted the way that just war discourse seems to occupy a particular niche in contemporary policy debates. Judging from historical studies, journalism, memoirs, and the like, one would have to say this niche is small, albeit sometimes significant.

It is interesting to think about why this is so. The invocation of just war notions sometimes seems to reflect the need of politicians to respond to specific constituencies. Thus one might judge George H. W. Bush's appeal to the tradition developed by Thomas Aquinas and others as a specific response to the public statement of the US Bishops' Conference. They had argued that any move from the purely defensive strategy of Desert Shield to the forward military action of Desert Storm would be unjust, not least because it would not satisfy the criterion of last resort. On this account, a sitting president would then be replying to the bishops and those who might be influenced by them, in an attempt to make the case for his chosen policy.[16] Similarly, President Obama's Nobel Peace Prize speech was widely considered a kind of apologetic for the expansion of US military power in Afghanistan. The president acknowledged as much in his own remarks, noting that there was some irony in the committee's selection of the commander in chief of a state involved simultaneously in two wars.

This does not mean that policymakers' references to just war are "merely" political, however. If one reads articles in foreign policy journals like *Survival* or *Foreign Policy*—sometimes, even *Foreign Affairs*—one finds occasional discussion of just war categories. Several articles by Steven Simon (who served as a National Security Council aide during the Bill Clinton years) provide an interesting case in point.[17] Simon and his various coauthors typically bring just war categories into play as one way of evaluating policy options. Often these are paired with considerations from international law, with the implication that assessing the moral and legal standing of actions is one component in policymaking, along with considerations of political and economic impact, diplomatic practice, and other factors. Because Simon does not typically tie moral and legal notions to constituencies, one is probably justified in thinking that just war and related ideas are being given a relatively independent standing in this conversation.

Independent, significant, but small—this last is important as well. Richard Haass's 2009 book—*War of Necessity, War of Choice*—is interesting in this regard.[18] Haass, the current president of the Council on Foreign Relations, makes the specific argument that Operations Desert Shield and Desert Storm were necessary, whereas the 2003 war to affect regime change in Iraq was not. He argues that the United States ought to follow the former precedent rather than the latter, so that military power is brought to bear only when there are no other good options—a kind of criterion of last resort, though not in the sense articulated by Jimmy Carter (see above).

Because Haass is a very public figure, it is not surprising that his book received considerable attention. Then, too, his language resonated with that of President Obama, who expressed several times during the 2008 campaign the view that the war to remove Saddam Hussein was a war of choice, whereas the effort in Afghanistan after the September, 11, 2001, terrorist attacks was something different. The war in Afghanistan had suffered by neglect due to the Bush administration's poor choice regarding Iraq. Afghanistan was not a war of choice but a truly necessary fight. In an Obama administration, candidate Obama promised, policy would reflect this priority.

In a number of interviews following the publication of his book, Haass noted that some readers called attention to the way his language reflected important precedents in his own Jewish faith. He professed to be unaware of those, for example in the discussion of *milhemet mitzvah* (obligatory war) and *milhemet rashut* (some-times rendered as "discretionary war") located (among other places) in Maimoni-des's *Mishneh Torah*. Haass did have some ideas about just war tradition, however. He did not consider it a particularly useful tool for statecraft, because it was overly restrictive.[19] One needs some way of distinguishing wars to which policymakers should commit the resources of their communities from others. But one needs to give them ample room to maneuver, not least because it is difficult to weigh the various factors involved—will war in a particular situation damage the state's capa-bility to fulfill other responsibilities, or not? Will it hurt or help existing alliances? How will it affect discussions of other initiatives, say, in matters of public health or finance? In this context, "necessity" is a measure susceptible of considerable varia-tion, so that one might envision a scale by which one has necessity level 1, level 2, and then 3 as a kind of ultimate standard.

It is reasonable to ask about the source of Haass's ideas of just war tradition. I do not know the answer, though it seems likely that he, like George H. W. Bush, may have been affected by the Catholic bishops' argument about Desert Storm. The fact that the bishops' argument was not a particularly good just war argument ought, then, to matter in thinking about the tradition's place in policymaking. As some put it in responding to the bishops, Iraq's invasion of Kuwait constituted a clear violation of international norms. Thus, the US and allied presence in the region should be considered an act of collective defense, and the requirement of last resort was not even in question.

I think that the just war tradition is a better resource for statecraft than Haass recognizes. In particular, the "overly restrictive" characterization seems to rest on notions of last resort that simply are not apt. The relationship between just war thinking and statecraft rests in large part on the connection of both with a realistic view of the world—one in which it is taken for granted that military force is not only an aspect of politics, but an aspect of "good" politics.[20] This means that a contemporary interpreter of just war tradition asks from the start whether military force is, in a given context, the most apt way of attaining certain goals. The respon-sibility of that interpreter is thus to comprehend in as complete a manner as possible what options are available, and what the likely impact of the various approaches will be with respect to the interests of justice. In this, the responsibilities of just war thinkers and policymakers overlap.

Now, what about "imperial overstretch"? If it is not true that just war tradition is overly restrictive, it may yet be true that it inclines people to support policy options that are unrealistic. This would have been, I think, the complaint of some-one like Reinhold Niebuhr, and one could certainly utilize the ideas of more con-temporary realists to develop similar criticisms.[21] It is interesting in this regard to consider how just war interpreters have responded to the debate regarding policy in Afghanistan. Early in 2009 President Obama asked General Stanley McChrystal to assess the situation and to make recommendations. As is well known, McChrystal described a dire situation, in which NATO efforts could be correlated with a revival of strength on the part of an alliance of insurgent groups, the largest group being the Taliban. Without a revision of NATO policy, the likelihood of continued gains by the Taliban was high.

In proposing specific reforms, McChrystal followed the ideas associated with COIN, particularly as developed by General David Petraeus and others during the post-2006 troop "surge" in Iraq. The approach rests on establishing protections for the general population—in effect, on driving the enemy out of designated areas, building security so that people cooperate and plan for the future, and also so that they may establish local police and other forces to protect themselves. As well, McChrystal's understanding of COIN required that NATO troops reduce their dependence on air power, and that the United States and other participants in the mission support a proportionate increase in ground forces, in financial and other forms of aid, and in programs aimed at the development of a cadre of local officials who might be deemed legitimated by Afghanis.

In 2009, the alternative to COIN was associated with Vice President Joe Biden, who argued that the primary objective of US policy ought to be the weakening of al-Qaeda. To that end, the kind of on the ground investment required by COIN could be deemed a distraction. Citing evidence that the use of aerial drones in a policy of targeted killings of known al-Qaeda commanders had seriously disrupted the organization's command and control structure, the vice president and others suggested that a policy organized around counterterrorism might be preferable to one based on COIN.

In the end, President Obama accepted much of General McChrystal's proposal. At the same time, the counterterrorism measures associated with Vice President Biden continued; arguably, these were strengthened through an increase of aid and cooperative measures undertaken with the Pakistani military. Which one should advocates of just war favor?[22]

My own, admittedly informal soundings suggest that a survey of opinion during the summer of 2009 would probably have shown that scholars knowledgeable about just war tradition favored General McChrystal's approach.[23] In this, one of the most important factors would have been COIN's focus on delimiting air power and the civilian casualties associated with collateral damage. That this is an important issue in the fighting is clear. In my own work, I followed not only McChrystal's recommendations but also a series of statements issued by Mullah Omar in which Taliban fighters were ordered to take the utmost care to avoid civilian casualties. In some of these, the leader of the largest group of Taliban forces took care to say that international aid workers ought not be considered military targets.[24] The fact that Mullah Omar thought it timely to speak in this way reflects important Shari'a precedents, of course. It is also clear that he understood, in ways similar to McChrystal, that the fighting had reached a point in which the side most clearly committed to (or perceived as so committed to) the protection of civilians stood to gain an advantage. In all, these developments suggested that COIN was an approach whose time had come in Afghanistan, whereas the counterterrorism approach ran the risk of connecting American and allied efforts to civilian deaths. Although no just war thinker actually stated that such deaths violated the criterion of discrimination (at least, not to my knowledge), one could certainly argue that the use of drones and other forms of air power runs afoul of *in bello* proportionality, as well as hurting NATO's possibility of success. As McChrystal argued in his assessment of existing policy, if too many civilians die, one loses the hearts and minds of the people, and thereby loses the war. Simply put, I am suggesting that the high moral tone presented in General McChrystal's statement of COIN was attractive to just war thinkers, and that the correlative stress on protection of civilians in Mullah Omar's pronouncements lent support to the judgment that such protection really would be a critical issue in determining the outcome of the conflict.

One factor lost, or at least obscured, in the 2009 discussion was simply put by Vice President Biden. He did not believe that COIN would work in Afghanistan. And looking at the situation objectively, it is easy to see why someone would think that. There were of course a number of books and articles reminding President Obama and others that Afghanistan is the "graveyard of empires." And there were those, including the vice president, who thought that the administration of Hamid Karzai was hopelessly corrupt, so that the COIN provision requiring a cadre of officials enjoying public trust would prove impossible to fulfill. Even more concretely, however, an assessment of the geography and political culture of Afghanistan suggests the difficulty of any policy designed to "clear, hold, and build." The terrain is in some places among the most forbidding on Earth; the sheer number of ethnic and linguistic groupings suggests a monumental task with respect to state building. In short, on the criterion of a reasonable hope of success, COIN deserved a closer inspection than many just war thinkers provided.[25]

Assuming that my informal survey is correct, it seems important to ask why just war thinkers tended to play up McChrystal's emphasis on the protection of civilians. Correspondingly, why did they play down Biden's appeal to a reasonable hope of success? I am not entirely sure of the answer; for now, however, I want to connect it to the notion of "imperial overstretch." Might it be the case that the just war tradition, or at least a certain reading of it, lends itself to the support of unrealistic policies? If the US bishops' version of just war tradition is overly restrictive (and thus, incorrect) in one way, might it be the case that a preference for policies like COIN with respect to delimiting civilian casualties obscures the more "realistic" measures associated with a reasonable hope of success and *ad bellum* proportionality?

CONCLUSION

I think the answer to these questions is "yes." And the lessons to be drawn, though simple (even obvious), are extremely difficult to put into practice. First, we should say that "good" just war thinking requires consideration of the range of concerns suggested by each and all of the criteria associated with the *jus ad bellum* and *jus in bello*. To fix on one or even several criteria in ways that raise it (or them) above the others leads to mistakes. Thus, if it is true that the US Conference of Catholic Bishops' recent pronouncements are less helpful because of an overemphasis on last resort, it can also be the case that others may err by playing down or ignoring the criteria of a reasonable hope of success and overall proportionality.

Second, it must be said that "good" just war thinking requires careful attention to the facts of particular conflicts. By this I mean not only questions of history—how did certain parties come into conflict? Whose claims resonate with the notion of just cause?—but also questions relevant to an evaluation of the possibilities of success and overall proportionality. Issues of terrain, the nature of the enemy, the match of skills and weaponry available to the parties—these are the kinds of things that many just war thinkers prefer to leave to policymakers. There are reasons for this reservation, to be sure. Nevertheless, such concerns are relevant to careful assessments of the justice of wars, and those who would engage in just war thinking do well to consider them. I have already mentioned some of the factors relevant to thinking about NATO's policy in Afghanistan; these should have given pause to anyone thinking about the possibilities of military action in that context. Similarly, just war thinking about US strategy with respect to al-Qaeda requires careful consideration of the nature of the group. As things stand, the debate between advocates of COIN and of counterterrorism seems to miss the fact that Osama bin Laden and his colleagues put together an organization that does not fit neatly with either response. Given that al-Qaeda is neither a classic insurgency nor a classic terrorist group, the particular sort of challenge it presents deserves careful analysis, and interpreters of the just war tradition must consider the question.[26]

Third, "good" just war thinking attends to the dynamic nature of conflicts. The criteria of the *jus ad bellum* and *jus in bello* guide reflection throughout a particular war. They are relevant at the beginning, end, and all the way through. In this sense, there is nothing odd about the notion that one might judge an initiative as just at the outset, unjust at some point in the course of fighting, and just at the end. Many interpreters focus primarily on the first phase—that is, whether it would be just to go to war in a particular case, as though answering that question settles the issue. If just war thinkers are to participate in policy discussions, however, they must enter into conversation at various points. In Afghanistan, for example, one might have deemed the original effort by the United States and its allies as just, particularly insofar as the aim was to defray al-Qaeda's ability to operate training camps and thus to produce fighters able to carry out operations analogous to the 9/11 attacks. The fact that this campaign also led to a change of regime in Kabul involves somewhat different considerations. Although I at least would not want to argue that the removal of Taliban leaders was unjust, it did set in motion a number of factors that led eventually to a campaign aimed at state building. As implied above, such a campaign, though noble, deserved careful consideration with respect to a reasonable hope of success and overall proportionality. In the summer of 2011 it seemed plausible to think that NATO's efforts in Afghanistan were at a turning point, in the sense that the scale of involvement by the United States and others might no longer be sustainable or, in the terms of the just war tradition, no longer justifiable. A different approach, with a different kind of investment, may be advisable.[27]

As these points suggest, I am interested in expanding the role of just war thinking in the making of policy. On my view, such thinking is a social practice, with relevance for discussions that take place among policymakers, among the citizens of democratic states, and in relation to the training and conduct of military professionals. At present, I am most interested in the first, so that just war discourse focuses on the question "When is war an apt means of statecraft?" Debates about the location of right authority, just cause, and right intention—this last construed as (at least in part) measured in terms of a conscientious effort to assess the criteria of a reasonable hope of success, overall proportionality, and the likely configuration of a postwar order (i.e., the concern associated with the criterion "aim of peace)— aim to assess the question "Is war timely or fitting?" in a particular set of circumstances. Construed in this way, right intention also provides a link between the *jus ad bellum* and *jus in bello*, because the planning and execution of strategy must involve an assessment of the means that will be necessary to achieve victory, and of the likelihood that these will be consistent with the criteria of discrimination and *in bello* proportionality.[28]

It is of course true that even the most intelligent and conscientious people can be wrong, and that careful thinking about the just war criteria may nevertheless be compromised by mistakes in judgment. This leads to a final lesson. "Good" just war thinking involves honesty about our limits. When it comes to thinking about justice and war, as about politics in general, Milton's lines seem apt: "So little knows any / Save God alone / To value right / The good before him."[29] Or, to put it another way, just war discourse can benefit from a healthy sense of what Reinhold Niebuhr described as the ironic nature of political action, where "virtue becomes vice due to some hidden defect in the virtue, . . . strength becomes weakness because of the vanity to which strength may prompt the mighty [person] or nation, . . . security is transmuted into insecurity because too much reliance is placed upon it, [and] . . . wisdom becomes folly because it does not know its own limits."[30]

In the end, this is perhaps why it is best that, in the assessment of war as a means of statecraft, advocates of the just war tradition state their case in a dialogue with others who speak in terms of international law and a variety of strategic doctrines. We need not hope for a "triumph" of just war thinking. Instead, we should hope to maintain a seat at the table where policy is made, offering a perspective that may contribute in the development of judgments that may be described as both wise and sane.

NOTES

1. Michael Walzer, *The Triumph of Just War (and the Dangers of Success)* (New Haven, CT: Yale University Press, 2004), 3–22.

2. See, e.g., James Turner Johnson, *Morality and Contemporary Warfare* (New Haven, CT: Yale University Press, 1999); James Turner Johnson, *Ethics and the Use of Force* (Burlington, VT: Ashgate, 2011); Jean Bethke Elshtain, *Just War against Terror* (New York: Basic Books, 2003); and George Weigel, *Against the Grain: Christianity and Democracy, War and Peace* (New York: Crossroad, 2008).

3. Jimmy Carter, "Just War—Or a Just War?" *New York Times*, March 9, 2003.

4. The speech was delivered Dec. 10, 2009. The text is available at www.white house.gov/the-press-office/remarks-president-acceptance-nobel-peace-prize.

5. In this, I take it that Nicholas Rengger's doubts about the "triumph" of the just war idea overlap with mine, as he discusses it in chapter 16 of the present volume.

6. The phrase is borrowed from Paul Kennedy, *The Rise and Fall of the Great Powers* (New York: Random House, 1987), though he meant something rather different than I do.

7. Because the present volume consists of essays originally presented at a conference sponsored by the US Institute of Peace, it seems fitting to note that the project on "Western and Islamic Religious and Cultural Traditions on War, Peace, and Statecraft" was carried out with the help of a grant from the US Institute of Peace. The two resulting volumes of essays— *Cross, Crescent, and Sword*, and *Just War and Jihad*—were published by Greenwood Press in, respectively, 1990 and 1991.

8. John Kelsay, "Just War, Jihad, and the Study of Comparative Ethics," *Ethics & International Affairs* 24, no. 3 (2010): 227–38.

9. Troeltsch stated this in his lectures (originally delivered 1912–13 in Heidelberg) published under the title *The Christian Faith*, trans. Garret Paul (Minneapolis: Fortress Press, 1991), cf. 81, among other places.

10. See, e.g., Donald Davidson, *Inquiries into Truth and Interpretation* (New York: Oxford University Press, 1984).

11. Those unfamiliar with these texts will get a sense of the issues connected with "form" by consulting an essay I wrote: John Kelsay, "Al-Shaybani and the Islamic Law of War," *Journal of Military Ethics* 2, no. 1 (2003): 63–75; more generally, see John Kelsay, *Arguing the Just War in Islam* (Cambridge, MA: Harvard University Press, 2007). Also see chapter 6 by Nahed Artoul Zehr in the present volume, as well as Nahed Artoul Zehr, "Responding to the *Call*: Just War and Jihad in the War against Al-Qaeda" (PhD diss., Florida State University, 2011).

12. See, e.g., Jeff McMahan, *Killing in War* (New York: Oxford University Press, 2009).

13. This is the approach taken by US Conference of Catholic Bishops, *The Challenge of Peace* (Washington, DC: US Conference of Catholic Bishops, 1983); US Conference of Catholic Bishops, *The Harvest of Justice Is Sown in Peace* (Washington, DC: US Conference of

Catholic Bishops, 1994); and US Conference of Catholic Bishops, "Statement on Iraq," November 13, 2002, www.ctbi.org.uk/intaff/iraq/uscath01.htm.

14. I discuss the role of history and precedent in Johnson's work in John Kelsay, "James Turner Johnson, Just War Tradition, and Forms of Practical Reasoning," *Journal of Military Ethics* 8, no. 3 (2009): 179–89. Many of the specific issues mentioned are addressed in Johnson's recent book *Ethics and the Use of Force* (Burlington, VT: Ashgate, 2011).

15. From *Tales of the Mighty Dead* (Cambridge, MA: Harvard University Press, 2002). These two quotations are from the introduction to the volume, the first at p. 13, the second at p. 15. The more elaborate discussion is in the two essays on Hegel at 178–209 and 210–34. I note here that the "historical" model in which appeals to precedent take priority need not involve a rejection of principles and rules, understood as a kind of "shorthand" signifying the norms implicit in precedent. As well, it is interesting to note the development by scholars somewhat later than al-Shaybani and others, by which it was held that the *maqasid al-shari'a* or "purposes" of the Lawgiver govern the connection between precedent and contemporary situation—that is, one is always asking whether a given scholar's ruling is actually in accord with the protection of life, property, religion, and other "goods" that it is the purpose of the Lawgiver to preserve.

Aside from the issues associated with comparison, it is appropriate at this point to note certain differences between Brandom's notion of tradition and that of MacIntyre. As O'Driscoll and Lang note in their fine introduction to this volume, the latter "argues that all traditions contain within them a standard of some sort that enables us to determine what counts as a persuasive interpretation or extension of that tradition." Brandom's approach makes this more difficult, not least because "reconstruction" leaves more room for creativity. To put it another way, a "Brandomian" version of tradition makes it difficult to locate the standard of which MacIntyre speaks. As an example, consider the question with which historians of Christianity were occupied in the late nineteenth and early twentieth centuries: Given all its variations through time, was there an "essence" of Christianity? Those working in the mode of Adolf Harnack thought there was; someone like Troeltsch was less certain. There is more here than I can work out at present, but my inclination is to think that the just war tradition does have some characteristics or vocabulary by which it may be distinguished. For example, it would be difficult to characterize discourse about war which ignores or sidesteps interest in war as a public act, authorized by recognizably political leaders as arguing in the vein of just war tradition. As the historical record shows, however, the precise content of right authority does shift in accord with changes in political institutions—Thomas Aquinas's prince who does not answer to any other prince is not quite the same as the contemporary notion of constitutionally designated representatives who may declare war. The greater flexibility of Brandom's comments (at least, on my account) makes responding to the question O'Driscoll and Lang raise about authority *in* the just war tradition more complex. I am grateful for conversations with Rosemary Kellison on these points. Her dissertation in progress will contribute to the just war conversation on this and other points.

16. Along these lines, it is interesting to note that this speech, delivered on January 28, 1991, was presented to a meeting of the National Association of Religious Broadcasters. If one consults the collection of Bush's speeches reproduced by Micah L. Sifry and Christopher Cerf, *The Gulf War: History, Documents, Opinions* (New York: Times Books, 1991), it seems clear that the speech was an exception to the president's general preference for the language of international law or of the reciprocal duties owed by one state to other participants in the international political order. The point was, or seems to have been, that the bishops and other religious groups are in some sense brokers of moral (as opposed to legal or other) legitimation, and that the just war idea is tied to this area of interest.

17. E.g., Steven Simon and Jonathan Stevenson, "Afghanistan: How Much Is Enough?" *Survival* 51, no. 5 (October–November 2009): 47–67; Steven Simon and Jonathan Stevenson, "The Real Shock of Fort Hood," *Foreign Policy*, November 18, 2009; and also Steven Simon, "Can the Right War Be Won?" *Foreign Affairs* 88, no. 4 (July–August 2009).

18. Richard Haass, *War of Necessity, War of Choice* (New York: Simon & Schuster, 2009).

19. This is at least my recollection of Haass's response to my query about the relationship between his way of speaking and the just war tradition, during May 28, 2009, Council on Foreign Relations audio conference on "Justifiable Wars." The recording is available at www.cfr.org/about/outreach/religioninitiative/audio.html?groupby = 3&id = 1355&filter = 2009.

20. This point was made by Paul Ramsey, among others; cf. Paul Ramsey, *The Just War* (New York: Charles Scribner's Sons, 1968).

21. John Mearsheimer goes to some lengths to distinguish his version of realism from that of Niebuhr, and so far as I know, does not directly engage just war thinkers. But one could certainly develop Mearsheimer's various critiques of recent US foreign policy along the lines I suggest. For Mearsheimer's systematic statement, see John Mearsheimer, *The Tragedy of Great Power Politics* (New York: W. W. Norton, 2001); for more popular articles on current topics, see Mearsheimer's website (http://mearsheimer.uchicago.edu/pub-affairs.html). I note in particular John Mearsheimer, "Afghanistan: No More the Good War," *Newsweek*, December 7, 2009; John Mearsheimer, "Hans Morgenthau and the Iraq War: Realism versus Neo-Conservatism," opendemocracy.com, May 19, 2005; and John Mearsheimer, "Hollow Victory," *Foreign Policy* (online), December 2, 2009. All these are available on Mearsheimer's website.

22. I wrote these lines in the fall of 2010 and, as the text indicates, I had in view the debates of 2009. I offered a brief comment on the reasons for and possible direction of a reassessment of US and NATO strategy in Afghanistan in the concluding section of this essay (below). The article came back for revisions in the summer of 2011, and at the editors' urging, I offered the following comment on the death of Osama bin Laden:

> Here it may be of interest to note that, in my view, the death of bin Laden, while significant in at least two ways, probably does not in itself constitute a reason for such reassessment. Rather, the death of al-Qaeda's most visible leader is important (1) psychologically, especially for war-weary Americans; and (2) in terms of the organization of al-Qaeda, particularly with respect to its ability to mount a truly global resistance. With respect to this latter point, reports of material found in the compound at Abbottabad seem to indicate the ongoing importance of bin Laden in directing and arranging financing for various operations. These are roles that he played early on, but which many analysts thought had passed to others. Particularly with respect to financing, it may prove difficult for a successor to make use of the range of contacts developed by bin Laden. In my view, this suggests the likelihood that bin Laden's "successor" will not be one person, but several, and that these will operate on a more regional base.

I confess now (March 2013) that I thought one of those regional leaders might be Anwar al-Awlaki, who at the time seemed to be moving into a prominent role in al-Qaeda in the Arabian Peninsula. While his subsequent death renders that suggestion moot, the more general point about the future of al-Qaeda holds, I think. With respect to these matters, and in particular as regards US policy in Afghanistan, interested persons may wish to consult my more recent article "Just War Thinking as a Social Practice," *Ethics & International Affairs* 27, no. 1 (2013): 67–86.

23. This rests on a number of lectures I gave at universities, where I had a chance to talk with people knowledgeable about the just war tradition. The judgments are thus impressionistic and open for correction based on more systematic surveys.

24. In the version of this chapter presented for discussion in August 2010, I noted the (at that point) recent killing of ten members of a group with a well-established mission in Afghanistan, and wondered whether this constituted a change in policy or a departure from Mullah Omar's statements. Given that the justification offered cited those killed for attempting to convert Muslims to Christianity, my own thought was and remains that Taliban leaders wanted to distinguish this case, basically by saying that the group had been allowed to carry out its work under an assurance of security (*al-aman*) which required them to respect the law (i.e., Muslim law as understood by the Taliban). Preaching Christianity would constitute a violation of this agreement.

25. Along these lines, see the argument of Bing West, *The Wrong War* (New York: Random House, 2011).

26. This point is well made by Zehr, "Responding to the *Call.*"

27. This is the point made in West, *Wrong War*, when he suggests that NATO forces be reduced by half, to approximately 50,000. These remaining forces would then be charged to advise and train Afghan military and police, rather than to "clear, hold, and build." The task of nation building would then fall to the US State Department and to a network of international organizations.

28. In terms of the typology articulated by O'Driscoll and Lang, this focus on policymaking suggests an emphasis on the political purpose of just war tradition. Those who speak and write about questions of war would then be aiming at an audience of policymakers and those who influence them—for example, citizens who pay taxes, vote, and express opinions about the justification and conduct of war. Such an emphasis need not rule out other purposes. O'Driscoll and Lang's prophetic type, for example, is perfectly consonant with an interest in advising policymakers, in that such an interest presupposes a robust discussion, in which people really do say what they think. This seems to be the political equivalent of "speaking truth to power." The danger in policy discussions, whether connected with just war or other issues, seems to be the possibility of "groupthink" or the delimitation of robust exchanges of reasons. Because O'Driscoll and Lang mention Old Testament or Hebrew Bible examples, readers might be interested in the story at I Kings 22, in which the desire of the king of Israel to hear a certain message leads to a certain amount of foot-dragging with respect to seeking the counsel of Micaiah ("I hate him, for he never prophesies anything favorable about me, but only disaster"). All the other prophets tell the king what he wants to hear—a nice example of groupthink, or so it seems to me!

There may be times and places when just war discourse is frozen out of policy discussion. In such cases, the less "connected" form of prophecy suggested by O'Driscoll and Lang may be appropriate. I should also note that the pastoral type, which O'Driscoll and Lang connect to military ethics, seems complementary to an emphasis on politics. As to the philosophical type of just war discourse, see my comments on just war thinking as a kind of historical rationality (above).

29. These lines from *Paradise Lost* may be found in Book 4 of any edition. My use of the quotation is inspired by James Gustafson's at the end of volume 2 of his *Theocentric Ethics* (Chicago: University of Chicago Press, 1984).

30. From Reinhold Niebuhr, "Preface," in *The Irony of American History*, by Reinhold Niebuhr, with a new introduction by Andrew Bacevich (Chicago: University of Chicago Press, 2008), xxiv.

CHAPTER 16

The Wager Lost by Winning?

On the "Triumph" of the Just War Tradition

Nicholas Rengger

THE PERIOD SINCE THE END of World War II, and most especially from the 1970s to the present, has seen a revival of normative theorizing about war unparalleled since the seventeenth century. And in the main, such theorizing has tended to fellow relatively well-worn paths. Both explicitly religious and, especially, secular theorizing have focused to a very large extent on working broadly within the parameters of the just war tradition, the most influential European tradition of thought connected with the ethical evaluation of war. This is even true where (as in some recent cosmopolitan work) the tradition is also greatly reworked and true also in the worlds of political rhetoric and military law, as witnessed by the constant recitation of central *in bello* principles by senior allied officers in Afghanistan and Iraq and by the regular invocation of the tradition by politicians of many different stripes (e.g., think of Tony Blair's 1999 Chicago speech).

Thus, it is perhaps understandable that for many, the just war tradition can be seen to have triumphed as the appropriate moral language for the evaluation of the use of force in the modern period, as it did—at least formally—in late medieval and early modern times in Europe. Indeed, in their introduction to this volume, in discussing a "state of the art" in the tradition, Tony Lang and Cian O'Driscoll argue that "the just war tradition is the predominant moral language through which we address questions pertaining to the rights and wrongs of the use of force in international society. . . . It furnishes us with a set of concepts, principles, and analytical devices for making sense of the moral-legal questions that war raises."

They emphasize further that "the just war tradition is central to the practice of international relations. Its influence is evident in the legal codes that govern how modern militaries perform their duties, and it has featured prominently in the rhetoric surrounding the war on terror and the recent invasions of Iraq, Afghanistan and Libya." And thus they conclude that the tradition

> reflects an enduring effort to sustain the idea that, even when he finds himself in the trenches, man occupies a moral world. As such, the tradition should not be misconstrued as a simple *techne* or set of guidelines stipulating what is permissible in war. Rather, it comprises a tradition of political theory that invites us to think about war in a philosophical register. It challenges us to peer beyond the possibility of a narrowly defined "ethics of war," toward a broader engagement with the practice of rules and responsibilities, and rights and duties, as they relate to the violent edge of world politics. Underpinning this is a sustained inquiry into the relation between the use of force in international life and political authority understood as a practice.

There is much in this, of course, with which I am sure we would all agree: that would certainly be true in my own case. But there are also some reasons for being rather more skeptical about some of these claims, and in this chapter it is this skepticism—my differences, in other words, with Lang and O'Driscoll, rather than my agreements with them—on which I want to dwell. One disagreement, in particular, will occupy me just below, but let me start by flagging a couple of other areas where I have some doubts.

In the first place, whereas it is true that in Europe and its cultural analogues elsewhere the just war tradition is probably "a predominant moral language through which we address questions pertaining to the rights and wrongs of the use of force," it is hardly the only one. There was much sneering on the part of some (so-called) neoconservative theorists and (indeed) policymakers at the time of the Iraq invasion and before, about the just war tradition and its antiquated sense of "playing by the rules." Victor Davis Hanson's *An Autumn of War*, written during the campaign in Afghanistan in late 2001, spoke for many in its contempt for the tradition, and there were many other (in my view rather risible) references to the need for a "pagan ethos" (or what have you) to govern the use of force in the twenty-first century.[1] Not, of course, that there is anything especially new about this; the tradition has always had its critics—a rowdy and contentious lot, for the most part—and the recent additions to their number do not I think add anything very new. But it is indication that, even in its heartland so to speak, the tradition is hardly unchallenged.

And that of course raises a second concern. If one moves beyond its heartland, it is even less likely to be dominant in the way Lang and O'Driscoll suggest. It goes without saying that jihadist fighters in Waziristan do not subscribe to the tenets of the just war tradition and, in a different context, I doubt that the Chinese political elite have much time for notions of the just war, whatever their public protestations of support for international law. The game is given away, of course, by the crucial—though rather unexamined—prefix that Lang and O'Driscoll use: "The just war tradition," they say, "is the predominant moral language through which *we* address questions pertaining to the rights and wrongs of the use of force in international society."

The crucial question therefore is who the "we" applies to. I do not think it can reasonably be extended beyond the modern West and perhaps some of its cultural analogues elsewhere, in which case I doubt the tradition could sensibly be described as *the* predominant moral language, though it is certainly *a* dominant one in some times and places.[2]

The third area of some disagreement points to the main theme I take up in this chapter. Lang and O'Driscoll rightly emphasize the extent to which there is a broad consensus among scholars of the tradition at least on the character of basic just war principles, but they admit that there is also considerable disagreement over which have priority in what contexts and so on. I want to suggest that one tension, present in the tradition from the beginning, has become especially significant in the con-temporary context and yet has not been given anything like the prominence it deserves: the tension, that is to say, between those who see the tradition as funda-mentally about the righting of a wrong—or in modern parlance, the elimination of injustice—and those who believe it is fundamentally about the limitation of destructiveness.

In a recent book I argue that the just war tradition historically was about both the limitation of destructiveness and the elimination, or punishment, of wrongdo-ing, but that these twin pillars of the tradition in fact have always sat very uneasily together. In writers like Augustine, the tension is noted but is explained as the inevitable dissonances of our "fallen world." With the emergence of what James Turner Johnson calls "just war doctrine" in the sixteenth century, however, and especially in the evolution of the distinction between *jus ad bellum* and *jus in bello*, the dichotomy becomes both more pronounced and over time begins to pull the tradition in very different directions.[3] In particular, I argue that for a variety of particular reasons in recent just war thinking, the "limitations of destructiveness" element becomes increasingly recessed.[4]

There are, as I say, many reasons for this. Historically, it is partly a reaction to the growing dominance of the *jus in bello*, a dominance strongly reinforced by the obvious fact that the emergent states system in the seventeenth and eighteenth cen-turies assumed that sovereigns had the right to use force to uphold their interests, an assumption that necessarily pushed the "*jus ad bellum*" into the background. It is also noteworthy that it is precisely at this point, I think, that the notion of author-ity, so central to every thinker from Augustine to Vitoria, becomes increasingly muddy—a point to which I return briefly at the close of this chapter, and that raises one of the most interesting underexplored questions in contemporary social and political theory: the character of, and the relations between, notions of authority and of legitimacy.[5]

This process was further deepened, I think, by the development in the nineteenth century of the codification of international law and especially by the development of the "laws of war," in that these were understood in the nineteenth century, and subsequently, in terms of a certain jurisprudential reading of law, grounded on state power—in other words to a particular form of legal positivism predicated, largely at least, on a particular framing of the idea of the state. In the book I call this conception, following Michael Oakeshott, a "teleocratic" understanding of the state—and suggest that such an understanding becomes the central framing orientation at least for secular versions of the tradition—as I say, the theological versions are rather more ambiguously related—a framing device that is still influential even in the emergent so-called cosmopolitan just war theory of today. This is largely due to the centrality of teleocratic conceptions of politics—what politics is for and what it should do—which, in the postwar period, become centrally entwined with notions about the promotion of justice and the elimination of its opposite, a development strongly enhanced by the burgeoning justice industry that followed the astonishing success of Rawls's *A Theory of Justice*.[6] So let me say something about this conception—and its opposite—as background for what I want to say in general about the just war.

TWO UNDERSTANDINGS OF POLITICAL ASSOCIATION

Oakeshott developed his account of this kind of politics—along with its rival conception, nomocratic politics—most especially in *On Human Conduct*, and I want to offer a brief consideration of it. In the process I shall also somewhat amend it.[7] It consists essentially in the claim that modern European states—now usually termed "liberal democratic states," though Oakeshott does not call them that—inherit a political vocabulary that is radically polarized between two different, and opposing, understandings of the *character of the political association and the office of its government*.[8] Oakeshott famously describes these two understandings by borrowing two Latin terms from Roman private law: *societas* and *universitas*:[9] The former term denotes a mode of association that has "agents who by choice or circumstance are related to one another so as to comprise an identifiable association of a certain sort. The tie which joins them . . . is not that of an engagement in an enterprise to pursue a common substantive purpose or to promote a common interest, but that of loyalty to one another, the conditions of which may achieve the formality denoted by the kindred word legality."[10]

For Oakeshott, a state understood in these terms is thus a *civitas*, a civil association, "and its government (*whatever its constitution*) is a nomocracy whose laws are
understood as conditions of conduct, not devices instrumental to the satisfaction of
preferred wants" (emphasis added).[11]

Universitas, by contrast, is understood as "persons associated in a manner such
as to constitute them a natural person; a partnership of persons which is itself a
person, or in some important respects like a person; . . . [and] a state understood
in terms of *universitas* is . . . an association of intelligent agents who recognize
themselves to be engaged upon the joint enterprise of seeking the satisfaction of
some common substantive want . . . government here may be said to be teleocratic,
the management of a purposive concern."[12]

Oakeshott's point in his essay is to emphasize the extent to which the modern
European political consciousness is a *polarized* one and that *these* are its poles.
Although Oakeshott denies that we should see these two poles as in any sense "dominant or recessive" and also is consistent in opposing the view that one pole—the
enterprise association "teleocratic" pole—is somehow *inevitably* destined to be
dominant, he also points out that it is the latter understanding that has been—by
far—the more popular over the course of the last two hundred or so years.[13] And
he suggests some powerful reasons for this. Chief among these is the claim—I think
indisputable—that it is the enterprise association that best fits what he calls "the
demands of modern war."[14]

"In war itself," he remarks,

> the latent or not so latent ingredient of managerial lordship in the office of
> the government of a modern state comes decisively to the surface and is mag-
> nified . . . and what is plenary in a condition of actual war is merely somewhat
> diminished in the intervals between wars. . . . War and military preparation
> imposes this character upon a state more or less completely, not in proportion
> to its destructiveness, but in proportion to the magnitude of the claims it
> makes upon the attention, the energies and the resources of subjects; and the
> wars of modern times have been progressively more demanding in this
> respect. . . . [In short], although it may be difficult to find any modern Euro-
> pean state recognizably the counterpart of Sparta in antiquity (that is a state
> whose reputed purpose is itself war), the condition of almost continuous war-
> fare in modern times has familiarized Europe with the spectacle of states,
> significantly, if intermittently, transformed into enterprise associations; and
> this has been the chief nourishment of the belief that the state is properly to
> be understood in these terms.[15]

In other words, if we may adapt a phrase of Charles Tilly, "war made the state
and the state made war," but the state that war made was a state understood in a
certain way, as a "teleocratic," enterprise association. To this needs to be added,

Oakeshott thinks, the increasingly powerful sense of modern states as agents of the distribution of goods that aim at the satisfaction of particular wants, a sense made progressively more powerful by the rise of mass politics and the interests that this itself generated.[16]

Taken together, I suggest (and I think Oakeshott wants to suggest), all these things have created in modern states an orientation that is heavily disposed to see itself in terms of an enterprise association, and a central component of this understanding is the ordering of a society for "war." Of course, the common enterprise for which force may be used will shift over time; it may be obviously material in one generation—access to the goods and services of the empire, the "expansion of England"; and so forth—and more ideational in another—"intervention for humanitarian purposes" perhaps, as we shall see. Nonetheless, central to the understanding of a modern state as an enterprise association is a willingness to see a "common purpose" for which, under at least some circumstances, force is an entirely appropriate response; as Oakeshott says, the habits learned through endless preparation for war are retained in times of relative peace.

But of course there is not only one way of conceptualizing the state as an enterprise association. In *On Human Conduct*, Oakeshott suggests that we might see four different idioms of teleocratic belief. The first considers the state as a religious and cultural enterprise (Oakeshott clearly has in mind Calvinist Geneva as the sine qua non of this idea, though other countries at different times and to different degrees also approximate it). The second idiom understands the state as a corporate enterprise for exploiting the recourses of the Earth. This idiom derives ultimately, Oakeshott thinks, from a Baconian vision of the state, though it is more fully developed by Bacon's successors, such as St. Simon, Fourier, Marx, and Lenin (and also, one might add, though Oakeshott does not, by many extreme free market productivists).[17] The third idiom combines, in a curious way, the first two to provide a model of "enlightened government," in which the productivist and materialist purpose of the second is yoked to a quasi-moral understanding derived from the first to produce what Oakeshott sees as "the strongest strand of teleocratic belief in modern European thought."[18] And finally, one might see the state in this light as a "therapeutic" corporation, the function of which is remedial: treating an association of invalids or victims (perhaps the version for which Oakeshott expresses most contempt in *On Human Conduct*).

Oakeshott suggests, correctly I think, that all versions of teleocratic belief in contemporary political thought combine, to some degree, these four idioms and though, as I remarked, he sees the model of enlightened government as the "strongest strand" in contemporary thought, it is the second—the state seen as a fully fledged *civitas cupiditas*—that he thinks is, over the long term, the greatest threat to civil association. I think that he is right about this, but I also think that he underestimates the extent to which this idiom has been subsumed in what might be seen as a version of teleocracy that unites a model of enlightened government with a model of the political community, however constituted as a therapeutic enterprise. It is, I suggest, this version of the state that we find coalescing in much of the twentieth century.

However, there is an additional point here to which Oakeshott only briefly alludes but is central to the argument I want to make. This is simply that though this polarization originated in the context of the European *state*, it has long since passed into a much more generalized conception of politics that is not tied to the state alone. As Oakeshott remarks in a footnote: "It is perhaps worth notice that notions of 'world peace' and 'world government' which in the eighteenth century were explored in terms of civil association have in this century become projects of world management concerned with the distribution of substantive goods. The decisive change took place in the interval between the League of Nations and the United Nations"[19]

In fact, I think Oakeshott is wrong here. I think this move can be traced back much further—back, in fact, to the mid–nineteenth century, as we will see—but the general point is crucial: This is no longer simply a matter of "the state and the office of government" but rather a generalized view of the character of politics tout court.

TELEOCRATIC POLITICS AND THE JUST WAR

Teleocratic conceptions of politics have, as Oakeshott says, bitten deep into understandings of contemporary politics. And just as they have put their mark on all aspects of liberal democratic politics in general, so they have also had a profound impact on how such polities understand the inherited traditions of thinking about the use of force. And what such conceptions have effectively underwritten, in the context of the just war tradition, is an understanding of the tradition that recesses ideas of the tradition as centrally about the limitation of destructiveness and foregrounds ideas of the tradition as fundamentally about the pursuit of wrongdoing, seen as the elimination of injustice. What is visible, in almost all the different ways of reading the just war tradition influential in moral and political theory today—as well as in a good deal of contemporary international law—is a conception of the ethics of force as predominantly about the elimination of injustice, as a priority *over and above* the restraint of force and that, as a natural corollary, in a violent and conflictual world, the tradition is becoming progressively *less* restrictive. Where injustice is everywhere, the reasons to use force to oppose it are not hard to find, even if they are not always politically apposite or, indeed, possible.

This trajectory became especially pronounced in the 1980s and 1990s through debates over what is now called "humanitarian" intervention.[20] By caparisoning the use of force with the high moral ground of the protection of rights and the responsibilities accruing thereof—most obviously in recent doctrines such as the "responsibility to protect"—the scope of the possible use of force has been extended, not restricted; and at least arguably, the conceptual restrictions on its illicit use have also been weakened (think of the justification offered by the Russian government for its operations in Chechnya and Ingushetia after the United States decided to invade Afghanistan). And moreover, I suggest we see the quite logical extension of this idea in the sudden burgeoning of discussions of the necessity of, the moral requirement for, and the possibilities of using "preventive" force.

Much of this discussion, of course, does not use the categories of the just war at all; there have long been advocates of the use of preventive force, going back at least to Gentili and arguably long before. What is most significant, however, in the current vogue of thinking about preventive war is not the reaction from skeptics about the just war tradition or the laws of war but rather the reaction of those who might in general terms be seen as supporters. Over the last few years a wide range of writers otherwise committed to the rule of law in international affairs, or to the just war tradition, or both, have begun to suggest that, though the manner in which (for example) the George W. Bush administration articulated it was clearly mistaken—and possibly deeply damaging—the instinct that the changing circumstances of contemporary conflict warrant revisiting the notion of preventive war is correct and that, as a result, we need to think how we can work in a legitimate notion of preventive war to our thinking about legitimate force. Robert Keohane, Allen Buchanan, Phillip Bobbitt, David Luban, and, perhaps in most detail, Michael Doyle have all made this case, and none are in the usual camp of skeptics about the tradition; quite the contrary.

Keohane and Buchanan, for example, have argued that "within an appropriate rule governed, institutional framework that is designed to help protect vulnerable countries against unjustified interventions without creating unacceptable risks of the costs of inaction, decisions to employ preventive force can be justified."[21] In the course of their argument they identify four contemporary positions on the use of force, which they term the just war blanket prohibition (the traditional just war view), the legal status quo, the national interest (the standard realist line that states do what they will), and the expanded right of self-defense (essentially the Bush administration's position as articulated in the 2002 *National Security Strategy*). All these views are insufficient, they argue, for the changed circumstances of the contemporary world; and so they propose a fifth, a cosmopolitan institutional view, predicated on a commitment to the human rights of all persons. Such a commitment, they argue, manifestly justifies the permissibility of force to prevent "presently occurring" massive human rights violations, and this has already been accepted by international actors, for example, in the context of the Kosovo intervention in 1999. They thus suggest—and I think that the logic is at one level impeccable—that there is, therefore, a prima facie argument for the permissibility of force to *prevent* massive violations of basic human rights. They stipulate that this argument applies not to any possible harms but to "situations where there is a significant risk of sudden and very serious harms on a massive scale" and add that "such a risk is inherent in weapons of mass destruction but not exclusive to them. Genocides may also erupt suddenly."[22]

For reasons that I will explain just below, it is, I think, exceptionally disturbing that among the contemporary advocates of preventive war, one finds both strong supporters of the just war tradition (which has always excoriated it) and also strong supporters of the international rule of law (which has always outlawed it). But I think that at one level they are correct. *If* one thinks of the just war (or the ethics of force) primarily in teleocratic terms as an instrument for the elimination of injustice, then the argument follows: that they do think this—and that, in large part, they have the warrant of the "secular just war theory" of the contemporary period to do so—is clear; the question, therefore, is whether we should think of it in that way.

WHAT IS WRONG WITH TELEOCRACY?

At this point, I do not doubt, there may very well be readers who are itching to tell me that though the "teleocratic" styles of politics to which I draw attention might, in some contexts, be susceptible to corruption or excess, they are also part of an important shift in international political sensibilities—and perhaps of political sensibilities more generally—toward a recognition that the international community must take a more proactive role in certain areas of global life than it traditionally has done. Thus, in a globalizing age, global order and good global governance *require* a more coordinated set of responses, at least on certain issue areas, than the classic "system of states" model provides, and therefore a more purposive international system, at least in principle, is not a bad thing at all.

We must regulate—such critics would suggest—the global economy or we will have endless repetition of the 2007–8 global financial crash. We need a system for managing international security problems that can react when necessary to large-scale threats; we need regional associations that can share the heavy lifting in particular contexts, and these need structure and oversight; and perhaps most significantly of all, we need to be able to address the large and growing challenges that cannot be met by any one country acting alone—climate change, environmental degradation, cross-border issues of many kinds, and so on.

To meet these challenges (my critics might well say) we *need* a teleocratic vision, a vision of politics that can put the resources of the community—be it state, regional, or global—behind the necessary common purposes that we *must* have. And only if we do have such a vision can we expect the slow civilizing of the "uncivil condition" that is, and has been, the default understanding of international politics for much of its history. As Andrew Hurrell, in one of the most sophisticated and thoughtful articulations of this position, puts it: "The conservative ideal, embodied in the work of Hayek and Oakeshott, that political life should be concerned only with limited procedural rules governing coexistence, cannot be satisfactorily applied to the conditions of global political life in the twenty-first century which *require the identification of substantive collective goals and the creation of institutionalized structures of governance to implement them*" (emphasis added).[23]

Leaving aside the question of whether it is entirely appropriate to yoke Oakeshott and Hayek together in this way, or whether the forms of Nomocratic politics that might be opposed to teleocracy are best seen as merely "limited procedural rules governing co-existence," it is clear that the vast majority of commentary on contemporary global order would broadly agree with Hurrell, without necessarily sharing the particular nuances of his argument (and probably without sharing his moral and intellectual capaciousness either).[24] Many, indeed, would go much further. Critical theorists such as Andrew Linklater, and advocates of cosmopolitan democracy such as David Held, would argue that Hurrell's broadly liberal internationalism does not go anything like far enough; that it gives too much ground to the Realists and the pluralists.[25] But still they would agree that here is no way back from a broadly teleocratic conception of politics (at all levels) if we are to address the challenges that face us.

And in this context they would also add that surely the trajectories I have identified in the just war tradition are surely a source of hope, not a reason for despair. What, they might argue, *should* we do in the event of genocide or the fact or the possibility of large-scale mass killing? Surely under some circumstances preventive war *will* be better than the alternatives, and the richness of recent just war writing gives us ample material to construct ways of assessing and evaluating the use of such force—whether by states, regional agencies, the UN, private security firms, or anyone else. If we have, as in theory we do now have, a "responsibility to protect," surely we should exercise that responsibility, and for that purpose the "new just war" is surely extraordinarily helpful.[26]

These are all powerful and serious points, well made, and I do not have, and certainly cannot attempt in the space available to me here, a complete response to them. Rather I want to gesture toward what I think a response might look like.

The point I would seek to emphasize is not to suggest that teleocratic conceptions of politics have no place in our accounts of politics: It is the *dominance* of teleocratic conceptions of politics to which I have objected, not their existence as such. As Oakeshott argues in *On Human Conduct*, the growth of conceptions of teleocratic politics in Europe came about very much as a response to an already-extant idea about the appropriate form of political association. So there may indeed be instances or contexts in which such conceptions provide a resource. But that is premised on the associated idea that such conceptions exist alongside other conceptions that can "balance" them. It is that which, I would argue, seems increasingly no longer to obtain.

Which brings me, of course, to the obvious question: *Why* do I think a predominantly teleocratic politics should be seen as a problem and not, as the above suggestion would suppose, part of the solution? In the space I have here, I can only outline my response to this question—and certainly cannot even begin to defend it—but the crucial point is to emphasize what we lose if teleocratic politics triumphs—as, in so many ways, I think it has.

The chief casualty of this process, Oakeshott thinks (and I agree), is the great achievement of modern European political thought: the idea of civil association. For Oakeshott, modern European political thought emerges not from classical or Roman models, however central these were in second-order terms, but rather from medieval ideas and practices. In particular, it emerges from what one might term the decay of the medieval synthesis. Civil association for Oakeshott was the kind of political association appropriate for the kinds of people we became as a result of that process: "self-determined autonomous human beings seeking the satisfaction of their wants in self-chosen transactions with others of their kind," adding that the *persona*, who is the counterpart of civil association, is the persona "who Montaigne and Rabelais celebrated."[27] And that, I suggest, is significant. For the persona that Montaigne and Rabelais celebrated was not, as Oakeshott is at pains to point out, "a savage egoist, nor a cold 'capitalist' nor the contemptible *bourgeois* of legend."[28]

Instead, he or she is an individual, a "self-determined autonomous human agent," who displays "a disposition to cultivate the 'freedom' inherent in agency, to enjoy individuality and . . . to readily concede virtue to this exercise of personal autonomy acquired in self-understanding."[29]

In terms Oakeshott uses elsewhere in *On Human Conduct*, such a *persona* displays a

> disposition to be "self-employed" in which a man recognizes himself and all others in terms of self determination: that is in terms of wants rather than slippery satisfactions and of adventures rather than uncertain outcomes. . . . And since men are apt to make gods whose characters reflect what they believe to be their own, the deity corresponding to this self understanding is an Augustinian god of majestic imagination who, when he might have devised an untroublesome universe, had the nerve to create one composed of self employed adventurers of unpredictable fancy, to announce to them some rules of conduct, and thus to acquire convives capable of answering back in civil tones with whom to spend an eternity in conversation.[30]

Such an individual requires, Oakeshott suggests, the unconditional and ethical noninstrumentalism guaranteed by civil association and denied in fact, if not always in name, by teleocracy. This "individual" and the mode of association appropriate for such, are, Oakeshott insists, a modern creation, but both are rooted in much older ideas; they are, he says, a "modification," of the conditions of medieval life and thought.

But there is, as well, a *persona*—or better, perhaps, a range of *personae*—appropriate to teleocracy. The animating disposition of these *personae* is to fear the "freedom inherent in agency" and to "prefer substantive satisfaction to the adventure and risk of self enactment."

And if we think of "world order" in general not as teleocrats (of any stripe) might do but as partners in civil association might do, we can see something else, I think. As Stephen Clark puts it,

> We all live within networks of familial and friendly relationships, that states gain such authority as they have only by embodying . . . values that transcend the merely economic and contractual, that business, sects and nations all have their part to play in a civilized world order whose lineaments are visible in times of war as well as in times of peace. . . . The world of our human experience . . . is still structured by familial affection, sexual desire and trade, by the demands of hospitality and word once given, by the spirits of our different nations, by war and innocence and the world's beauty.[31]

It is precisely such a conception of international order that a teleocratic conception of politics can never allow. For Oakeshott, civil association is to the "self-enacted" individual, an opening out toward that wider world, in which, as Clark suggests, "the gods . . . keep just their ancient places"; teleocracy represents a closing down of it.[32]

Civil understandings of politics require, as both Oakeshott and Clark emphasize, an Augustinian recognition of the limits of our knowledge and a humility toward our capacity to alter the conditions of our existence—an "anti-Pelagian" recognition, if you will—a recognition that accommodates us to the continuing importance of charity and mercy and the possibilities that exist for us to make spaces for these and related virtues in our world. Teleocratic understandings, however, close off such options and emphasize the common purposes that would trump the plurality and many-sided "uncenteredness" of a genuinely civil international order.

My reason for being very suspicious of claims that expand the *provenance* of war—even when the claims are predicated on admirable moral assumptions—is that such claims are always going to be the enemy of civil politics understood in this sense. As we have seen, claims about humanitarian intervention and about preventive war often arise from very understandable, and in many respects very welcome, ethical concerns. But such concerns in themselves should also make us wary, because one of the central assumptions of seeing politics as civil (and therefore limited) is that in general terms people cannot be trusted with too much power, and expanding the power of the state—or, indeed, of other agencies as proxies for states—to make war, even for very good reasons, *necessarily* (and not just contingently) *will* give them too much power. As I say, this does not mean that war can never be justified—sometimes the danger is indeed enough to warrant the risk, and the lineaments of a civil world order are (or should be) visible in times of war as well as times of peace—but it does mean that trajectories, policies, and institutional schemes devised with the intent of making war more permissible—even in very limited contexts—should always be viewed with real skepticism and suspicion. By definition, such schemes run the very real risk—even when its advocates are unambiguously of good intent—of creating a situation where the cure is worse than the disease.

The basic problem with the teleocratic conception of politics is that it turns what is (and should be) an understanding of, and welcoming of, plurality into a monistic conception—though of course the substance of that monism will be very different for different teleocrats. And it will do this not just contingently but necessarily. And in the context of the just war tradition, it will expand, and not limit, the scope of legitimate force. And in doing that, not only will the possibility of civil politics at all levels be weakened—which for those of us who see the *persona* of civil association as one we should welcome and adopt would be bad enough—but it would also I think profoundly weaken one of the central elements of the just war tradition itself: its emphasis on the limitation of the destructiveness of war.

One other thing is, I think, relevant here, given one of the concerns this book has had from the introductory chapter onward, and so I just want to gesture toward it in a few final remarks. In that introduction, Lang and O'Driscoll, citing Johnson, point out that it is (to put it no stronger) rather odd that the notion of proper authority has been so little explored in the modern just war literature. They suggest, in my view quite correctly, that one of the central reasons for this was the effective equivalence in the modern period of notions of state sovereignty and proper authority and go on to map out a richer notion of "authority" that they hope to deploy in connection with the just war tradition. In his fine contribution James Turner Johnson also points out that "classic just war thinking was right to hold that use of arms is just only when authorized by a ruler responsible for the common good, employed for the purposes of protecting the common good and punishing threats to it, and intended to produce or restore peace."[33]

But it is also worth considering that the notion of the common good is very different when considered from the standpoint of a teleocracy, on the one hand, or a nomocracy, on the other. In the latter case, what is "common" will be by definition noninstrumental and nonpurposive. In the former case, however, "common" goods will be targets to aim at, purposes to be pursued, ends to be sought. A properly constituted authority in the nomocratic case, however, will possess "authority" because, as Oakeshott remarks, "authority will be the only conceivable attribute it could be indisputably acknowledged to have."[34] In the teleocratic case, however, because teleocracy thinks of the common good in instrumental terms, the point will precisely be the content of the "purposes," whatever they might be said to be.

Why is this significant in the present context? Because it seems to me that, given the dominance of teleocratic conceptions of politics, "authority" in the sense required by the tradition will itself be essentially contested. Indeed, to put it perhaps a little provocatively, it might be said that in contemporary international relations and law, we have no "authority," only "legitimacy"—which can be bound to the desirability of particular states of affairs, and thus common goals or purposes. Although it is important enough in its own right, of course, legitimacy should not be confused with authority. And in the context of the decision to use force, in the modern world at least, this suggests that though there may be "legitimate" decisions to use force, there will be very few that are truly "authoritative."[35]

And this brings me back to the wager I mention in my title. By wagering on a teleocratic conception of the just war, the tradition may have well adapted itself to the prevailing mores of the contemporary world and thereby at least begun to achieve, and at least in certain contexts, the "triumph" of which Lang and O'Driscoll spoke. But in "winning," the tradition would also lose, I think, for ultimately a teleocratic world is a functional one, and the language of functionalism is always ultimately one of power. As Noel O'Sullivan points out in his subtle and illuminating study of the evolution of postwar European political thought, power can of course be used benignly; but even if and when it is, something is still lost: the possibility of civil association and all that goes with it.[36] As he remarks, one might recall, in this context, the situation of Rome after the Battle of Actium: "When Augustus effected a revolutionary shift from republic to empire with such subtlety that few noticed the dramatic change that had occurred. . . . For two centuries thereafter Romans enjoyed an imperial golden age. They enjoyed it, however, by sacrificing *libertas* to non-accountable *imperium*."[37]

In the contemporary context, the just war tradition may well have "triumphed" as the preferred language for the moral assessment of the use of force. But inasmuch as it has triumphed in alliance with a teleocratic conception of politics and all that brings with it, its triumph will, I suspect, ultimately be a defeat: a wager lost by winning.

NOTES

Elements of this chapter are drawn from Rengger, *Just War and International Order: The Uncivil Condition in World Politics* (Cambridge: Cambridge University Press, 2013). I should also acknowledge that the inspiration for my title comes from the wonderful short story "A Wager Lost by Winning," by John Brunner. He bears no responsibility for the use to which I have put it here!

1. This reference is to Robert Kaplan's short book *Warrior Politics: Why Leadership Demands a Pagan Ethos* (New York: Vintage, 2003), actually one of the better and more literate of such arguments.

2. This point is admirably developed, though obviously in ways that would in some respects differ from mine, by John Kelsay in chapter 15 of this volume.

3. I do not mean to imply by this that Johnson is thinking of the tradition simply as a "doctrine." He is very clear—much clearer than many others—that it is a tradition. The

point is merely to emphasize that its recognizable form takes shape roughly between the thirteenth and the sixteenth centuries.

4. See Nicholas Rengger, *Just War and International Order: The Uncivil Condition in World Politics* (Cambridge: Cambridge University Press, 2013). The point about the growth of the *jus in bello* and its significance was also aired in some detail in an earlier paper that fed into the book. See Nicholas Rengger, "The Jus in Bello in Historical and Philosophical Perspective," in *War and Philosophy*, ed. Larry May (Cambridge: Cambridge University Press, 2008).

5. I have discussed this point in general terms in a paper focusing on Fritz Kratochwil's signal engagement with the topics. See Nicholas Rengger, "Rules, Norms, Revisions?" in *On Rules, Politics, and Knowledge*, ed. Cecilia Lynch, Oliver Kessler, Rodney Bruce Hall, and Nicholas Onuf (London: Palgrave Macmillan, 2010).

6. John Rawls, *A Theory of Justice* (Cambridge, MA: Harvard University Press, 1971).

7. However, it is worth adding that Oakeshott developed his ideas on these two understandings over many years, and earlier versions appear in many places in his unpublished writings and lectures. See Michael Oakeshott, *On Human Conduct* (Oxford: Clarendon Press, 1975).

8. Similar in form, though not at all in content, is Quentin Skinner's development of two equally differing accounts of what he calls "our common life"; one which sees sovereignty as a possession of the people, the other of the state; one emphasizes the citizen, the other the sovereign. This is implied, of course, by Quentin Skinner, *The Foundations of Modern Political Thought* (Cambridge: Cambridge University Press, 1978), but is developed much more explicitly in his three-volume *Visions of Politics* (Cambridge: Cambridge University Press, 2003) and is crucial to his development of "republican political thought," as noted earlier. Note, for interest, Oakeshott's critique of Skinner in his review of *The Foundations* in the *Historical Journal* 23, no. 2 (1980): 449–53.

9. A rather different deployment of these ideas, in connection with international relations—indeed as modes of understanding international society itself—is given by Terry Nardin, *Law, Morality and the Relations of States* (Princeton, NJ: Princeton University Press, 1983).

10. Oakeshott, *On Human Conduct*, 202.

11. Ibid., 203.

12. Ibid.

13. The best general discussion of this can be found in the excellent book by Paul Franco, *The Political Philosophy of Michael Oakeshott* (New Haven, CT: Yale University Press, 1990), esp. 215–22.

14. Oakeshott, *On Human Conduct*, 322.

15. Ibid., 272–74.

16. This is discussed in many places in Oakeshott's work—see, e.g., his essay "The Masses in Representative Government" in the expanded edition of *Rationalism in Politics* (Indianapolis: Liberty Fund, 1991). For another interesting, if idiosyncratic, reading of this phenomenon, see Christopher Lasch, *The True and Only Heaven: Progress and Its Critics* (New York: W. W. Norton, 1991).

17. Best discussed in Bacon's *The New Atlantis*.

18. Oakeshott, *On Human Conduct*, 286.

19. Ibid., 313n1.

20. Among an avalanche of commentary, for an especially sober and well-thought-out account, see Nicholas Wheeler, *Saving Strangers: Humanitarian Intervention and International Society* (Oxford: Oxford University Press, 2000).

21. Allen Buchanan and Robert Keohane, "The Preventive Use of Force: A Cosmopolitan Institutional Proposal," *Ethics and International Affairs* 18, no. 1 (2004): 1–22, at 1.

22. Ibid., 5.

23. Andrew Hurrell, *On Global Order: Power, Values and the Constitution of International Society* (Oxford: Oxford University Press, 2007), 298. It is worth pointing out that Hurrell is very far from being an uncritical supporter of teleocracy. In many respects he has affinities with the "pluralist" version of the Realistic response above.

24. My own view is that it is not entirely appropriate to yoke Oakeshott and Hayek together in this way, in that Hayek, although advocating a minimal and procedural order, did so for instrumental reasons almost wholly at variance with Oakeshott's understanding. However, that is a matter for another day. In reference to the last point, again, I do not think it is—certainly not in Oakeshott's case.

25. For Linklater, this was argued perhaps most obviously in Andrew Linklater, *The Transformation of Political Community* (Cambridge: Polity Press, 1997); but see also his ongoing three-volume study of the problem of harm and global civilizing processes, the first volume of which is now published. Also see Andrew Linklater, *The Problem of Harm in World Politics: Theoretical Investigations* (Cambridge: Cambridge University Press, 2011). For Held, this was originally advocated in David Held, *Democracy and the Global Order* (Cambridge: Polity Press, 1995), but also in many subsequent works.

26. The literature on "R2P," as it is now known, has become in a stunningly short time immense and it is growing all the time—a sure sign of its rhetorical power, if nothing else. Good and nonhysterical accounts are given by Gareth Evans, *The Responsibility to Protect: Ending Mass Atrocity Crimes Once and for All* (Washington, DC: Brookings Institution Press, 2008); and Alex Bellamy, *Responsibility to Protect: The Global Effort to End Mass Atrocities* (Cambridge: Polity Press, 2009).

27. Oakeshott, *On Human Conduct*, 315.

28. Ibid., 322.

29. Ibid., 239.

30. Ibid., 324.

31. Stephen Clark, *Civil Peace and Sacred Order* (Oxford: Clarendon Press, 1989), 159.

32. Ibid.

33. Johnson, chapter 1 of this volume.

34. Oakeshott, *On Human Conduct*, 154.

35. This is the merest sketch of a distinction that I hope to develop in subsequent work.

36. See Noel O'Sullivan, *European Political Thought since 1945* (London: Palgrave 2004), especially the argument of chapter 7.

37. Ibid., 189.

Conclusion

Reclaiming the Just War Tradition for International Political Theory

Cian O'Driscoll

WE OPENED THIS VOLUME with a brief discussion of President Obama's remarks upon the receipt of his Nobel Peace Prize in December 2009. These remarks, the reader will recall, challenged members of the international community to find new ways of thinking about "just war" and how it should apply to the battlefields of the twenty-first century. It was in light of these remarks that we, the editors and various contributors to this volume, agreed to meet in Washington in the summer of 2010 to discuss the current state of play and future prospects of that tradition. The conversation that we began in Washington has since carried on for two years, resulting in many rich debates. The essays gathered in this volume are the result of these exchanges—but they also function as a freeze-frame or snapshot of a dialogue that is still ongoing, and will hopefully have a life beyond this particular installment.

On a personal note, the urgency and importance of this dialogue was brought home to me on a recent field trip, undertaken with graduate students in my university's global security program, to Brussels. The highlight of the trip was undoubtedly a visit to SHAPE—Supreme Headquarters Allied Powers Europe—during which a senior member of NATO's top brass addressed our delegation. Recently returned from NATO's Chicago Summit, the official (whom I am not at liberty to name) generously shared his views on the challenges NATO will confront in the coming decade.[1] At the top of his concerns was NATO's working relationship with the United Nations. This was a topic, he confided, that had been foremost in the minds of NATO planners since the 1999 Kosovo mission, which had raised troublesome questions about the scope of NATO's authority and jurisdiction vis-à-vis the use of force in the service of international peace and security. But this is apparently not the only matter that looms large on NATO's radar. The rise of cybercrime and the related threat of cyberwarfare are also liable to keep officials awake at night. Because

the control of the internet lies overwhelmingly (95 percent) in private hands, orthodox security actors such as NATO and its member states must think long and hard
about how to tackle the specter of cyberattacks (e.g., the one that targeted Estonia
in 2007) and who should be assigned this responsibility. The question, once again,
is one of authority and jurisdiction. The final concern stated by the NATO official
was about the issues that arise in relation to piracy and the privatization of security,
with special reference to the recent publication of plans for the assembly of a private
navy (funded by Martin Reith, the founder and former chief executive officer of the
Lloyd's of London insurer Ascot Underwriting) comprising eighteen ships to escort
merchant ships through the Gulf of Aden, a piracy hot spot.[2]

This NATO official's views are interesting, I think, because they reveal both the
centrality and difficulty of questions of authority as they pertain to the use of military force in today's complex security environment. These are, it is important to
stress, the questions that are currently keeping our political and military leaders
busy. Following from this, I would like to use these concluding remarks to reflect
upon whether the chapters in this volume offer us any purchase on these questions.
Or, at the very least, do they suggest to us how—if at all—the just war tradition
might function as a resource for addressing them? Although one could speak at
great length on this topic, I restrict myself to four key points related to the four
approaches to authority that dominate this volume.

THE AUTHORITY OF THE JUST WAR TRADITION

We can begin with the authority of the just war tradition as a site of moral discourse
in international affairs. From where is this authority derived? Turning back to Obama's Nobel address, it is interesting to note that he secured his reference to just war
by invoking the historical tradition out of which it emerged over time: "And over
time, as codes of law sought to control violence within groups, so did philosophers
and clerics and statesmen seek to regulate the destructive power of war. The concept
of 'just war' emerged." Obama's own appeals to the just war tradition in relation to
the challenges of the twenty-first century should be afforded respect, he went on to
imply, as both faithful to this heritage and an attempt to build upon it. Indeed, it
was in this spirit that his remarks were judged—favorably by some, less so by
others.[3] What unifies both Obama and his supporters and detractors, however, is
the common conviction that his just war talk derives its authority from the tradition
it invokes.

Some contributors to this volume—James Turner Johnson, John Kelsay, and
Gregory Reichberg, for example—endorse Obama's view. Others, however, would
likely frame the matter in a subtly different way. Nigel Biggar, for instance, without
discounting the importance of history as a repository of human experience, offers
a Christian theological account of love and natural flourishing as a source of just

war values. And Chris Brown, for his part, places less stock in the precise form of the historical canon of just war thought than in its capacity to continue evolving and guiding moral judgment now and into the future. Others, like Laura Sjoberg, go even further and challenge the basis of the tradition's ostensible authority.

What are we to make of these differences and disagreements? Do they indicate a fracturing of the just war idea such that it becomes nigh impossible to talk about a coherent just war tradition? The experience of compiling this volume suggests otherwise. It rather suggests that the diversity of approaches showcased here is not necessarily a problem, and may even be beneficial. The pluralism among our contributors functioned as a spur to dialogue, a stimulus for clarity of argumentation, and a safeguard against reductive monism. Moreover, this pluralism is reflective of the context within which contemporary just war thought takes place—as such, it is probably something to celebrate rather than bemoan.

AUTHORITIES ON THE JUST WAR TRADITION

The second point follows directly from the first. It is the contention that the question—raised in the introduction—of how to determine who qualifies as an authoritative interpreter of the just war tradition is both somewhat beside the point but also, as we shall see, productive. It is beside the point because, if we value pluralism and see it as a source of inspiration for dialogue and exchange, we should not cavil excessively about the credentials (or lack thereof) of those who seek to join our conversations. To draw on the language we employed in the introduction to this volume, one does not need to be *an* authority on the just war tradition in order to engage with it. To insist otherwise would disaggregate the tradition from its democratic context and reduce it to an elite affair.[4] Of course, not all the contributors to this volume will agree with this point. Many will argue that the tradition is in danger of being hollowed out or diminished by those who show no understanding of it and use it loosely; that is to say that the tradition must be preserved from those who do not have expert knowledge of it but would invoke (and thereby corrupt) it all the same.

But whichever side of the argument one adopts, the question of how to determine who qualifies as an authoritative interpreter of the just war tradition is fruitful to ponder. It prods us to think about what we value most about the tradition, and what kind of tradition we wish to cultivate. Do we, for example, strive for a tradition that remains true to its sources? Or do we wish to encourage a tradition that is protean and adaptive to the shifting norms of international politics? And are these ends incommensurable, or are they reconcilable? Viewed in concert, the chapters in this volume both demonstrate the significance of these questions and provide instructive examples for how we might go about tackling them.

AUTHORITY AS A CATEGORY OF
THE JUST WAR TRADITION

The third point refers to how we conceive of authority as a category or principle of the *jus ad bellum*. It follows a refrain that has echoed throughout this volume: that we should not treat authority in relation to the right to war in algorithmic terms.[5] That is, we should not seek a technical or tick-box definition of authority that could be used in a checklist approach to determining whether a war was justified or not. We should not, then, fool ourselves into thinking that we can devise a rote definition of proper authority, attach it some entities such as the UN Security Council or sovereign states, and be done with it. The matter is much more complex than this. Because political authority is itself a site of contestation—one that bears an intimate relation with both power and legitimacy—and because it can take many forms— pastoral, philosophical, prophetic, and political—it ought to invite problematization rather than (to use another ugly word) operationalization.[6] The point that I am reaching for here is that when we see the concept of proper authority invoked in just war writings, our response should not be to ask whether it is "satisfied" or not, whatever that might mean. Instead, our response should be to investigate the predicates of this postulation. This entails asking more questions. What work is the reference to authority intended to do in the context of this claim? What legal or normative claims does it rest upon? What are its parameters and conditions of possibility? And what possible political aims are achieved (and obviated) by deploying authority in this manner? Our hope is that the chapters in this volume provide the willing and interested scholar with a sense of how one might go about not only asking but also pursuing such questions.

THE JUST WAR TRADITION AS
A PRACTICE OF AUTHORITY

The fourth and final point brings us full circle, back to the fact that leaders like President Obama have—when it has suited them—adopted the terminology of the just war tradition as their own.[7] Whether we perceive this development as (following Michael Walzer) a good to be celebrated or (following Ken Booth) as a pernicious abuse of moral rhetoric to be resisted, it seems to be the case that the just war tradition is best understood not only (to borrow Paul Ramsey's memorable phrase) as a matter of "Christian conscience" but also as a practice of political authority.[8] When we conceive of the just war tradition in these terms, we do not set questions of moral obligation aside from the vicissitudes of international political life. Rather, we connect them with both the ebb and flow of international norms and institutions and the cut and thrust of realpolitik. This is, we would argue, a forthright and ambitious agenda to set before anyone interested in the just war tradition.

Our view is that the adoption of such an approach would enrich the field of just war studies. Some scholars, however, will disagree, claiming that this approach risks framing the tradition too broadly, such that—to paraphrase Stephen Walt's critique of the contemporary inclination to expand the concept of security to include non-traditional issues—it simultaneously becomes everything and nothing.[9] At stake here is nothing less than the question of what kind of just war tradition we wish to cultivate. Thus we will be interested to see if this approach provokes any response or commentary from the community of just war scholars.

CONCLUSION

What kind of response would we like to see this book generate? Although it is not in our gift to determine such things, suffice it to say that we would be very happy if this book prompted scholars of the just war tradition to think a little bit more deeply about how they treat the principle of proper authority in their writings on just war. As the preceding pages hopefully indicate, this is not as modest an ambition as it first appears. On the one hand, it signals a refusal to treat the requirement of proper authority as a proxy for state sovereignty, a formal box to be ticked but not opened up. On the other hand, it invites us to think about proper authority as a concept that both situates and problematizes the practice of just war within the normative-institutional and hard-power dynamics of international society. In this respect, we might even go so far as to tweak Walzer's well-known formulation and suggest that the aim of this book is to reclaim the just war tradition for *international political theory*.[10]

NOTES

1. On the NATO summit at Chicago, see NATO, "Summit Meetings of Heads of State and Government," Chicago, May 20–21, 2012, www.nato.int/cps/en/natolive/events_84074 .htm. On SHAPE, see Supreme Headquarters Allied Powers Europe, "What Is SHAPE?" www.aco.nato.int/shape.aspx.

2. Ocean Protection Services, "Private Fleet Worth 30m Set to Fight Somali Pirates," www.oceanprotectionservices.com/articles/?p = 1647.

3. E.g., George Weigel, "The Just-War Tradition," *National Review Online*, December 12, 2009, www.nationalreview.com/articles/228786/just-war-tradition/george-weigel.

4. On the democratic context within which contemporary just war thinking takes place, see chapter 4 in this volume by John Williams.

5. This term is used by Chris Brown and Joseph Boyle in chapters 2 and 10, respectively. It is echoed elsewhere in the volume, but referred to with different terminology.

6. On the relationship between power, authority, and legitimacy, see chapter 7 in this volume by Tarik Kochi.

7. For more on this, see chapters 15 and 16 by, respectively, John Kelsay and Nicholas Rengger.

8. Paul Ramsey, *War and the Christian Conscience: How Shall Modern War Be Conducted Justly?* (Durham, NC: Duke University Press, 1961).

9. Stephen M. Walt, "The Renaissance of Security Studies," *International Studies Quarterly* 35, no. 2 (1991): 211–39.

10. Michael Walzer, *Just and Unjust Wars: A Moral Argument with Historical Illustrations* (New York: Basic Books, 1992).

Contributors

Nigel Biggar is Regius Professor of Moral and Pastoral Theology at the University of Oxford, where he is also director of the McDonald Centre for Theology, Ethics, and Public Life. His publications include *In Defence of War: Christian Realism and the Use of Force* (2013); *Behaving in Public: How to Do Christian Ethics* (2011); *Religious Voices in Public Places* (coeditor, with Linda Hogan, 2009); *Aiming to Kill: The Ethics of Suicide and Euthanasia* (2004); and *Burying the Past: Making Peace and Doing Justice after Civil Conflict* (editor, 2003).

Joseph Boyle is professor of philosophy at the University of Toronto, where he is a fellow and former principal (1991–2002) at St. Michael's College. He does research in the area of moral philosophy, particularly in the Roman Catholic moral tradition. He has collaborated with Germain Grisez and John Finnis in developing and applying a distinctive version of natural law theory, and is coauthor with them of *Nuclear Deterrence, Morality, and Realism* (1988). The focus in his current work is on double effect and intention. He received a PhD in philosophy from Georgetown University.

Chris Brown is professor of international relations at the London School of Economics and Political Science. He is the author of numerous articles in international political theory and of *Practical Judgement in International Political Theory* (2010); *Sovereignty, Rights, and Justice* (2002); *International Relations Theory: New Normative Approaches* (1992); *Political Restructuring in Europe: Ethical Perspectives* (editor, 1994); and *International Relations in Political Thought: Texts from the Greeks to the First World War* (coeditor, with Terry Nardin and Nicholas Rengger, 2002). His textbook *Understanding International Relations* (4th edition, 2009) has been translated into Arabic, Turkish, Chinese, and Portuguese. He was chair of the British International Studies Association in 1998–99 and previously taught at Kent and Southampton universities.

Martin L. Cook is the Admiral James Bond Stockdale Professor of Professional Military Ethics at the US Naval War College. He previously served as a professor of philosophy and deputy head of the Department of Philosophy at the US Air Force Academy, as a professor of ethics and Elihu Root Chair of Military Studies at the US Army War College, and as a tenured member of the faculty at Santa Clara University in California. He has also taught at St. Xavier University in Illinois; Gustavus Adolphus College in Minnesota; the College of William and Mary in Virginia; and the Graduate Institute of St. John's College in New Mexico. He serves as an editor of *The Journal of Military Ethics* and as a member of the editorial board of *Parameters*, the scholarly journal of the US Army War College. He has written more than forty scholarly articles and has lectured on topics of military ethics in the United Kingdom, Australia, Singapore, Hong Kong, France, the Netherlands, and Norway. He is the author of *The Moral Warrior: Ethics and Service in the US Military* (2004) and *Issues in Military Ethics: To Support and Defend the Constitution* (2013).

Neta C. Crawford is a professor of political science at Boston University. She is the author of articles in professional journals, including *International Security, Perspectives on Politics, Orbis*, and *Ethics & International Affairs*. Her books include *Argument and Change in World Politics: Ethics, Decolonization, and Humanitarian Intervention* (2002) and *Collateral Damage* (2013).

Michael L. Gross is professor of political science in the Division of International Relations at the University of Haifa in Israel. He has published widely in medical ethics, military ethics, and at the intersection of the two as they come together in military medical ethics and related questions of medicine and national security. His articles have appeared in the *American Journal of Bioethics, Journal of Military Ethics, Cambridge Quarterly of Healthcare Ethics, Hastings Center Report, Journal of Medical Ethics*, and *Journal of Applied Philosophy*. His books include *Ethics and Activism* (1997); *Bioethics and Armed Conflict* (2006); *Moral Dilemmas of Modern War: Torture, Assassination and Blackmail in an Age of Asymmetric Conflict* (2010); and *Military Medical Ethics for the 21st Century* (coeditor, with Don Carrick, 2013).

James Turner Johnson is Distinguished Professor of Religion and Associate of the Graduate Program in Political Science at Rutgers—the State University of New Jersey, where he has been on the faculty since 1969. His research and teaching have focused principally on the historical development and application of the Western and Islamic moral traditions related to war, peace, and the practice of statecraft. He has received Rockefeller Foundation, Guggenheim Foundation, and National Endowment for the Humanities fellowships and various other research grants and has directed two of the Endowment's summer seminars for college teachers. His most recent books are *Ethics and the Use of Force: Just War in Historical Perspective* (2011); *The War to Oust Saddam Hussein: Just War and the New Face of Conflict* (2005); and *Morality and Contemporary Warfare* (2001). His other books include

Ideology, Reason, and the Limitation of War; Just War Tradition and the Restraint of War; Can Modern War Be Just?; The Quest for Peace: Three Moral Traditions in Western Cultural History; The Holy War Idea in Western and Islamic Traditions; Cross, Crescent, and Sword: The Justification and Limitation of War in Western and Islamic Tradition (coeditor, with John Kelsay); and *Just War and Jihad: Historical and Theoretical Perspectives on War and Peace in Western and Islamic Traditions* (coeditor, with John Kelsay). He is currently writing a book with the working title *The Idea of Sovereignty in Moral and Historical Perspective*. He received his PhD from Princeton University.

John Kelsay is Distinguished Research Professor and Lucius Moody Bristol Professor of Religion and Ethics at Florida State University. His publications include *Islam and War: A Study in Comparative Ethics* (1993); *Arguing the Just War in Islam* (2009); and two coedited volumes (with James Turner Johnson), *Cross, Crescent, and Sword: The Justification and Limitation of War in Western and Islamic Tradition*; and *Just War and Jihad: Historical and Theoretical Perspectives on War and Peace in Western and Islamic Traditions*. He serves as editor of *Soundings: An Interdisciplinary Journal*.

Tarik Kochi is senior lecturer of law at the University of Sussex. His research and teaching interests lie in international law, political theory, and global security, with a focus on contemporary problems of war and terror. His publications include *The Other's War: Recognition of Violence and Ethics* (2009), which was awarded the International Ethics Book Prize by the International Studies Association; numerous articles in distinguished journals; and several book chapters. He is currently working on a second monograph, *Power, Property, and International Law*.

Anthony F. Lang Jr. is a reader in the School of International Relations at the University of St. Andrews, where he also serves as director of the Centre for Global Constitutionalism. His research and teaching focus on international political theory, broadly defined, with special attention to the intersection of law, politics, and ethics at the global level. He has published two scholarly books and edited five others, as well as a number of articles and book chapters.

Cian O'Driscoll is lecturer on politics at the University of Glasgow. He has published widely on the subject of the just war tradition. He is the author of *Renegotiation of the Just War Tradition in the Twenty-First Century* (2008). He has also published articles in leading journals, including the *European Journal of Political Theory, International Relations, Millennium: Journal of International Studies, Journal of International Political Theory*, and *Cambridge Review of International Affairs*. He is a fellow of the Royal Society of Edinburgh, Young Academy; was a Snell Exchange

Fellow at Balliol College, Oxford; and is currently conducting research on the precursors to the just war tradition in the ancient world.

Gregory M. Reichberg is Research Professor at the Peace Research Institute Oslo (PRIO). He is a specialist in the thought of Thomas Aquinas, and has published widely on the ethics of war and peace. In addition to numerous articles, his published work includes several coedited volumes: *World Religions and Norms of War* (2009); *Ethics, Nationalism, and Just War: Medieval and Contemporary Perspectives* (2007); and *The Ethics of War: Classic and Contemporary Readings* (2006). He has a book in press, *Religion, War, and Ethics: A Sourcebook;* and he is currently writing a book with the working title *Peace and War in the Ethics of Thomas Aquinas.*

Nicholas Rengger is professor of political theory and international relations at the University of St. Andrews, and a Carnegie Council Global Ethics Fellow at the Carnegie Council for Ethics and International Affairs in New York. He has published in many areas of political theory, social thought, and international relations. His most recent study is of the teleocratic roots of the contemporary just war tradition, *Just War and International Order: The Uncivil Condition in World Politics* (2013), and he is currently completing a collection of essays titled *Dealing in Darkness: The Anti-Pelagian Imagination in Political Theory and International Relations.*

Laura Sjoberg is associate professor of political science at the University of Florida, where her teaching and research focus on issues of gender and international security. She is the author of *Gender, Justice, and the Wars in Iraq* (2006); *Gendering Global Conflict: Towards a Feminist Theory of War* (2013); and, with Caron Gentry, *Mothers, Monsters, Whores: Women's Violence in Global Politics* (2007). She has edited several books, and her work has been published in more than thirty peer-reviewed journals, including most recently the *Feminist Review, International Theory*, and *International Political Sociology.*

Brent J. Steele is an associate professor of political science and international relations at the University of Kansas, where he is also director of faculty programs for the Office of International Programs. His research has focused on a variety of issues dealing with US foreign policy, just war theory, torture, and accountability in global politics. He teaches courses on international relations theory, international ethics, US foreign policy, and critical security studies. He is the author of three books, *Ontological Security in International Relations: Self-Identity and the IR State* (2007); *Defacing Power: The Aesthetics of Insecurity in Global Politics* (2010); and *Alternative Accountabilities in Global Politics: The Scars of Violence* (2012). He is also the coeditor of two volumes, *Ethics, Authority and War: Non-State Actors and the Just War Tradition* (with Eric A. Heinze, 2009); and *Theory and Application of the "Generation" in International Relations and Politics* (with Jonathan M. Acuff, 2012). His research has been published in a number of international studies journals, with articles appearing most recently in *Millennium, International Studies Review, Journal of International Political Theory*, and *Review of International Studies*.

John Williams is professor of international relations at Durham University, which he joined in 2001 following five years as a lecturer in international relations at the University of Aberdeen. His research interests include international relations theory, particularly the "English school," and international ethics, particularly the ethics of territorial boundaries and the ethics of violence. He is the author of *Legitimacy in International Relations and the Rise and Fall of Yugoslavia* (1998) and *The Ethics of Territorial Borders: Drawing Lines in the Shifting Sands* (2006). He is coeditor of *Global Citizenship: A Critical Introduction* (with Nigel Dower, 2002); *Hannah Arendt and International Relations: Readings across the Lines* (with Anthony F. Lang Jr., 2005); and *The Anarchical Society in a Globalized World* (with Richard Little, 2006); as well as author or coauthor of twenty articles and chapters in journals and collections.

Nahed Artoul Zehr spent the 2011–12 academic year as Minerva Research Chair at the US Naval War College and became assistant professor of Islam and religious studies at Western Kentucky University in the fall of 2012. She has published on issues of religious ethics, the just war tradition, and Islam in the *Journal of Military Ethics* and the *Journal of Religious Ethics*. She is currently working on a manuscript on al-Qaeda and the American military response in the war on terrorism.

Index